GRANT MORRISON'S
18 DAYS™

VOLUME 3: DARK SECRETS

GRANT MORRISON'S 18 DAYS™

Created by Grant Morrison

CHAPTER 1 - **KRISHNA'S ALLIANCE**

Script Samit Basu
Art Jeevan J. Kang
Color S. Sundarakannan

CHAPTER 2 - **THE BIRTH OF GATOK**

Script Samit Basu
Art Saumin Patel
Color Saumin Patel

CHAPTER 3 - **CHARGE OF THE ELEPHANTS**

Script Sarwat Chadda
Art Saumin Patel
Color S. Sundarakannan

CHAPTER 4 - **BHIMA STRIKES BACK**

Script Sarwat Chadda
Art Saumin Patel
Color S. Sundarakannan

CHAPTER 5 - **THE DARK SECRETS OF KINGS**

Script Samit Basu
Art Jeevan J. Kang
Color Sesha Sainan Devarajan

Readers of NOMEN OMEN,

I'm writing you a warning letter about the authors of this series, Jacopo Camagni and Marco Bucci.

My first meeting with them took place in 2017 at the Lucca Comics and Games festival, on a wet Autumn day. To tell you the whole story, two years earlier I had not given the best picture of myself in a virtual exchange, so Jacopo took me for a completely snobbish and unworthy soul, hence our interaction during a signing session at our common publisher's booth was as cold as an iceberg. As for Marco... Being the tireless verbal storyteller that he is, he was far too busy overwhelming people approaching their table with words to pay attention to me (and my astral predispositions made me hate it more than I hate the taste of beets).

But believe it or not, after this unpleasant first encounter in Tuscany, in a very short time Jacopo and Marco have become such precious friends that now I can say I would follow them blindfolded over any mortal precipice. There can be only one explanation for this: they have bewitched me. This is exactly why I feel the urge to warn you: through NOMEN OMEN, it is very likely that the same spell will hit you!

It could result in an addiction enchantment, or it may open a portal within you, or change your perception of gravity forever. This is a very hard delight to avoid because the ingredients that Marco and Jacopo brewed in their pot created a very powerful recipe. In NOMEN OMEN, magic, poetry and pop culture are one in the same language.

These two managed to introduce the idea that ancient magic and modern magic are part of the same continuum, thus making them inseparable. Concocting a way to blend the pagan mythological worlds with mainstream culture is no small feat either: here fauns shave their legs with their sickle between two games of *Labyrinth* pinball, while trolls dressed in *Harry Potter* T-shirts are more than often than not big computer geeks.

Thanks to their ability to understand alchemy and magic as a transformative art, with NOMEN OMEN Marco and Jacopo show that all the various kinds of networks we deal with in our everyday life make our era a decisive magic springboard, in the spiritual, energetic and divine sense, as they're all are based on one core notion: connection.

I have no advice to give you that would help ward off the narrative spell that will take hold of you. But don't you worry, this is still white magic or rather some kind of colored magic whose exact gamut you will discover as the chapters progress. In short: it's definitely not black magic. Actually, I can only wish you such a spell. Like the one I fell for two years ago, it's imbued with love for the magical and sacred dimension that resides in everyone.

Julie Maroh
(Jul, for Jacopo and Marco)

Julie Maroh is one of the most appreciated and acclaimed comic book authors in Europe. Aer first comic book, *Blue is the Warmest Color*, won the Audience Award at the Angoulême festival in 2011. Its movie adaptation won the Palme d'Or at the Cannes film festival in 2013. Some of aer best-selling graphic novels include *Body Music* (2017) and *Skandalon* (2013) and *You Brought Me the Ocean* (2020), an Aqualad OGN written by Alex Sanchez and published by DC Comics.

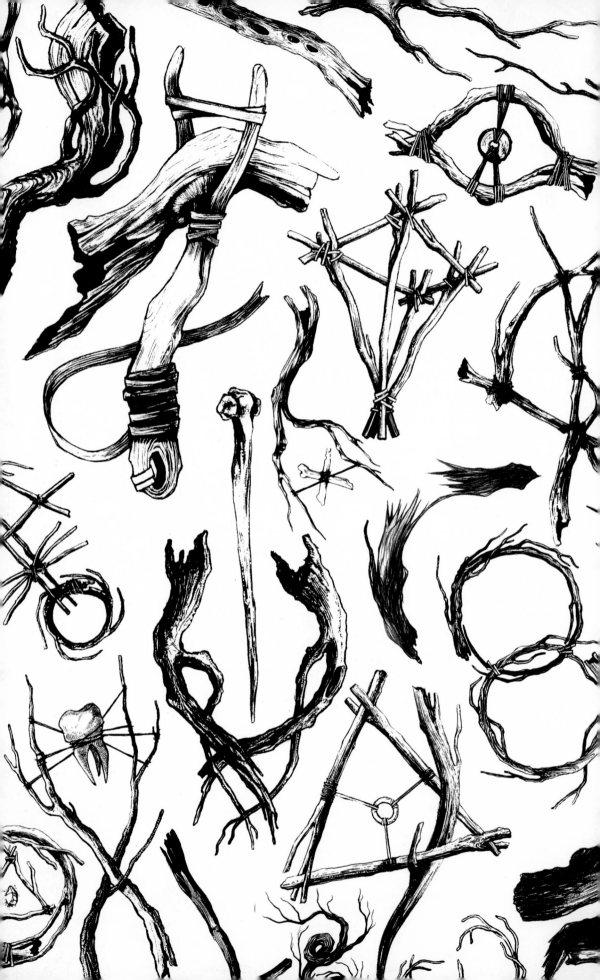

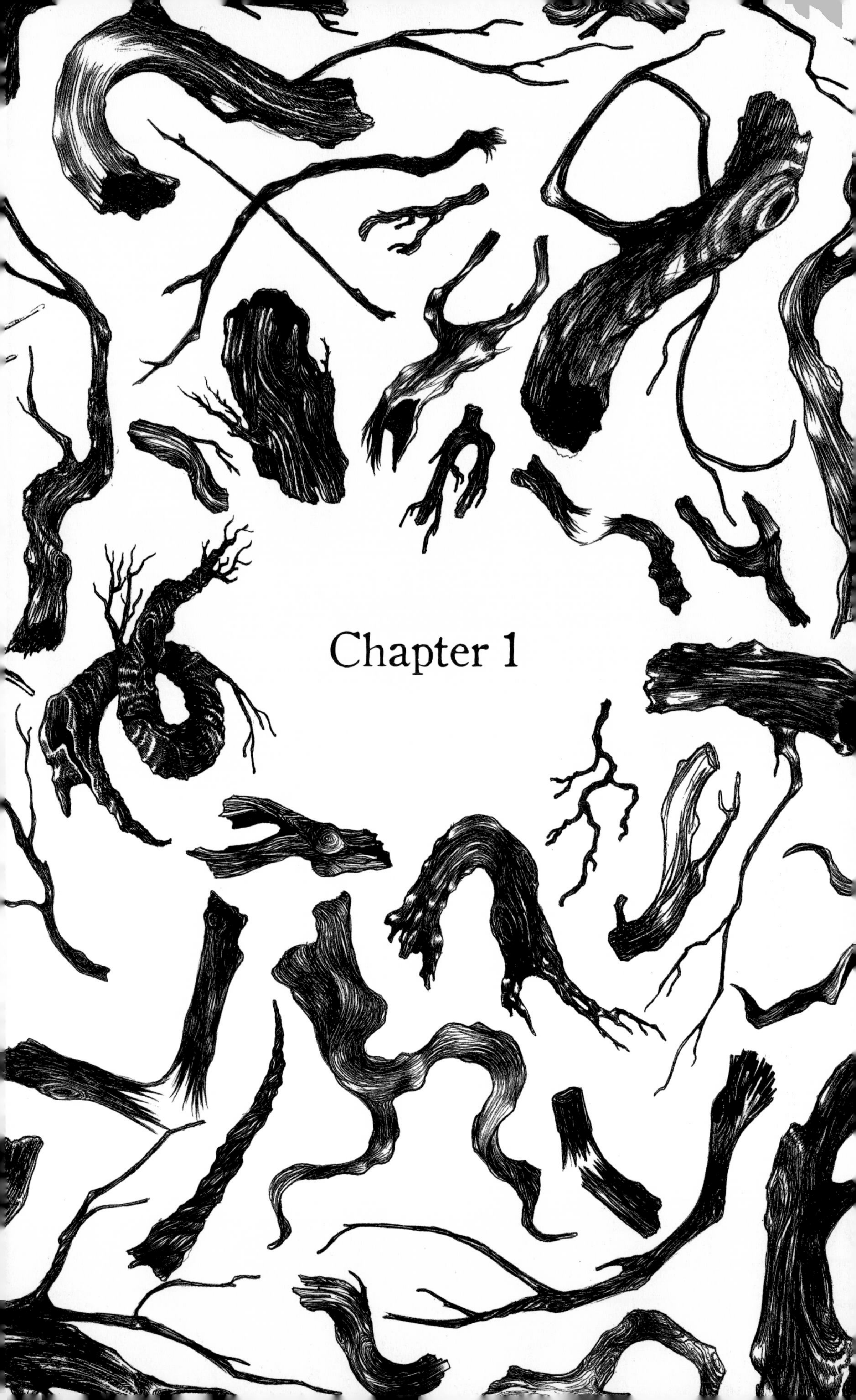

Chapter 1

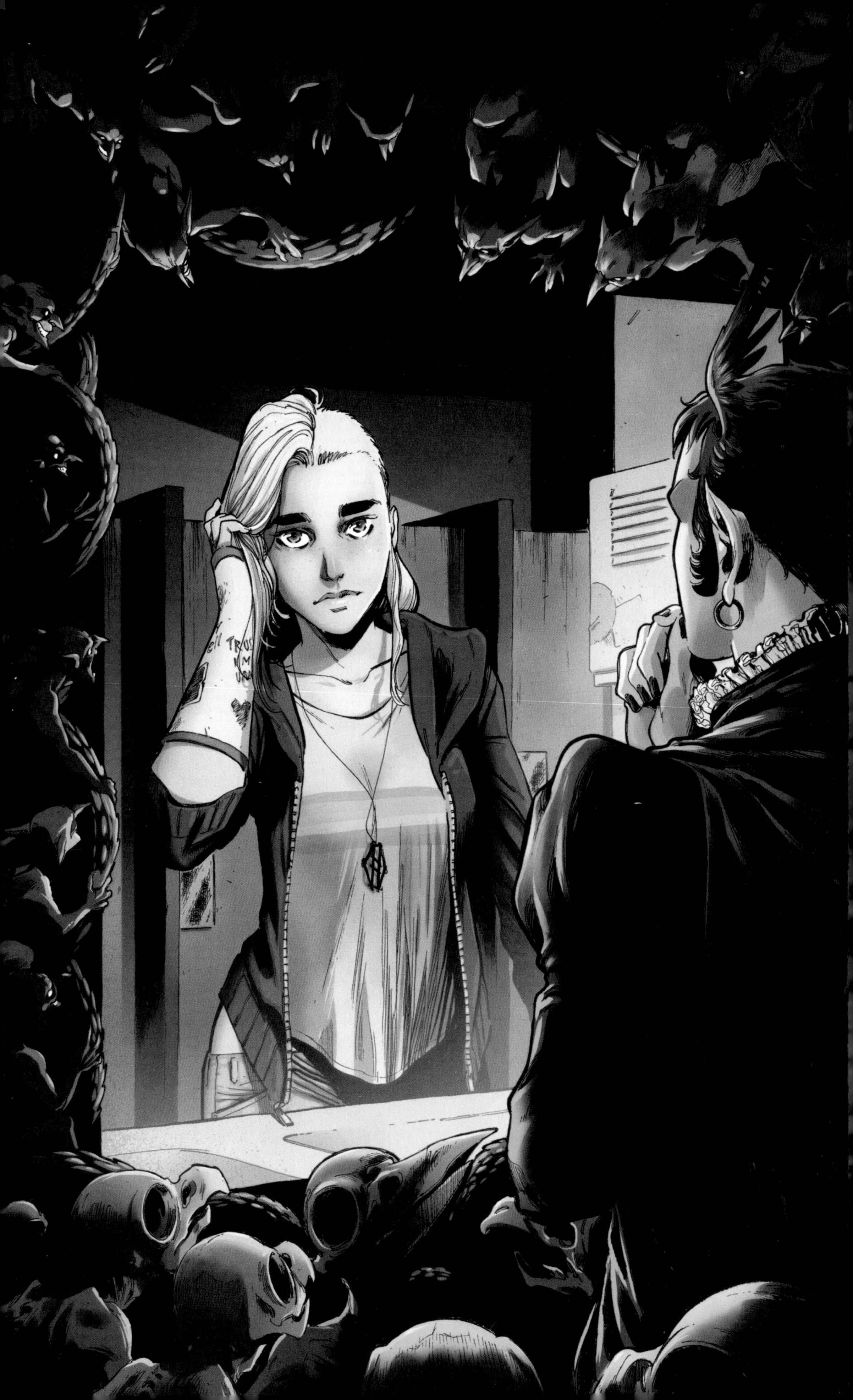

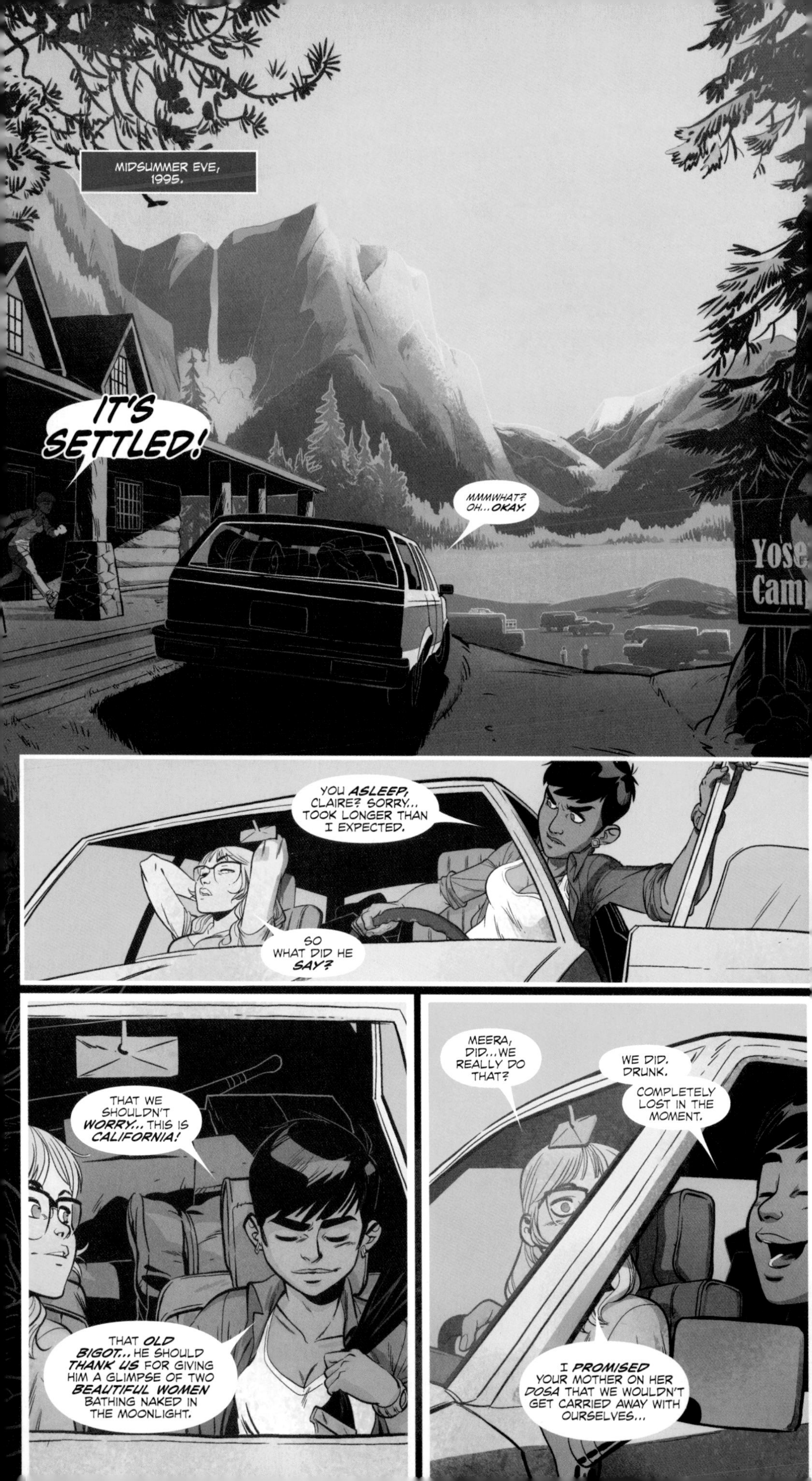
MIDSUMMER EVE, 1995.
IT'S SETTLED!
MMMWHAT? OH...OKAY.
Yose
Camp
YOU ASLEEP, CLAIRE? SORRY... TOOK LONGER THAN I EXPECTED.
SO WHAT DID HE SAY?
THAT WE SHOULDN'T WORRY... THIS IS CALIFORNIA!
THAT OLD BIGOT... HE SHOULD THANK US FOR GIVING HIM A GLIMPSE OF TWO BEAUTIFUL WOMEN BATHING NAKED IN THE MOONLIGHT.
MEERA, DID...WE REALLY DO THAT?
WE DID. DRUNK.
COMPLETELY LOST IN THE MOMENT.
I PROMISED YOUR MOTHER ON HER DOSA THAT WE WOULDN'T GET CARRIED AWAY WITH OURSELVES...

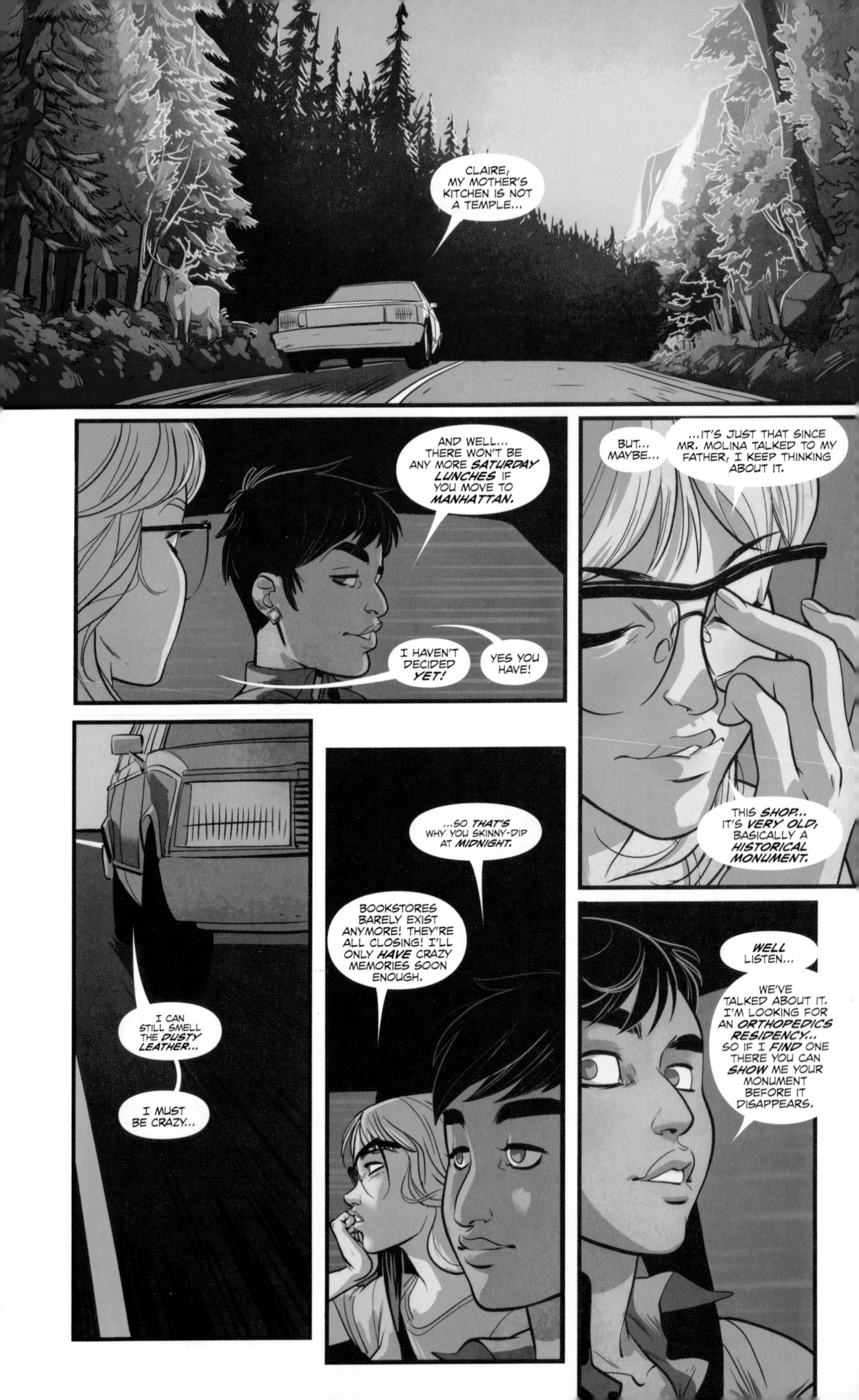
CLAIRE, MY MOTHER'S KITCHEN IS NOT A TEMPLE...
AND WELL... THERE WON'T BE ANY MORE *SATURDAY LUNCHES* IF YOU MOVE TO *MANHATTAN.*
I HAVEN'T DECIDED *YET!*
YES YOU HAVE!
BUT... MAYBE...
...IT'S JUST THAT SINCE MR. MOLINA TALKED TO MY FATHER, I KEEP THINKING ABOUT IT.
THIS *SHOP...* IT'S *VERY OLD,* BASICALLY A *HISTORICAL MONUMENT.*
I CAN STILL SMELL THE *DUSTY LEATHER...*
I MUST BE CRAZY...
...SO *THAT'S* WHY YOU SKINNY-DIP AT *MIDNIGHT.*
BOOKSTORES BARELY EXIST ANYMORE! THEY'RE ALL CLOSING! I'LL ONLY *HAVE* CRAZY MEMORIES SOON ENOUGH.
WELL LISTEN...
WE'VE TALKED ABOUT IT. I'M LOOKING FOR AN *ORTHOPEDICS RESIDENCY...* SO IF I *FIND* ONE THERE YOU CAN *SHOW* ME YOUR MONUMENT BEFORE IT DISAPPEARS.

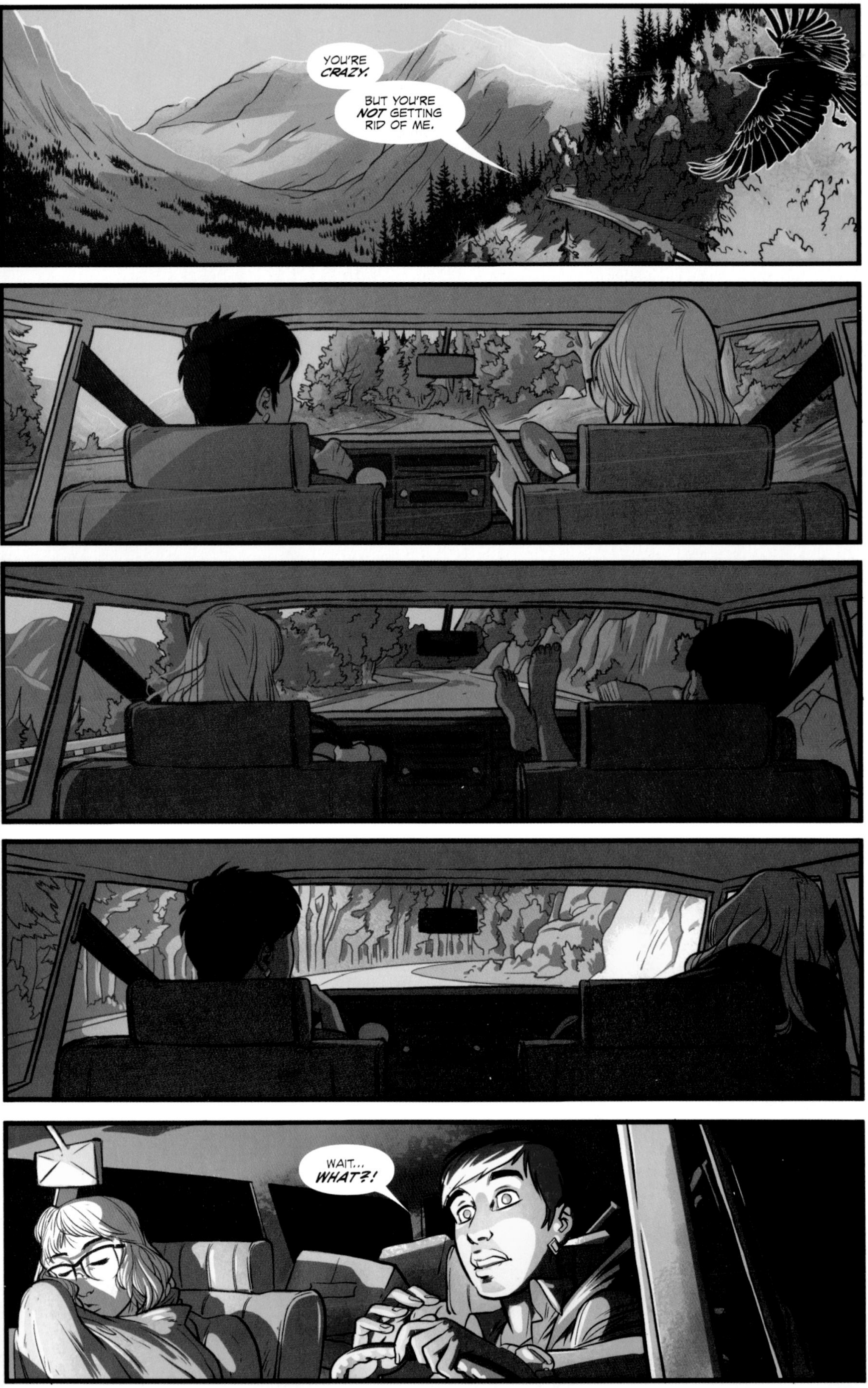
YOU'RE *CRAZY.*
BUT YOU'RE *NOT* GETTING RID OF ME.
WAIT... *WHAT?!*

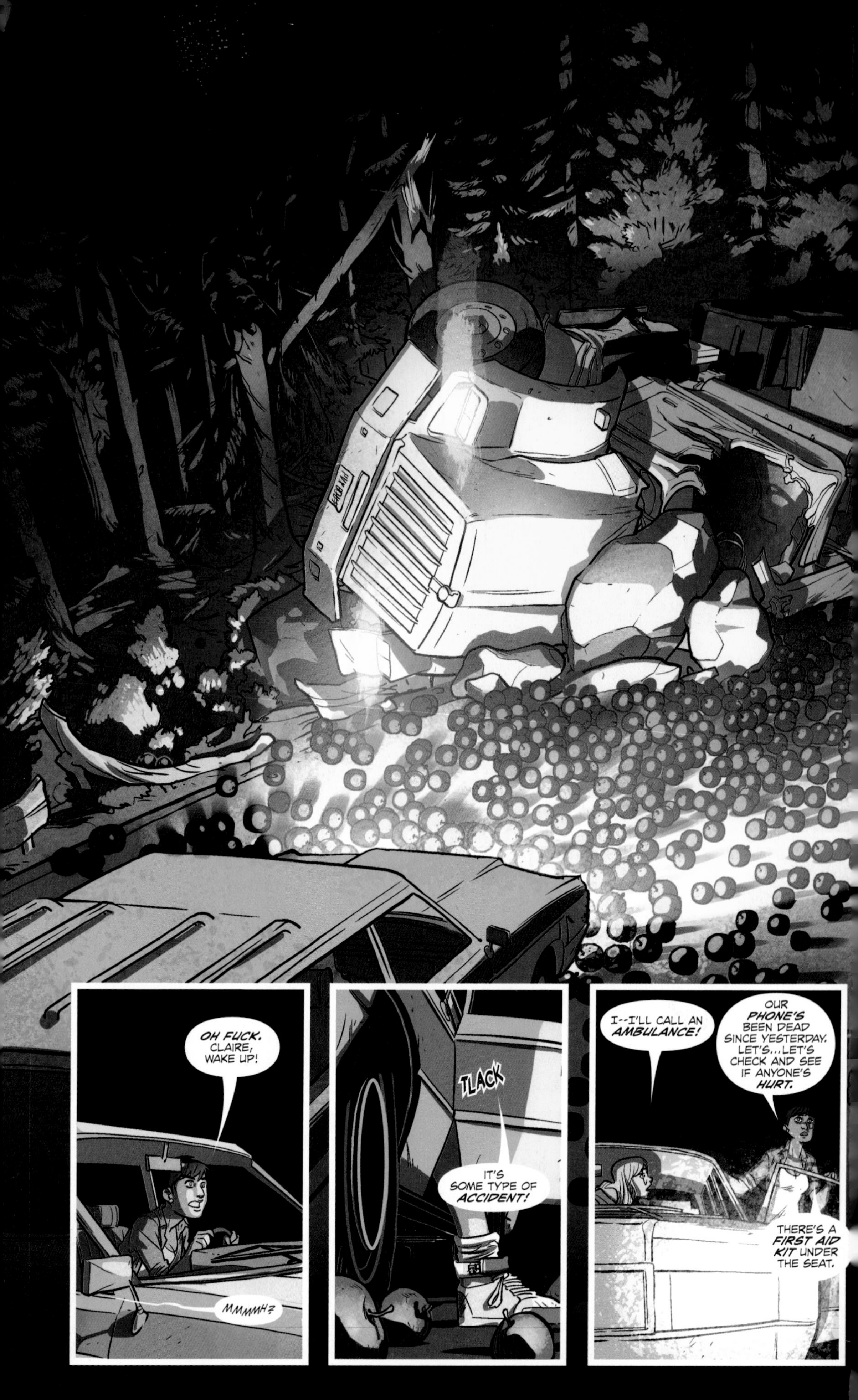
OH FUCK. CLAIRE, WAKE UP!
MMMMH?
TLACK
IT'S SOME TYPE OF ACCIDENT!
I--I'LL CALL AN AMBULANCE!
OUR PHONE'S BEEN DEAD SINCE YESTERDAY. LET'S...LET'S CHECK AND SEE IF ANYONE'S HURT.
THERE'S A FIRST AID KIT UNDER THE SEAT.

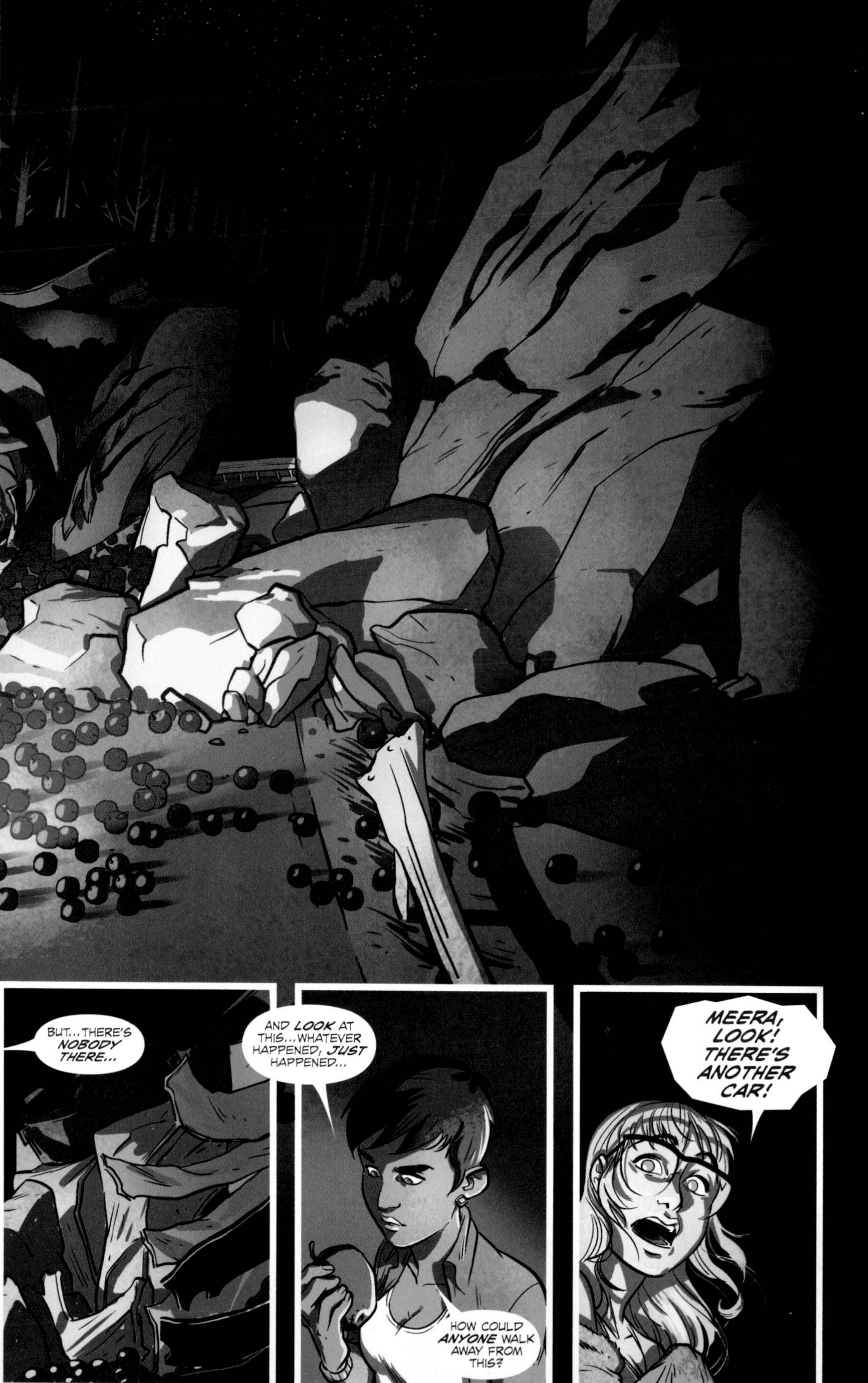
BUT... THERE'S NOBODY THERE...
AND LOOK AT THIS... WHATEVER HAPPENED, JUST HAPPENED...
HOW COULD ANYONE WALK AWAY FROM THIS?
MEERA, LOOK! THERE'S ANOTHER CAR!

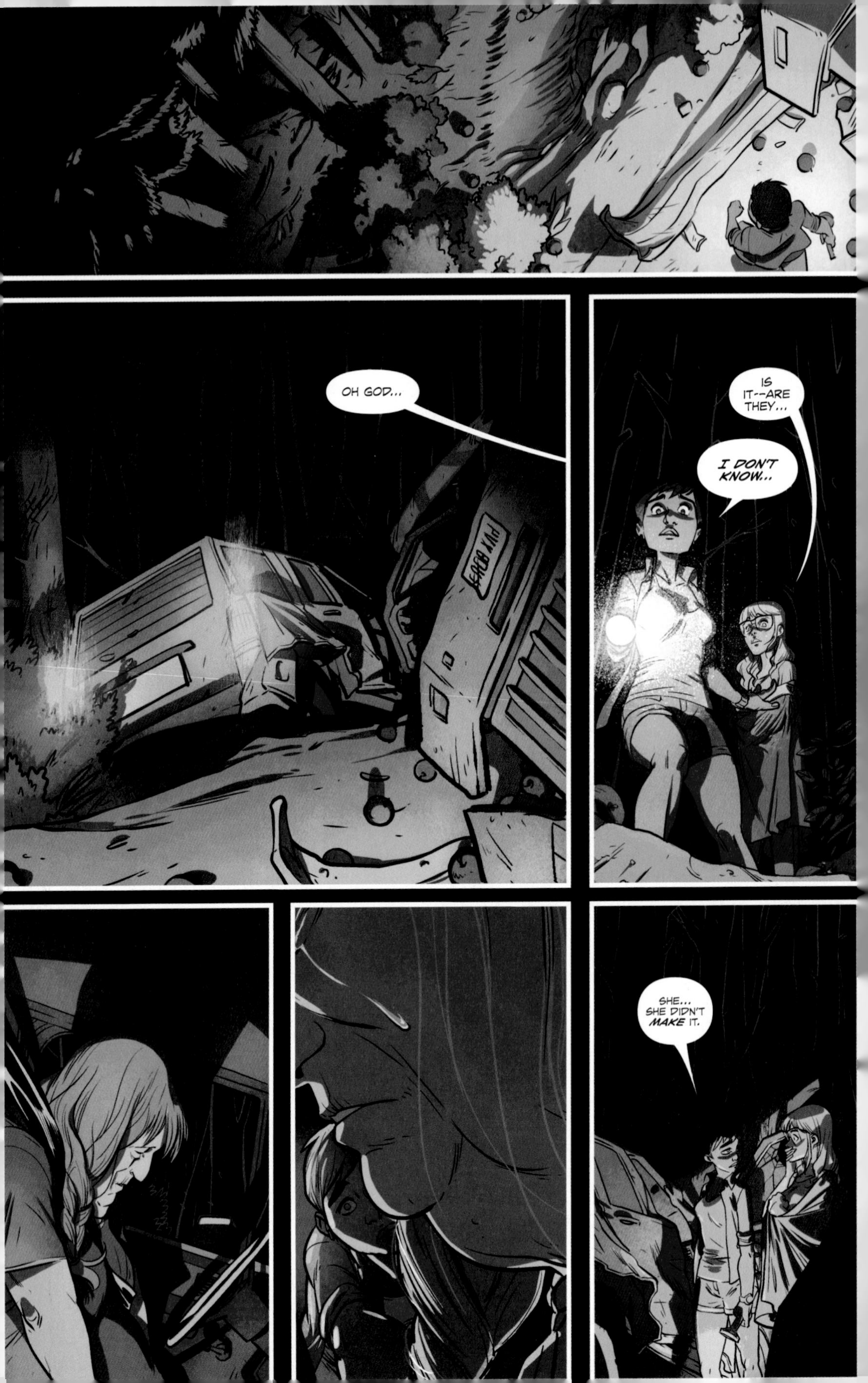
OH GOD...
IS IT--ARE THEY...
I DON'T KNOW...
SHE... SHE DIDN'T MAKE IT.

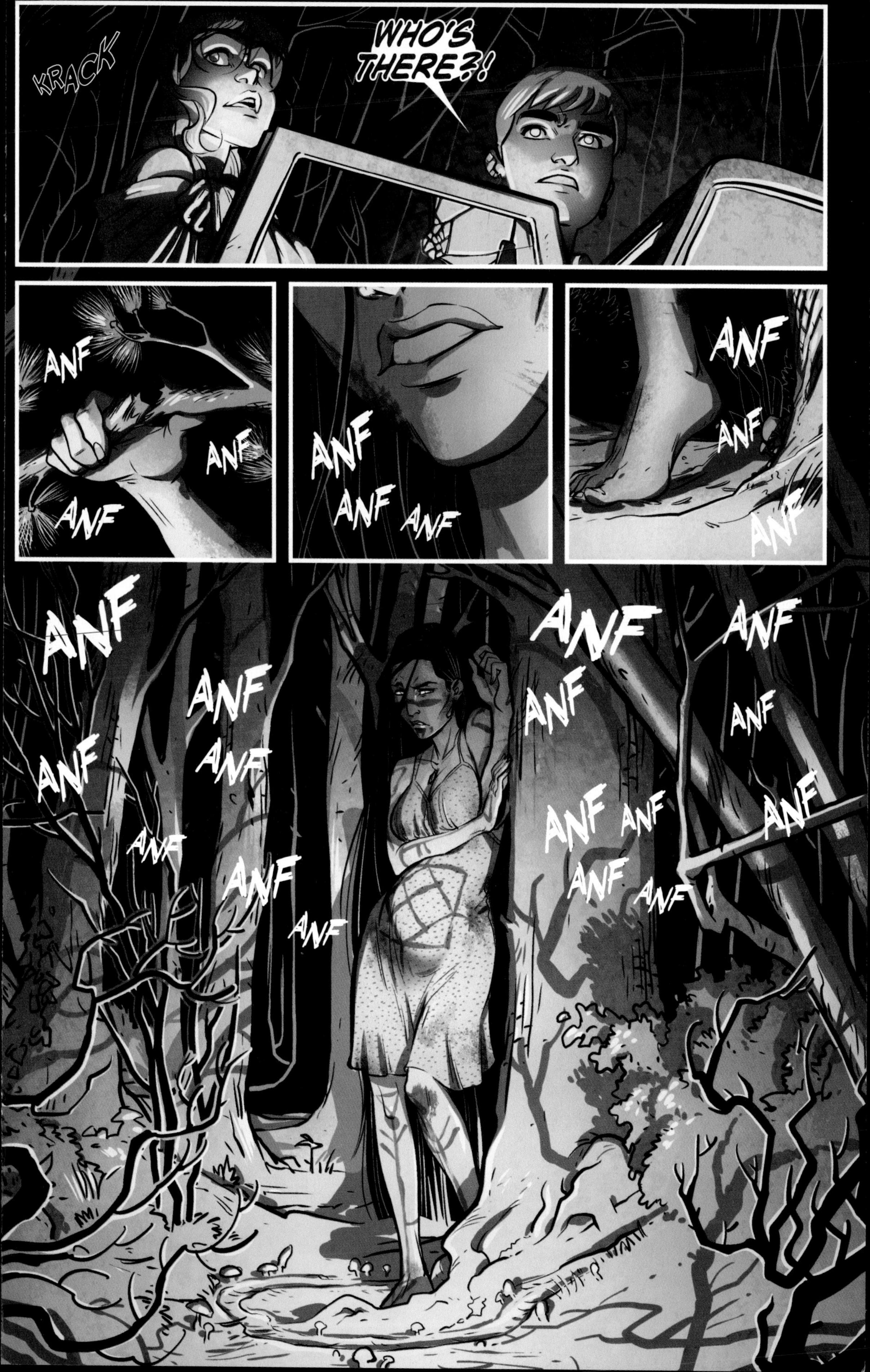
KRACK
WHO'S THERE?!
ANF
ANF
ANF
ANF
ANF
ANF
ANF
ANF
ANF
ANF
ANF ANF
ANF ANF
ANF
ANF ANF
ANF
ANF
ANF
ANF
ANF
ANF
ANF ANF
ANF ANF
ANF

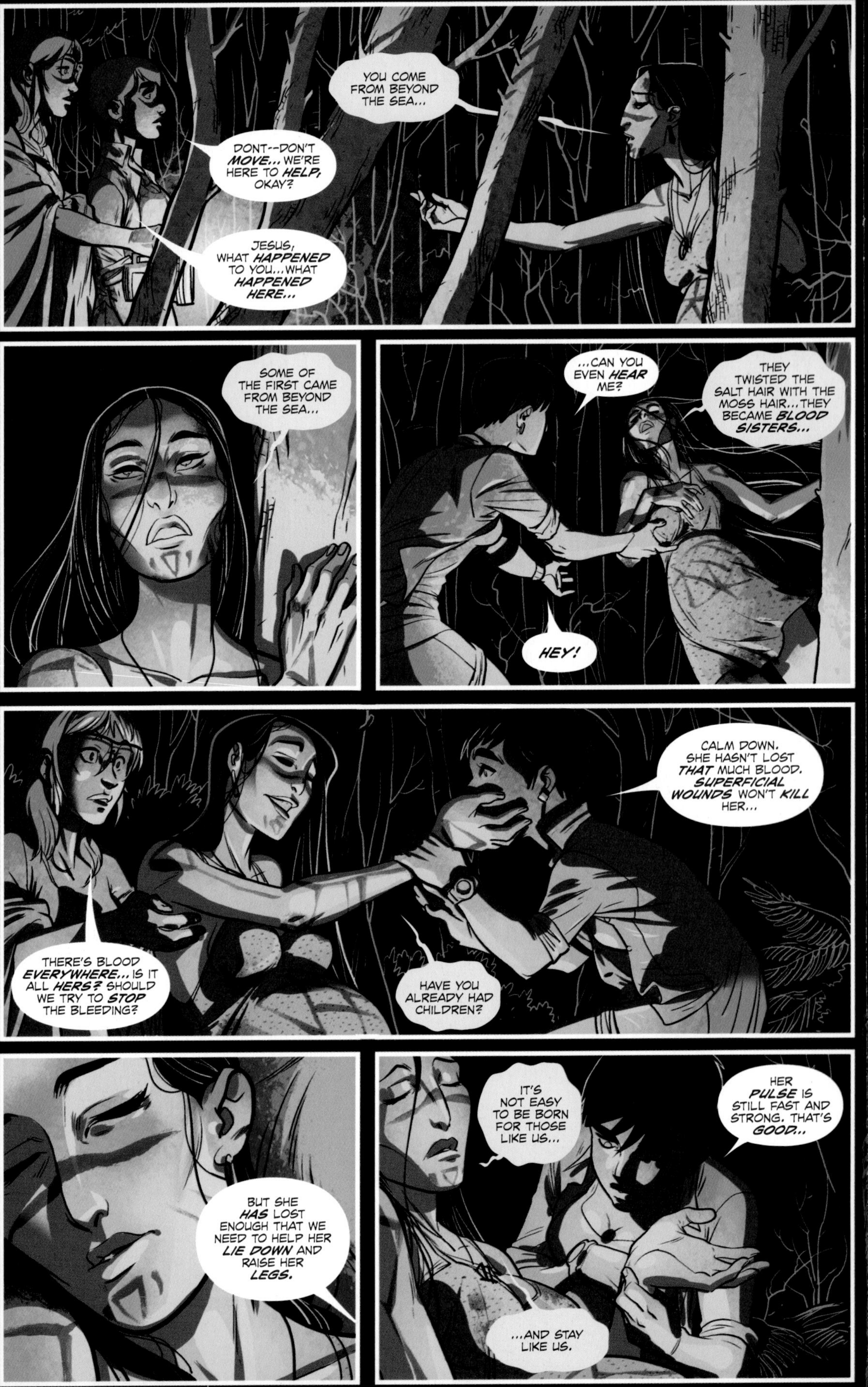
YOU COME FROM BEYOND THE SEA...
DONT--DON'T MOVE... WE'RE HERE TO HELP, OKAY?
JESUS, WHAT HAPPENED TO YOU... WHAT HAPPENED HERE...
SOME OF THE FIRST CAME FROM BEYOND THE SEA...
...CAN YOU EVEN HEAR ME?
THEY TWISTED THE SALT HAIR WITH THE MOSS HAIR... THEY BECAME BLOOD SISTERS...
HEY!
CALM DOWN. SHE HASN'T LOST THAT MUCH BLOOD. SUPERFICIAL WOUNDS WON'T KILL HER...
THERE'S BLOOD EVERYWHERE... IS IT ALL HERS? SHOULD WE TRY TO STOP THE BLEEDING?
HAVE YOU ALREADY HAD CHILDREN?
BUT SHE HAS LOST ENOUGH THAT WE NEED TO HELP HER LIE DOWN AND RAISE HER LEGS.
IT'S NOT EASY TO BE BORN FOR THOSE LIKE US...
HER PULSE IS STILL FAST AND STRONG. THAT'S GOOD...
...AND STAY LIKE US.

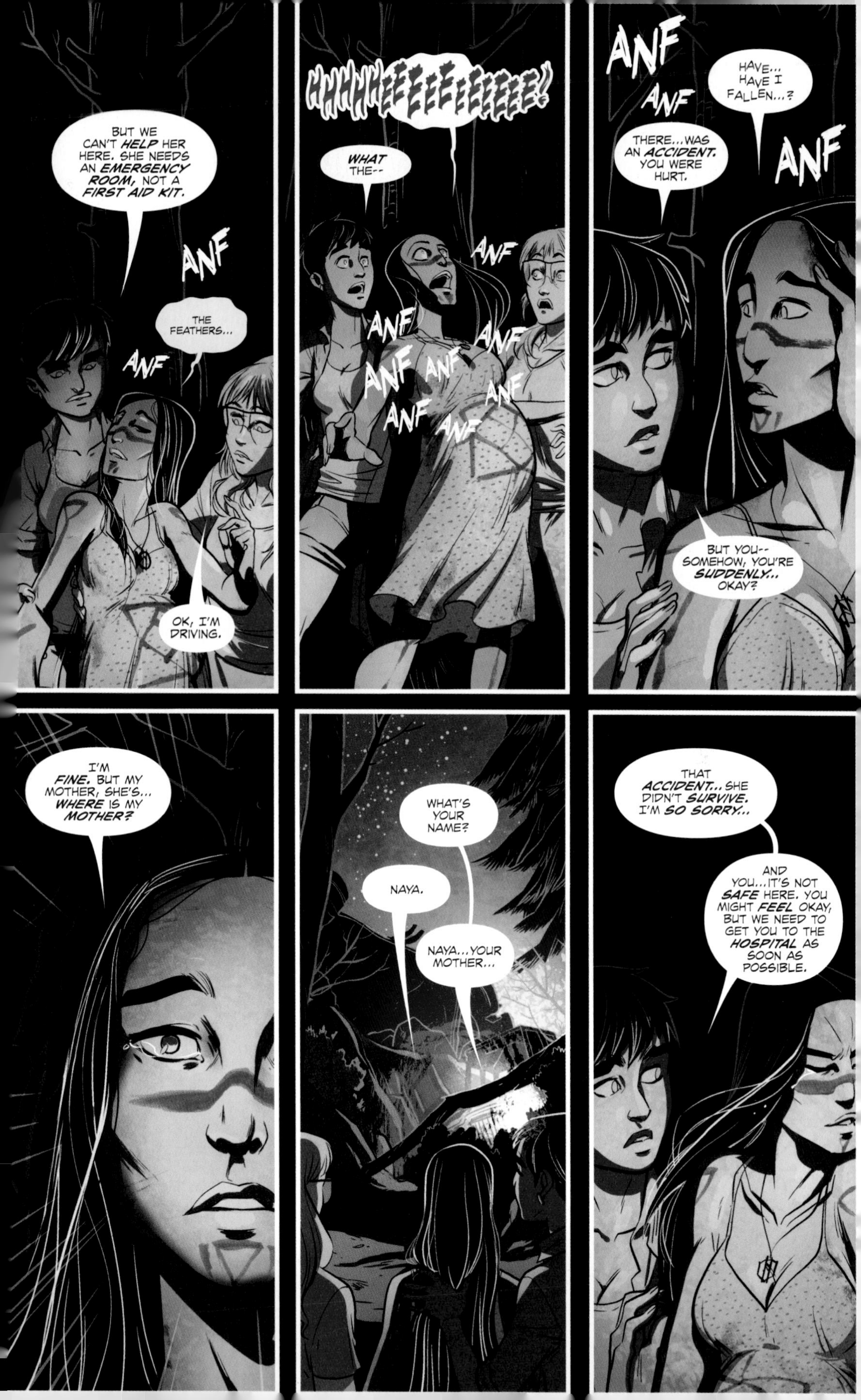
BUT WE CAN'T HELP HER HERE. SHE NEEDS AN EMERGENCY ROOM, NOT A FIRST AID KIT.
ANF
THE FEATHERS...
ANF
OK, I'M DRIVING.
HHHHHEEEEEEEEEEE!
WHAT THE--
ANF ANF ANF ANF ANF ANF ANF ANF
ANF
ANF
HAVE... HAVE I FALLEN...?
THERE...WAS AN ACCIDENT. YOU WERE HURT.
ANF
BUT YOU--SOMEHOW, YOU'RE SUDDENLY... OKAY?
I'M FINE. BUT MY MOTHER, SHE'S... WHERE IS MY MOTHER?
WHAT'S YOUR NAME?
NAYA.
NAYA...YOUR MOTHER...
THAT ACCIDENT... SHE DIDN'T SURVIVE. I'M SO SORRY...
AND YOU...IT'S NOT SAFE HERE. YOU MIGHT FEEL OKAY, BUT WE NEED TO GET YOU TO THE HOSPITAL AS SOON AS POSSIBLE.

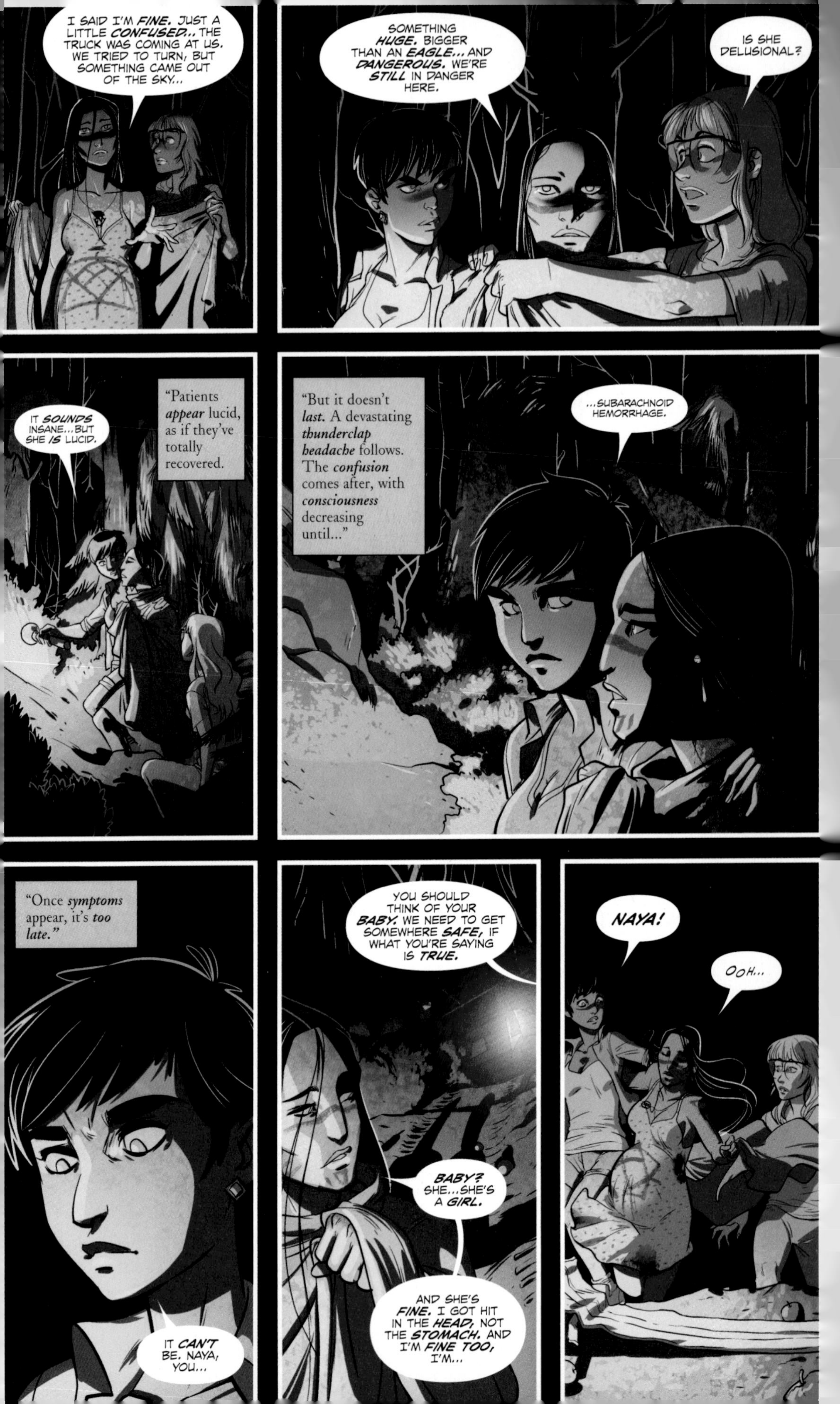
I SAID I'M FINE. JUST A LITTLE CONFUSED... THE TRUCK WAS COMING AT US. WE TRIED TO TURN, BUT SOMETHING CAME OUT OF THE SKY...
SOMETHING HUGE. BIGGER THAN AN EAGLE... AND DANGEROUS. WE'RE STILL IN DANGER HERE.
IS SHE DELUSIONAL?
IT SOUNDS INSANE...BUT SHE IS LUCID.
"Patients appear lucid, as if they've totally recovered.
"But it doesn't last. A devastating thunderclap headache follows. The confusion comes after, with consciousness decreasing until..."
...SUBARACHNOID HEMORRHAGE.
"Once symptoms appear, it's too late."
IT CAN'T BE. NAYA, YOU...
YOU SHOULD THINK OF YOUR BABY. WE NEED TO GET SOMEWHERE SAFE, IF WHAT YOU'RE SAYING IS TRUE.
BABY? SHE...SHE'S A GIRL.
AND SHE'S FINE. I GOT HIT IN THE HEAD, NOT THE STOMACH. AND I'M FINE TOO, I'M...
NAYA!
OOH...

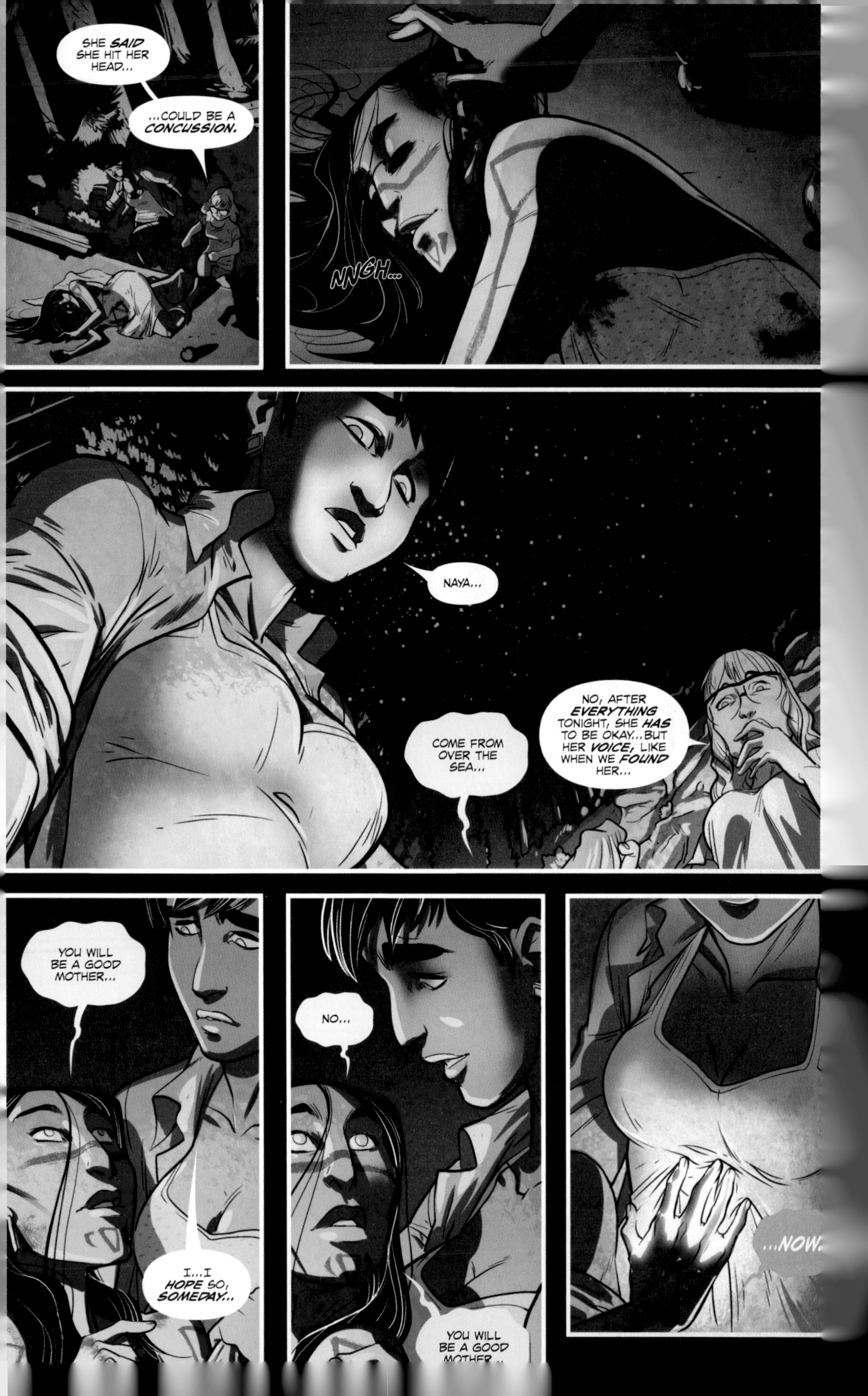
SHE SAID SHE HIT HER HEAD...
...COULD BE A CONCUSSION.
NNGH...
NAYA...
COME FROM OVER THE SEA...
NO, AFTER EVERYTHING TONIGHT, SHE HAS TO BE OKAY...BUT HER VOICE, LIKE WHEN WE FOUND HER...
YOU WILL BE A GOOD MOTHER...
I...I HOPE SO, SOMEDAY...
NO...
YOU WILL BE A GOOD MOTHER...
...NOW.

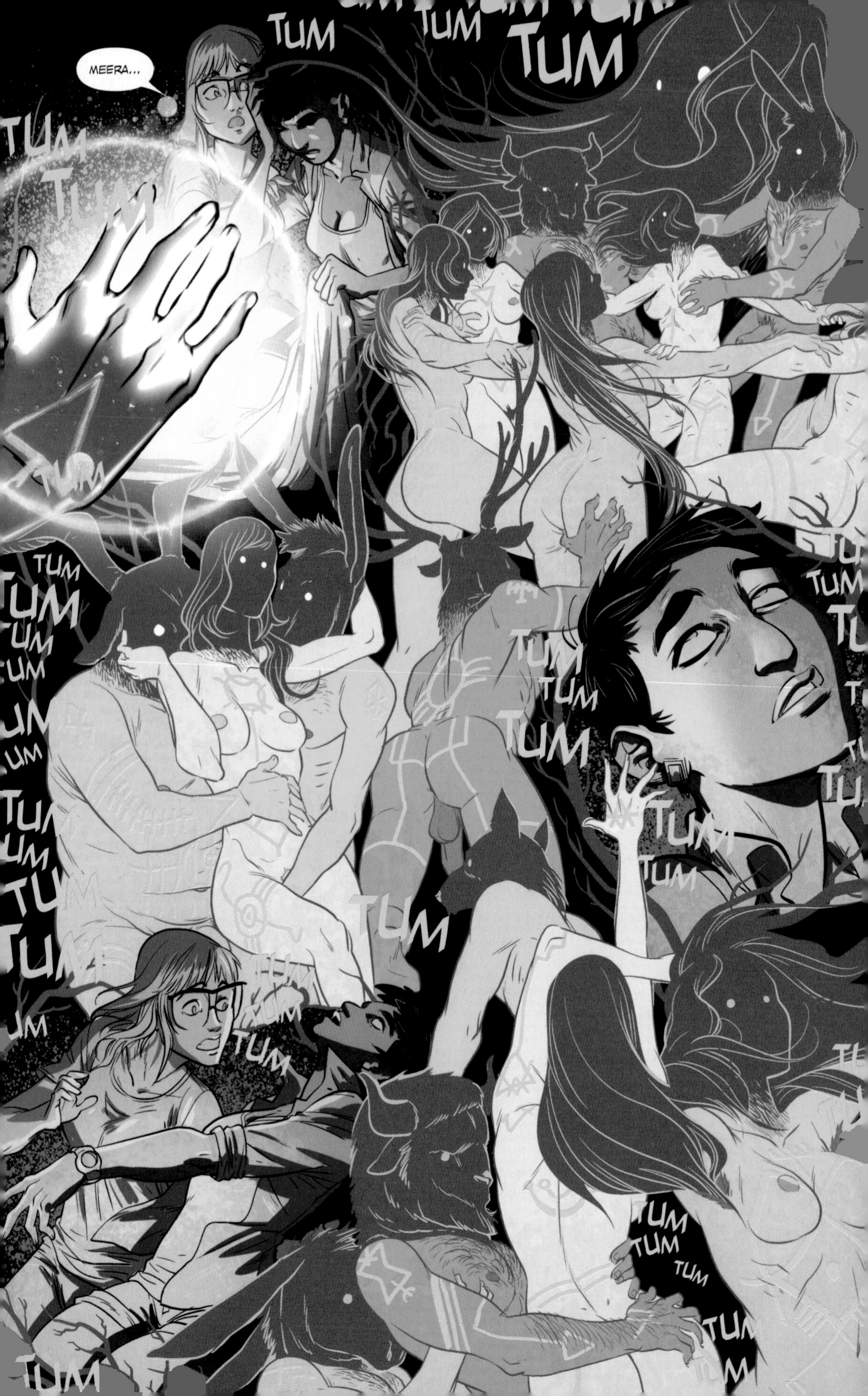
MEERA...
TUM
TUM
TUM
TUM
TUM
TUM
TUM
TUM
TUM
TUM
TUM
TUM
TUM
TUM
TUM
TUM
TUM
TUM
TUM
TUM
TUM
TUM
TUM

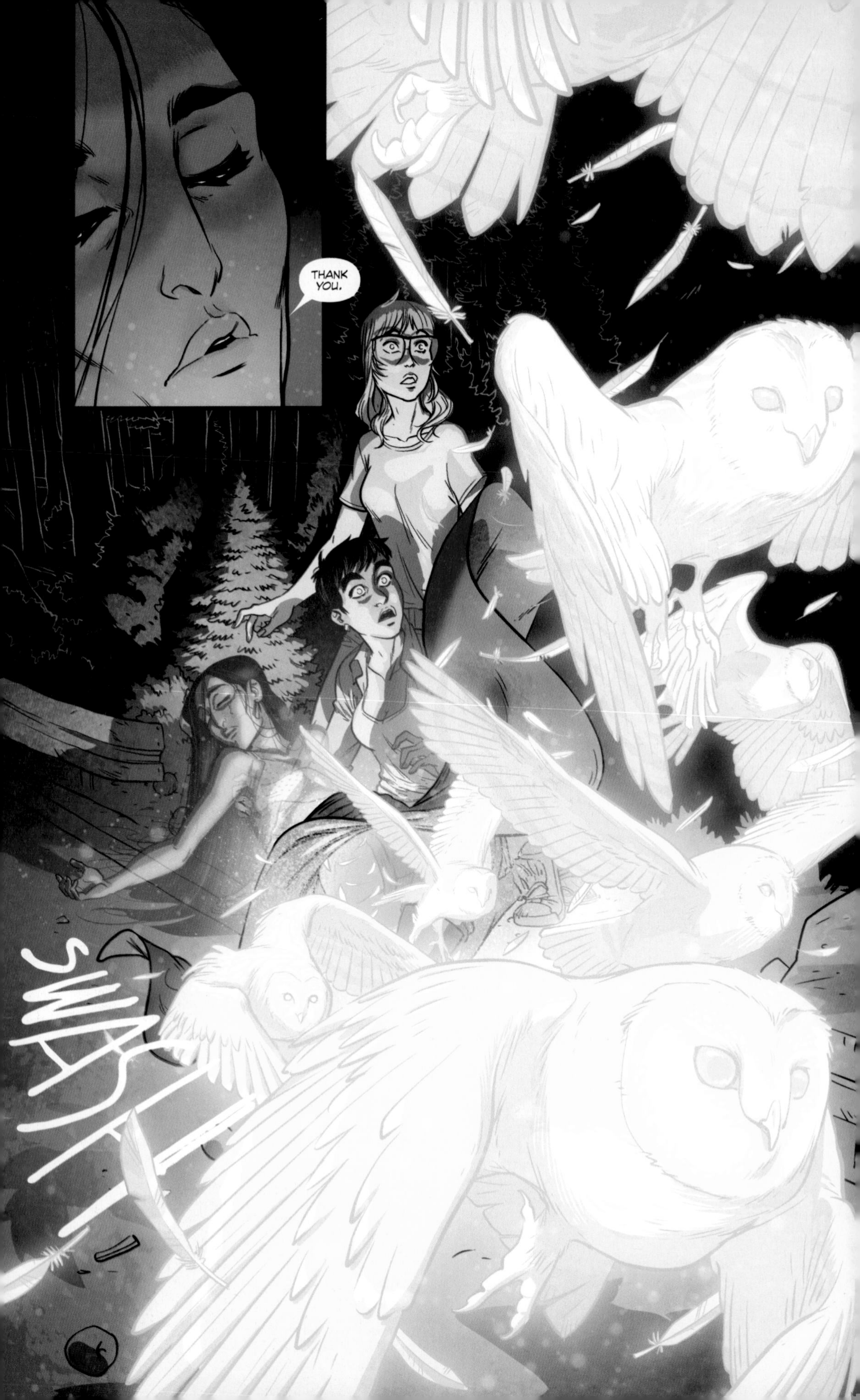
THANK YOU.
SWASH

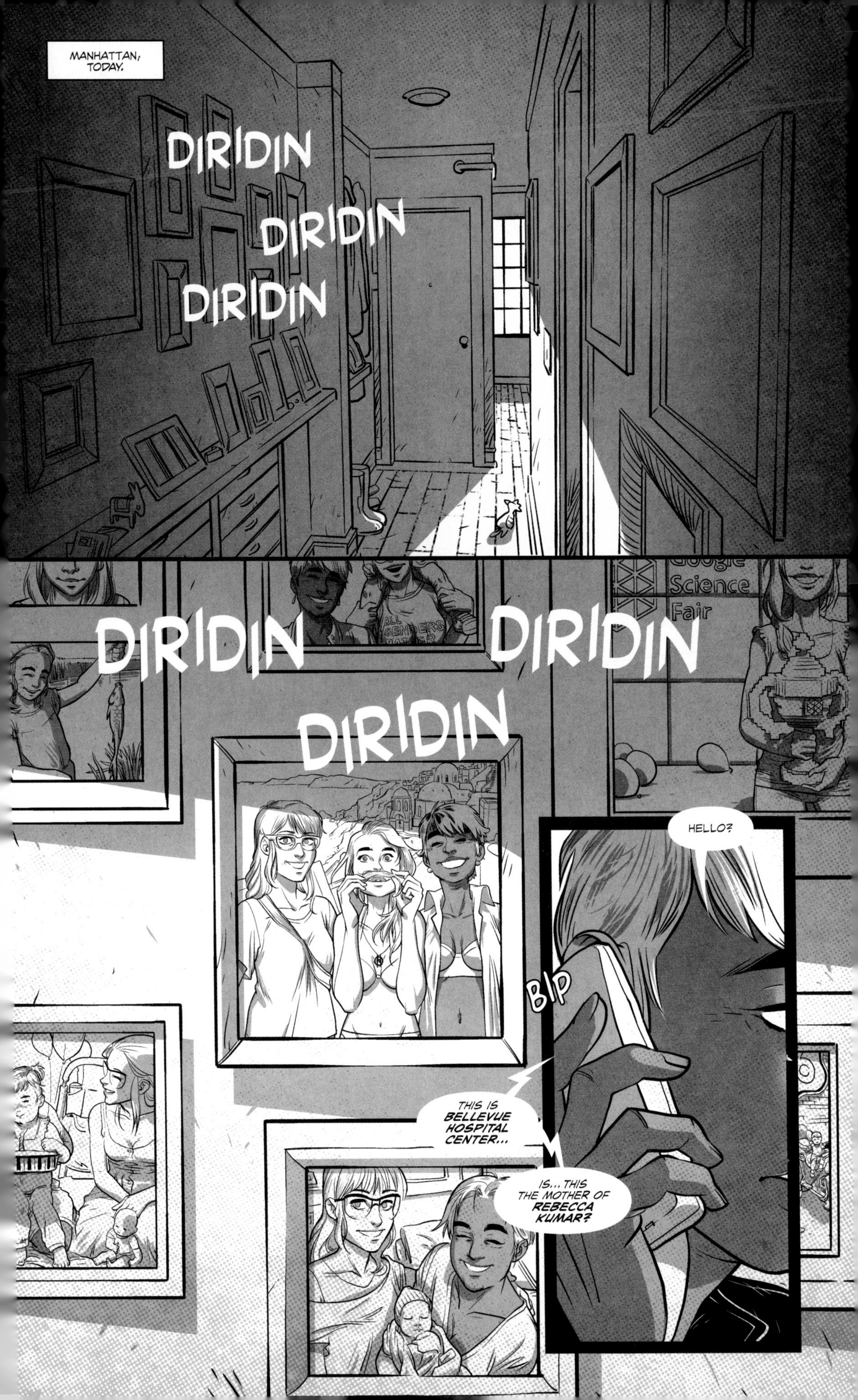
MANHATTAN, TODAY.
DIRIDIN
DIRIDIN
DIRIDIN
ALL GENDERS MATTER
Google Science Fair
DIRIDIN
DIRIDIN
DIRIDIN
HELLO?
BIP
THIS IS BELLEVUE HOSPITAL CENTER...
IS... THIS THE MOTHER OF REBECCA KUMAR?

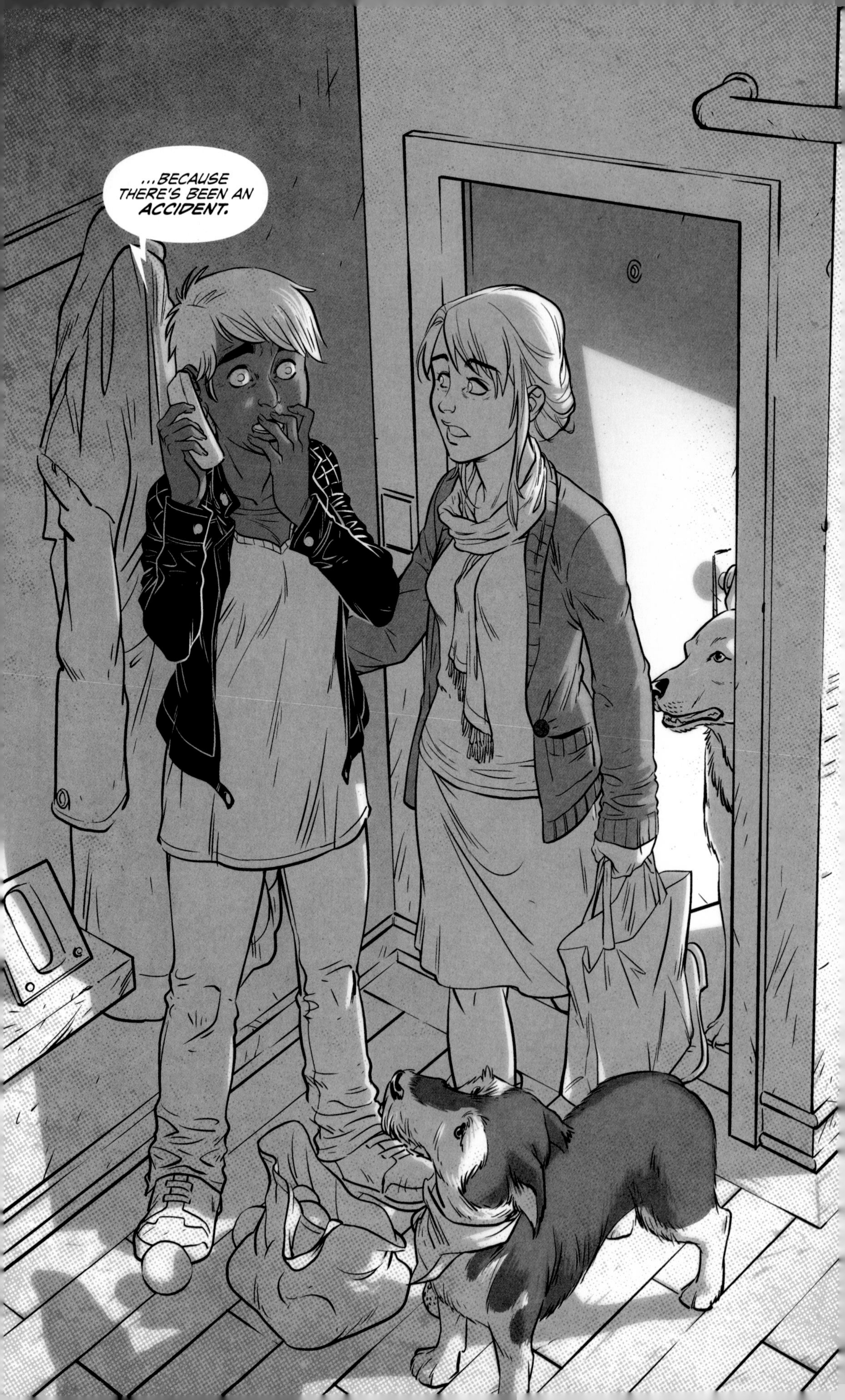
...BECAUSE THERE'S BEEN AN ACCIDENT.

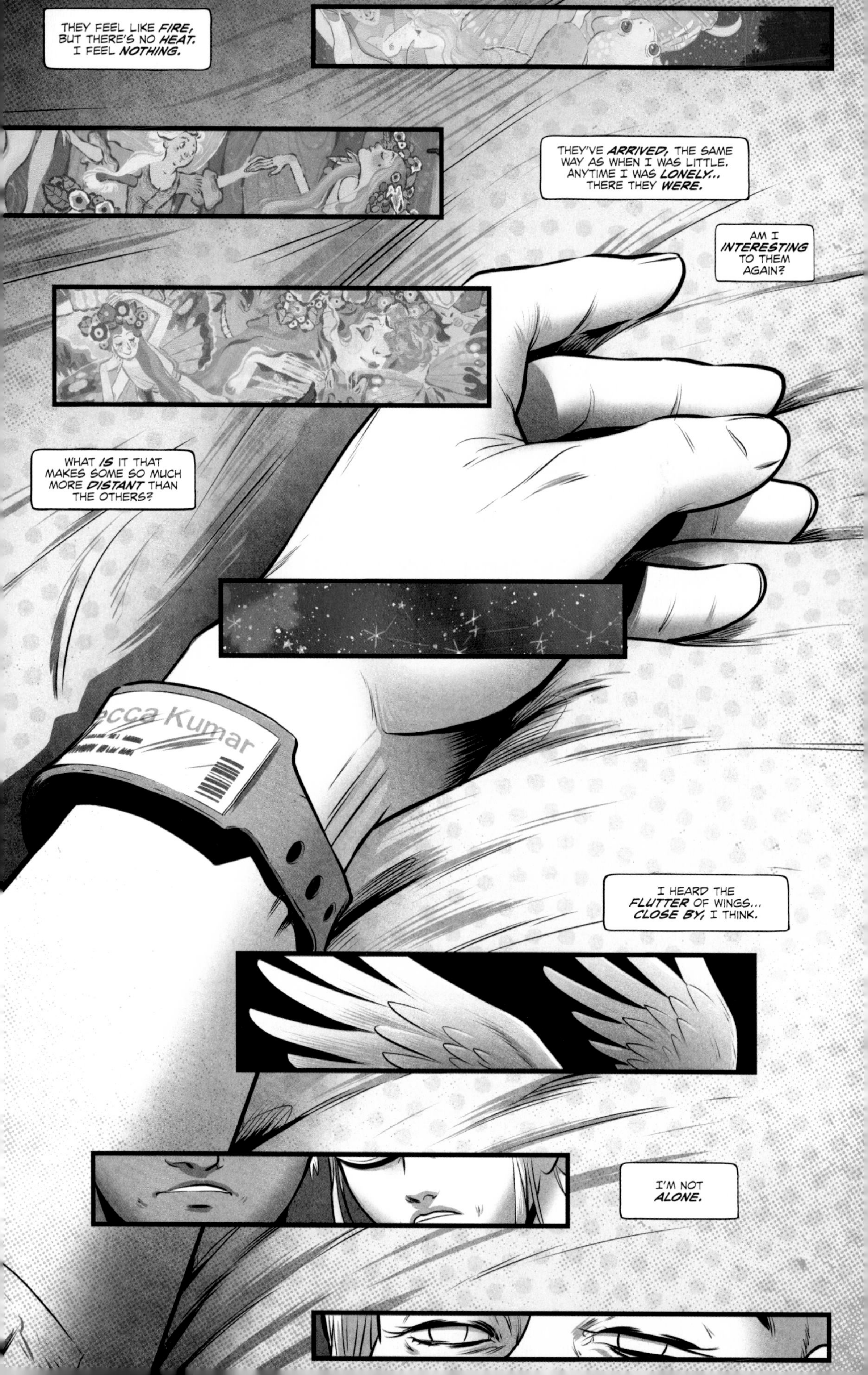
THEY FEEL LIKE *FIRE,* BUT THERE'S NO *HEAT.* I FEEL *NOTHING.*
THEY'VE *ARRIVED,* THE SAME WAY AS WHEN I WAS LITTLE. ANYTIME I WAS *LONELY...* THERE THEY *WERE.*
AM I *INTERESTING* TO THEM AGAIN?
WHAT *IS* IT THAT MAKES SOME SO MUCH MORE *DISTANT* THAN THE OTHERS?
I HEARD THE *FLUTTER* OF WINGS... *CLOSE BY,* I THINK.
I'M NOT *ALONE.*

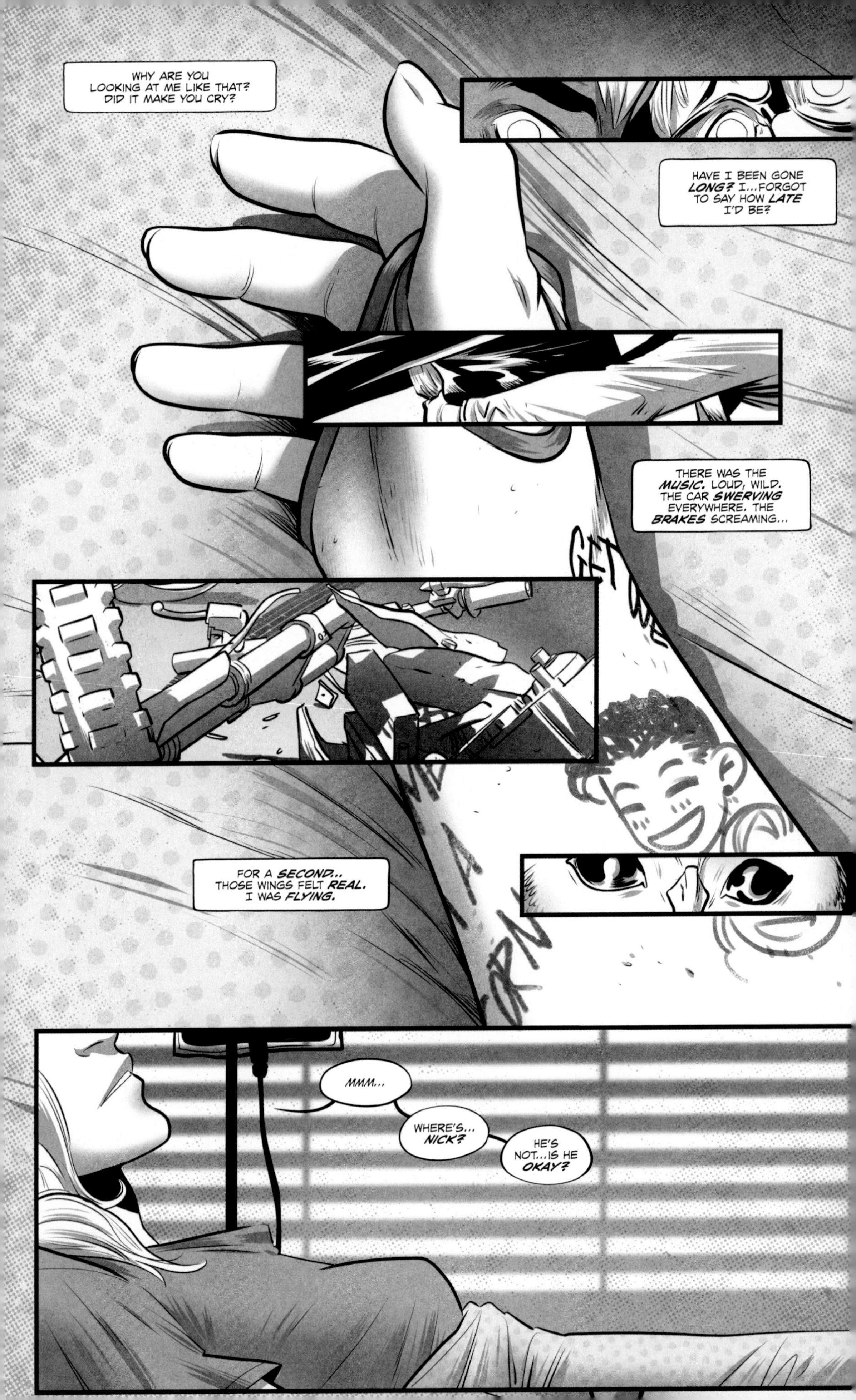
WHY ARE YOU LOOKING AT ME LIKE THAT? DID IT MAKE YOU CRY?
HAVE I BEEN GONE LONG? I...FORGOT TO SAY HOW LATE I'D BE?
THERE WAS THE MUSIC. LOUD, WILD. THE CAR SWERVING EVERYWHERE. THE BRAKES SCREAMING...
FOR A SECOND... THOSE WINGS FELT REAL. I WAS FLYING.
MMM...
WHERE'S... NICK?
HE'S NOT...IS HE OKAY?

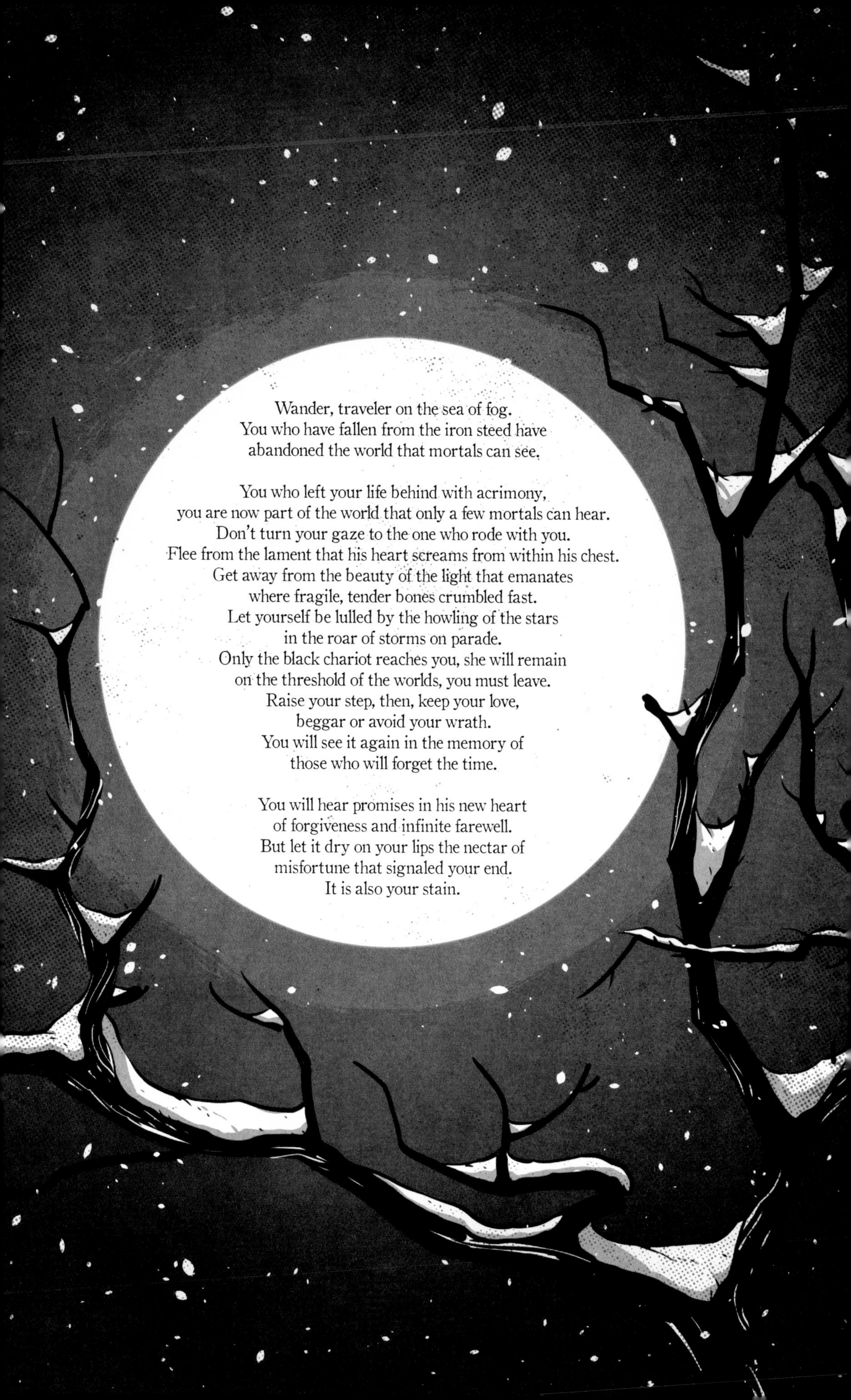

Wander, traveler on the sea of fog.
You who have fallen from the iron steed have
abandoned the world that mortals can see.

You who left your life behind with acrimony,
you are now part of the world that only a few mortals can hear.
Don't turn your gaze to the one who rode with you.
Flee from the lament that his heart screams from within his chest.
Get away from the beauty of the light that emanates
where fragile, tender bones crumbled fast.
Let yourself be lulled by the howling of the stars
in the roar of storms on parade.
Only the black chariot reaches you, she will remain
on the threshold of the worlds, you must leave.
Raise your step, then, keep your love,
beggar or avoid your wrath.
You will see it again in the memory of
those who will forget the time.

You will hear promises in his new heart
of forgiveness and infinite farewell.
But let it dry on your lips the nectar of
misfortune that signaled your end.
It is also your stain.

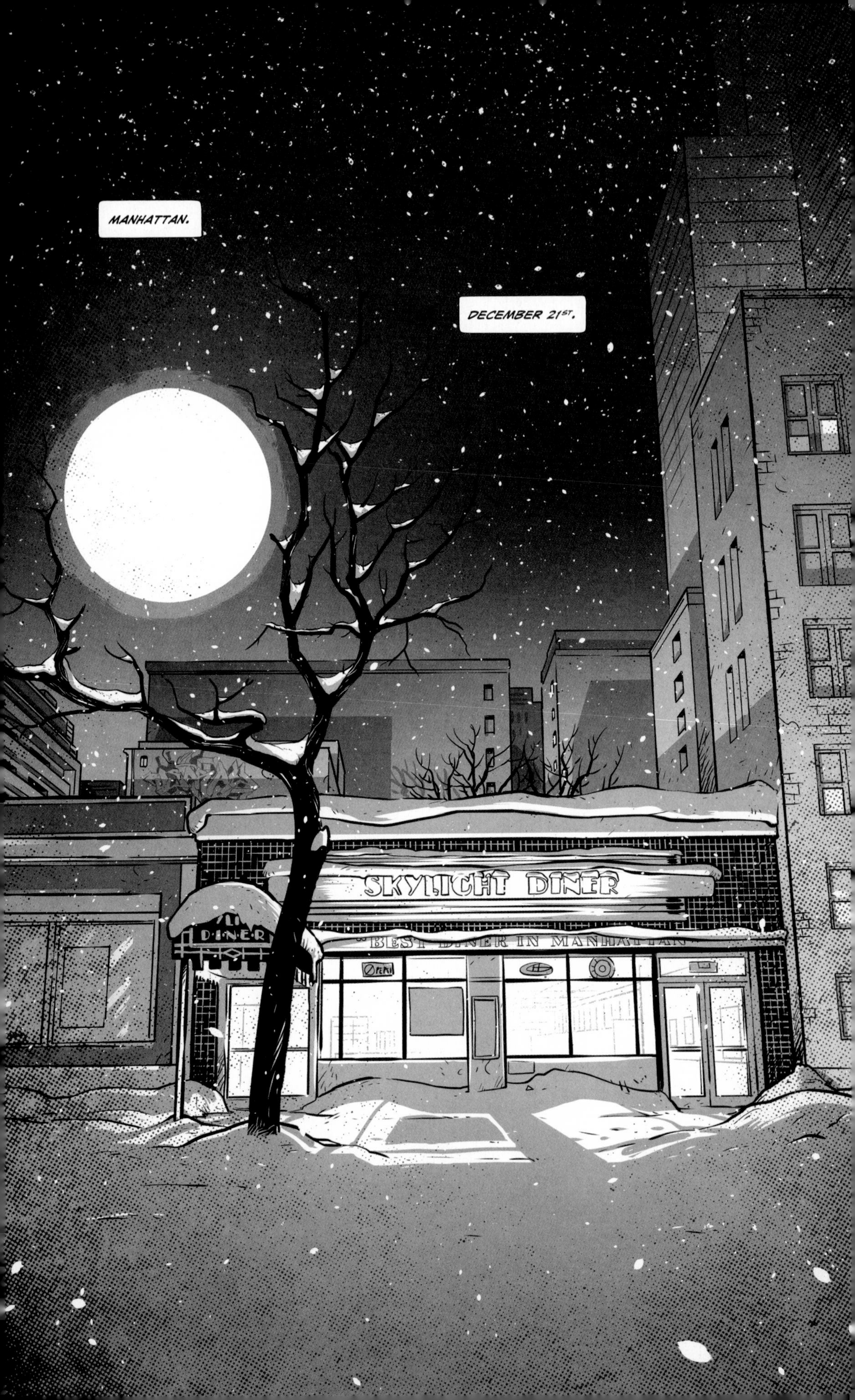
MANHATTAN.
DECEMBER 21ST.
SKYLIGHT DINER
"BEST DINER IN MANHATTAN"
DINER

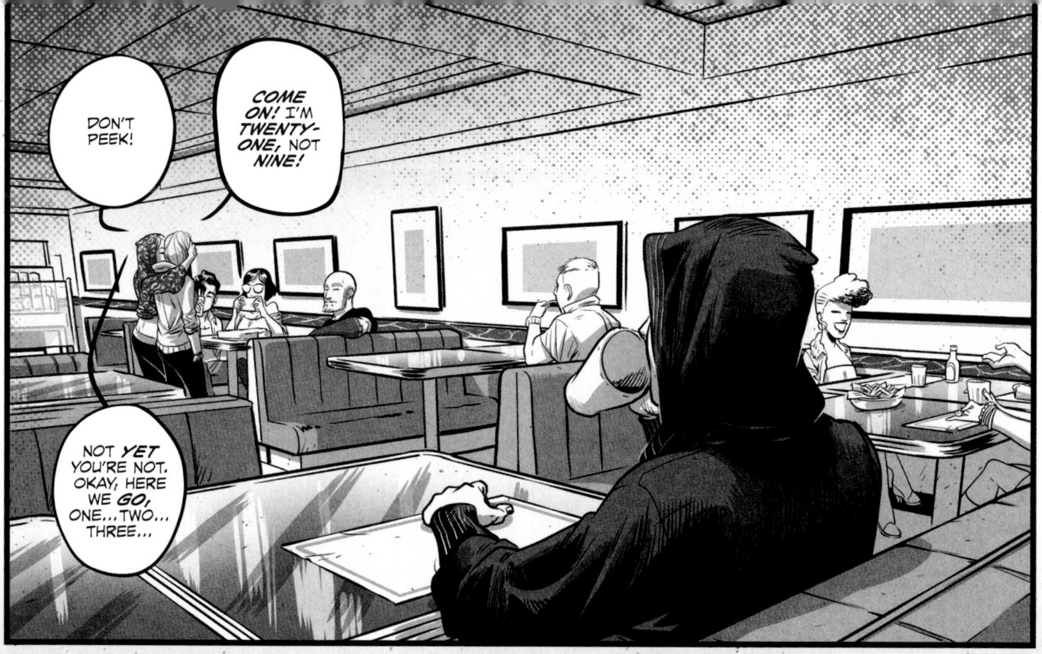
DON'T PEEK!
COME ON! I'M TWENTY-ONE, NOT NINE!
NOT YET YOU'RE NOT. OKAY, HERE WE GO, ONE... TWO... THREE...

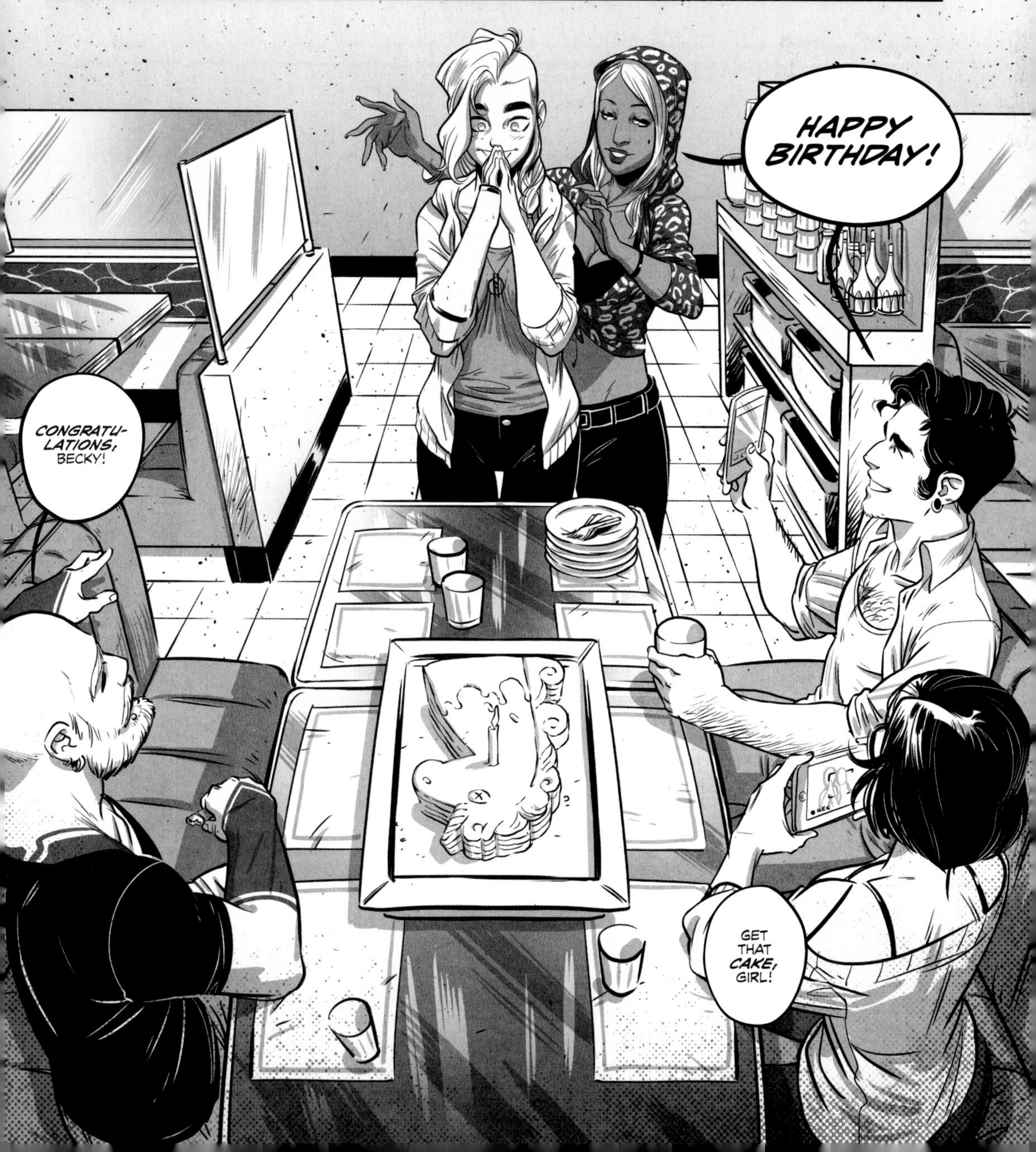
HAPPY BIRTHDAY!
CONGRATU-LATIONS, BECKY!
GET THAT CAKE, GIRL!

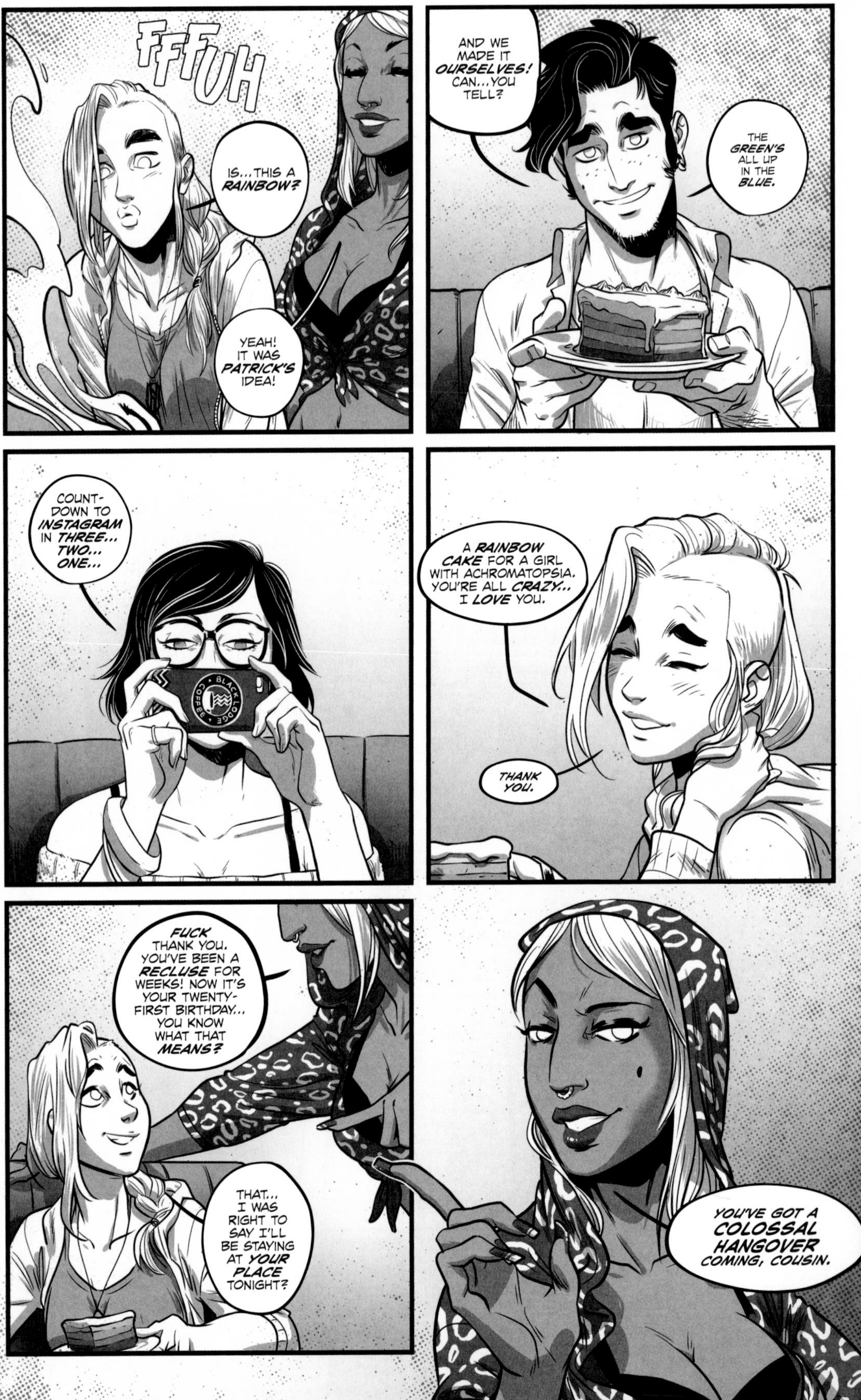
FFFUH
IS...THIS A RAINBOW?
YEAH! IT WAS PATRICK'S IDEA!
AND WE MADE IT OURSELVES! CAN...YOU TELL?
THE GREEN'S ALL UP IN THE BLUE.
COUNT-DOWN TO INSTAGRAM IN THREE... TWO... ONE...
BLACK LODGE COFFEE
A RAINBOW CAKE FOR A GIRL WITH ACHROMATOPSIA. YOU'RE ALL CRAZY... I LOVE YOU.
THANK YOU.
FUCK THANK YOU. YOU'VE BEEN A RECLUSE FOR WEEKS! NOW IT'S YOUR TWENTY-FIRST BIRTHDAY... YOU KNOW WHAT THAT MEANS?
THAT... I WAS RIGHT TO SAY I'LL BE STAYING AT YOUR PLACE TONIGHT?
YOU'VE GOT A COLOSSAL HANGOVER COMING, COUSIN.

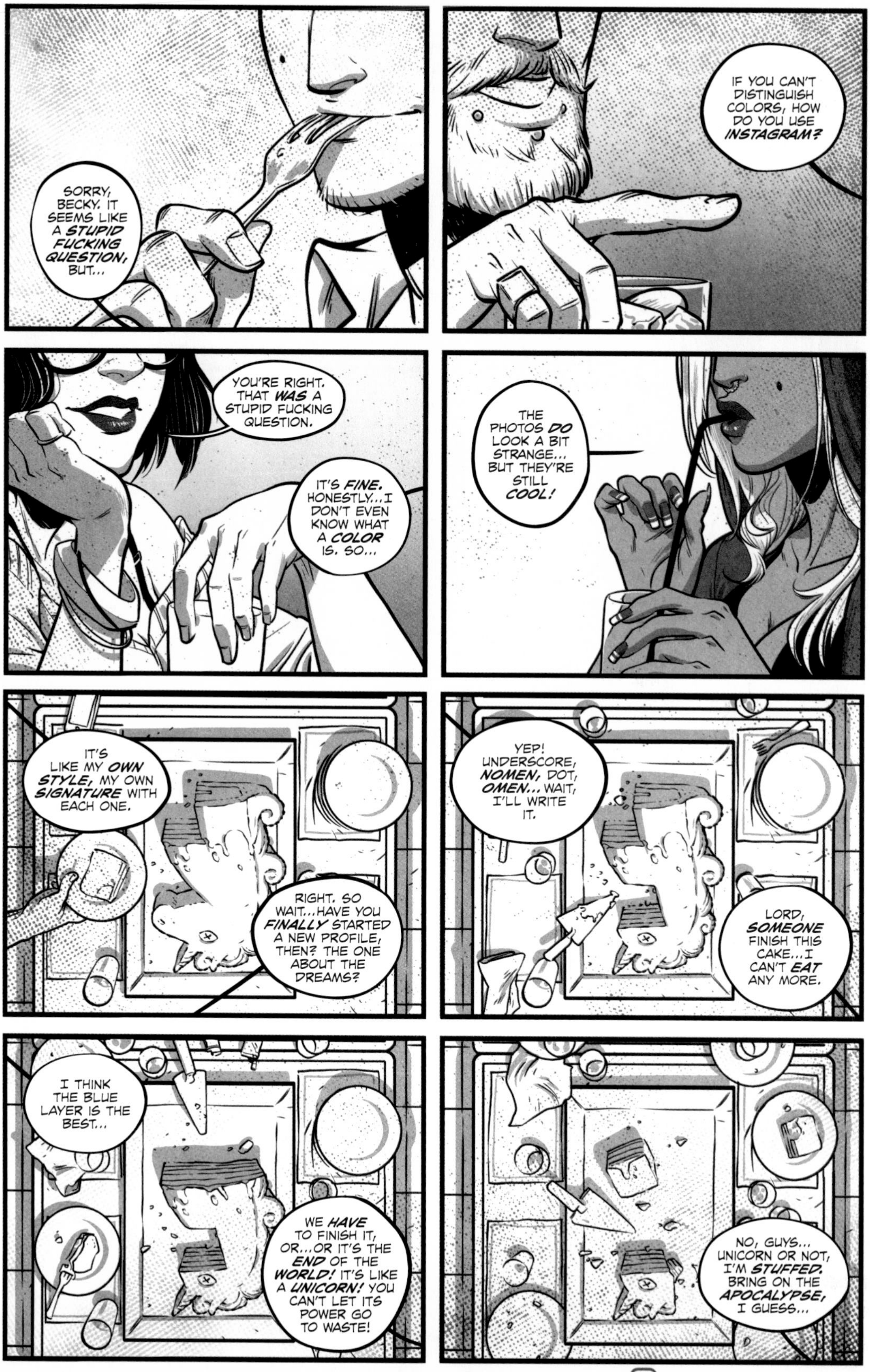
SORRY, BECKY. IT SEEMS LIKE A STUPID FUCKING QUESTION, BUT...
IF YOU CAN'T DISTINGUISH COLORS, HOW DO YOU USE INSTAGRAM?
YOU'RE RIGHT. THAT WAS A STUPID FUCKING QUESTION.
IT'S FINE. HONESTLY...I DON'T EVEN KNOW WHAT A COLOR IS. SO...
THE PHOTOS DO LOOK A BIT STRANGE... BUT THEY'RE STILL COOL!
IT'S LIKE MY OWN STYLE, MY OWN SIGNATURE WITH EACH ONE.
RIGHT. SO WAIT...HAVE YOU FINALLY STARTED A NEW PROFILE, THEN? THE ONE ABOUT THE DREAMS?
YEP! UNDERSCORE, NOMEN, DOT, OMEN... WAIT, I'LL WRITE IT.
LORD, SOMEONE FINISH THIS CAKE...I CAN'T EAT ANY MORE.
I THINK THE BLUE LAYER IS THE BEST...
WE HAVE TO FINISH IT, OR...OR IT'S THE END OF THE WORLD! IT'S LIKE A UNICORN! YOU CAN'T LET ITS POWER GO TO WASTE!
NO, GUYS... UNICORN OR NOT, I'M STUFFED. BRING ON THE APOCALYPSE, I GUESS...

nomen.omen

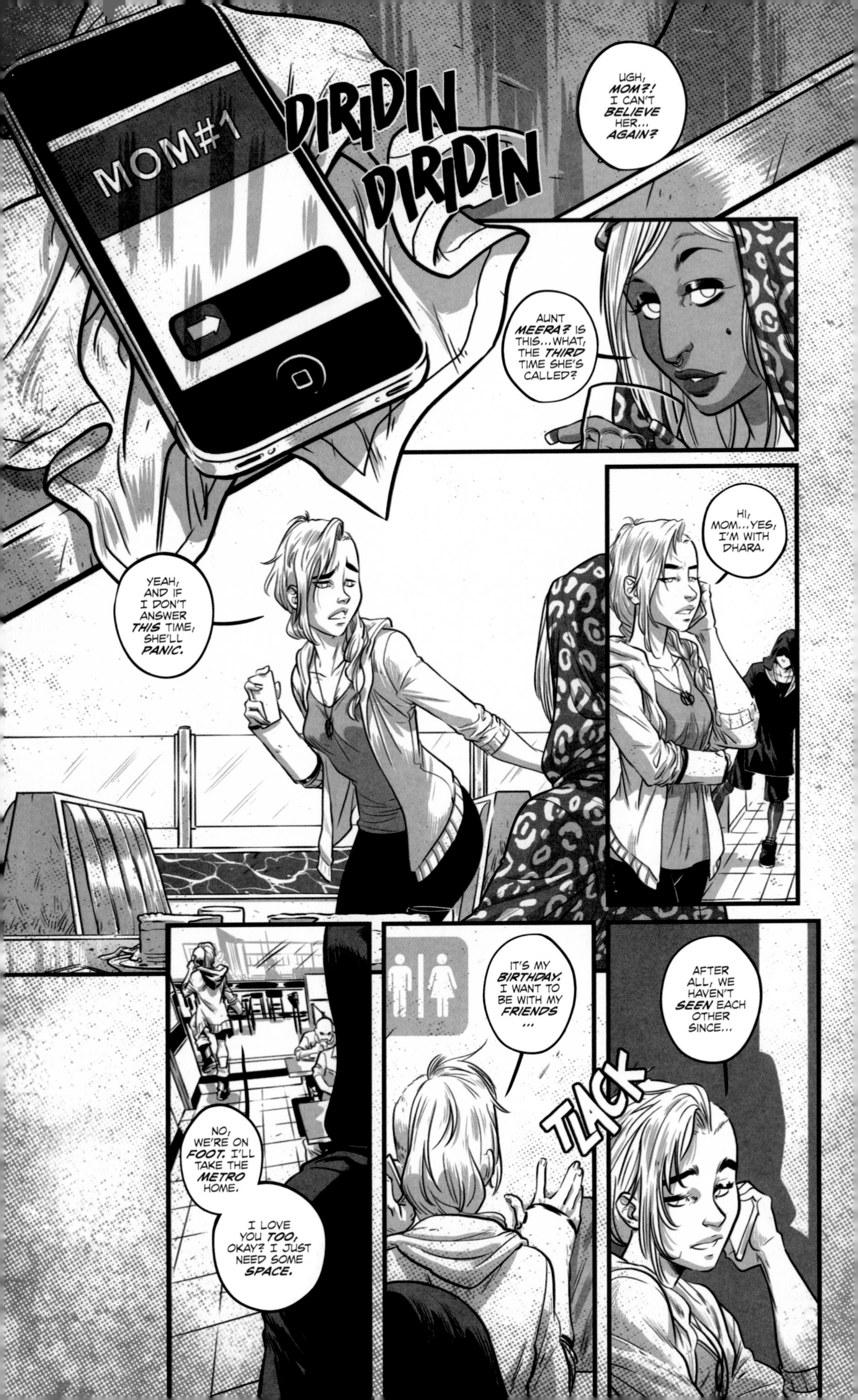
MOM#1
DIRIDIN DIRIDIN
UGH, MOM?! I CAN'T BELIEVE HER... AGAIN?
AUNT MEERA? IS THIS...WHAT, THE THIRD TIME SHE'S CALLED?
YEAH, AND IF I DON'T ANSWER THIS TIME, SHE'LL PANIC.
HI, MOM...YES, I'M WITH DHARA.
NO, WE'RE ON FOOT. I'LL TAKE THE METRO HOME.
I LOVE YOU TOO, OKAY? I JUST NEED SOME SPACE.
IT'S MY BIRTHDAY. I WANT TO BE WITH MY FRIENDS ...
AFTER ALL, WE HAVEN'T SEEN EACH OTHER SINCE...
TLACK

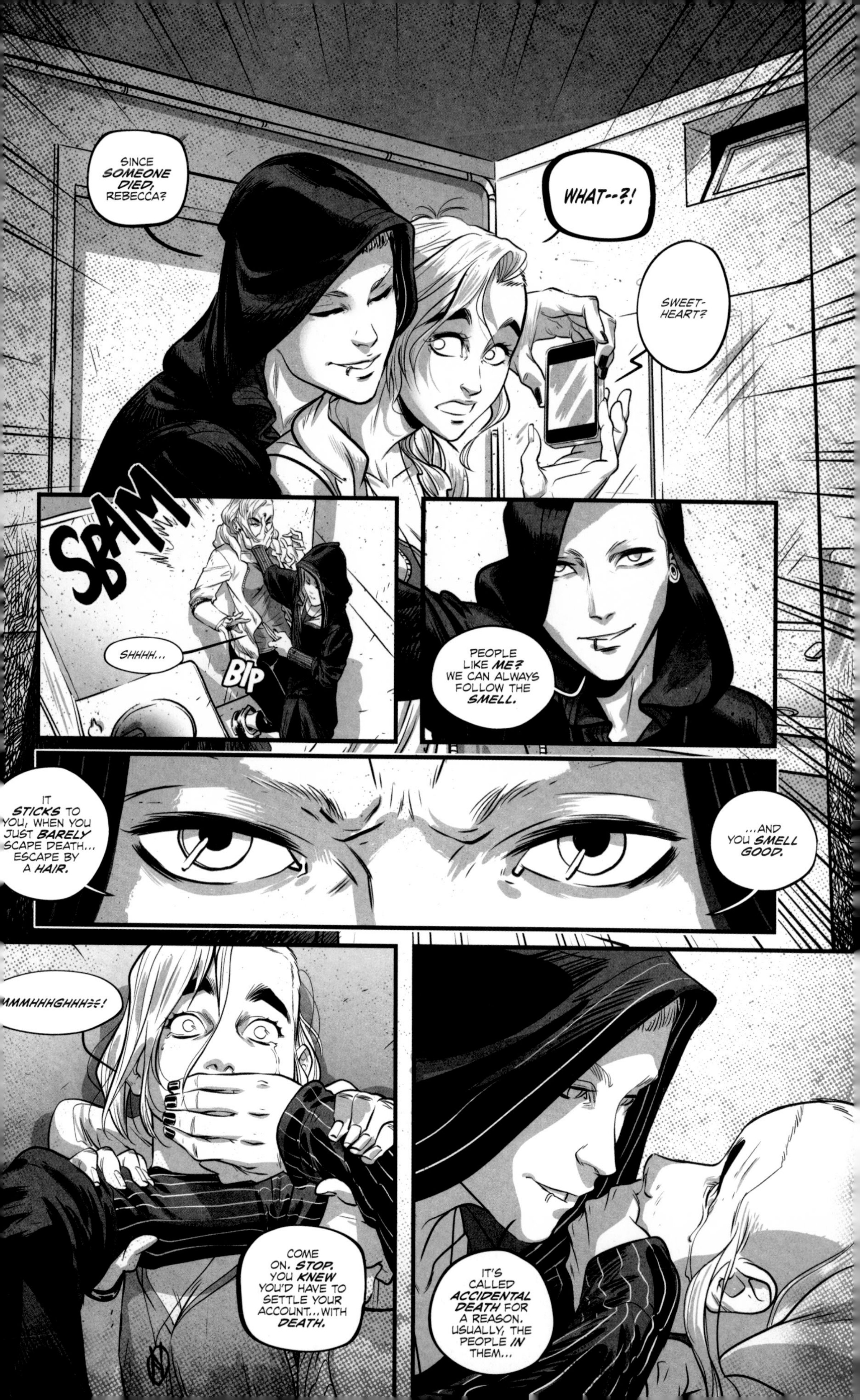
SINCE SOMEONE DIED, REBECCA?
WHAT--?!
SWEET-HEART?
SBAM
SHHHH...
BIP
PEOPLE LIKE ME? WE CAN ALWAYS FOLLOW THE SMELL.
IT STICKS TO YOU, WHEN YOU JUST BARELY SCAPE DEATH... ESCAPE BY A HAIR.
...AND YOU SMELL GOOD.
MMMHHHGHHH!!
COME ON. STOP. YOU KNEW YOU'D HAVE TO SETTLE YOUR ACCOUNT...WITH DEATH.
IT'S CALLED ACCIDENTAL DEATH FOR A REASON. USUALLY, THE PEOPLE IN THEM...

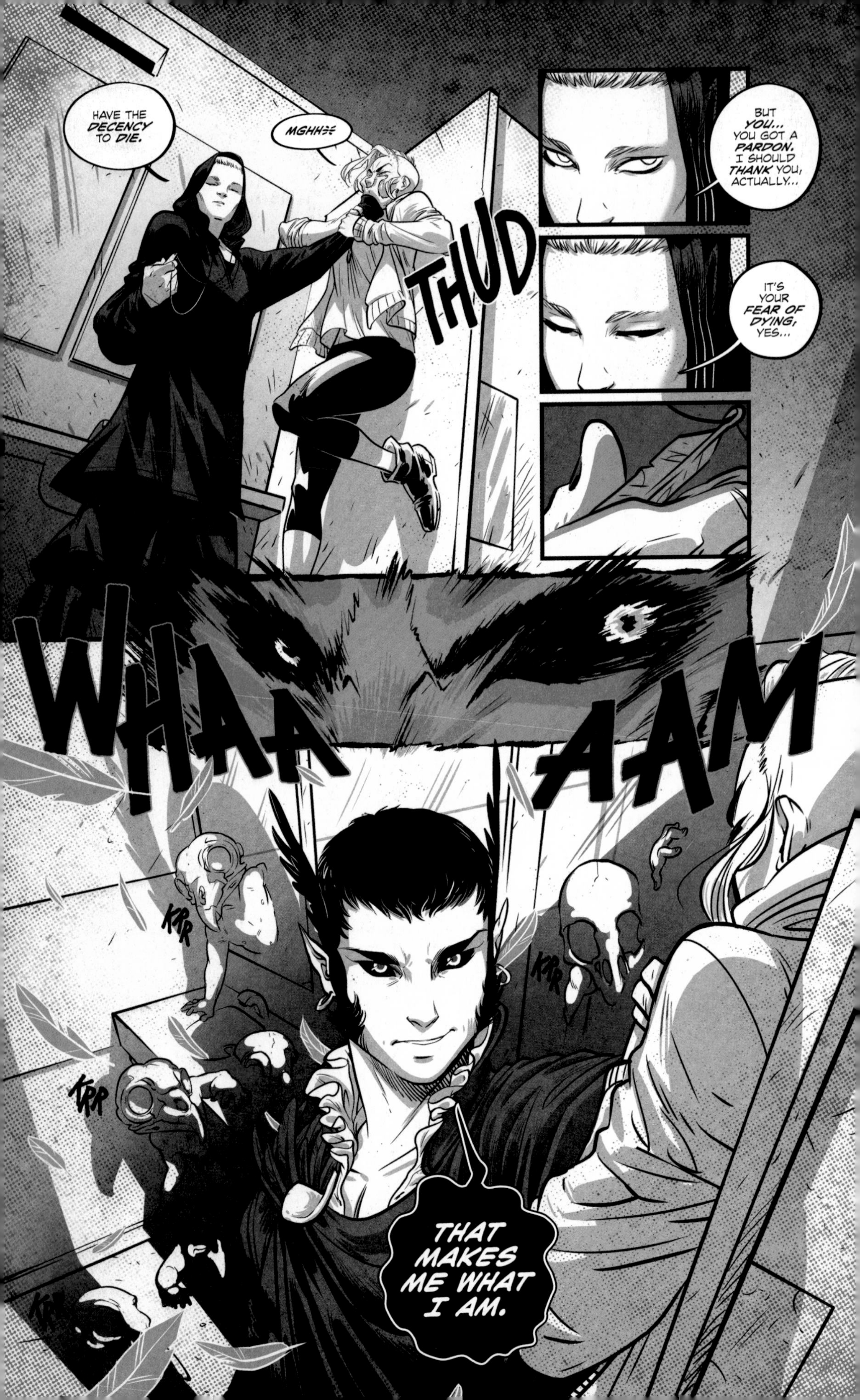

HAVE THE *DECENCY* TO *DIE.*
MGHH≠
THUD
BUT *YOU...* YOU GOT A *PARDON.* I SHOULD *THANK* YOU, ACTUALLY...
IT'S YOUR *FEAR OF DYING,* YES...
WHAAAAM
KRR
KRR
KRR
THAT MAKES ME WHAT I AM.

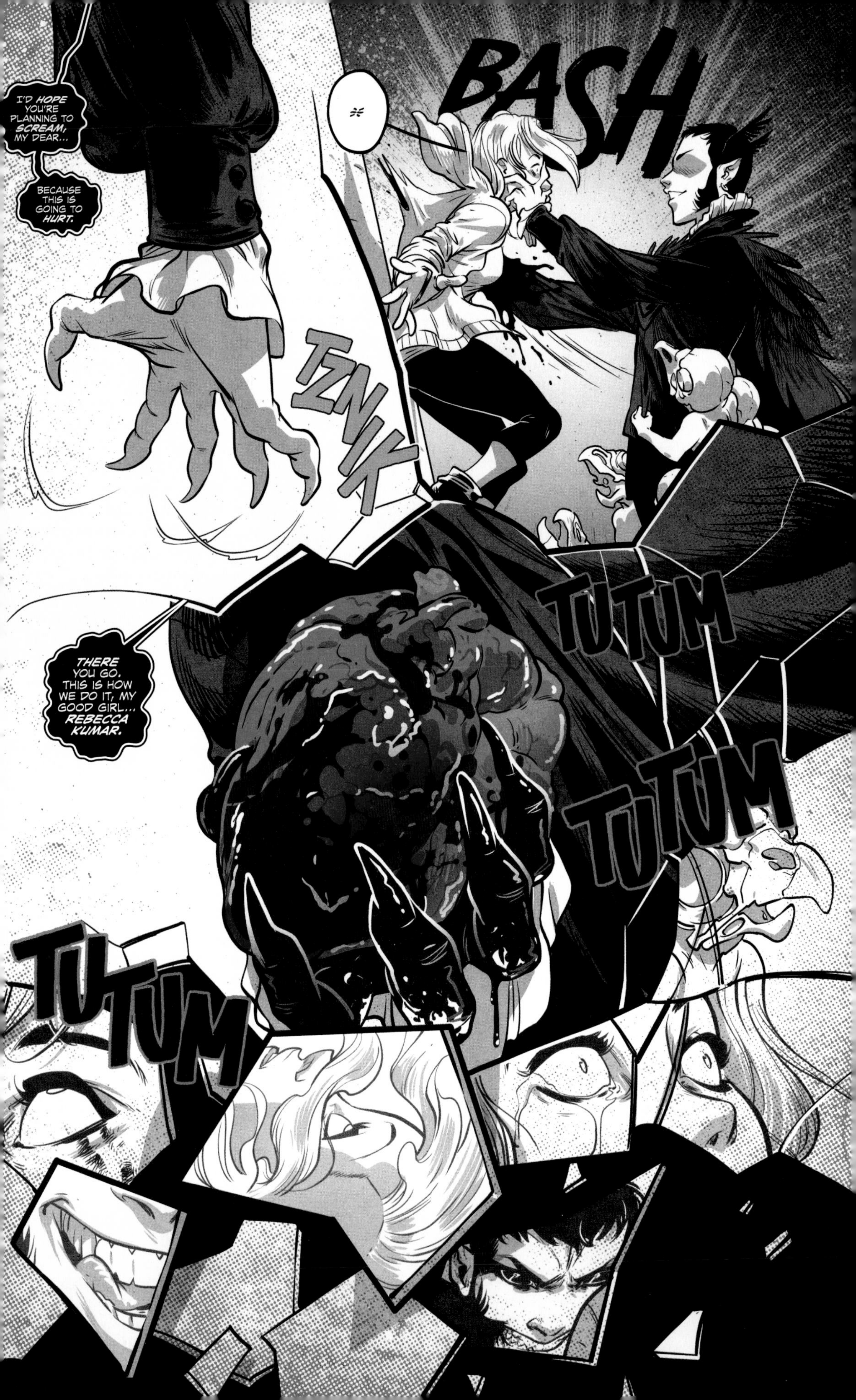
I'D HOPE YOU'RE PLANNING TO SCREAM, MY DEAR...
BECAUSE THIS IS GOING TO HURT.
BASH
TZNIK
THERE YOU GO. THIS IS HOW WE DO IT, MY GOOD GIRL... REBECCA KUMAR.
TUTUM
TUTUM
TUTUM

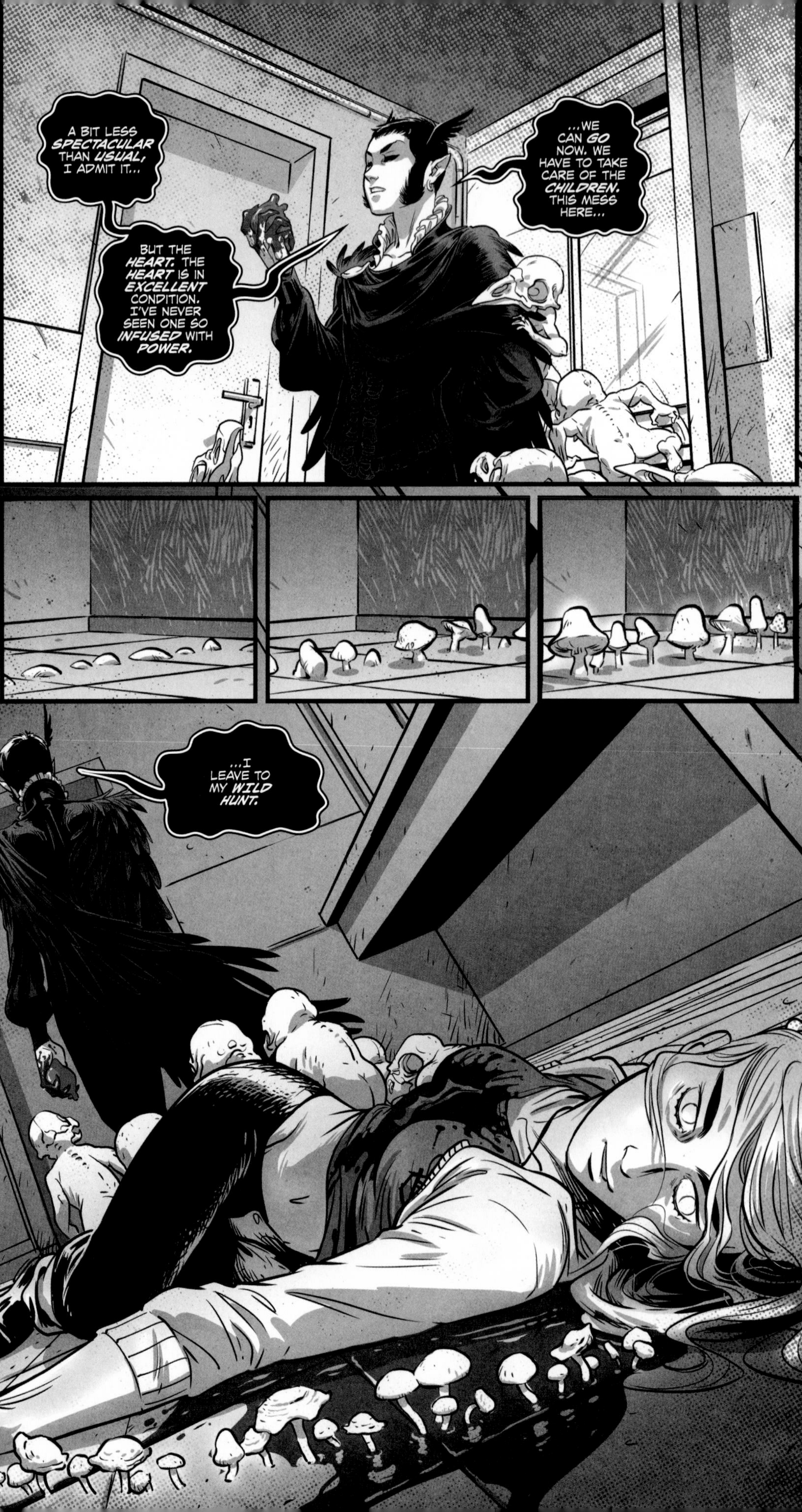
A BIT LESS SPECTACULAR THAN USUAL, I ADMIT IT...
BUT THE HEART. THE HEART IS IN EXCELLENT CONDITION. I'VE NEVER SEEN ONE SO INFUSED WITH POWER.
...WE CAN GO NOW. WE HAVE TO TAKE CARE OF THE CHILDREN. THIS MESS HERE...
...I LEAVE TO MY WILD HUNT.

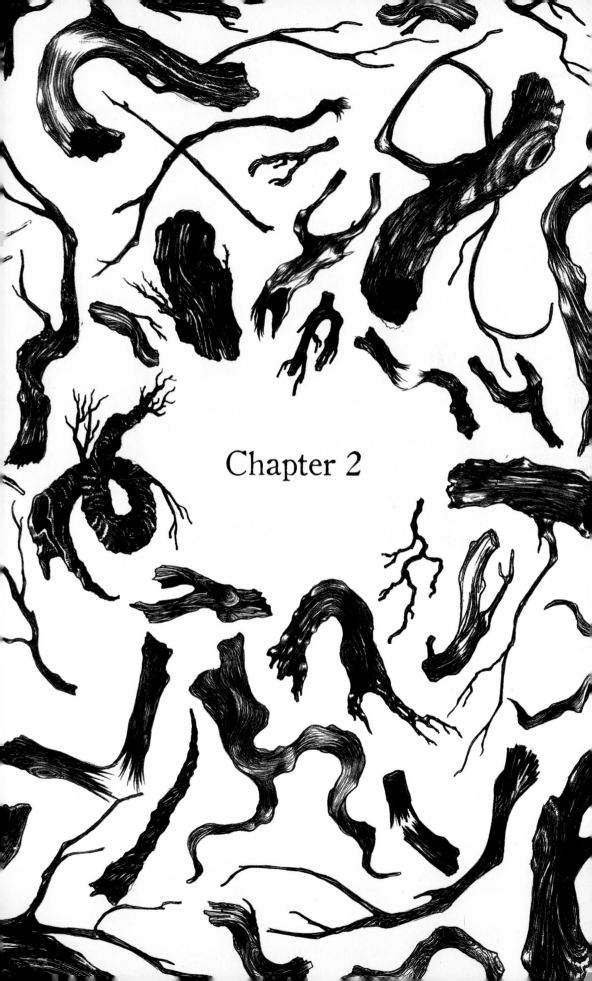

Chapter 2

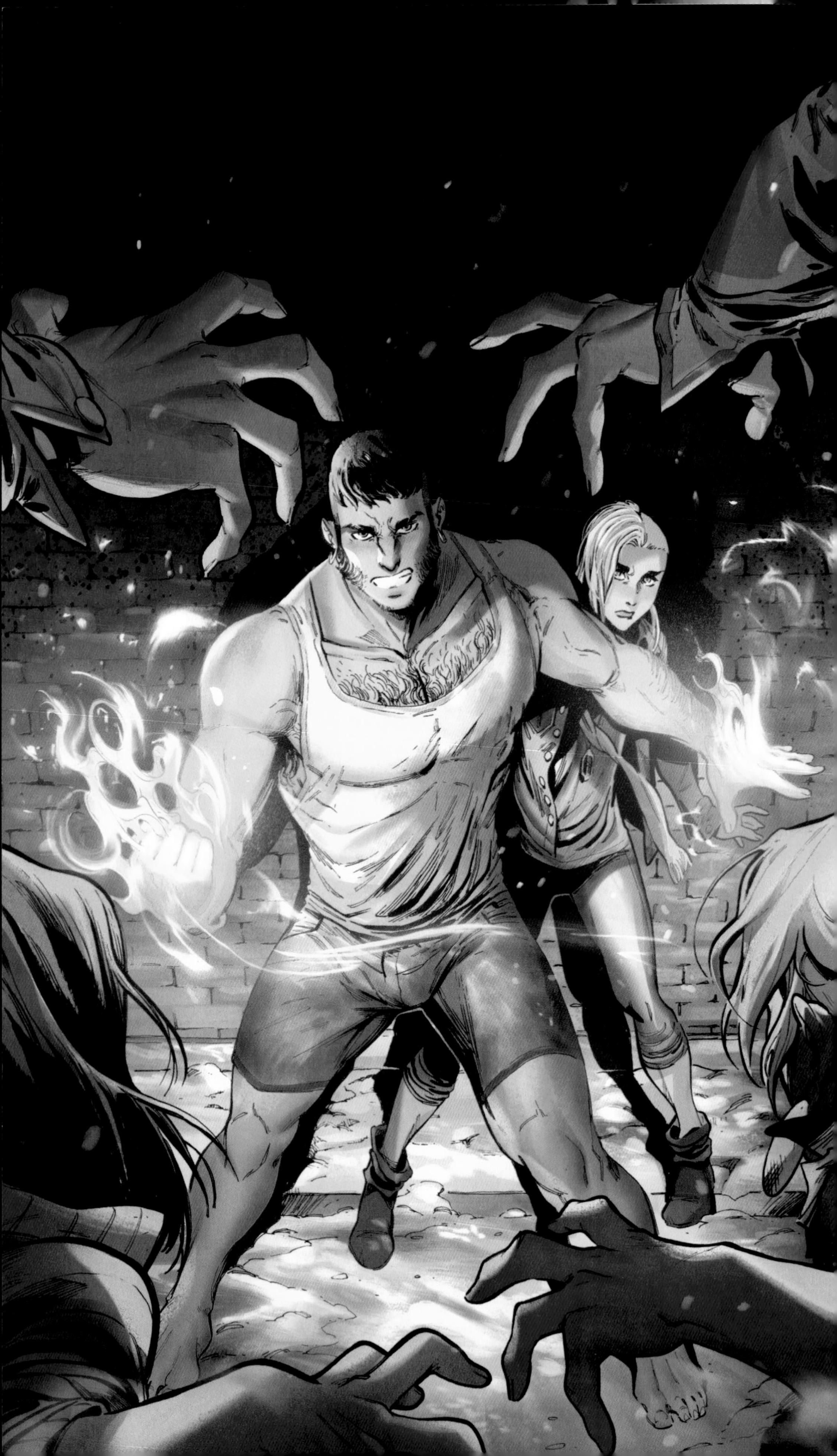

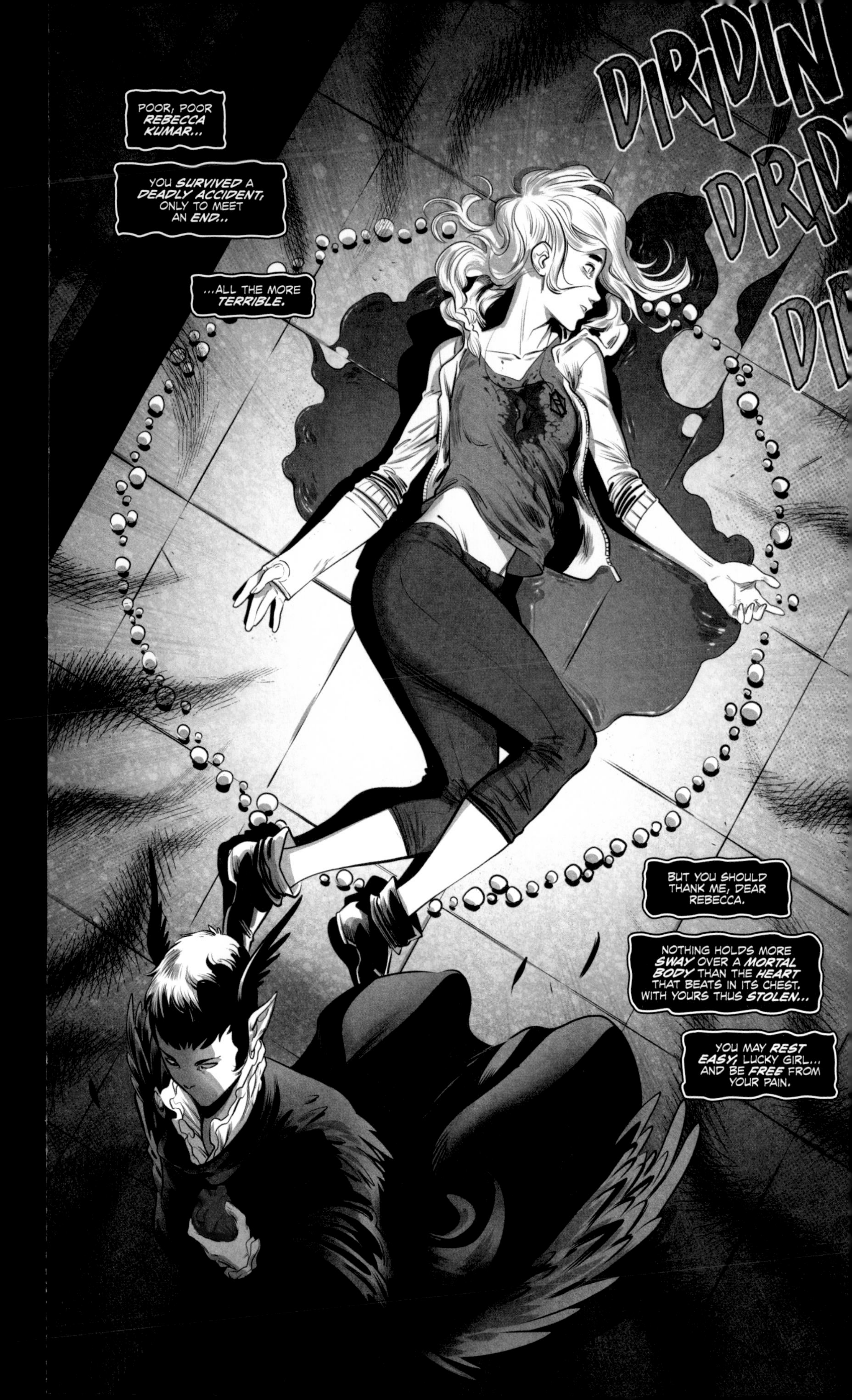

DIRIDIN DIRID DIR
POOR, POOR REBECCA KUMAR...
YOU SURVIVED A DEADLY ACCIDENT, ONLY TO MEET AN END...
...ALL THE MORE TERRIBLE.
BUT YOU SHOULD THANK ME, DEAR REBECCA.
NOTHING HOLDS MORE SWAY OVER A MORTAL BODY THAN THE HEART THAT BEATS IN ITS CHEST. WITH YOURS THUS STOLEN...
YOU MAY REST EASY, LUCKY GIRL... AND BE FREE FROM YOUR PAIN.

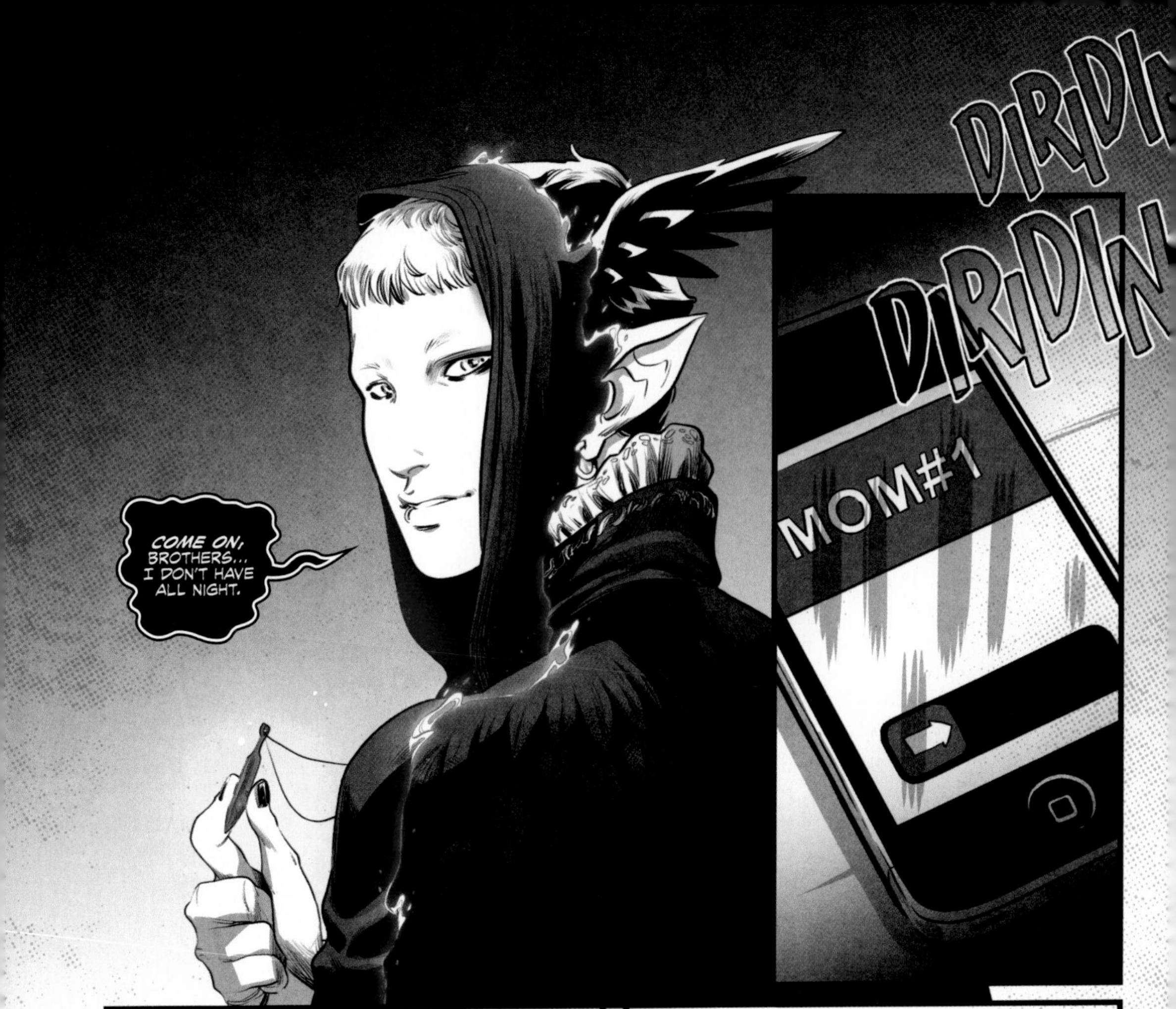
DIRIDIN
DIRIDIN
MOM#1
COME ON, BROTHERS... I DON'T HAVE ALL NIGHT.

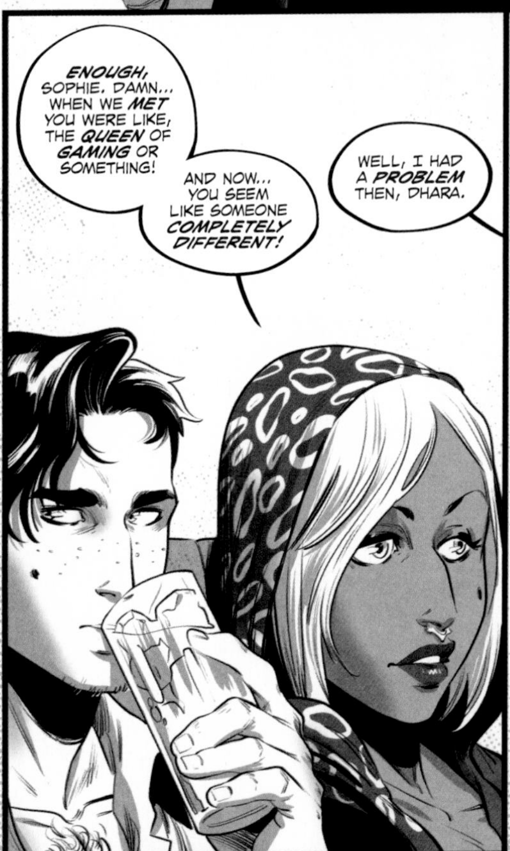
ENOUGH, SOPHIE. DAMN... WHEN WE MET YOU WERE LIKE, THE QUEEN OF GAMING OR SOMETHING!
AND NOW... YOU SEEM LIKE SOMEONE COMPLETELY DIFFERENT!
WELL, I HAD A PROBLEM THEN, DHARA.

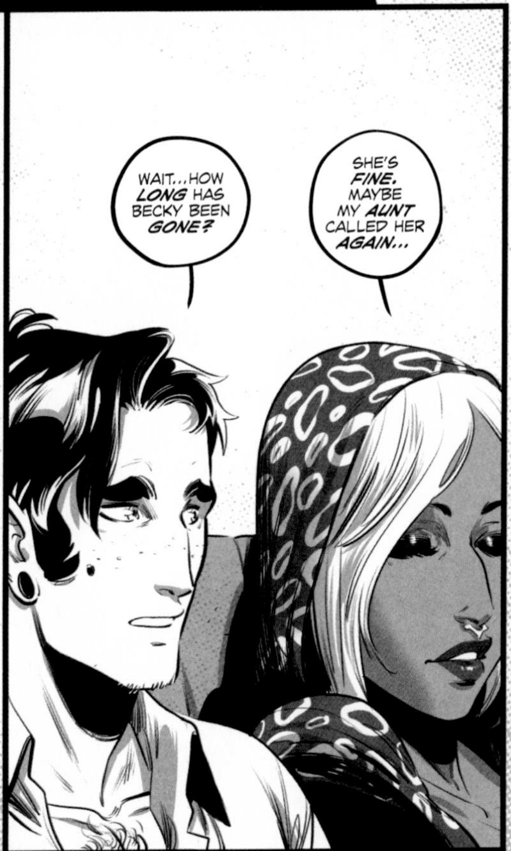
WAIT...HOW LONG HAS BECKY BEEN GONE?
SHE'S FINE. MAYBE MY AUNT CALLED HER AGAIN...

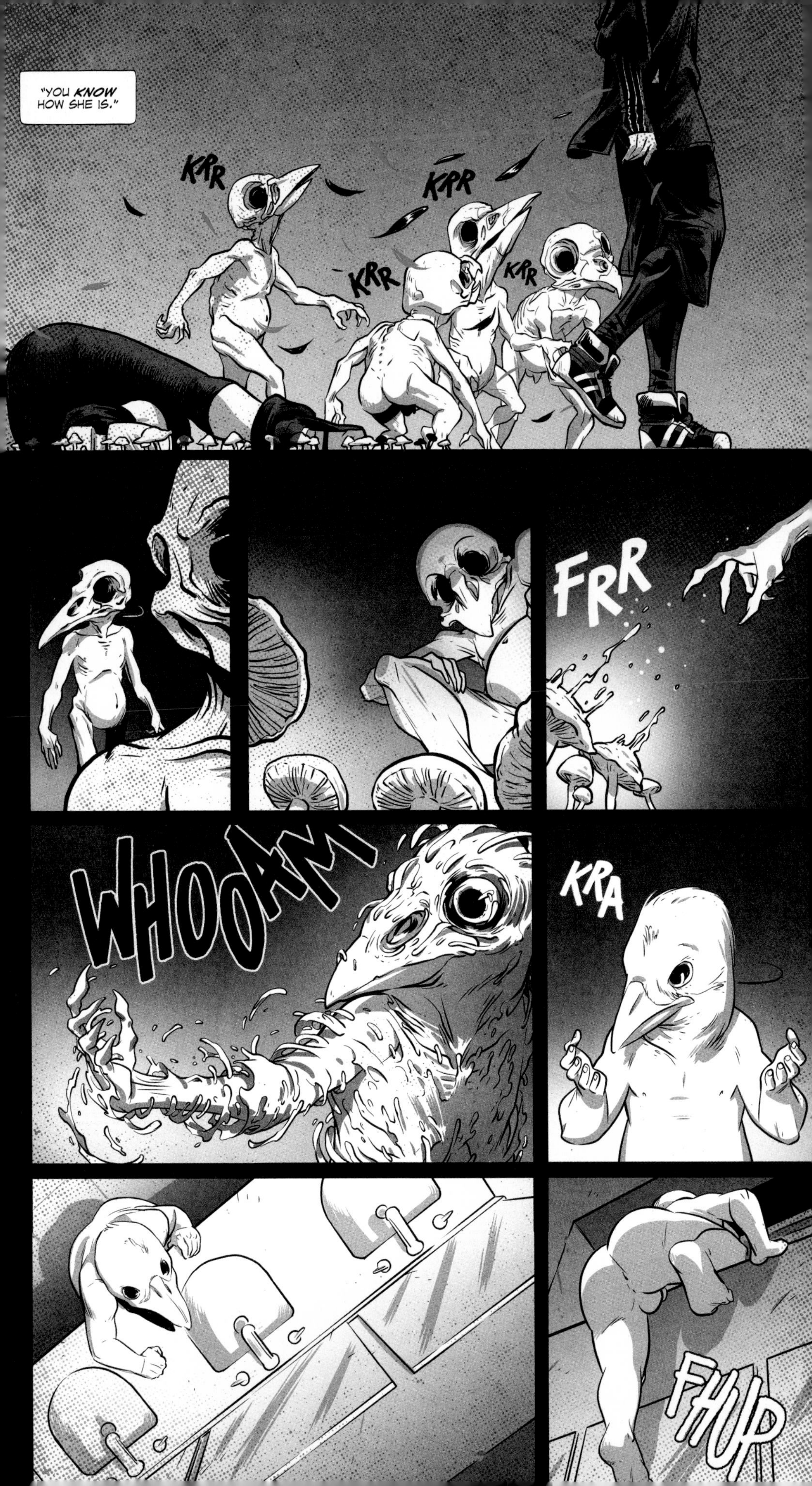
"YOU KNOW HOW SHE IS."
KRR
KRR
KRR
KRR
FRR
WHOOAM
KRA
FHUP

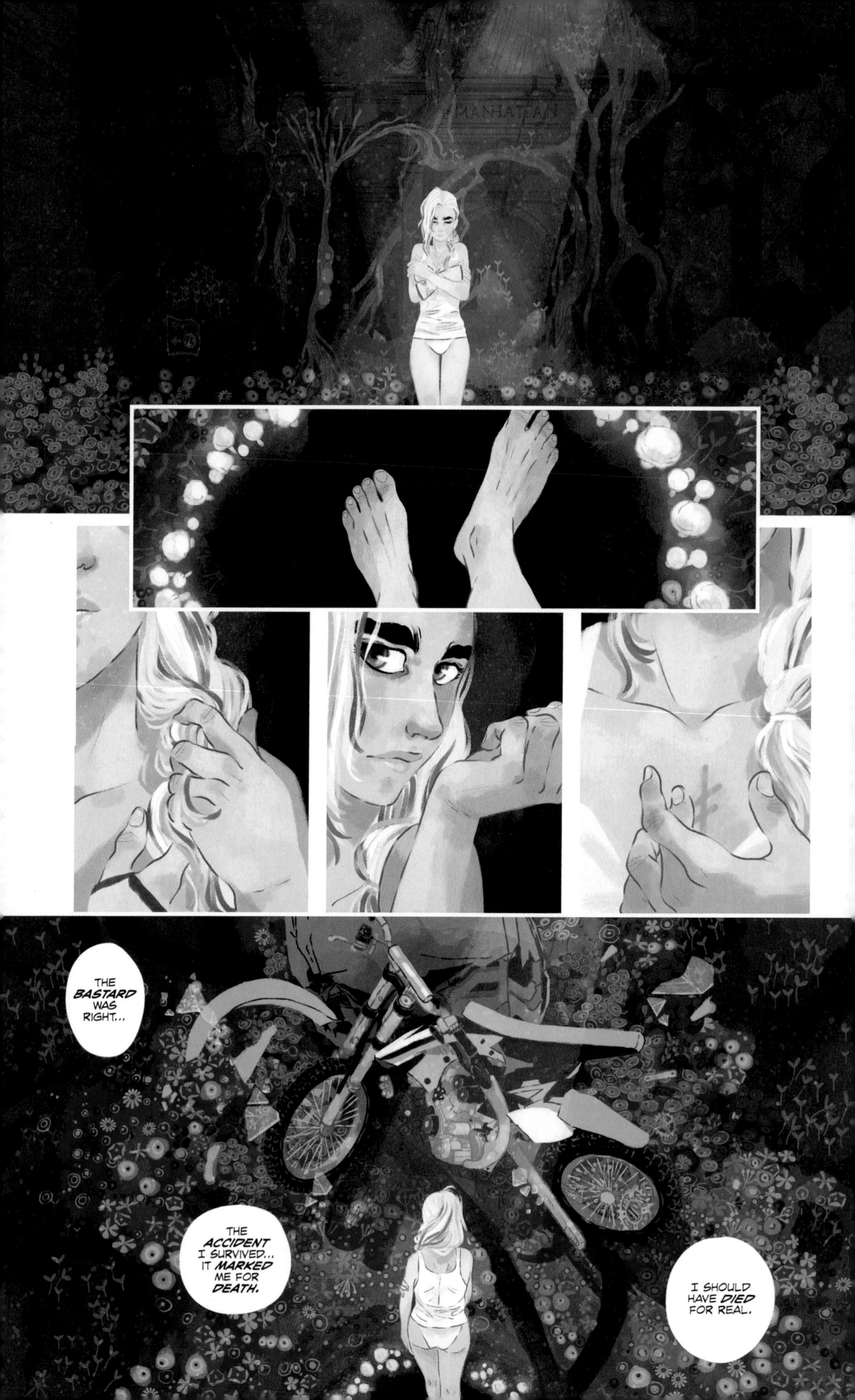
MANHATTAN
THE BASTARD WAS RIGHT...
THE ACCIDENT I SURVIVED... IT MARKED ME FOR DEATH.
I SHOULD HAVE DIED FOR REAL.

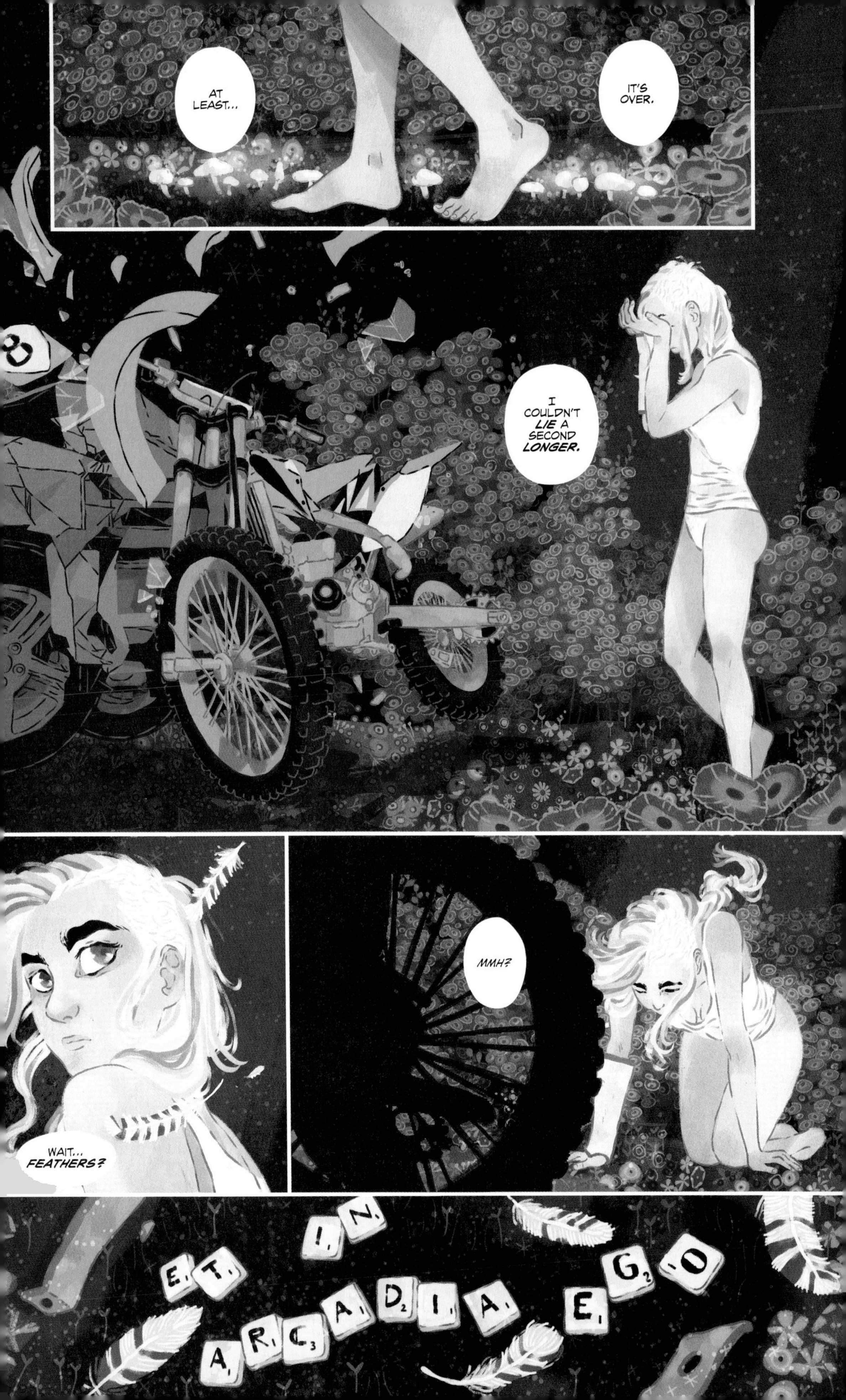
AT LEAST...
IT'S OVER.
I COULDN'T *LIE* A SECOND *LONGER.*
WAIT... *FEATHERS?*
MMH?
ET IN ARCADIA EGO

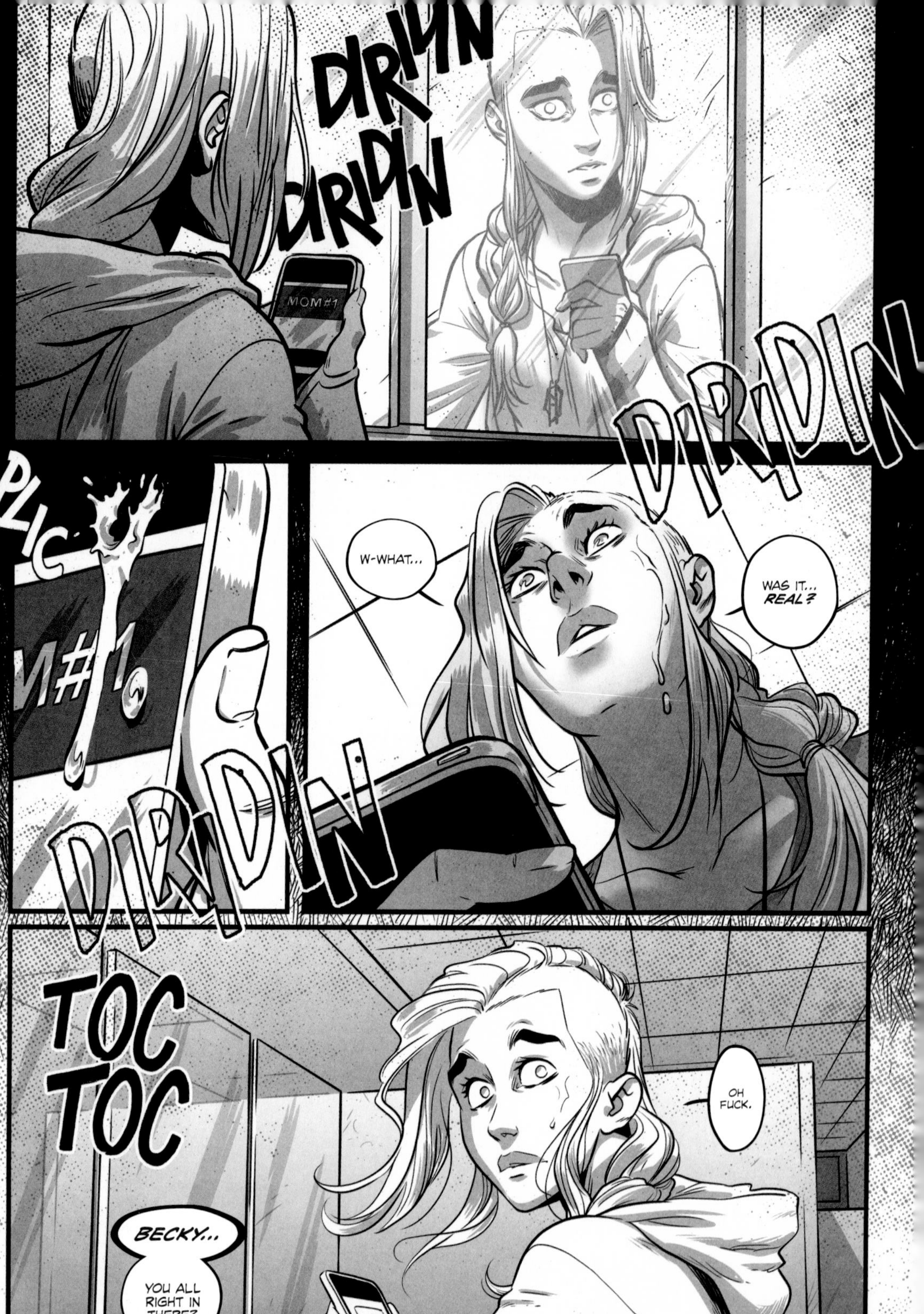
DIRIYN
DIRIDIN
MOM#1
DIRIDIN
PLIC
M#1
W-WHAT...
WAS IT... REAL?
DIRIDIN
TOC TOC
OH FUCK.
BECKY...
YOU ALL RIGHT IN THERE?
1 MISSED CALL

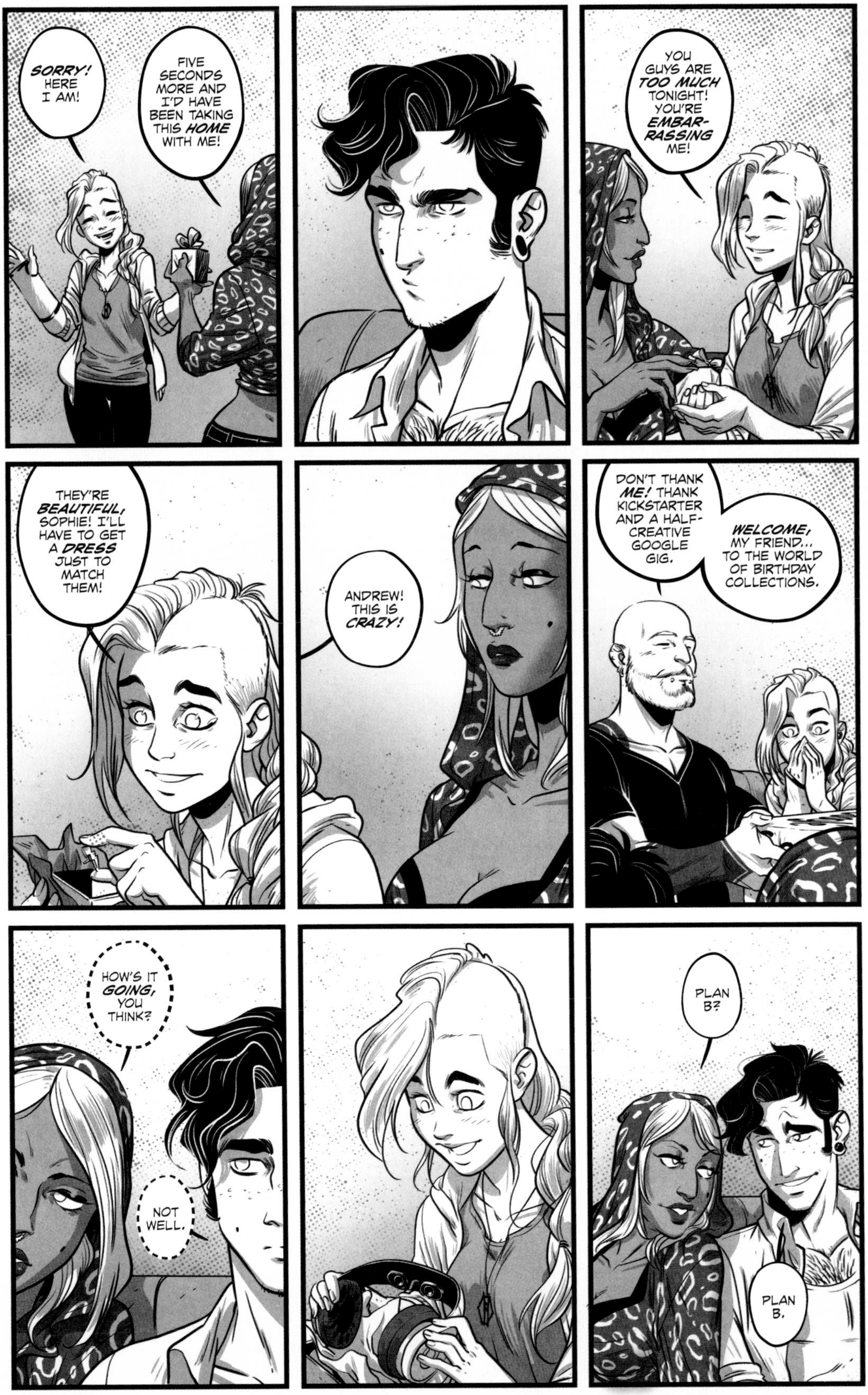
SORRY! HERE I AM!
FIVE SECONDS MORE AND I'D HAVE BEEN TAKING THIS HOME WITH ME!
YOU GUYS ARE TOO MUCH TONIGHT! YOU'RE EMBAR-RASSING ME!
THEY'RE BEAUTIFUL, SOPHIE! I'LL HAVE TO GET A DRESS JUST TO MATCH THEM!
ANDREW! THIS IS CRAZY!
DON'T THANK ME! THANK KICKSTARTER AND A HALF-CREATIVE GOOGLE GIG.
WELCOME, MY FRIEND... TO THE WORLD OF BIRTHDAY COLLECTIONS.
HOW'S IT GOING, YOU THINK?
NOT WELL.
PLAN B?
PLAN B.

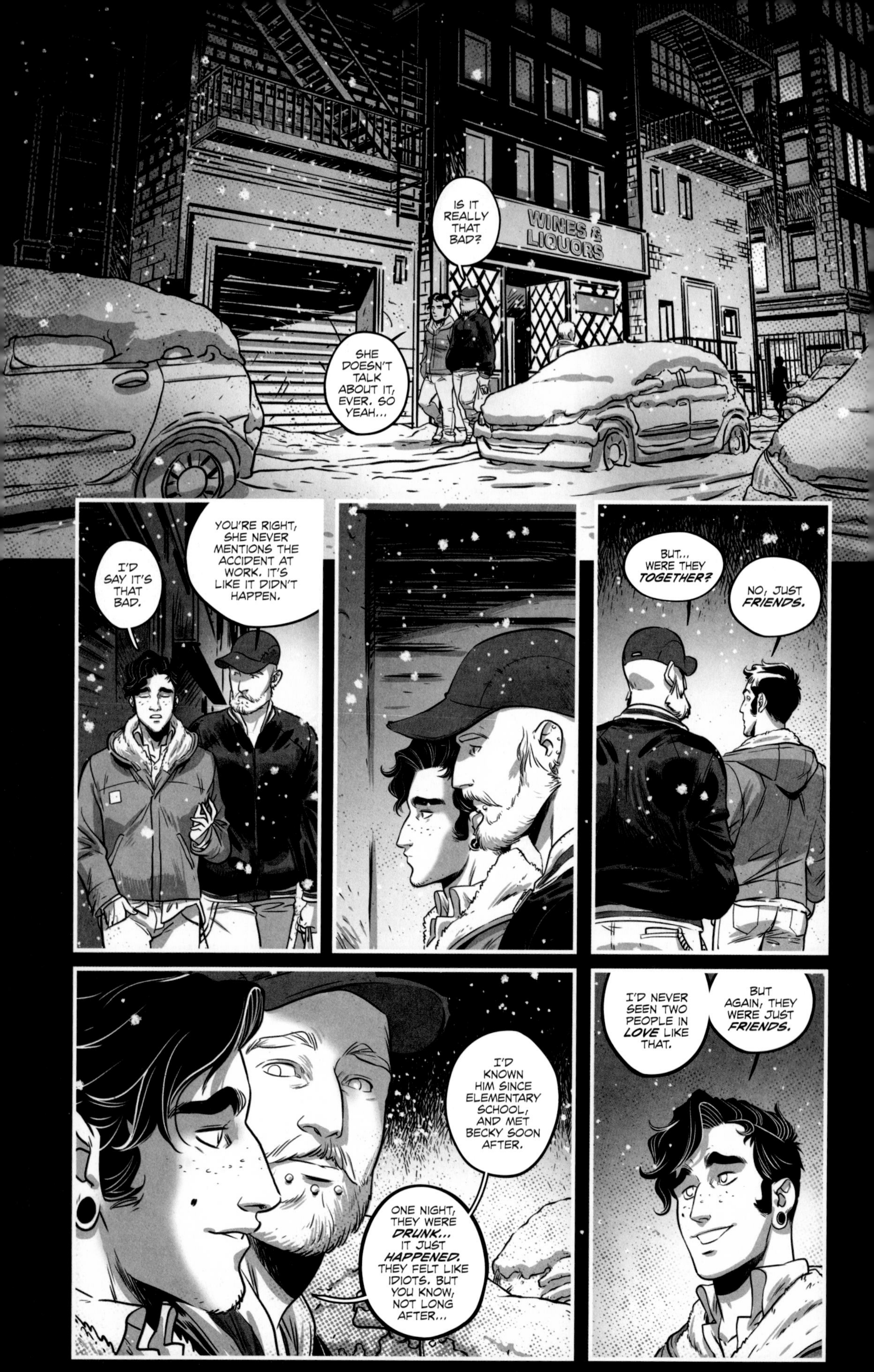
WINES & LIQUORS
IS IT REALLY THAT BAD?
SHE DOESN'T TALK ABOUT IT, EVER. SO YEAH...
I'D SAY IT'S THAT BAD.
YOU'RE RIGHT, SHE NEVER MENTIONS THE ACCIDENT AT WORK. IT'S LIKE IT DIDN'T HAPPEN.
BUT... WERE THEY TOGETHER?
NO, JUST FRIENDS.
I'D KNOWN HIM SINCE ELEMENTARY SCHOOL, AND MET BECKY SOON AFTER.
ONE NIGHT, THEY WERE DRUNK... IT JUST HAPPENED. THEY FELT LIKE IDIOTS. BUT YOU KNOW, NOT LONG AFTER...
I'D NEVER SEEN TWO PEOPLE IN LOVE LIKE THAT.
BUT AGAIN, THEY WERE JUST FRIENDS.

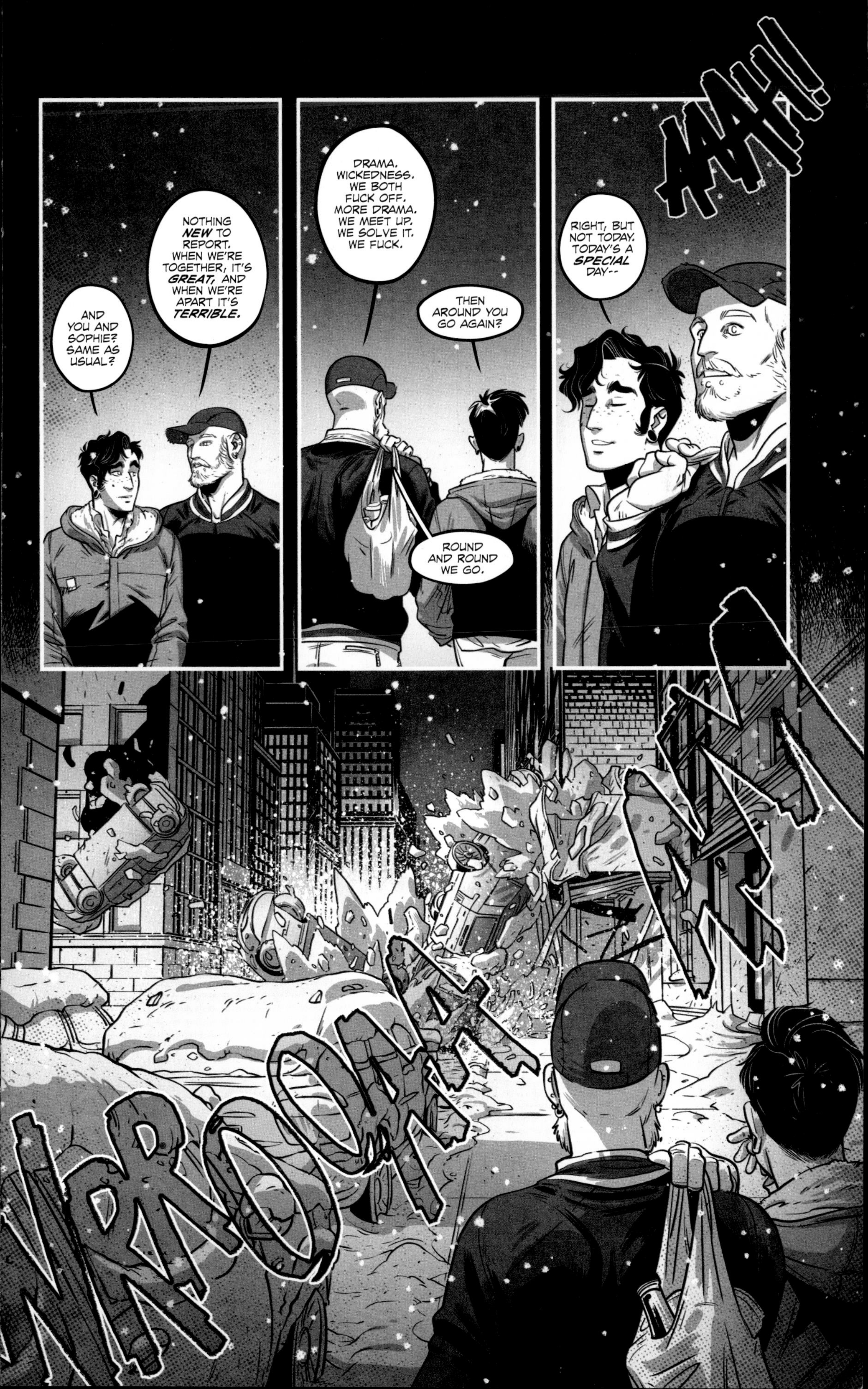
AND YOU AND SOPHIE? SAME AS USUAL?
NOTHING *NEW* TO REPORT. WHEN WE'RE TOGETHER, IT'S *GREAT,* AND WHEN WE'RE APART IT'S *TERRIBLE.*
DRAMA. WICKEDNESS. WE BOTH FUCK OFF. MORE DRAMA. WE MEET UP. WE SOLVE IT. WE FUCK.
THEN AROUND YOU GO AGAIN?
ROUND AND ROUND WE GO.
RIGHT, BUT NOT TODAY. TODAY'S A *SPECIAL* DAY--
AAAH!!
WRROOOM
KRASH!

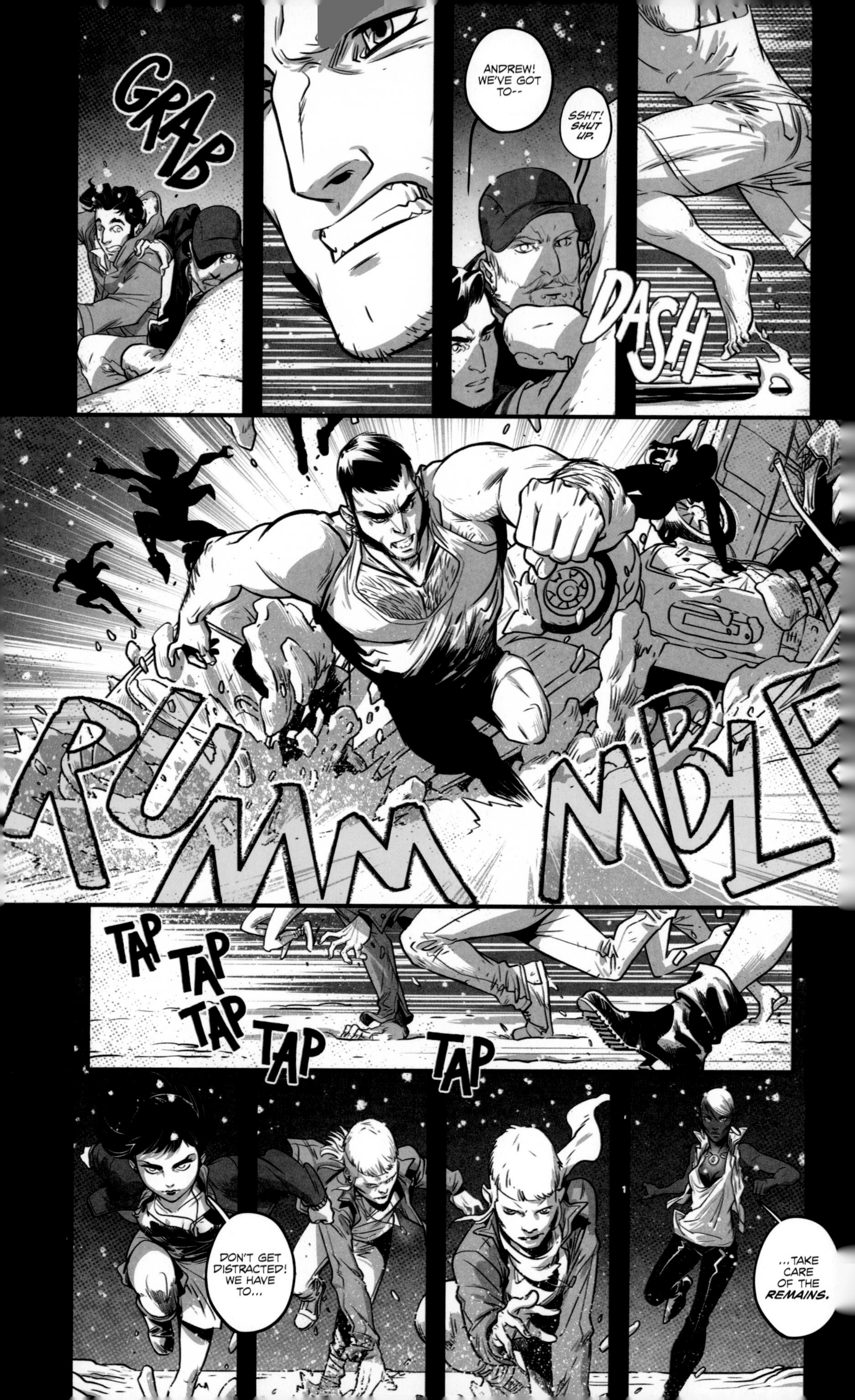
GRAB
ANDREW! WE'VE GOT TO--
SSHT! SHUT UP.
DASH
RUMMMBLE
TAP TAP TAP TAP TAP
DON'T GET DISTRACTED! WE HAVE TO...
...TAKE CARE OF THE REMAINS.

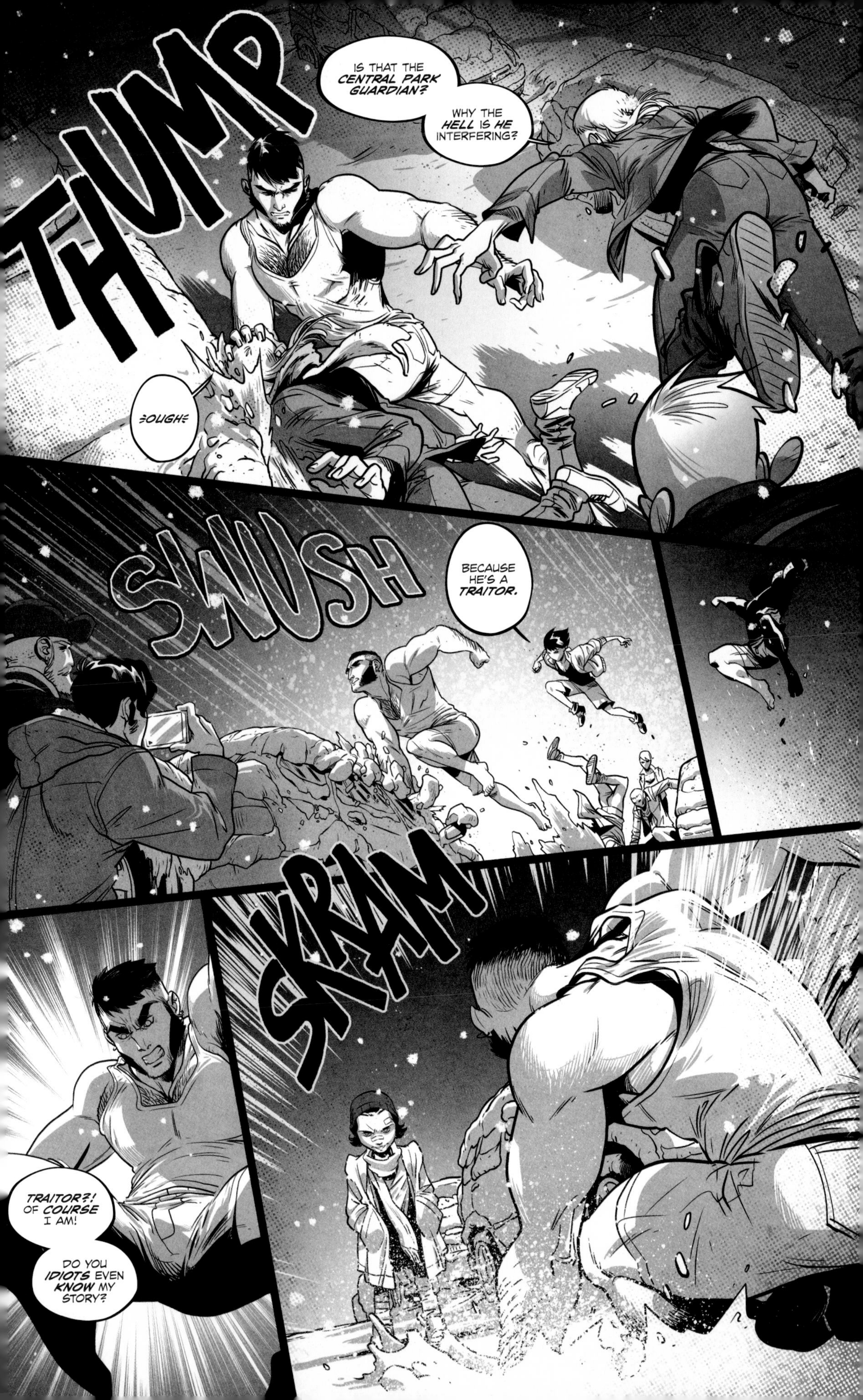
THUMP
IS THAT THE CENTRAL PARK GUARDIAN?
WHY THE HELL IS HE INTERFERING?
OUGH
SWUSH
BECAUSE HE'S A TRAITOR.
SKRAM
TRAITOR?! OF COURSE I AM!
DO YOU IDIOTS EVEN KNOW MY STORY?

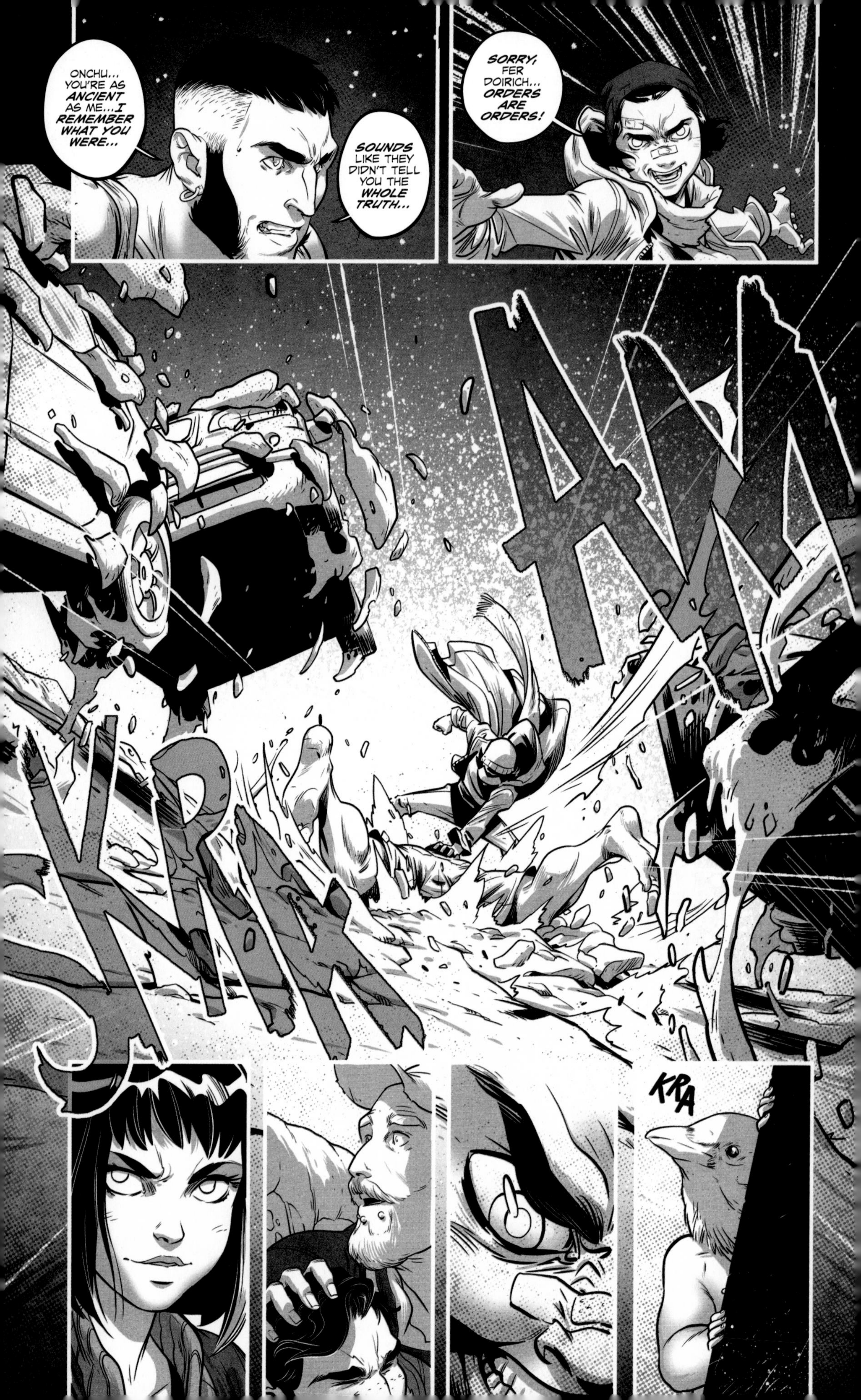
ONCHU... YOU'RE AS ANCIENT AS ME...I REMEMBER WHAT YOU WERE...
SOUNDS LIKE THEY DIDN'T TELL YOU THE WHOLE TRUTH...
SORRY, FER DOIRICH... ORDERS ARE ORDERS!
KRA

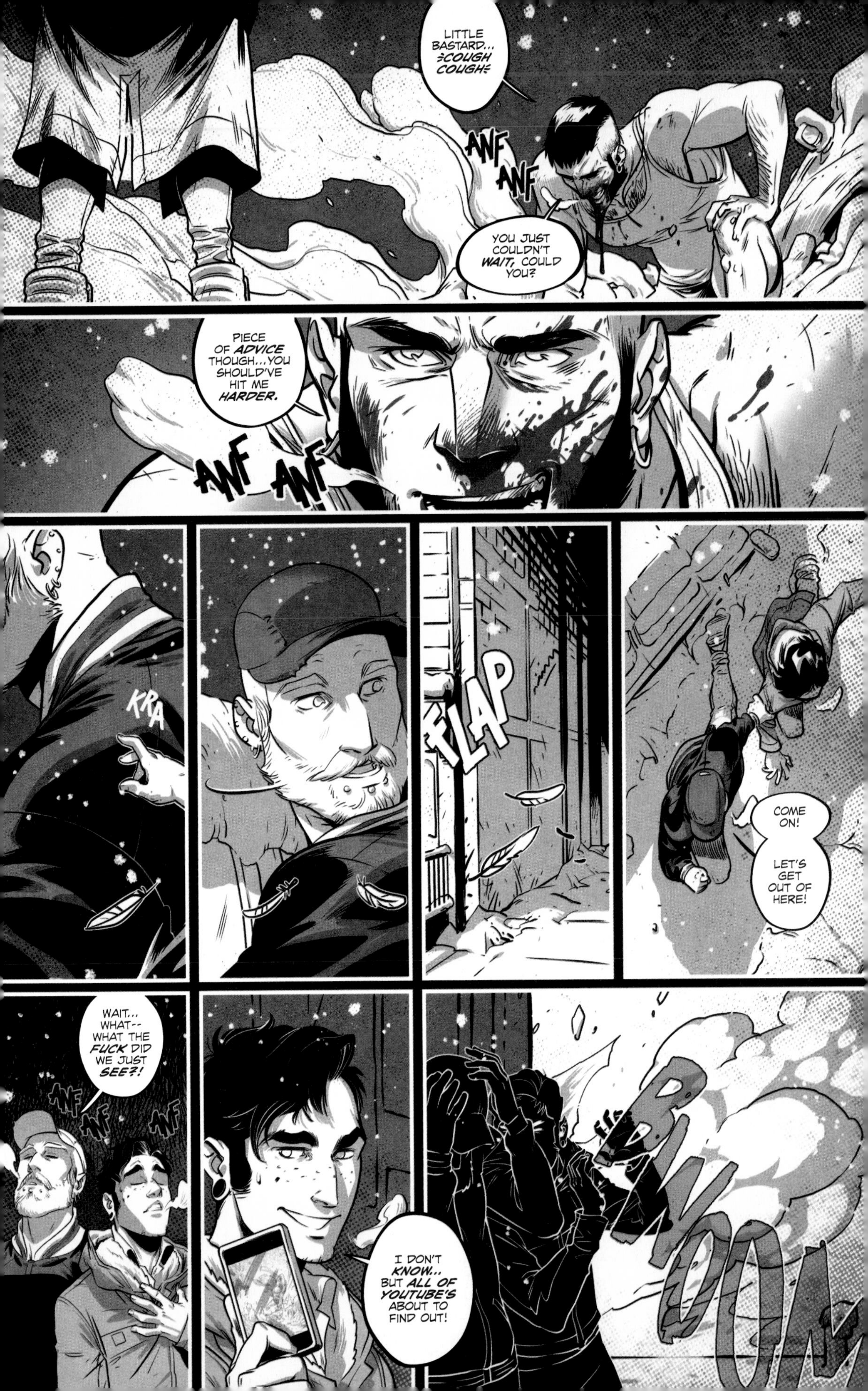
LITTLE BASTARD... *COUGH COUGH*
ANF ANF
YOU JUST COULDN'T WAIT, COULD YOU?
PIECE OF ADVICE THOUGH...YOU SHOULD'VE HIT ME HARDER.
ANF ANF
KRA
FLAP
COME ON!
LET'S GET OUT OF HERE!
WAIT... WHAT-- WHAT THE FUCK DID WE JUST SEE?!
ANF ANF ANF
I DON'T KNOW... BUT ALL OF YOUTUBE'S ABOUT TO FIND OUT!
BOOM

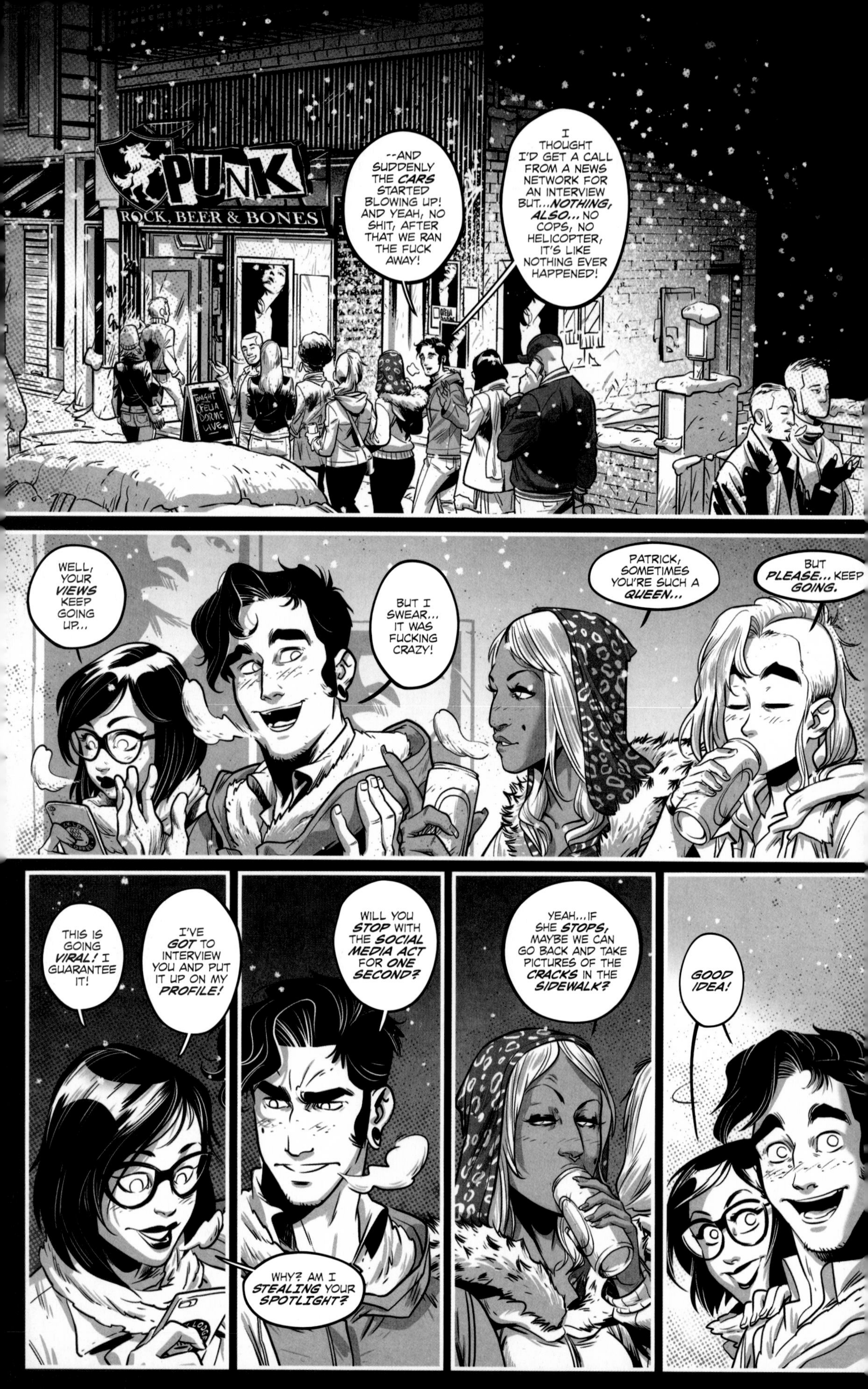
PUNK
ROCK, BEER & BONES
TONIGHT OFELIA DORME LIVE
--AND SUDDENLY THE CARS STARTED BLOWING UP! AND YEAH, NO SHIT, AFTER THAT WE RAN THE FUCK AWAY!
I THOUGHT I'D GET A CALL FROM A NEWS NETWORK FOR AN INTERVIEW BUT...NOTHING, ALSO... NO COPS, NO HELICOPTER, IT'S LIKE NOTHING EVER HAPPENED!
WELL, YOUR VIEWS KEEP GOING UP...
BUT I SWEAR... IT WAS FUCKING CRAZY!
PATRICK, SOMETIMES YOU'RE SUCH A QUEEN...
BUT PLEASE... KEEP GOING.
THIS IS GOING VIRAL! I GUARANTEE IT!
I'VE GOT TO INTERVIEW YOU AND PUT IT UP ON MY PROFILE!
WILL YOU STOP WITH THE SOCIAL MEDIA ACT FOR ONE SECOND?
WHY? AM I STEALING YOUR SPOTLIGHT?
YEAH...IF SHE STOPS, MAYBE WE CAN GO BACK AND TAKE PICTURES OF THE CRACKS IN THE SIDEWALK?
GOOD IDEA!

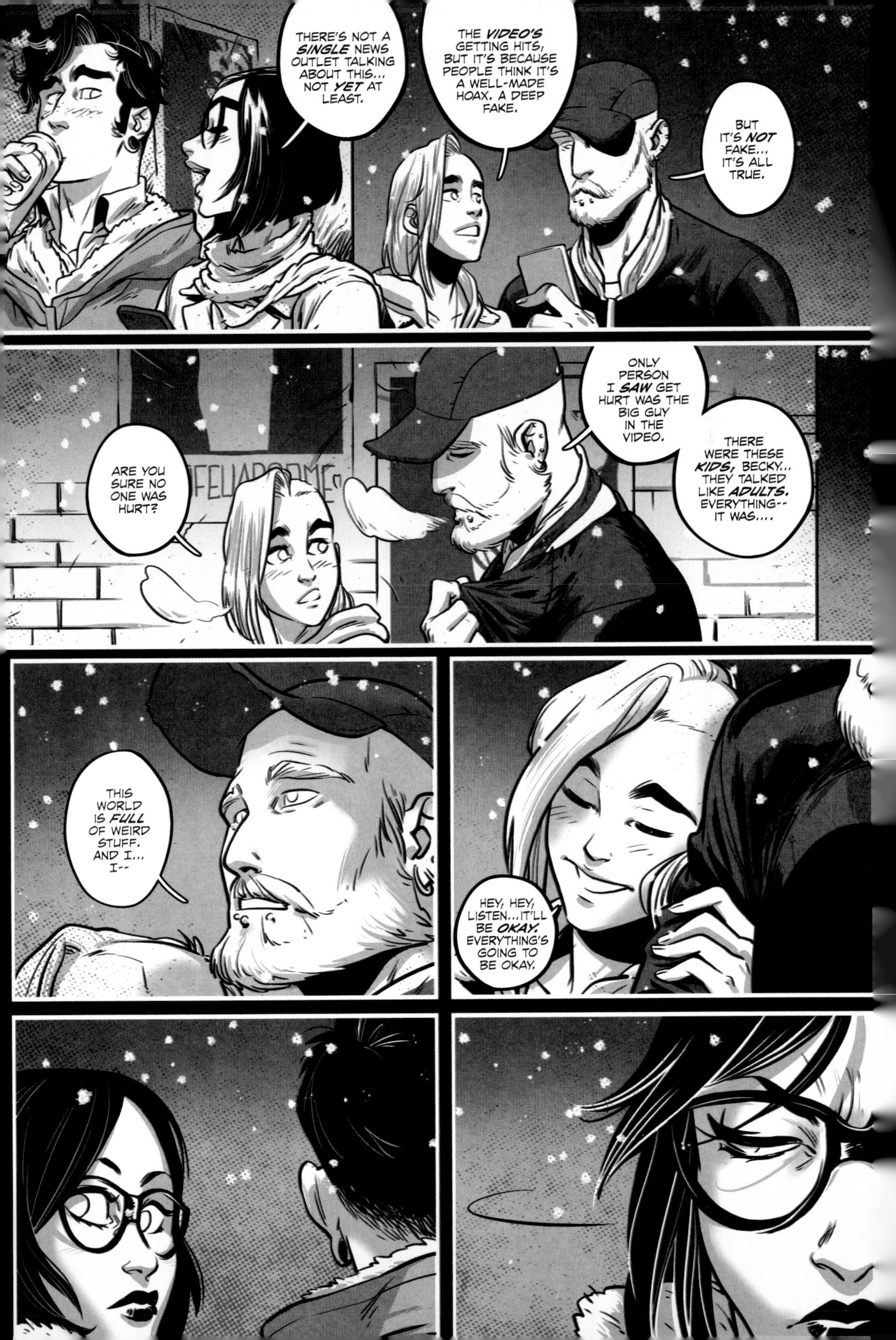

THERE'S NOT A SINGLE NEWS OUTLET TALKING ABOUT THIS... NOT YET AT LEAST.
THE VIDEO'S GETTING HITS, BUT IT'S BECAUSE PEOPLE THINK IT'S A WELL-MADE HOAX. A DEEP FAKE.
BUT IT'S NOT FAKE... IT'S ALL TRUE.
ARE YOU SURE NO ONE WAS HURT?
ONLY PERSON I SAW GET HURT WAS THE BIG GUY IN THE VIDEO.
THERE WERE THESE KIDS, BECKY... THEY TALKED LIKE ADULTS. EVERYTHING-- IT WAS....
THIS WORLD IS FULL OF WEIRD STUFF. AND I... I--
HEY, HEY, LISTEN...IT'LL BE OKAY. EVERYTHING'S GOING TO BE OKAY.

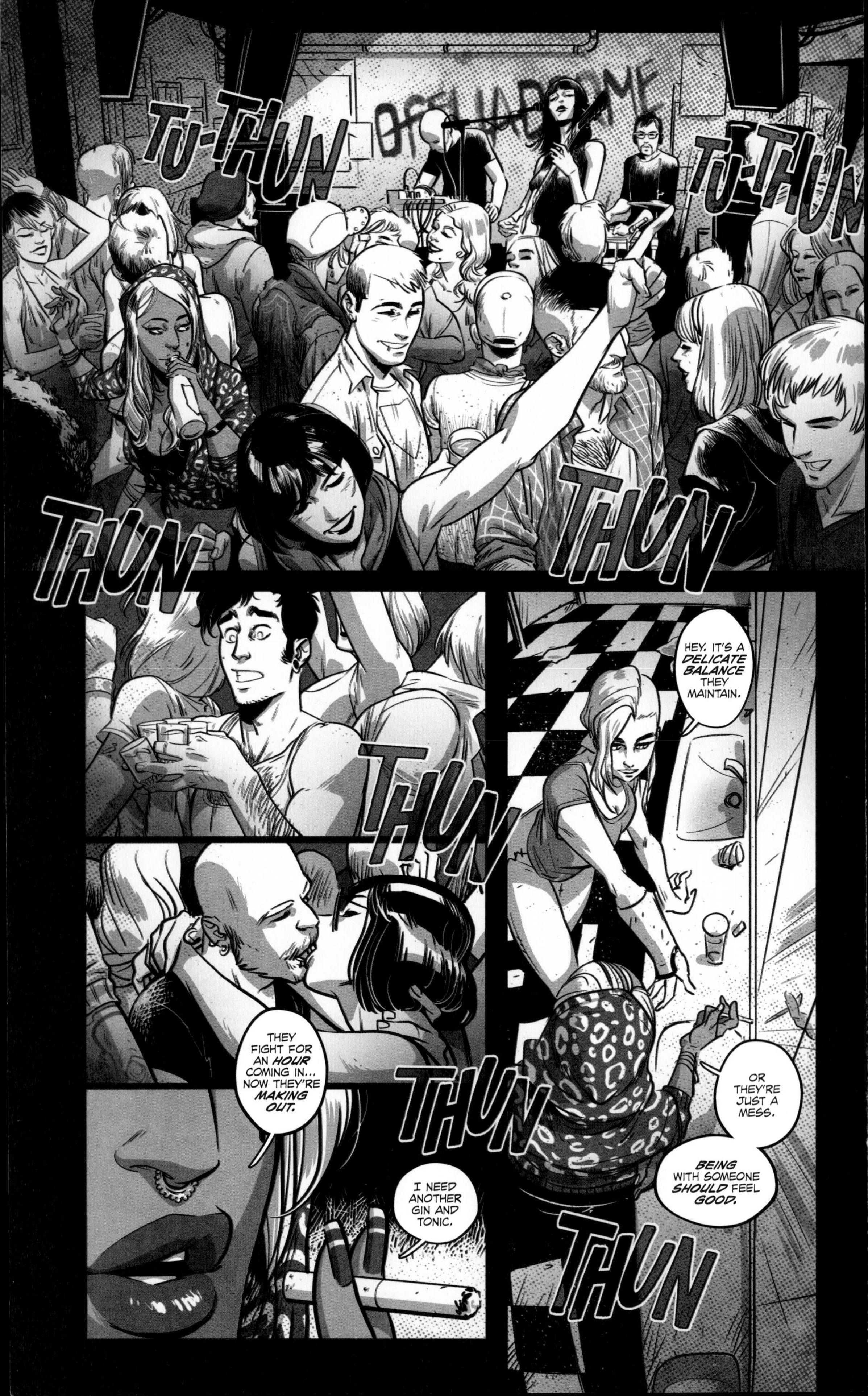
TU-THUN
TU-THUN
THUN
THUN
THUN
HEY. IT'S A DELICATE BALANCE THEY MAINTAIN.
THEY FIGHT FOR AN HOUR COMING IN... NOW THEY'RE MAKING OUT.
THUN
OR THEY'RE JUST A MESS.
BEING WITH SOMEONE SHOULD FEEL GOOD.
I NEED ANOTHER GIN AND TONIC.
THUN

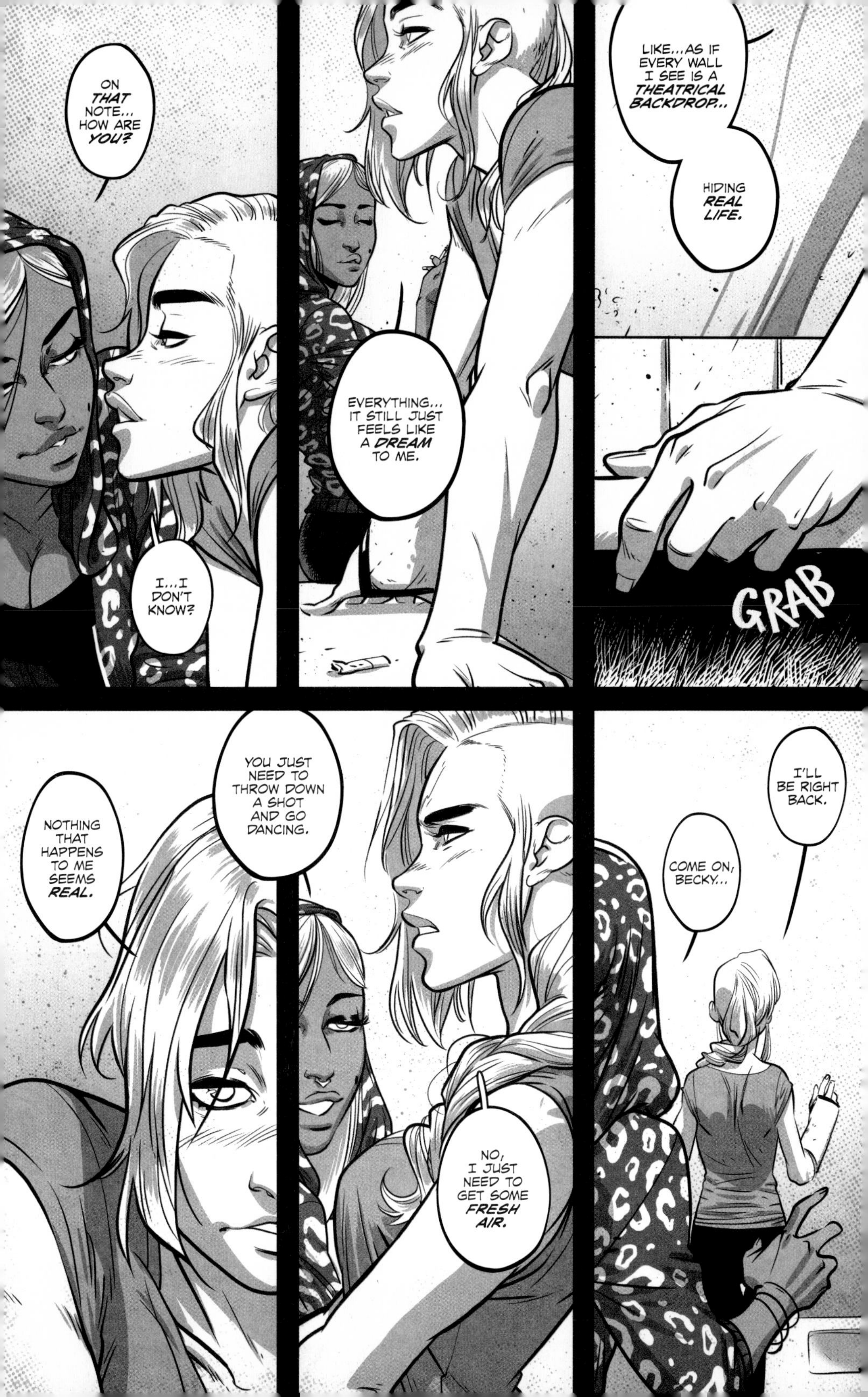
ON THAT NOTE... HOW ARE YOU?
I...I DON'T KNOW?
EVERYTHING... IT STILL JUST FEELS LIKE A DREAM TO ME.
LIKE...AS IF EVERY WALL I SEE IS A THEATRICAL BACKDROP...
HIDING REAL LIFE.
GRAB
NOTHING THAT HAPPENS TO ME SEEMS REAL.
YOU JUST NEED TO THROW DOWN A SHOT AND GO DANCING.
NO, I JUST NEED TO GET SOME FRESH AIR.
I'LL BE RIGHT BACK.
COME ON, BECKY...

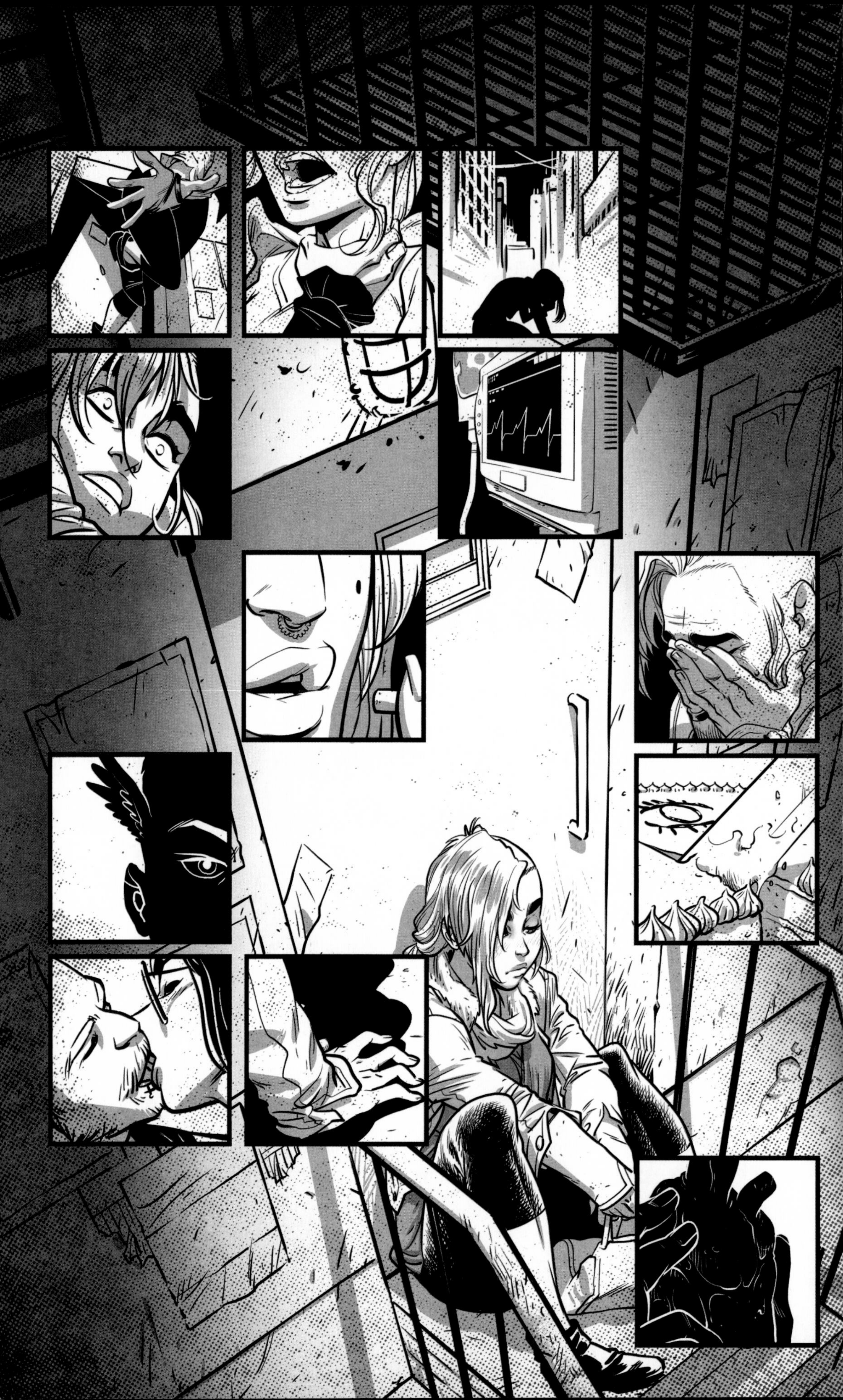

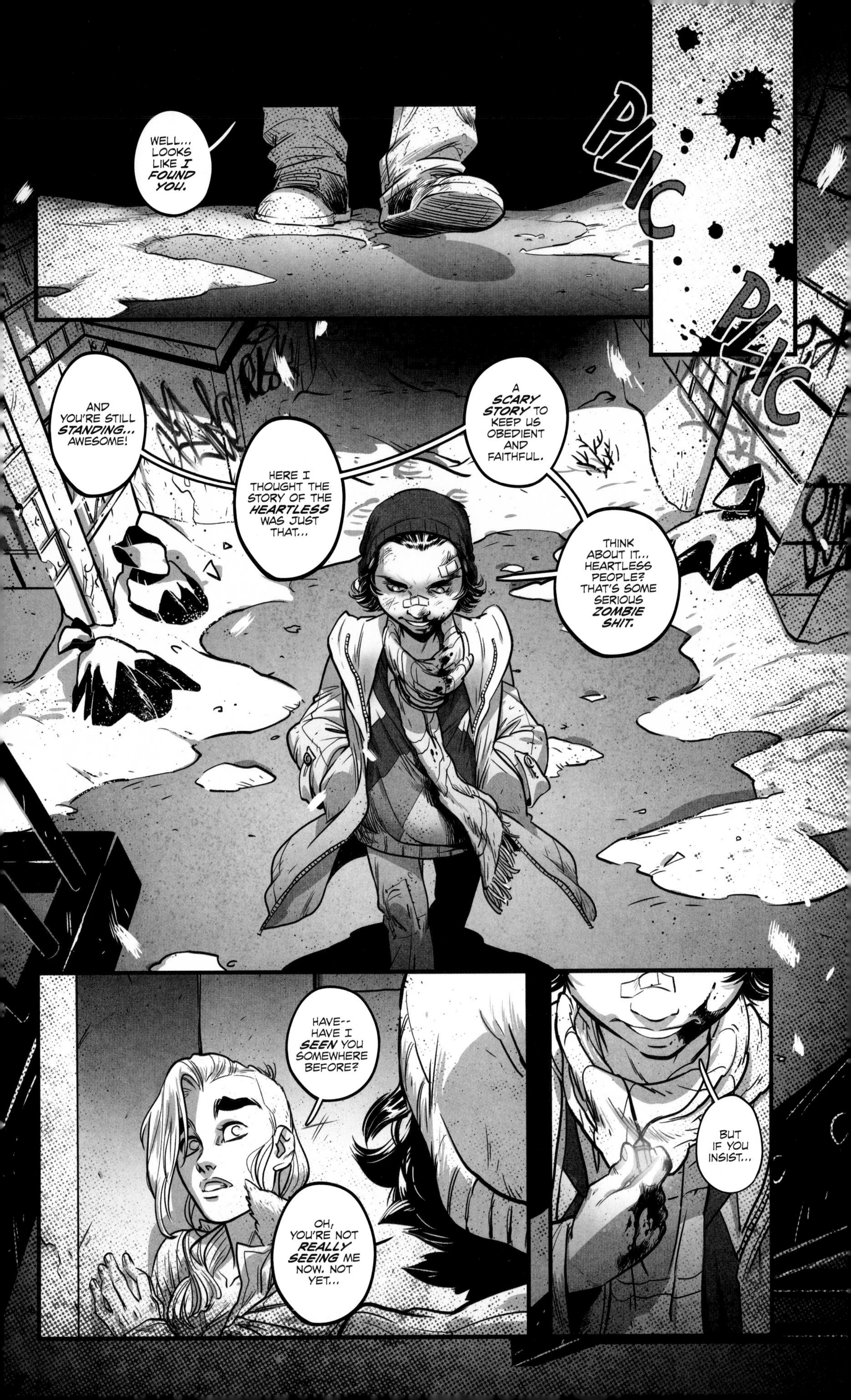
WELL... LOOKS LIKE I FOUND YOU.
PLIC
PLIC
PLIC
AND YOU'RE STILL STANDING... AWESOME!
HERE I THOUGHT THE STORY OF THE HEARTLESS WAS JUST THAT...
A SCARY STORY TO KEEP US OBEDIENT AND FAITHFUL.
THINK ABOUT IT... HEARTLESS PEOPLE? THAT'S SOME SERIOUS ZOMBIE SHIT.
HAVE-- HAVE I SEEN YOU SOMEWHERE BEFORE?
OH, YOU'RE NOT REALLY SEEING ME NOW. NOT YET...
BUT IF YOU INSIST...

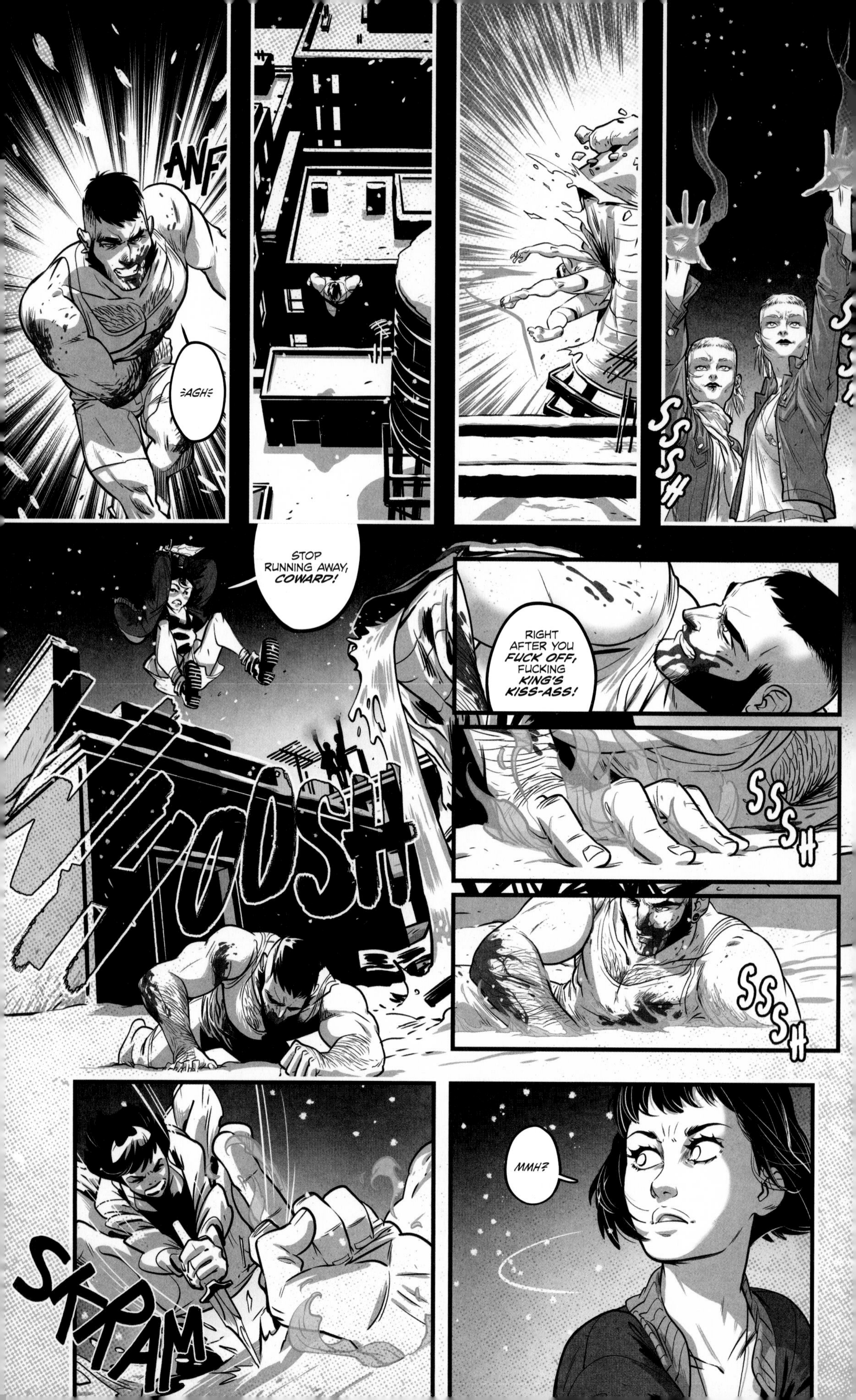
ANF
AGH
SSSH
STOP RUNNING AWAY, COWARD!
RIGHT AFTER YOU FUCK OFF, FUCKING KING'S KISS-ASS!
WOOSH
SSSH
SSSH
SKRAM
MMH?

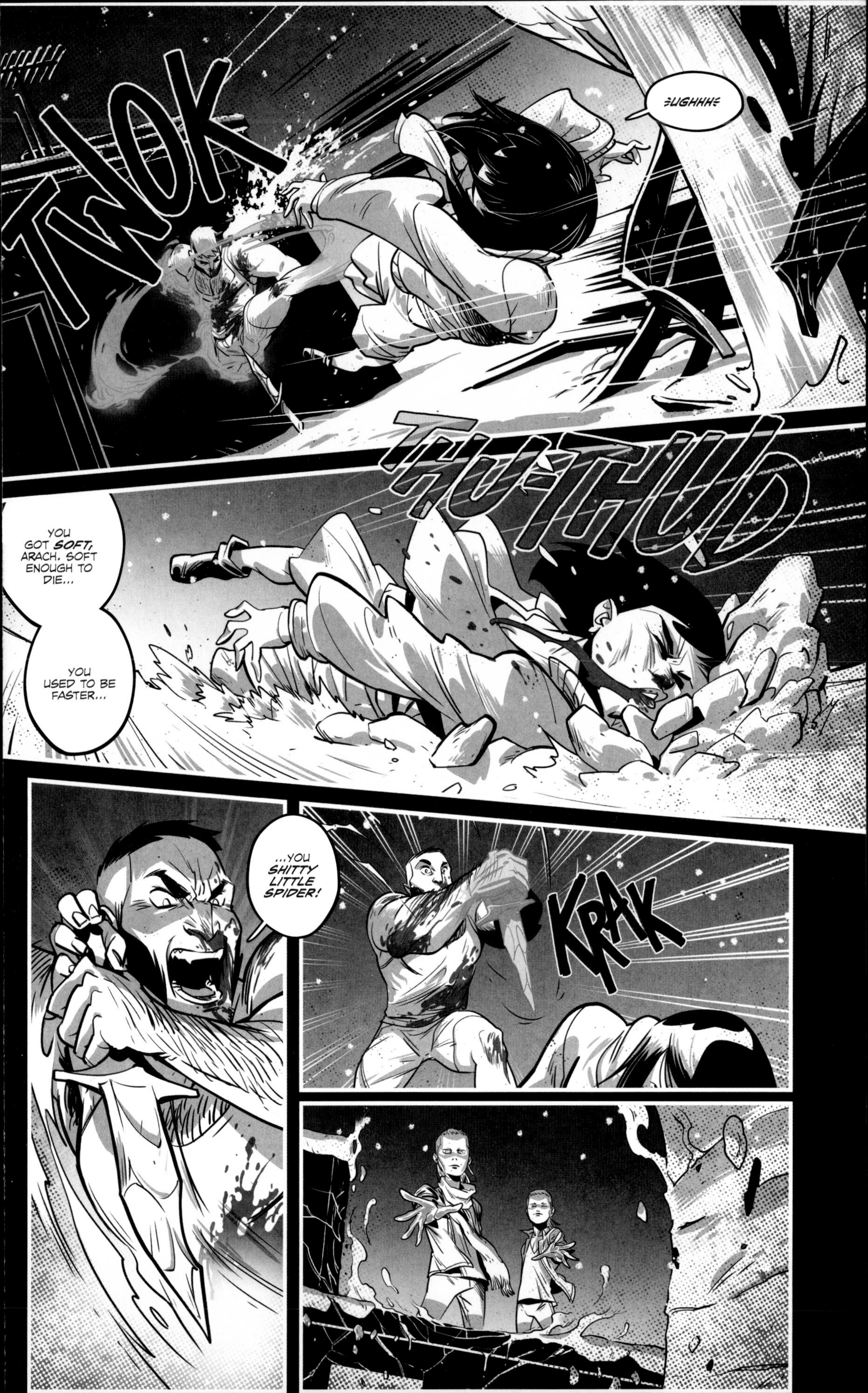
TWOK
=UGHHH=
THUTHUD
YOU GOT SOFT, ARACH. SOFT ENOUGH TO DIE...
YOU USED TO BE FASTER...
...YOU SHITTY LITTLE SPIDER!
KRAK

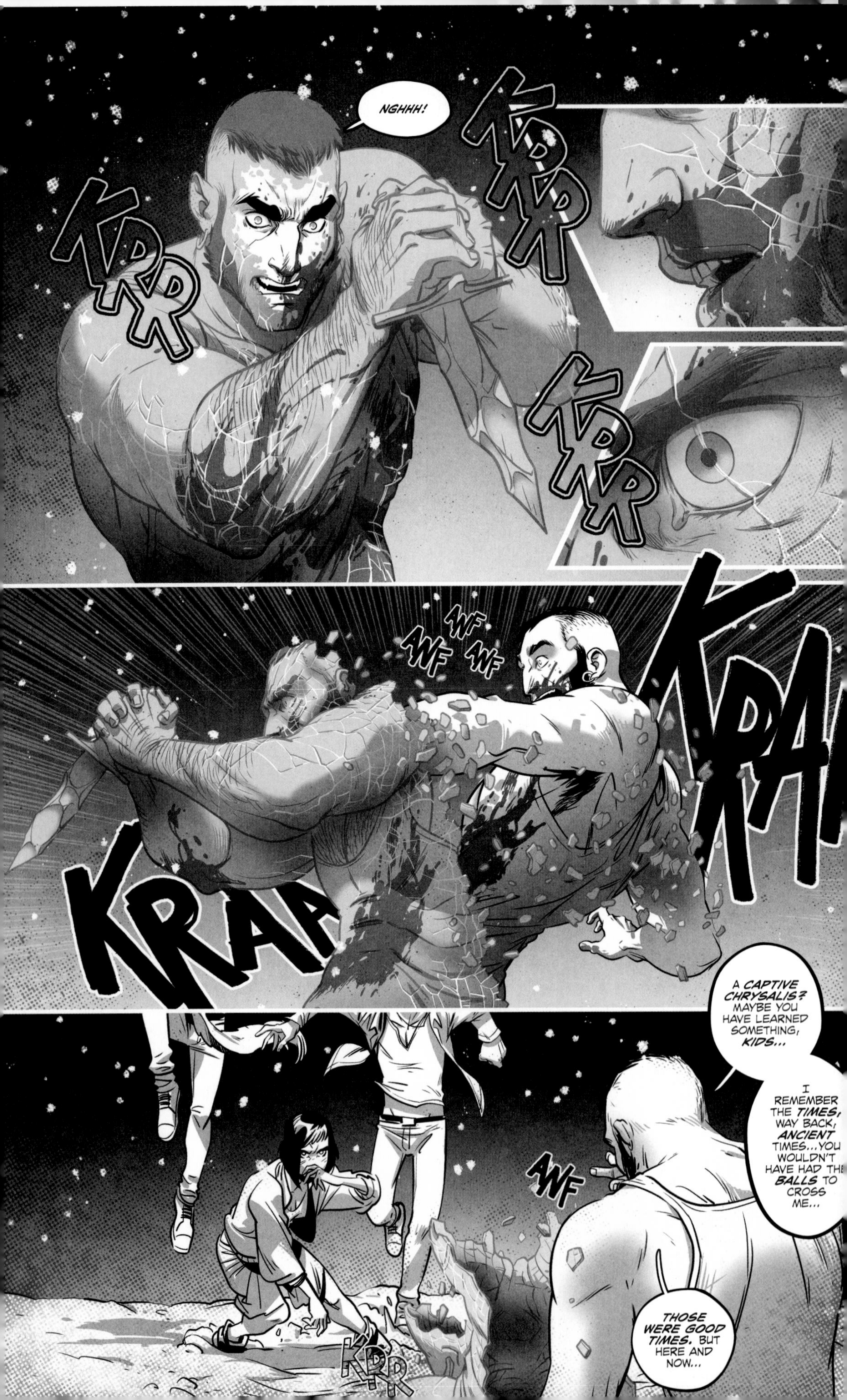
NGHHH!
KRRR
KRRR
KRRR
AWF
AWF
AWF
KRAA
KRAA
A CAPTIVE CHRYSALIS? MAYBE YOU HAVE LEARNED SOMETHING, KIDS...
I REMEMBER THE TIMES, WAY BACK, ANCIENT TIMES...YOU WOULDN'T HAVE HAD THE BALLS TO CROSS ME...
AWF
THOSE WERE GOOD TIMES. BUT HERE AND NOW...
KRRR

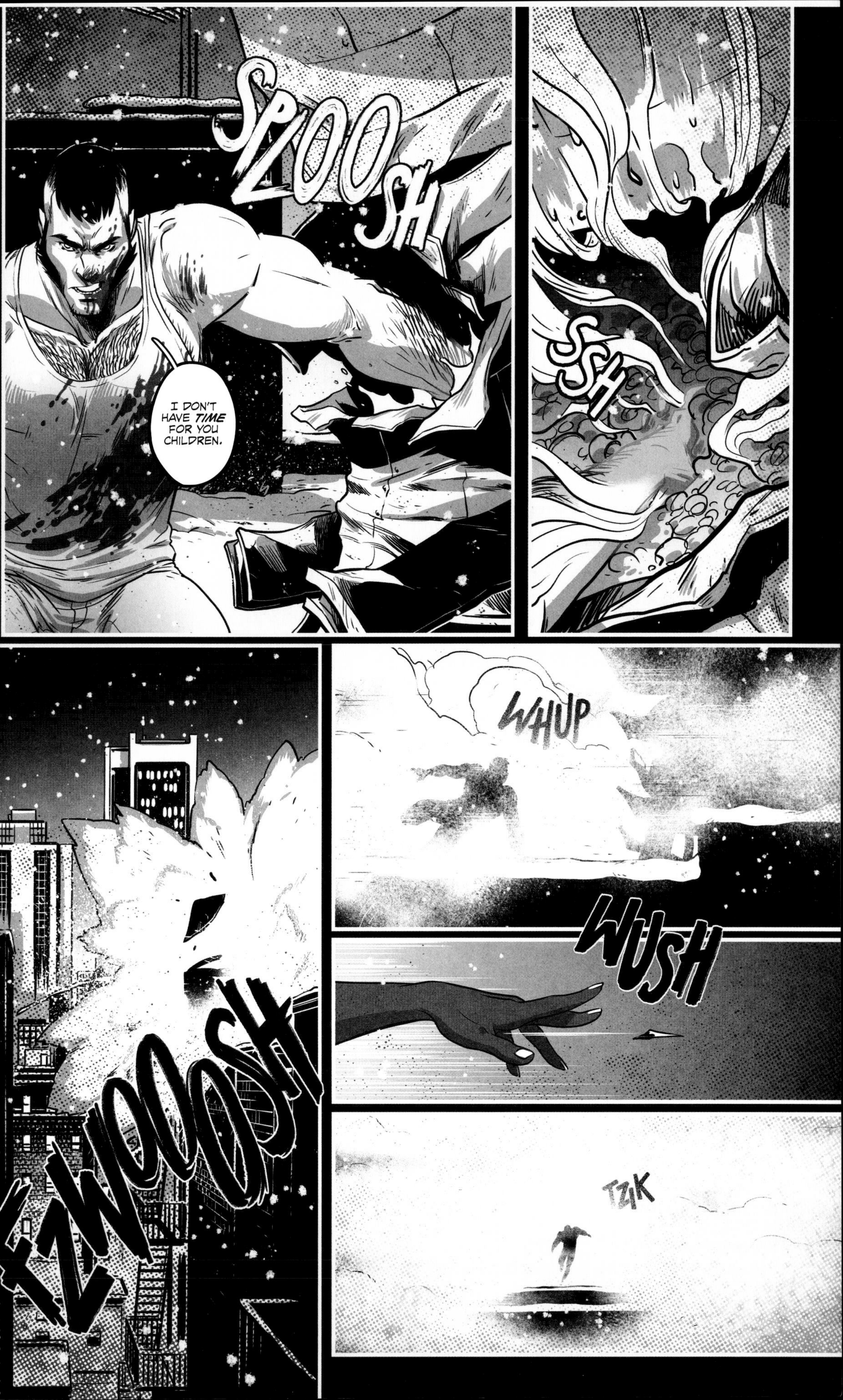
SPLOOSH
I DON'T HAVE *TIME* FOR YOU CHILDREN.
SSH
FZWOOOSH
WHUP
WUSH
TZIK

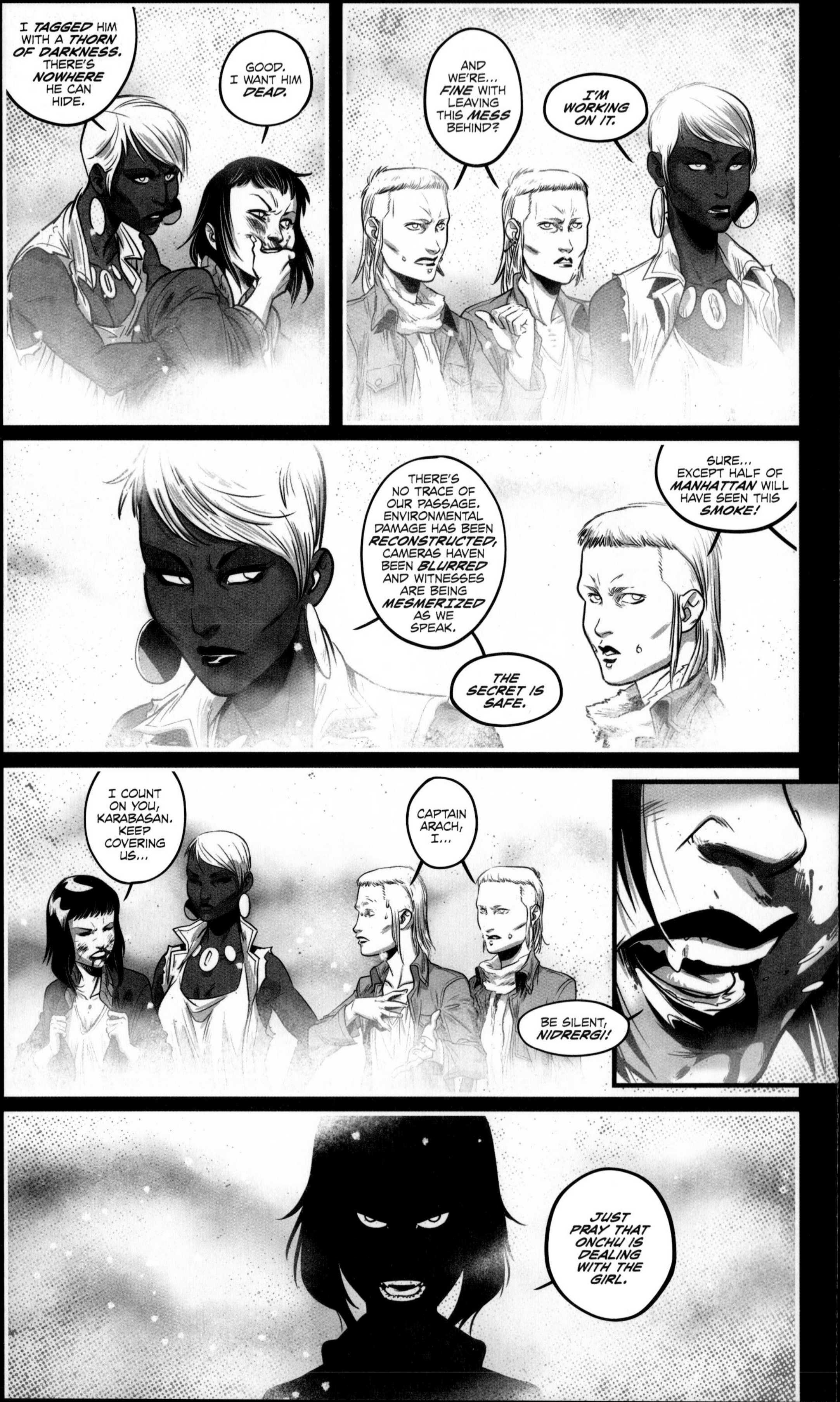
I TAGGED HIM WITH A THORN OF DARKNESS. THERE'S NOWHERE HE CAN HIDE.
GOOD. I WANT HIM DEAD.
AND WE'RE... FINE WITH LEAVING THIS MESS BEHIND?
I'M WORKING ON IT.
THERE'S NO TRACE OF OUR PASSAGE. ENVIRONMENTAL DAMAGE HAS BEEN RECONSTRUCTED, CAMERAS HAVEN BEEN BLURRED AND WITNESSES ARE BEING MESMERIZED AS WE SPEAK.
THE SECRET IS SAFE.
SURE... EXCEPT HALF OF MANHATTAN WILL HAVE SEEN THIS SMOKE!
I COUNT ON YOU, KARABASAN. KEEP COVERING US...
CAPTAIN ARACH, I...
BE SILENT, NIDRERGI!
JUST PRAY THAT ONCHU IS DEALING WITH THE GIRL.

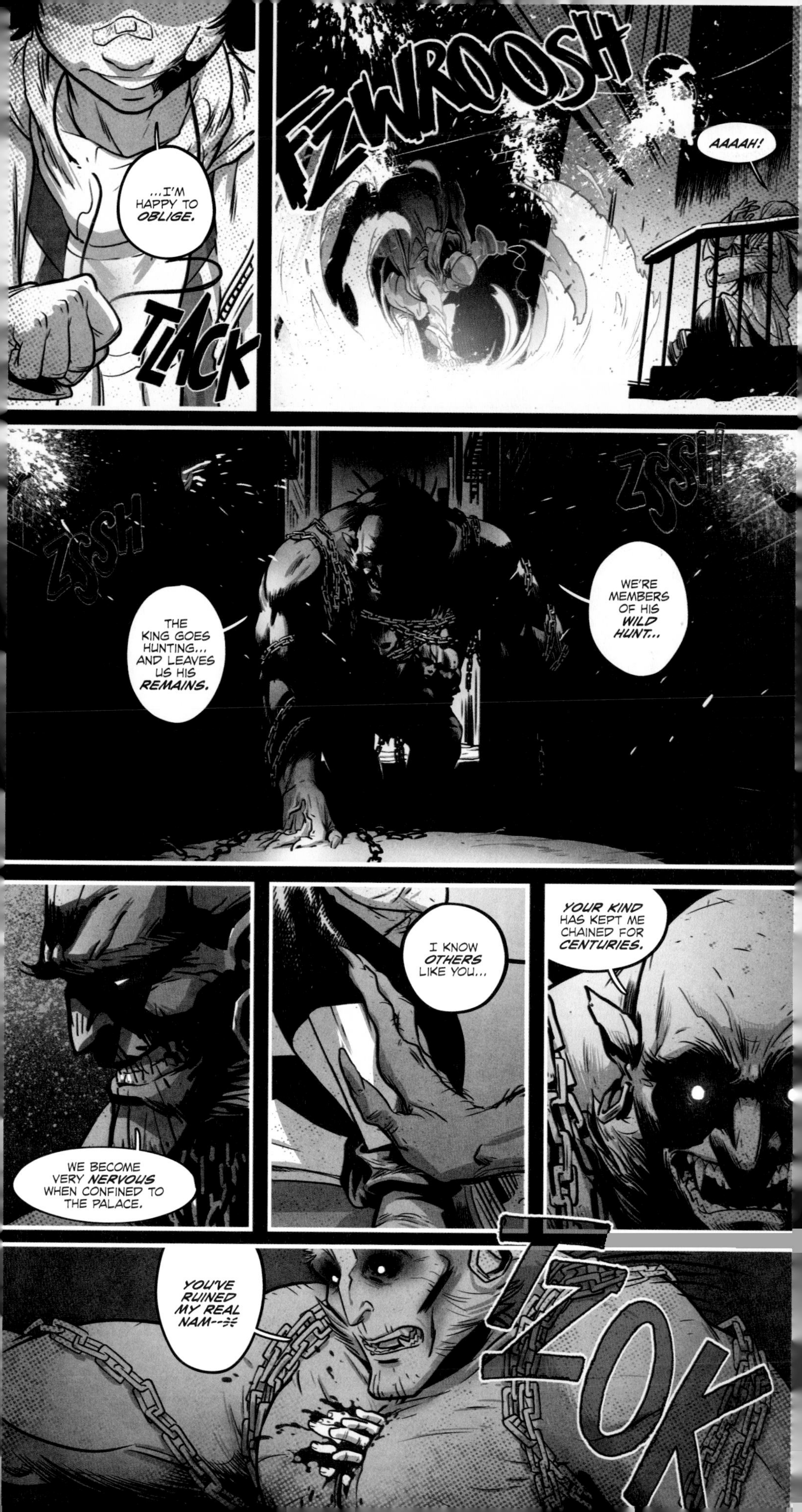
...I'M HAPPY TO OBLIGE.
TLACK
FZWROOSH
AAAAH!
ZSSH
ZSSH
THE KING GOES HUNTING... AND LEAVES US HIS REMAINS.
WE'RE MEMBERS OF HIS WILD HUNT...
WE BECOME VERY NERVOUS WHEN CONFINED TO THE PALACE.
I KNOW OTHERS LIKE YOU...
YOUR KIND HAS KEPT ME CHAINED FOR CENTURIES.
YOU'VE RUINED MY REAL NAM--
ZOK

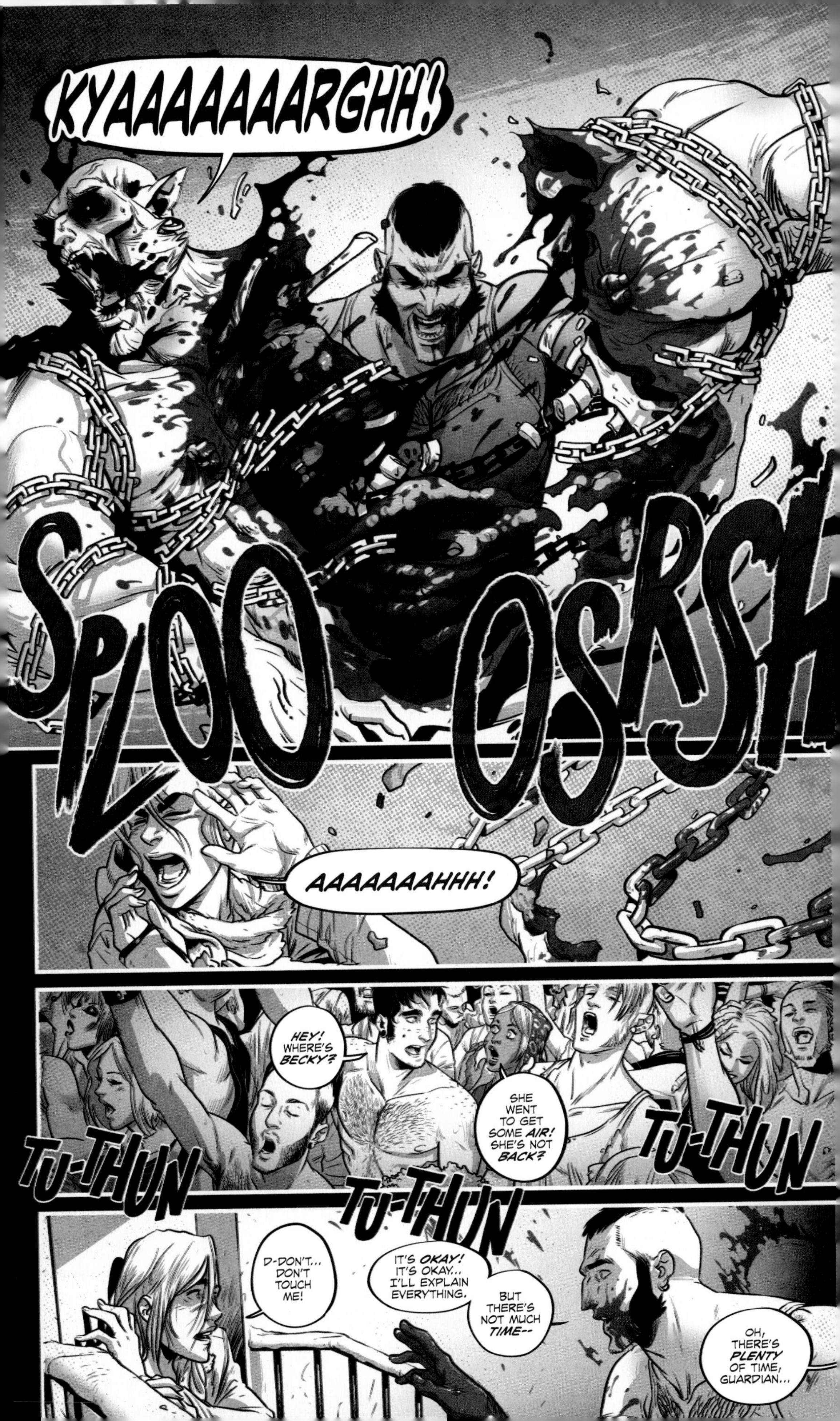
KYAAAAAAARGHH!
SPLOO-OSRSH
AAAAAAAHHH!
HEY! WHERE'S BECKY?
SHE WENT TO GET SOME AIR! SHE'S NOT BACK?
TU-THUN
TU-THUN
TU-THUN
D-DON'T... DON'T TOUCH ME!
IT'S OKAY! IT'S OKAY... I'LL EXPLAIN EVERYTHING.
BUT THERE'S NOT MUCH TIME--
OH, THERE'S PLENTY OF TIME, GUARDIAN...

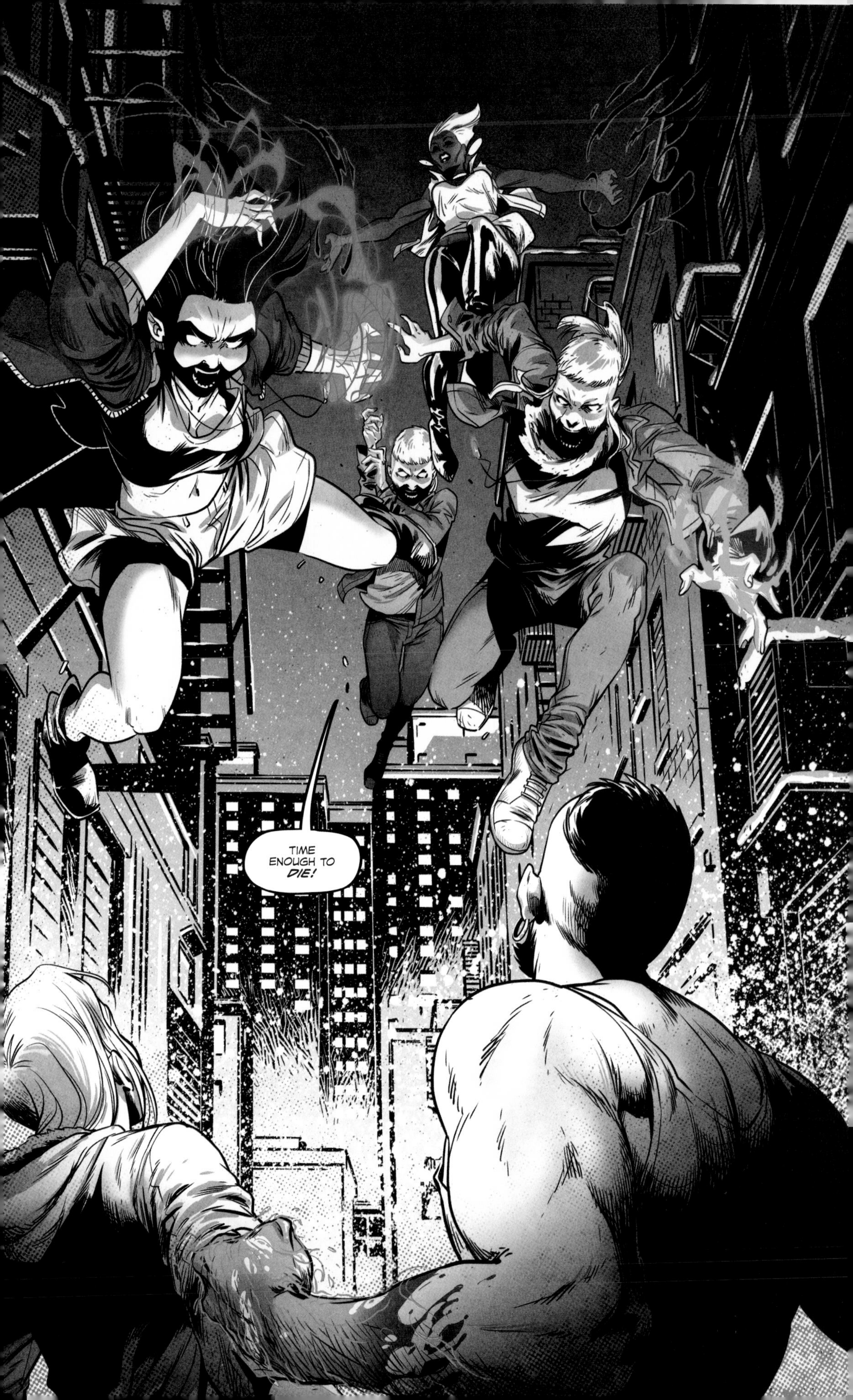
TIME ENOUGH TO DIE!

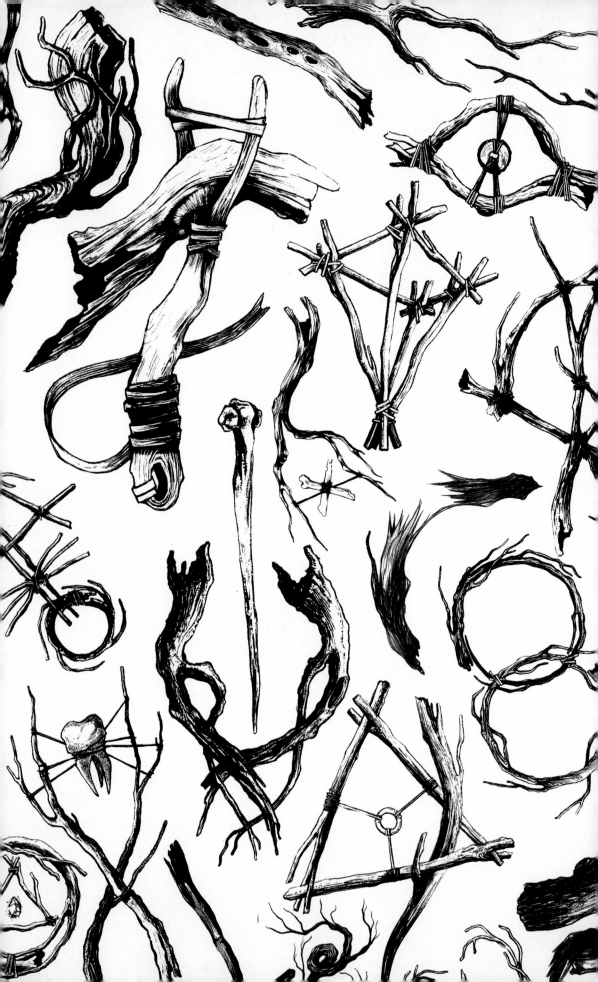

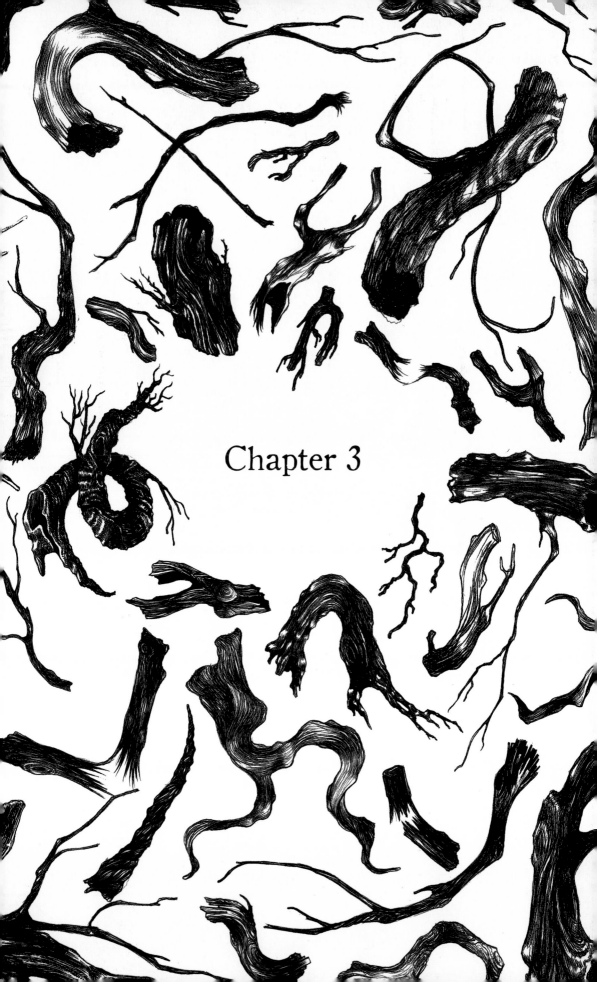

Chapter 3

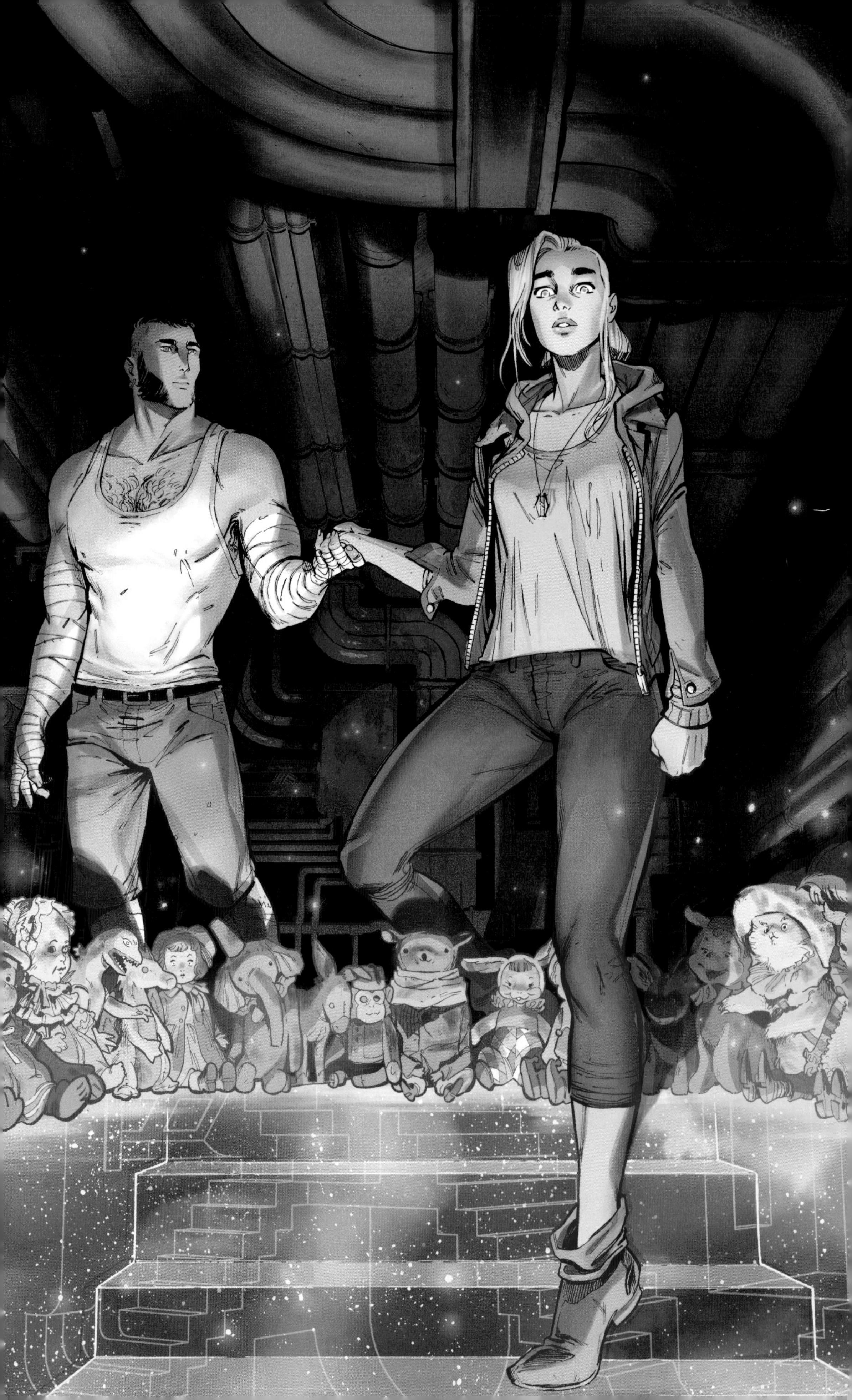

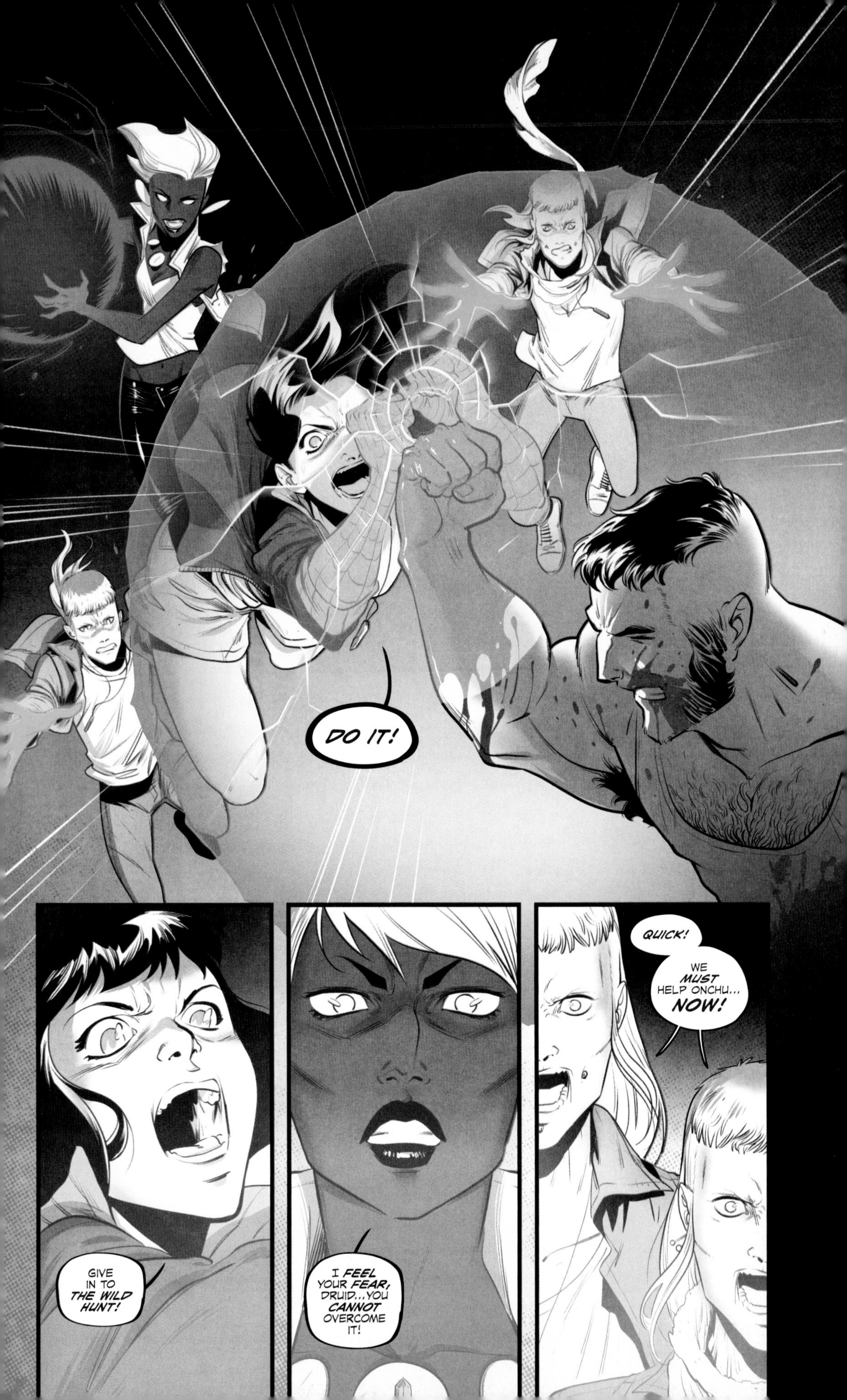
DO IT!
GIVE IN TO THE WILD HUNT!
I FEEL YOUR FEAR, DRUID...YOU CANNOT OVERCOME IT!
QUICK!
WE MUST HELP ONCHU... NOW!

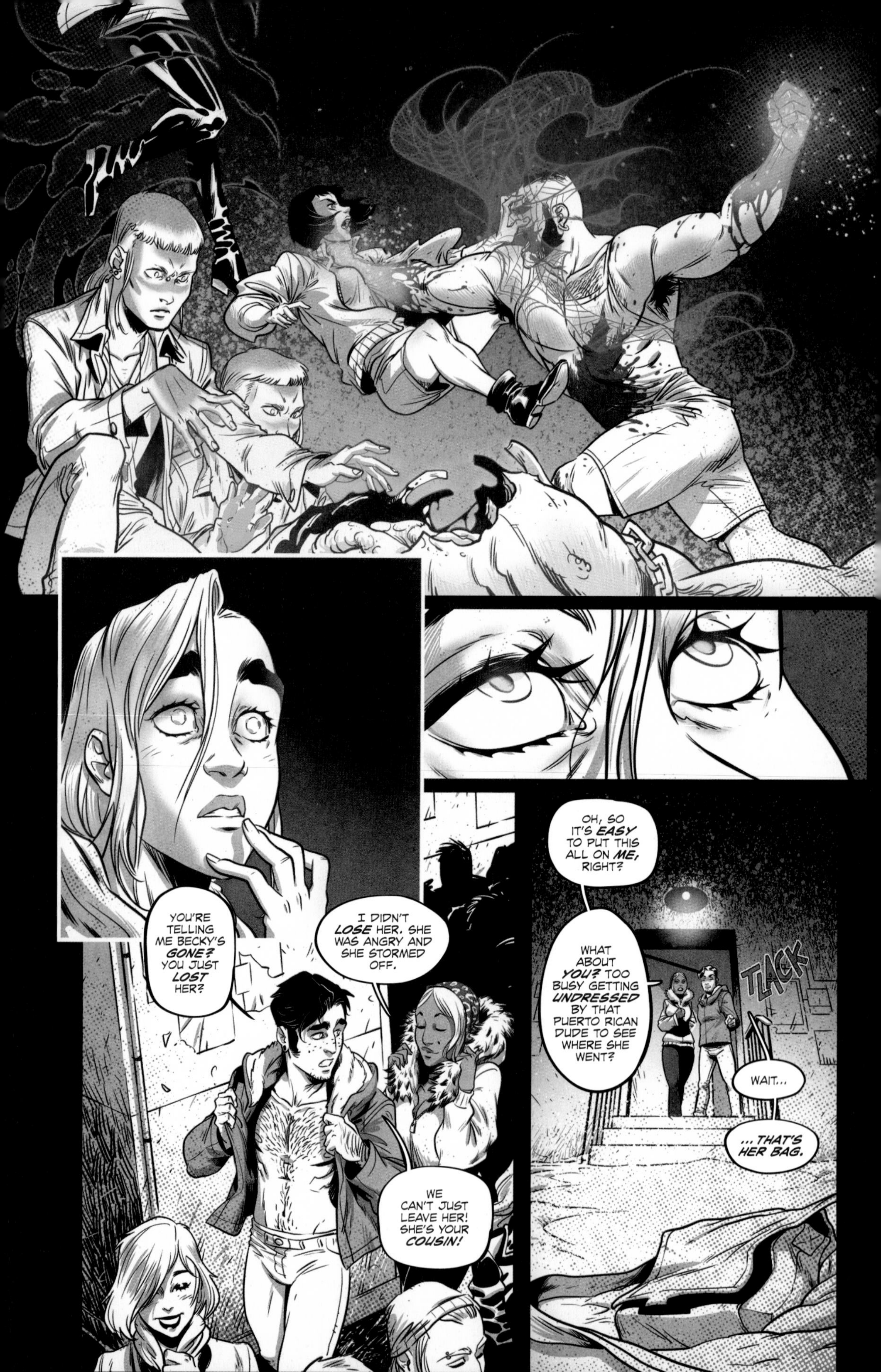
YOU'RE TELLING ME BECKY'S GONE? YOU JUST LOST HER?
I DIDN'T LOSE HER. SHE WAS ANGRY AND SHE STORMED OFF.
WE CAN'T JUST LEAVE HER! SHE'S YOUR COUSIN!
OH, SO IT'S EASY TO PUT THIS ALL ON ME, RIGHT?
WHAT ABOUT YOU? TOO BUSY GETTING UNDRESSED BY THAT PUERTO RICAN DUDE TO SEE WHERE SHE WENT?
TLACK
WAIT...
...THAT'S HER BAG.

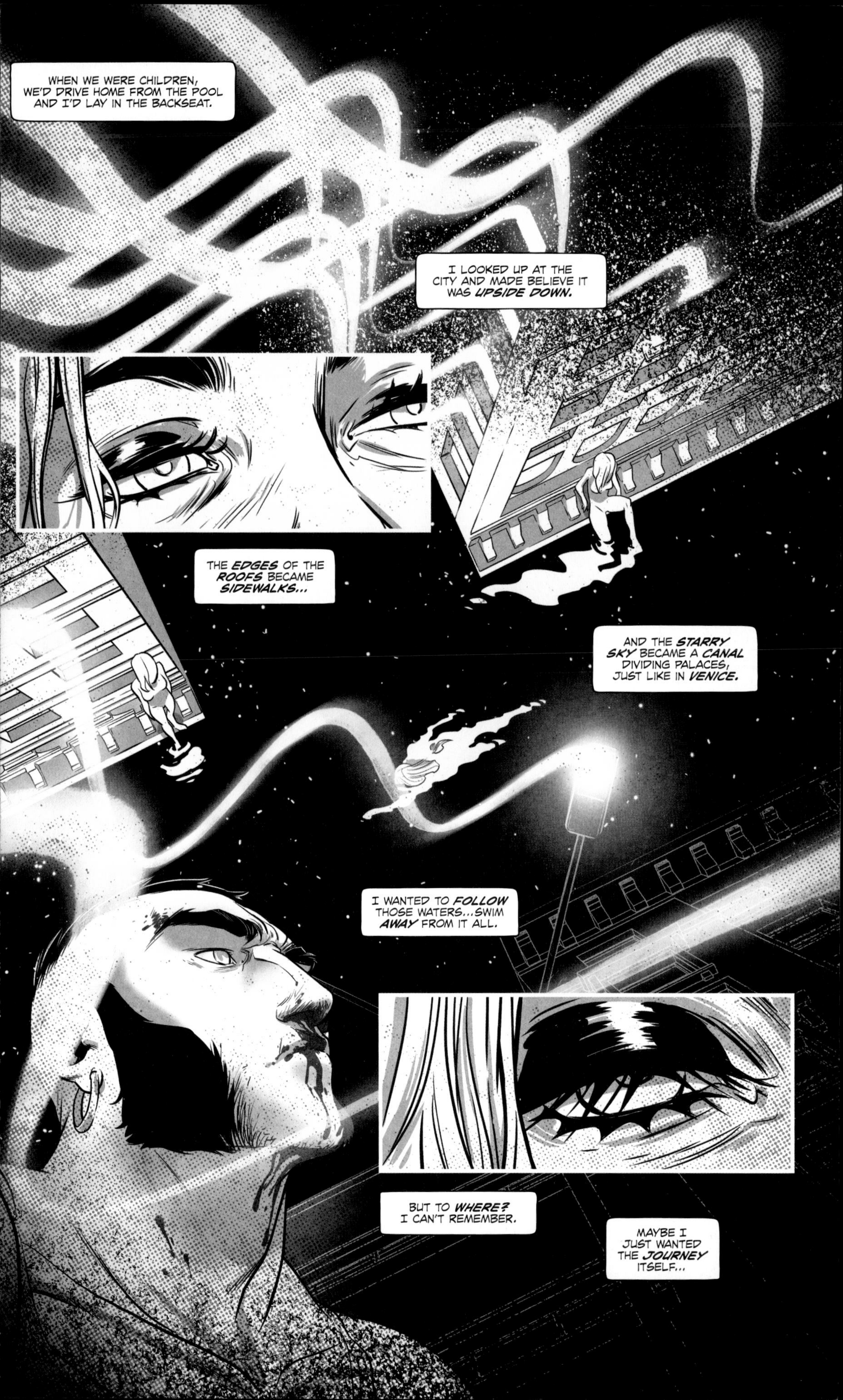
WHEN WE WERE CHILDREN, WE'D DRIVE HOME FROM THE POOL AND I'D LAY IN THE BACKSEAT.
I LOOKED UP AT THE CITY AND MADE BELIEVE IT WAS UPSIDE DOWN.
THE EDGES OF THE ROOFS BECAME SIDEWALKS...
AND THE STARRY SKY BECAME A CANAL DIVIDING PALACES, JUST LIKE IN VENICE.
I WANTED TO FOLLOW THOSE WATERS...SWIM AWAY FROM IT ALL.
BUT TO WHERE? I CAN'T REMEMBER.
MAYBE I JUST WANTED THE JOURNEY ITSELF...

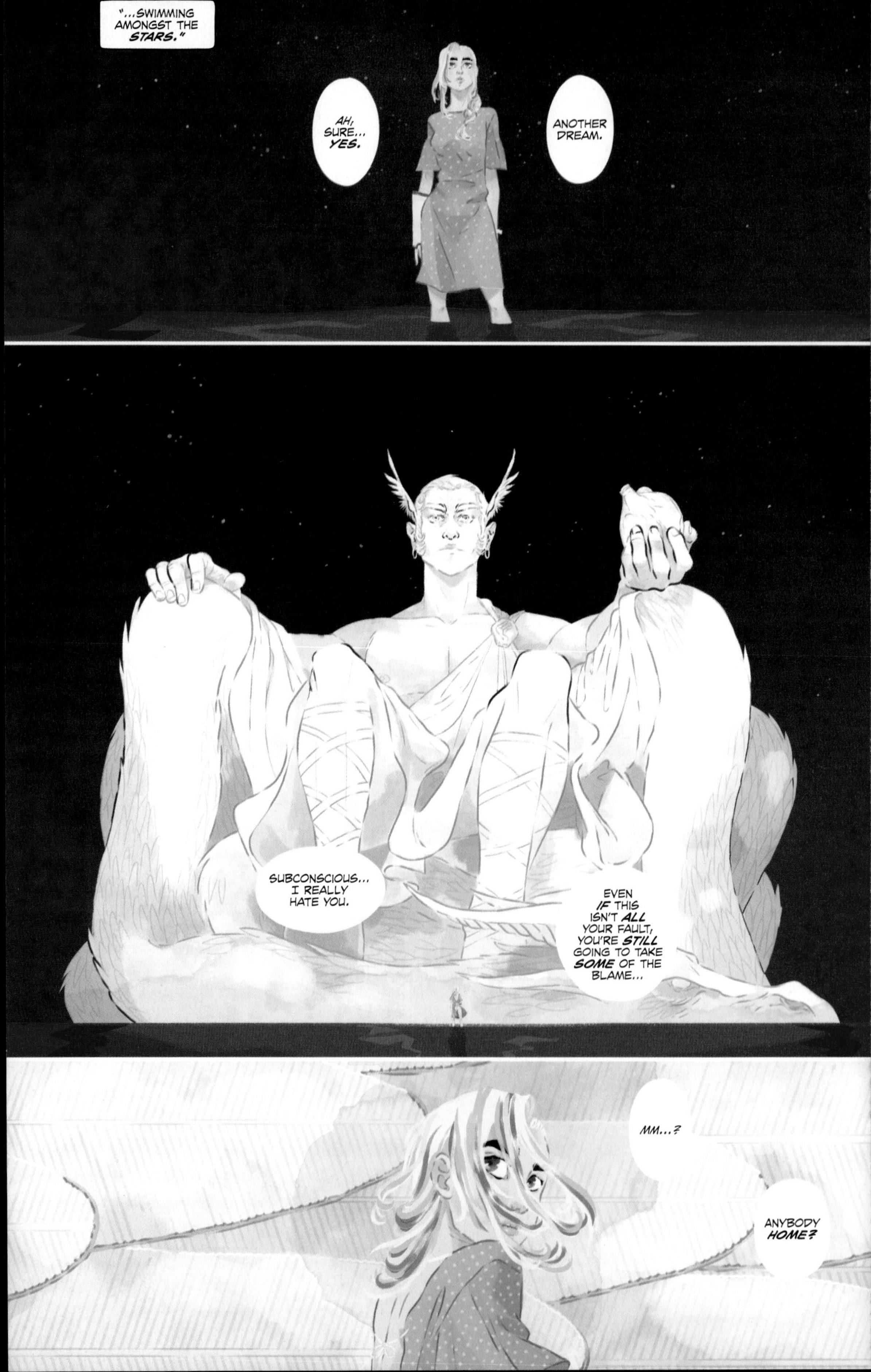
"...SWIMMING AMONGST THE STARS."
AH, SURE... YES.
ANOTHER DREAM.
SUBCONSCIOUS... I REALLY HATE YOU.
EVEN IF THIS ISN'T ALL YOUR FAULT, YOU'RE STILL GOING TO TAKE SOME OF THE BLAME...
MM...?
ANYBODY HOME?

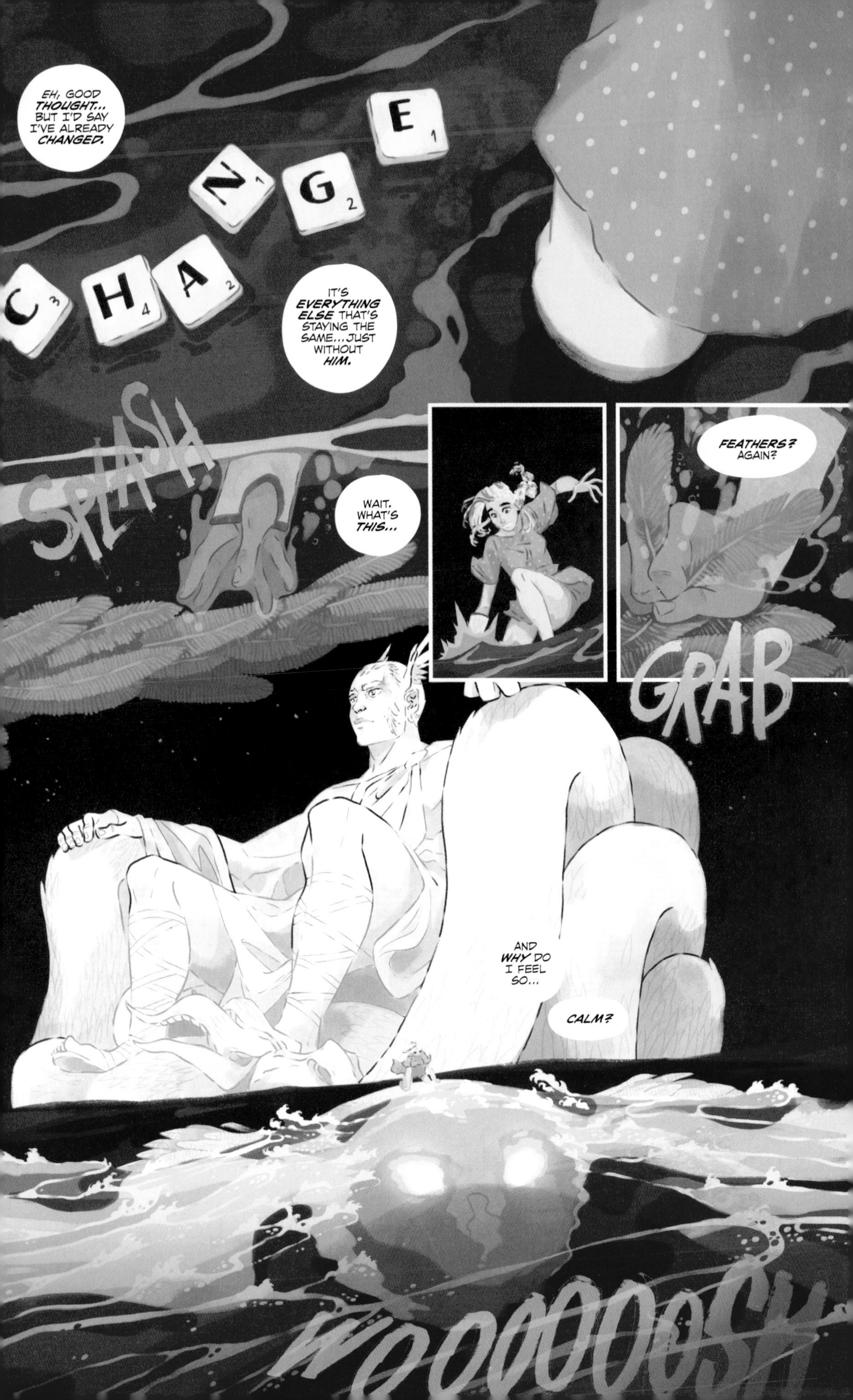
EH, GOOD THOUGHT... BUT I'D SAY I'VE ALREADY CHANGED.
CHANGE
IT'S EVERYTHING ELSE THAT'S STAYING THE SAME... JUST WITHOUT HIM.
SPLASH
WAIT. WHAT'S THIS...
FEATHERS? AGAIN?
GRAB
AND WHY DO I FEEL SO...
CALM?
WOOOOOOSH

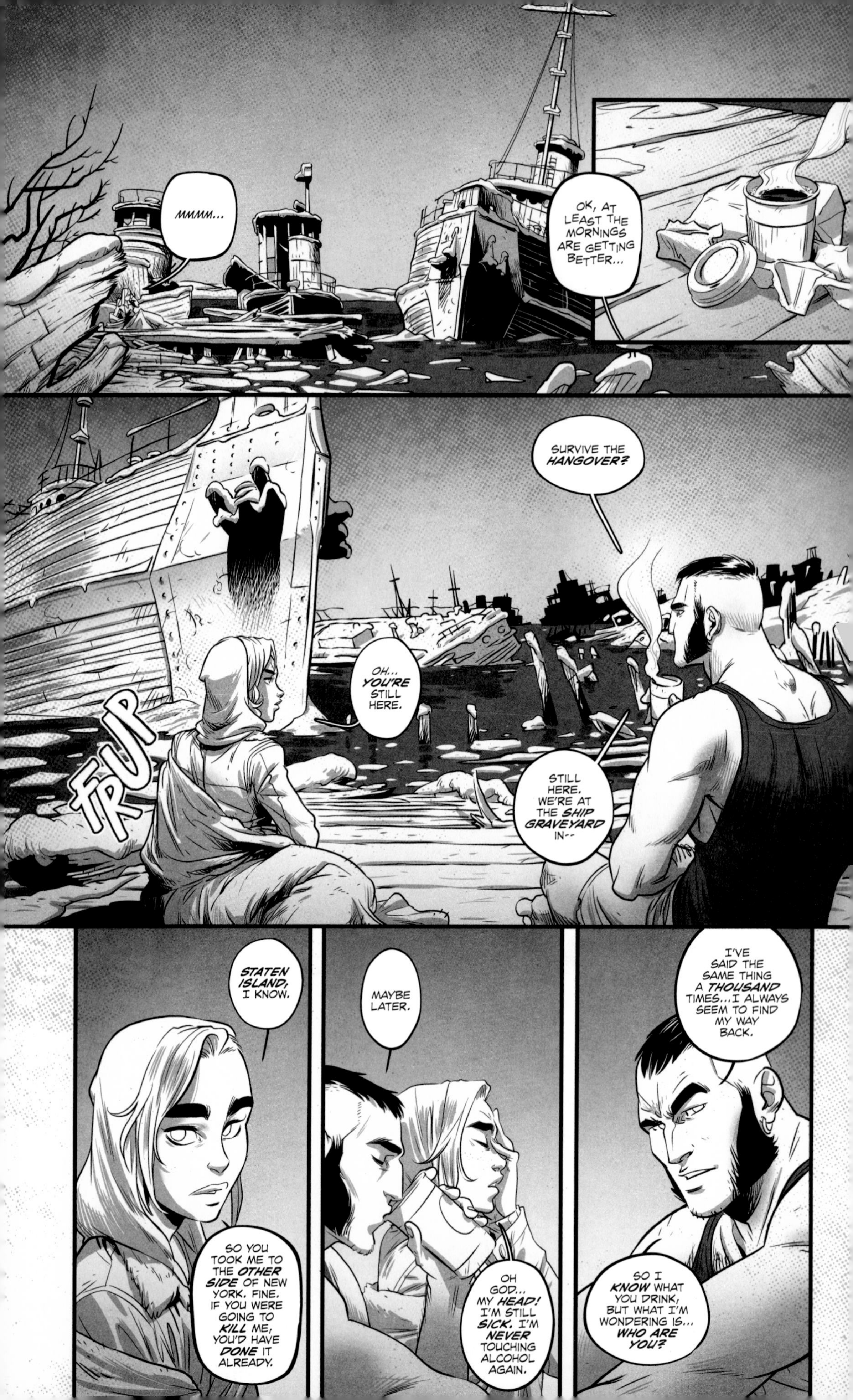
MMMM...
OK, AT LEAST THE MORNINGS ARE GETTING BETTER...
SURVIVE THE HANGOVER?
OH... YOU'RE STILL HERE.
FRUP
STILL HERE. WE'RE AT THE SHIP GRAVEYARD IN--
STATEN ISLAND, I KNOW.
SO YOU TOOK ME TO THE OTHER SIDE OF NEW YORK. FINE. IF YOU WERE GOING TO KILL ME, YOU'D HAVE DONE IT ALREADY.
MAYBE LATER.
OH GOD... MY HEAD! I'M STILL SICK. I'M NEVER TOUCHING ALCOHOL AGAIN.
I'VE SAID THE SAME THING A THOUSAND TIMES...I ALWAYS SEEM TO FIND MY WAY BACK.
SO I KNOW WHAT YOU DRINK, BUT WHAT I'M WONDERING IS... WHO ARE YOU?

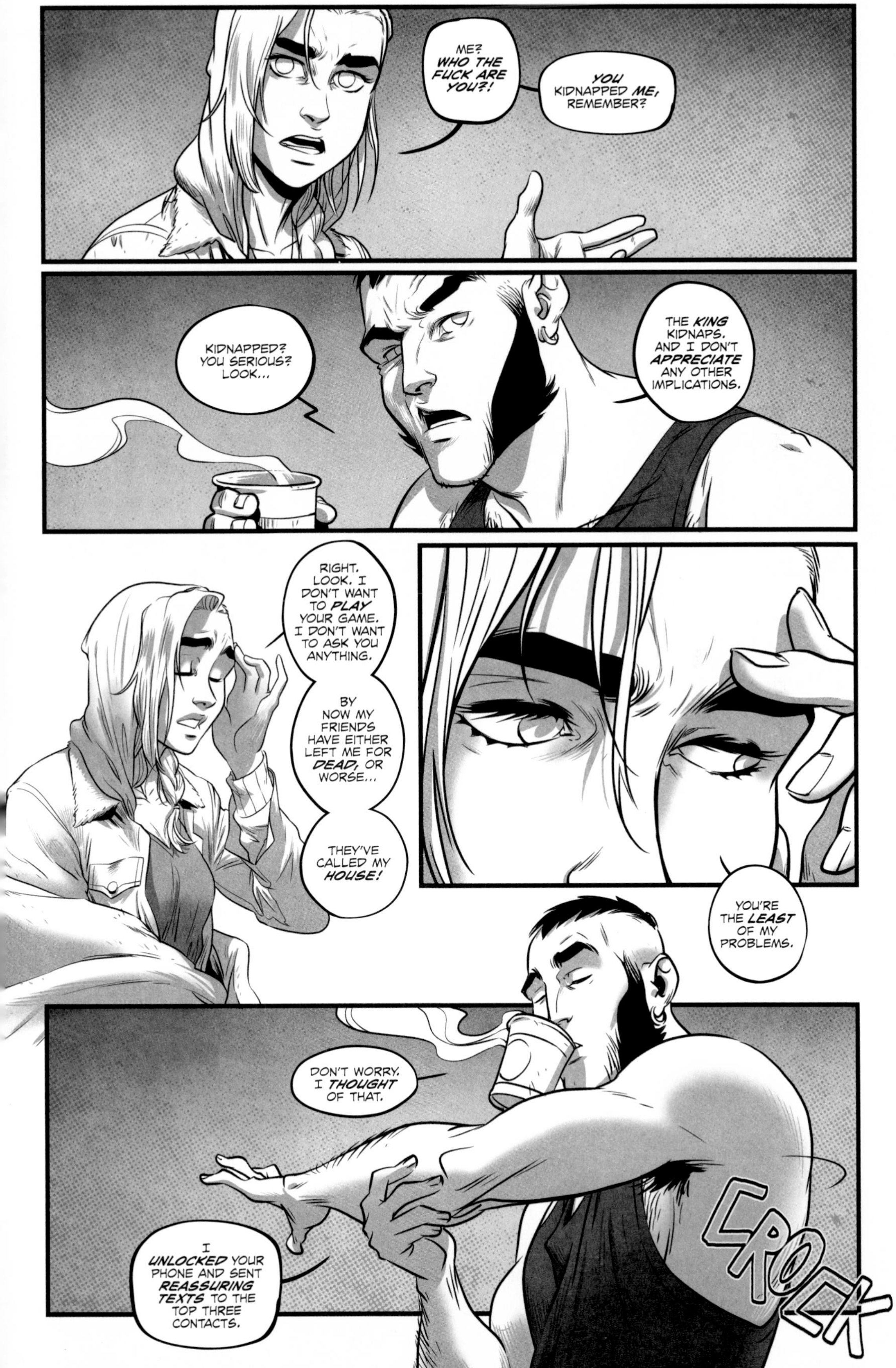
ME?
WHO THE FUCK ARE YOU?!
YOU KIDNAPPED ME, REMEMBER?
KIDNAPPED? YOU SERIOUS? LOOK...
THE KING KIDNAPS. AND I DON'T APPRECIATE ANY OTHER IMPLICATIONS.
RIGHT. LOOK. I DON'T WANT TO PLAY YOUR GAME. I DON'T WANT TO ASK YOU ANYTHING.
BY NOW MY FRIENDS HAVE EITHER LEFT ME FOR DEAD, OR WORSE...
THEY'VE CALLED MY HOUSE!
YOU'RE THE LEAST OF MY PROBLEMS.
DON'T WORRY. I THOUGHT OF THAT.
I UNLOCKED YOUR PHONE AND SENT REASSURING TEXTS TO THE TOP THREE CONTACTS.
CROCK

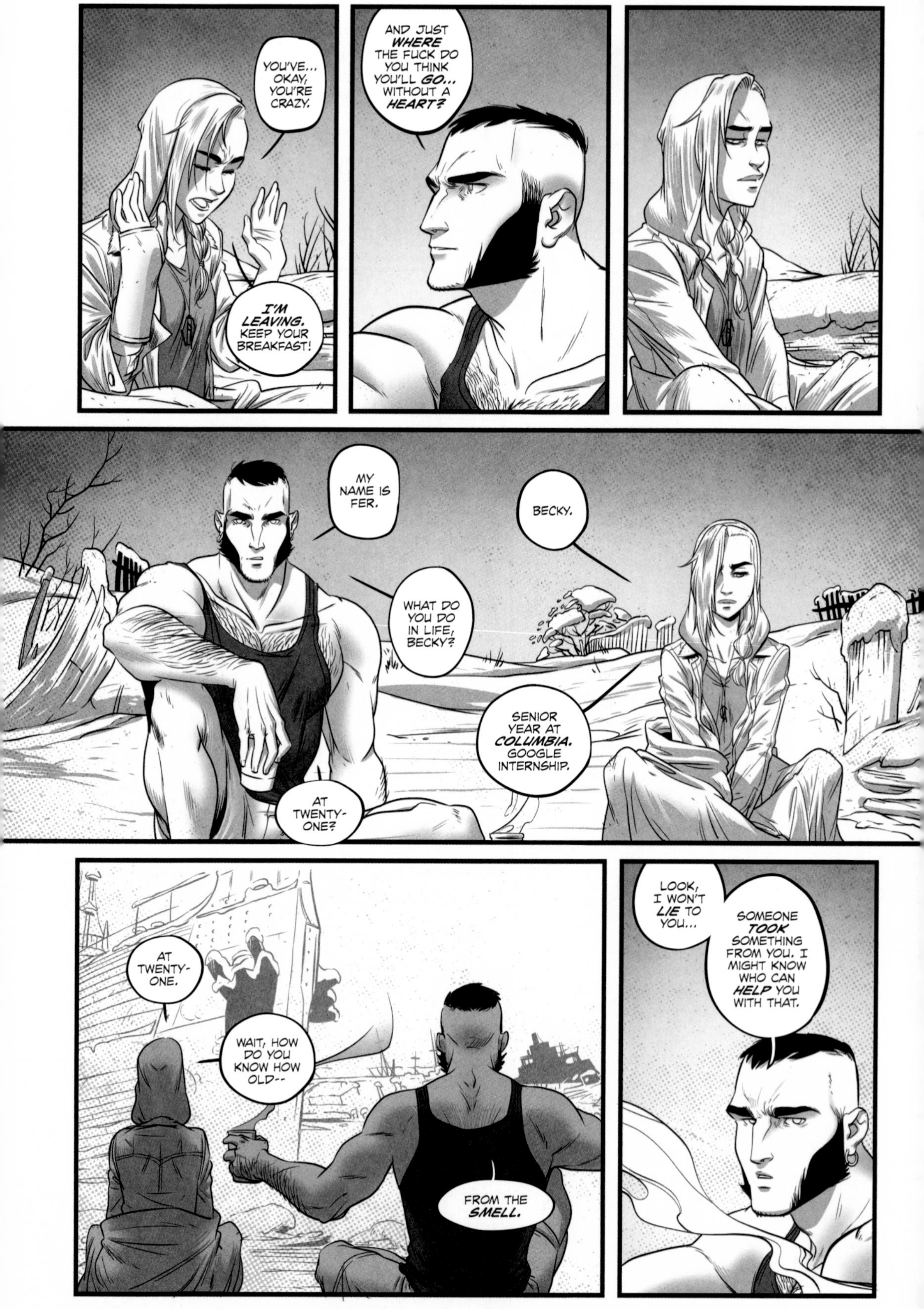
YOU'VE... OKAY, YOU'RE CRAZY.
I'M LEAVING. KEEP YOUR BREAKFAST!
AND JUST WHERE THE FUCK DO YOU THINK YOU'LL GO... WITHOUT A HEART?
MY NAME IS FER.
BECKY.
WHAT DO YOU DO IN LIFE, BECKY?
SENIOR YEAR AT COLUMBIA. GOOGLE INTERNSHIP.
AT TWENTY-ONE?
AT TWENTY-ONE.
WAIT, HOW DO YOU KNOW HOW OLD--
FROM THE SMELL.
LOOK, I WON'T LIE TO YOU...
SOMEONE TOOK SOMETHING FROM YOU. I MIGHT KNOW WHO CAN HELP YOU WITH THAT.

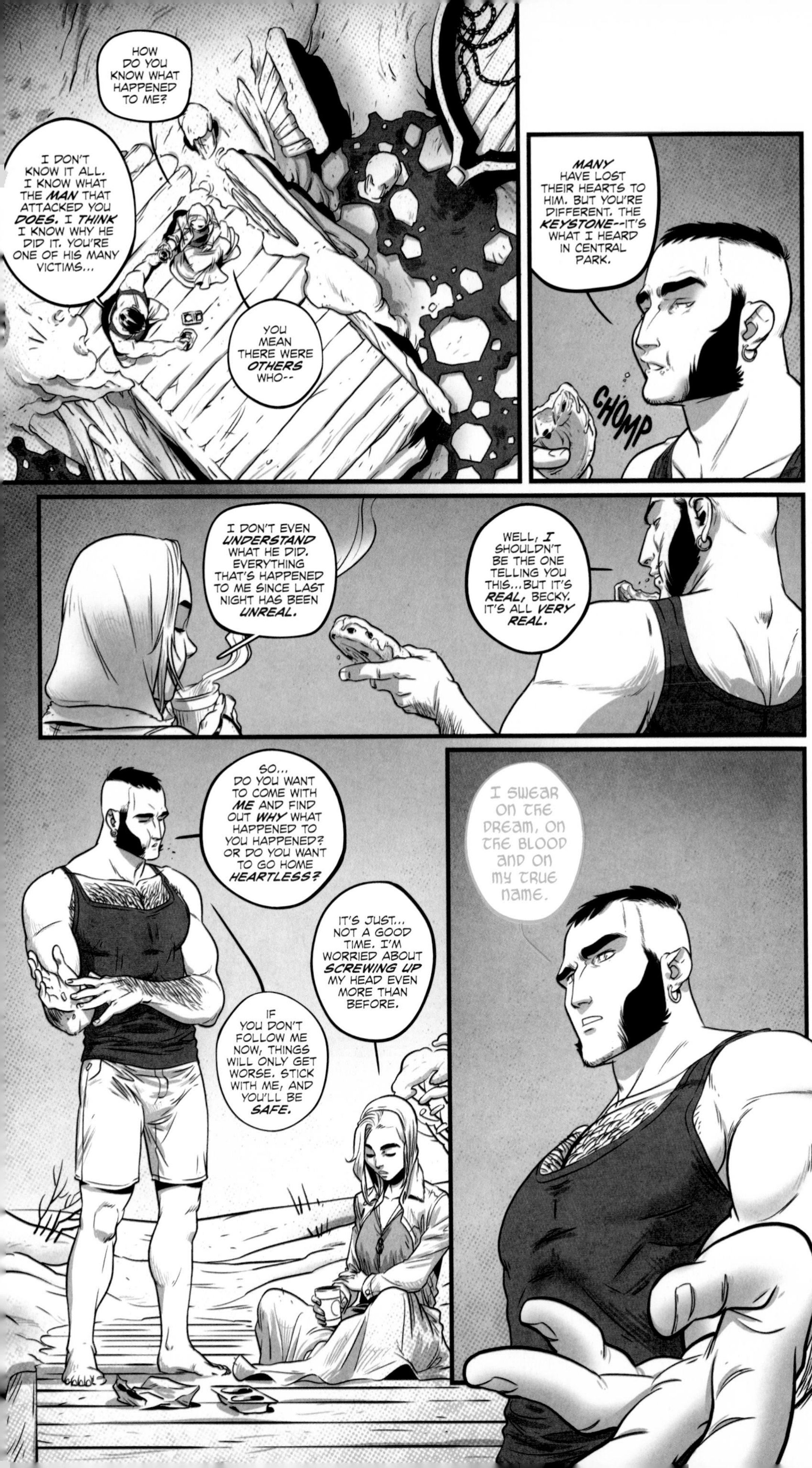
HOW DO YOU KNOW WHAT HAPPENED TO ME?
I DON'T KNOW IT ALL. I KNOW WHAT THE MAN THAT ATTACKED YOU DOES. I THINK I KNOW WHY HE DID IT. YOU'RE ONE OF HIS MANY VICTIMS...
YOU MEAN THERE WERE OTHERS WHO--
MANY HAVE LOST THEIR HEARTS TO HIM. BUT YOU'RE DIFFERENT. THE KEYSTONE--IT'S WHAT I HEARD IN CENTRAL PARK.
CHOMP
I DON'T EVEN UNDERSTAND WHAT HE DID. EVERYTHING THAT'S HAPPENED TO ME SINCE LAST NIGHT HAS BEEN UNREAL.
WELL, I SHOULDN'T BE THE ONE TELLING YOU THIS...BUT IT'S REAL, BECKY. IT'S ALL VERY REAL.
SO... DO YOU WANT TO COME WITH ME AND FIND OUT WHY WHAT HAPPENED TO YOU HAPPENED? OR DO YOU WANT TO GO HOME HEARTLESS?
IT'S JUST... NOT A GOOD TIME. I'M WORRIED ABOUT SCREWING UP MY HEAD EVEN MORE THAN BEFORE.
IF YOU DON'T FOLLOW ME NOW, THINGS WILL ONLY GET WORSE. STICK WITH ME, AND YOU'LL BE SAFE.
I SWEAR ON THE DREAM, ON THE BLOOD AND ON MY TRUE NAME.

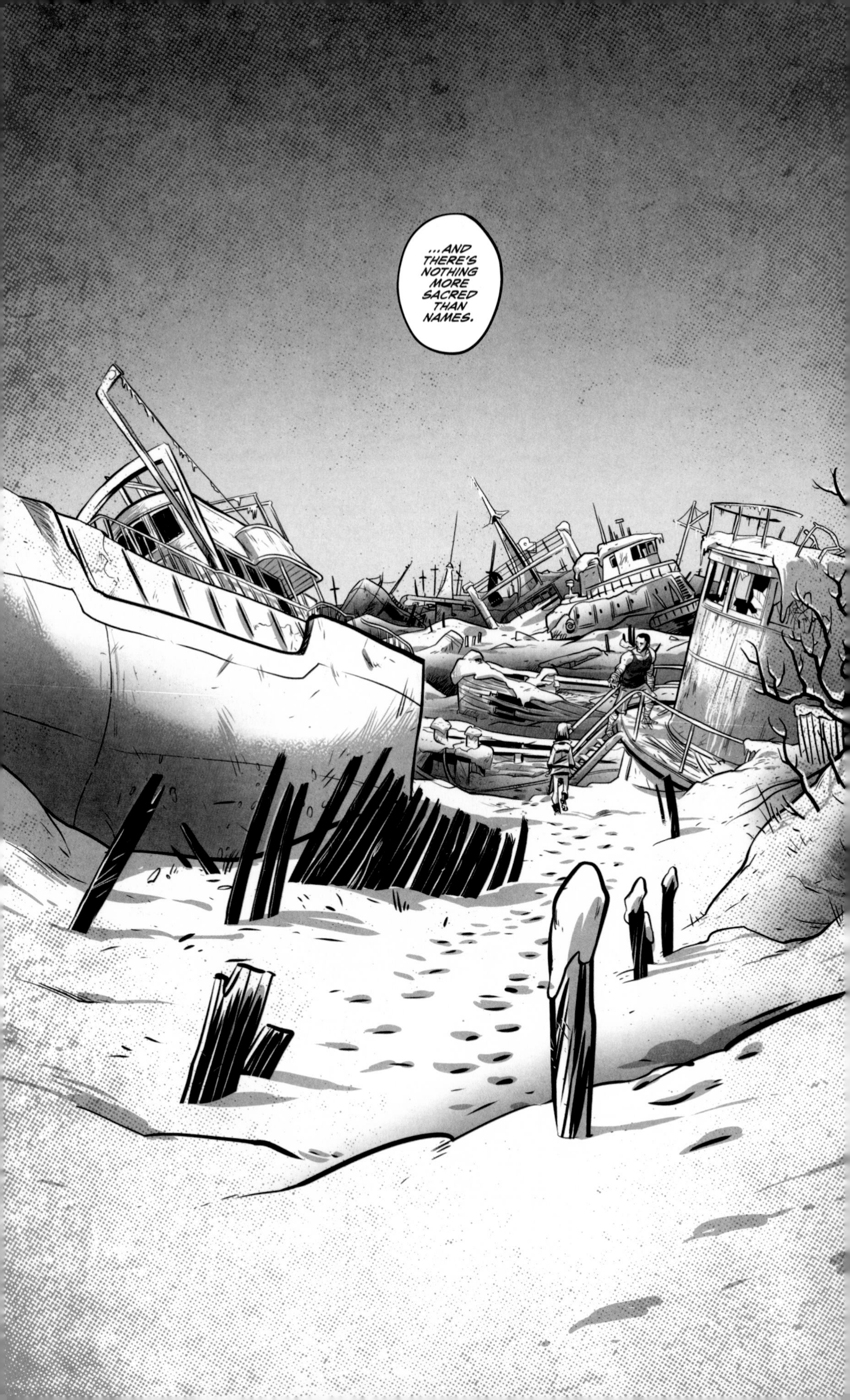
...AND THERE'S NOTHING MORE SACRED THAN NAMES.

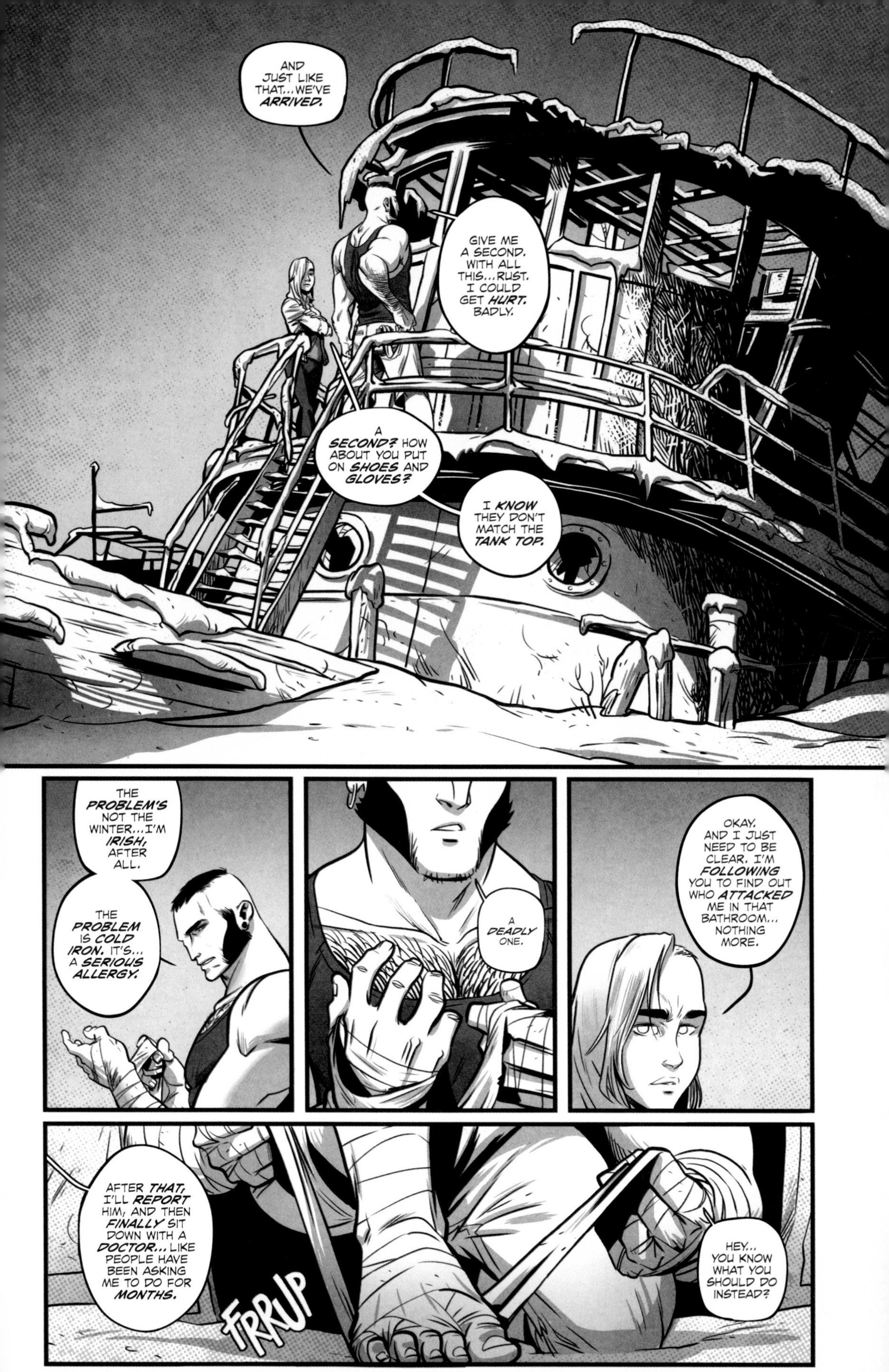
AND JUST LIKE THAT...WE'VE ARRIVED.
GIVE ME A SECOND. WITH ALL THIS...RUST. I COULD GET HURT. BADLY.
A SECOND? HOW ABOUT YOU PUT ON SHOES AND GLOVES?
I KNOW THEY DON'T MATCH THE TANK TOP.
THE PROBLEM'S NOT THE WINTER...I'M IRISH, AFTER ALL.
THE PROBLEM IS COLD IRON. IT'S... A SERIOUS ALLERGY.
A DEADLY ONE.
OKAY. AND I JUST NEED TO BE CLEAR. I'M FOLLOWING YOU TO FIND OUT WHO ATTACKED ME IN THAT BATHROOM... NOTHING MORE.
AFTER THAT, I'LL REPORT HIM, AND THEN FINALLY SIT DOWN WITH A DOCTOR... LIKE PEOPLE HAVE BEEN ASKING ME TO DO FOR MONTHS.
FRRUP
HEY... YOU KNOW WHAT YOU SHOULD DO INSTEAD?

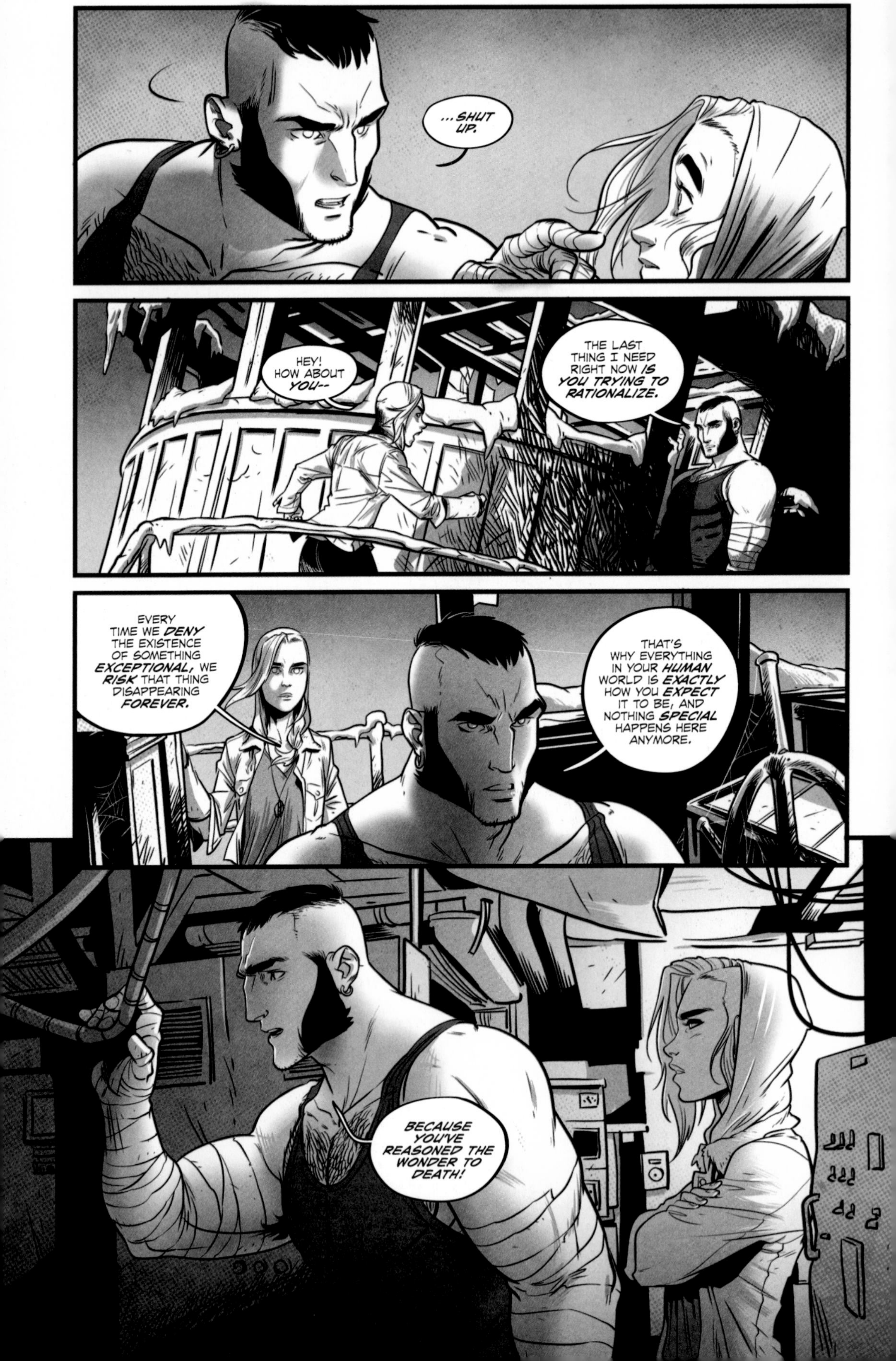
...SHUT UP.
HEY! HOW ABOUT YOU--
THE LAST THING I NEED RIGHT NOW IS YOU TRYING TO RATIONALIZE.
EVERY TIME WE DENY THE EXISTENCE OF SOMETHING EXCEPTIONAL, WE RISK THAT THING DISAPPEARING FOREVER.
THAT'S WHY EVERYTHING IN YOUR HUMAN WORLD IS EXACTLY HOW YOU EXPECT IT TO BE, AND NOTHING SPECIAL HAPPENS HERE ANYMORE.
BECAUSE YOU'VE REASONED THE WONDER TO DEATH!

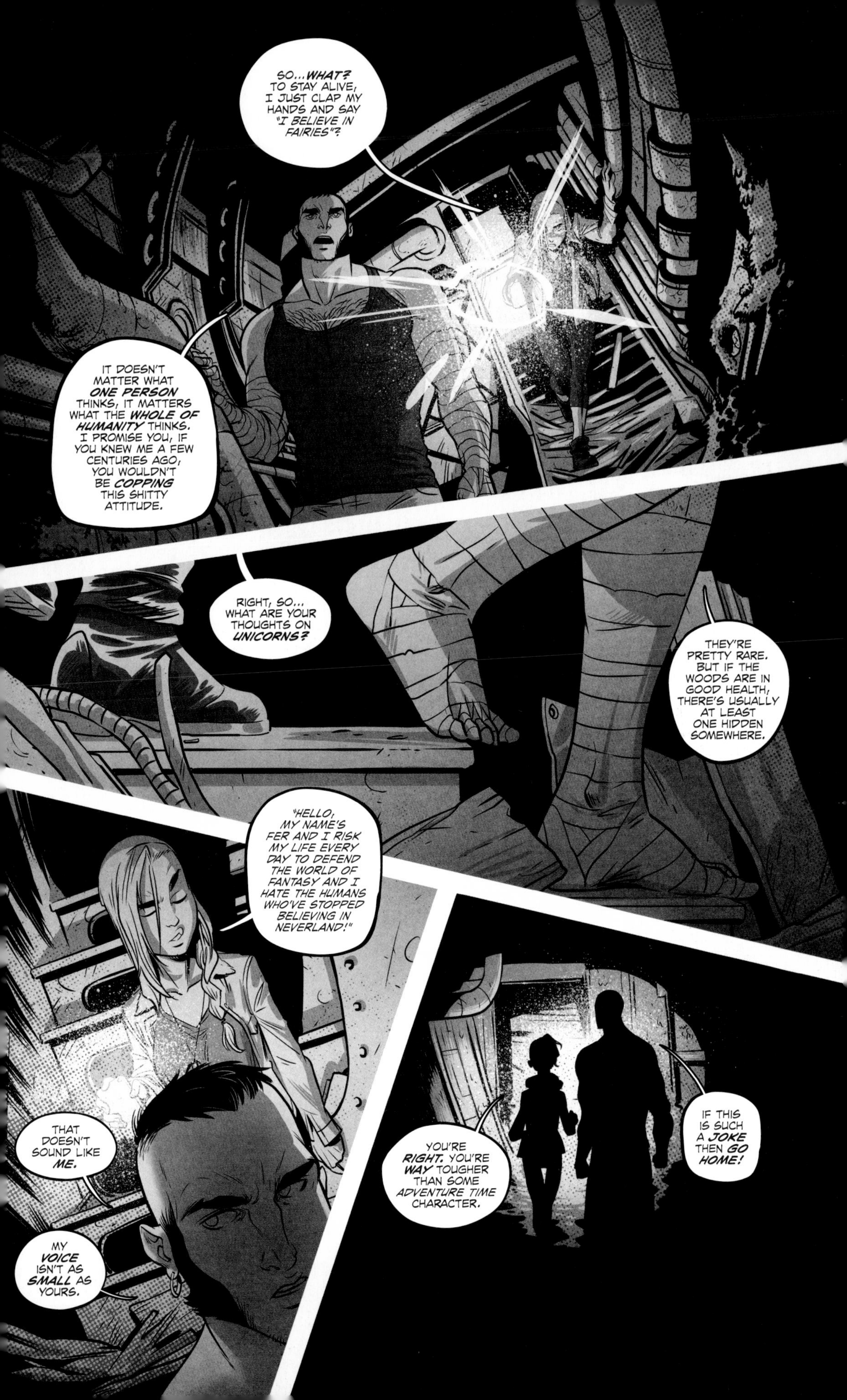
SO... WHAT? TO STAY ALIVE, I JUST CLAP MY HANDS AND SAY "I BELIEVE IN FAIRIES"?
IT DOESN'T MATTER WHAT ONE PERSON THINKS, IT MATTERS WHAT THE WHOLE OF HUMANITY THINKS. I PROMISE YOU, IF YOU KNEW ME A FEW CENTURIES AGO, YOU WOULDN'T BE COPPING THIS SHITTY ATTITUDE.
RIGHT, SO... WHAT ARE YOUR THOUGHTS ON UNICORNS?
THEY'RE PRETTY RARE. BUT IF THE WOODS ARE IN GOOD HEALTH, THERE'S USUALLY AT LEAST ONE HIDDEN SOMEWHERE.
"HELLO, MY NAME'S FER AND I RISK MY LIFE EVERY DAY TO DEFEND THE WORLD OF FANTASY AND I HATE THE HUMANS WHO'VE STOPPED BELIEVING IN NEVERLAND!"
THAT DOESN'T SOUND LIKE ME.
MY VOICE ISN'T AS SMALL AS YOURS.
YOU'RE RIGHT. YOU'RE WAY TOUGHER THAN SOME ADVENTURE TIME CHARACTER.
IF THIS IS SUCH A JOKE THEN GO HOME!

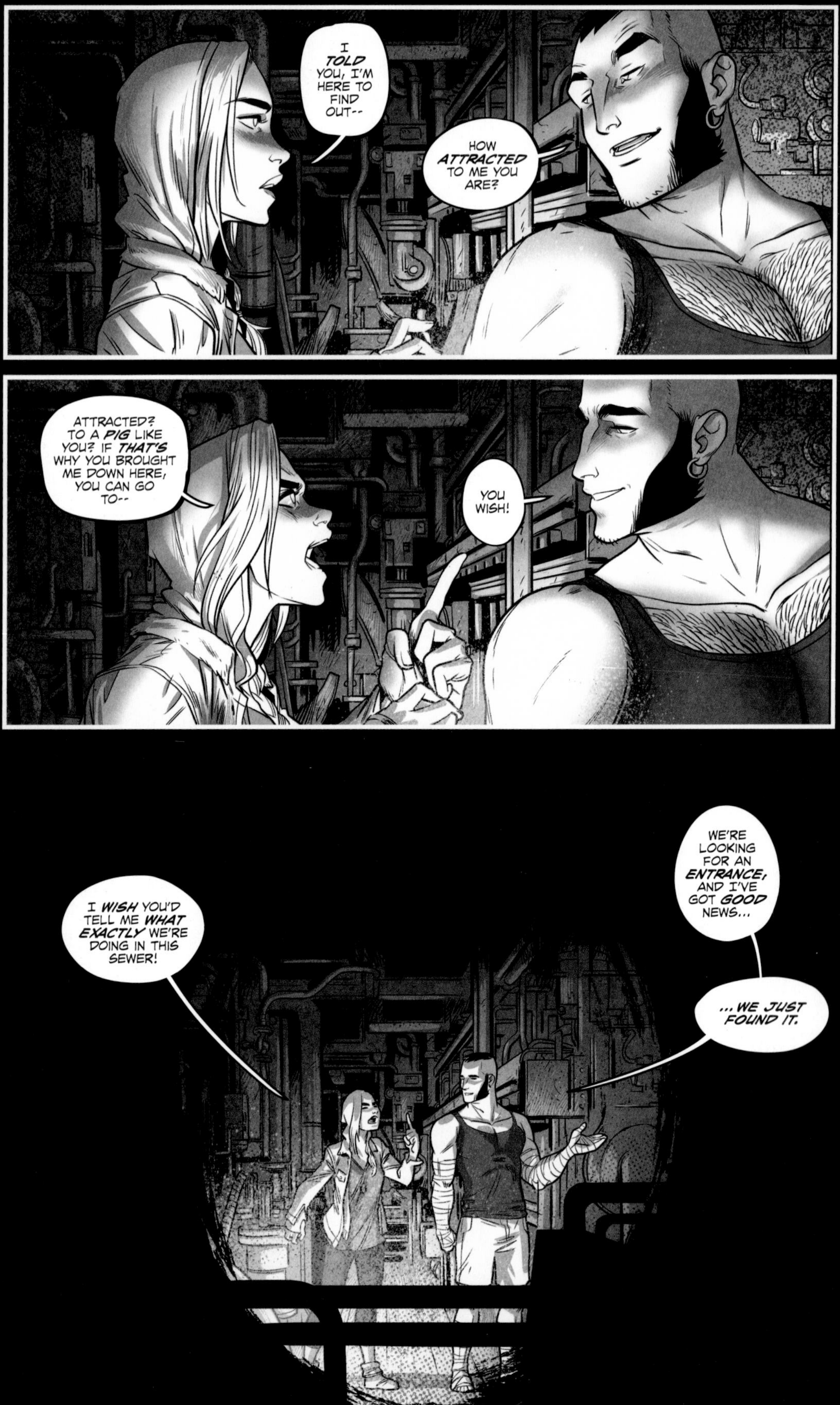
I TOLD YOU, I'M HERE TO FIND OUT--
HOW ATTRACTED TO ME YOU ARE?
ATTRACTED? TO A PIG LIKE YOU? IF THAT'S WHY YOU BROUGHT ME DOWN HERE, YOU CAN GO TO--
YOU WISH!
I WISH YOU'D TELL ME WHAT EXACTLY WE'RE DOING IN THIS SEWER!
WE'RE LOOKING FOR AN ENTRANCE, AND I'VE GOT GOOD NEWS...
...WE JUST FOUND IT.

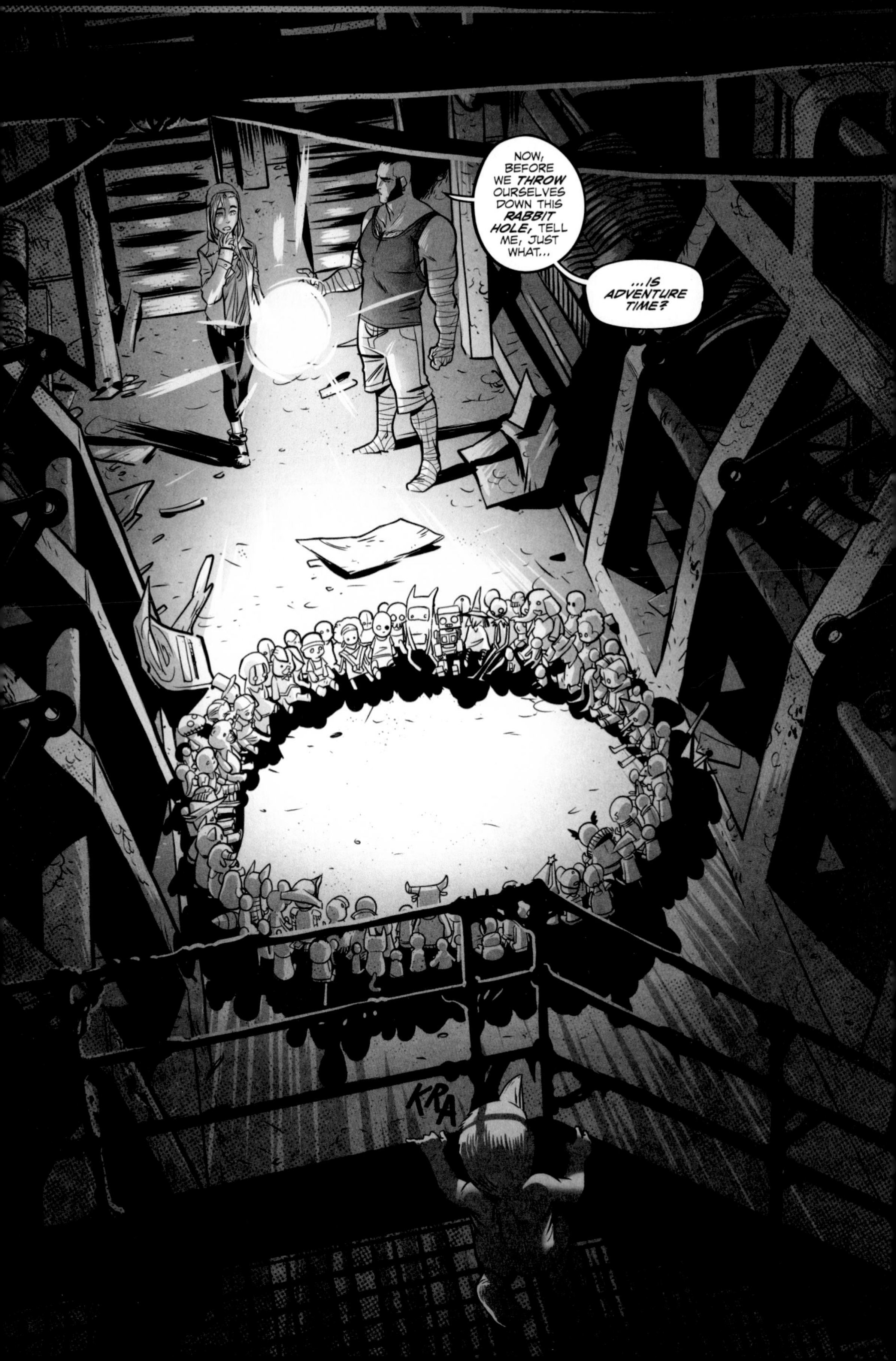
NOW, BEFORE WE THROW OURSELVES DOWN THIS RABBIT HOLE, TELL ME, JUST WHAT...
...IS ADVENTURE TIME?
KRA

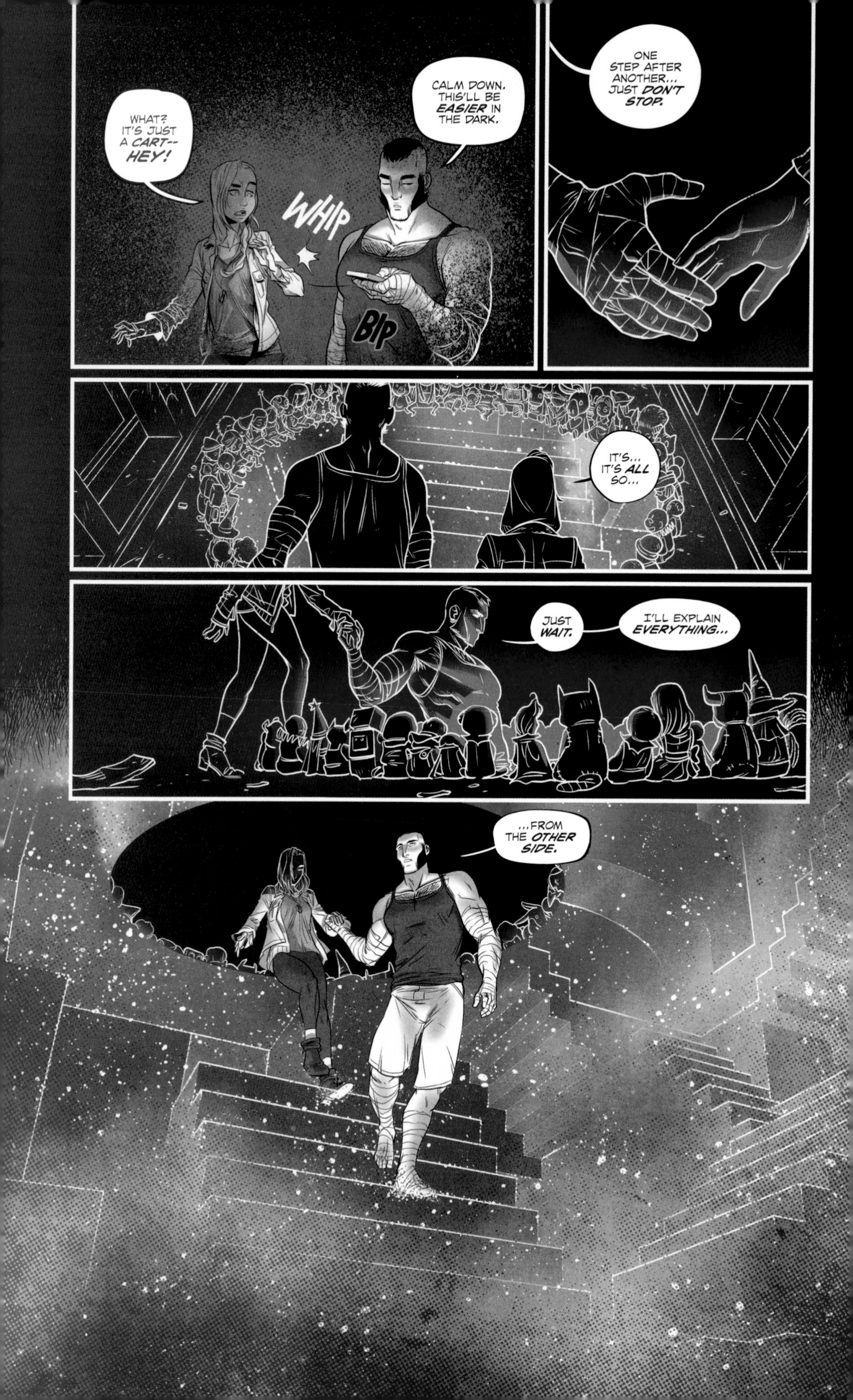
WHAT? IT'S JUST A CART-- HEY!
CALM DOWN. THIS'LL BE EASIER IN THE DARK.
WHIP
BIP
ONE STEP AFTER ANOTHER... JUST DON'T STOP.
IT'S... IT'S ALL SO...
JUST WAIT.
I'LL EXPLAIN EVERYTHING...
...FROM THE OTHER SIDE.

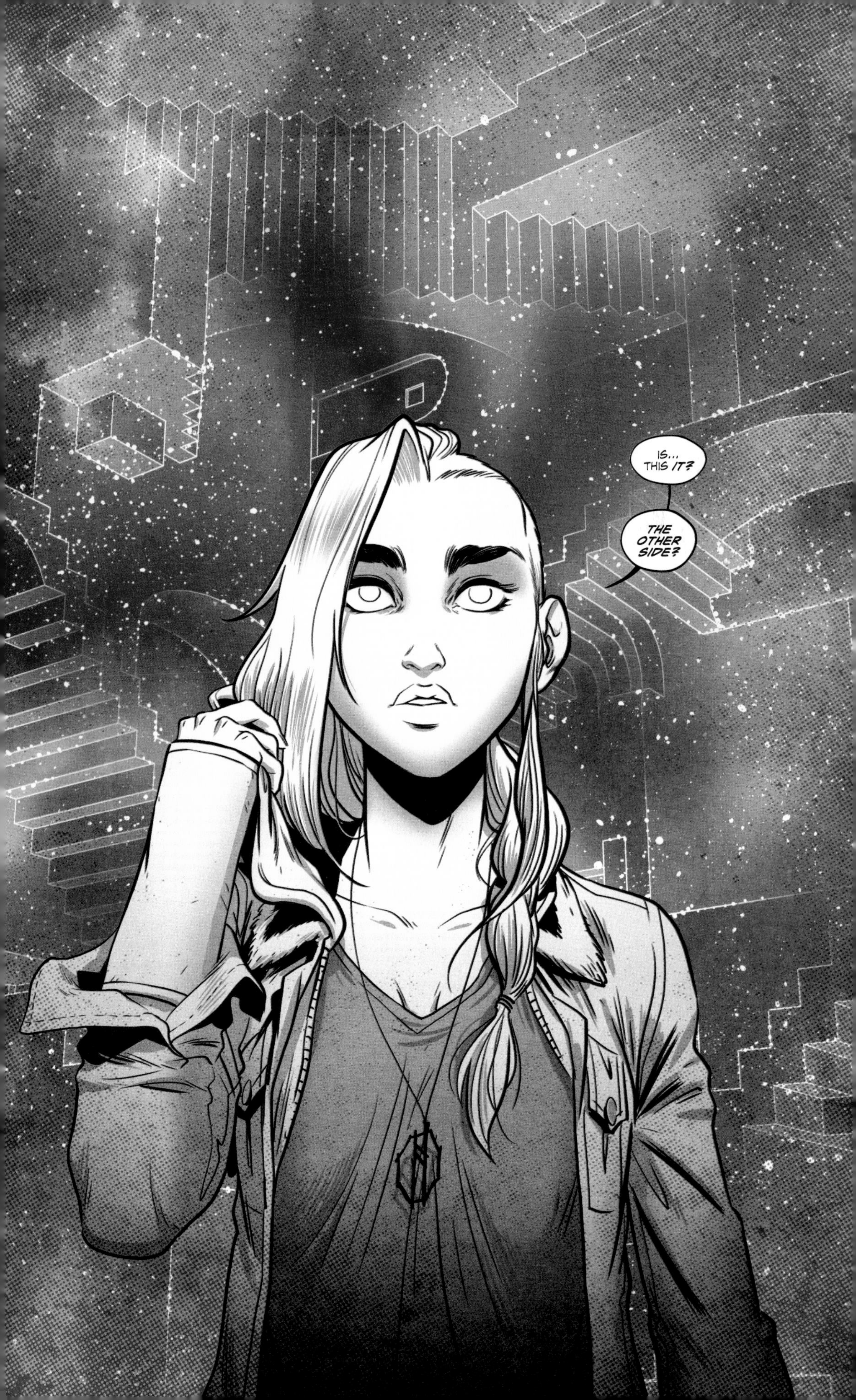
IS... THIS IT?
THE OTHER SIDE?

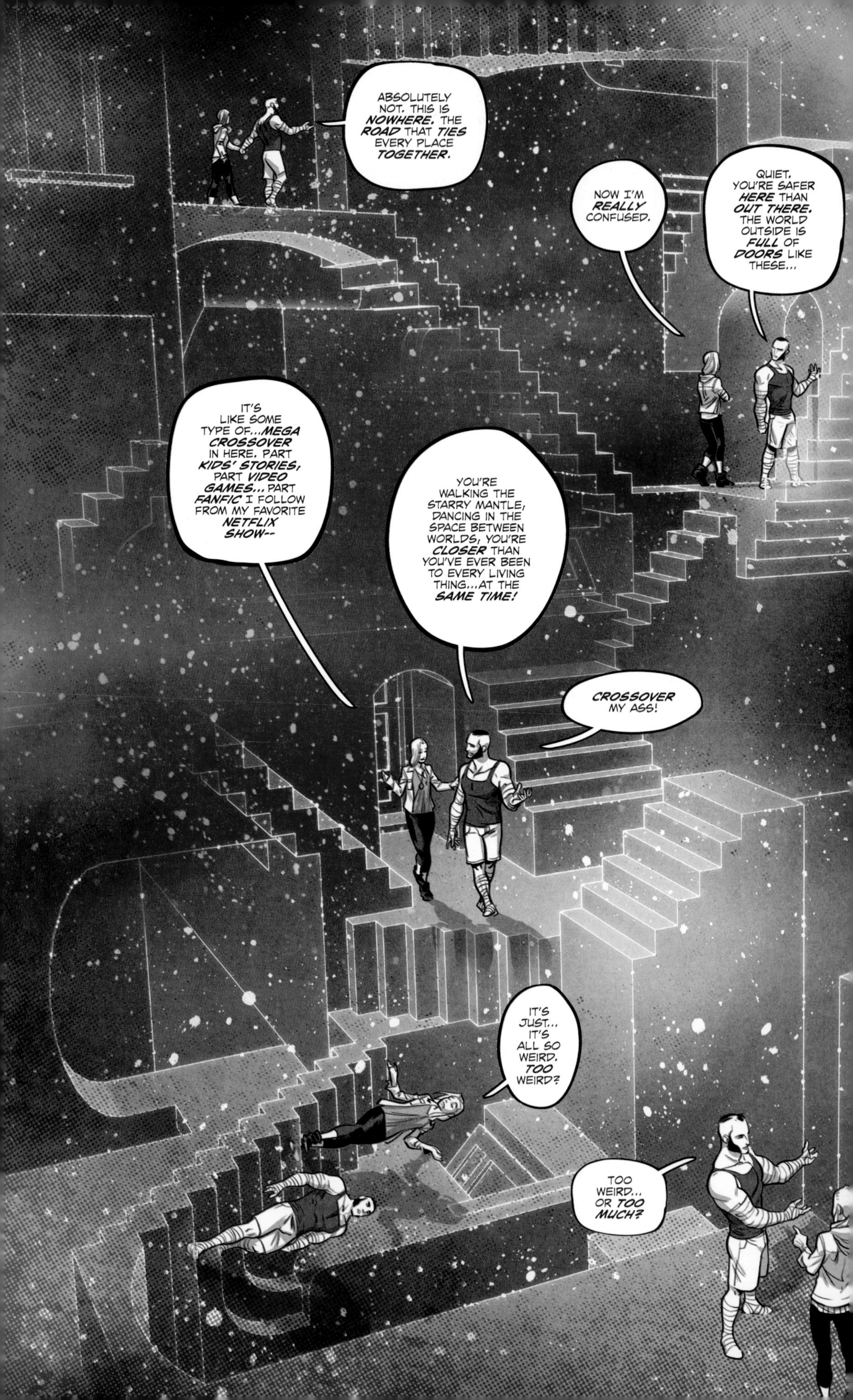

ABSOLUTELY NOT. THIS IS NOWHERE. THE ROAD THAT TIES EVERY PLACE TOGETHER.
NOW I'M REALLY CONFUSED.
QUIET. YOU'RE SAFER HERE THAN OUT THERE. THE WORLD OUTSIDE IS FULL OF DOORS LIKE THESE...
IT'S LIKE SOME TYPE OF...MEGA CROSSOVER IN HERE. PART KIDS' STORIES, PART VIDEO GAMES... PART FANFIC I FOLLOW FROM MY FAVORITE NETFLIX SHOW--
YOU'RE WALKING THE STARRY MANTLE, DANCING IN THE SPACE BETWEEN WORLDS, YOU'RE CLOSER THAN YOU'VE EVER BEEN TO EVERY LIVING THING...AT THE SAME TIME!
CROSSOVER MY ASS!
IT'S JUST... IT'S ALL SO WEIRD. TOO WEIRD?
TOO WEIRD... OR TOO MUCH?

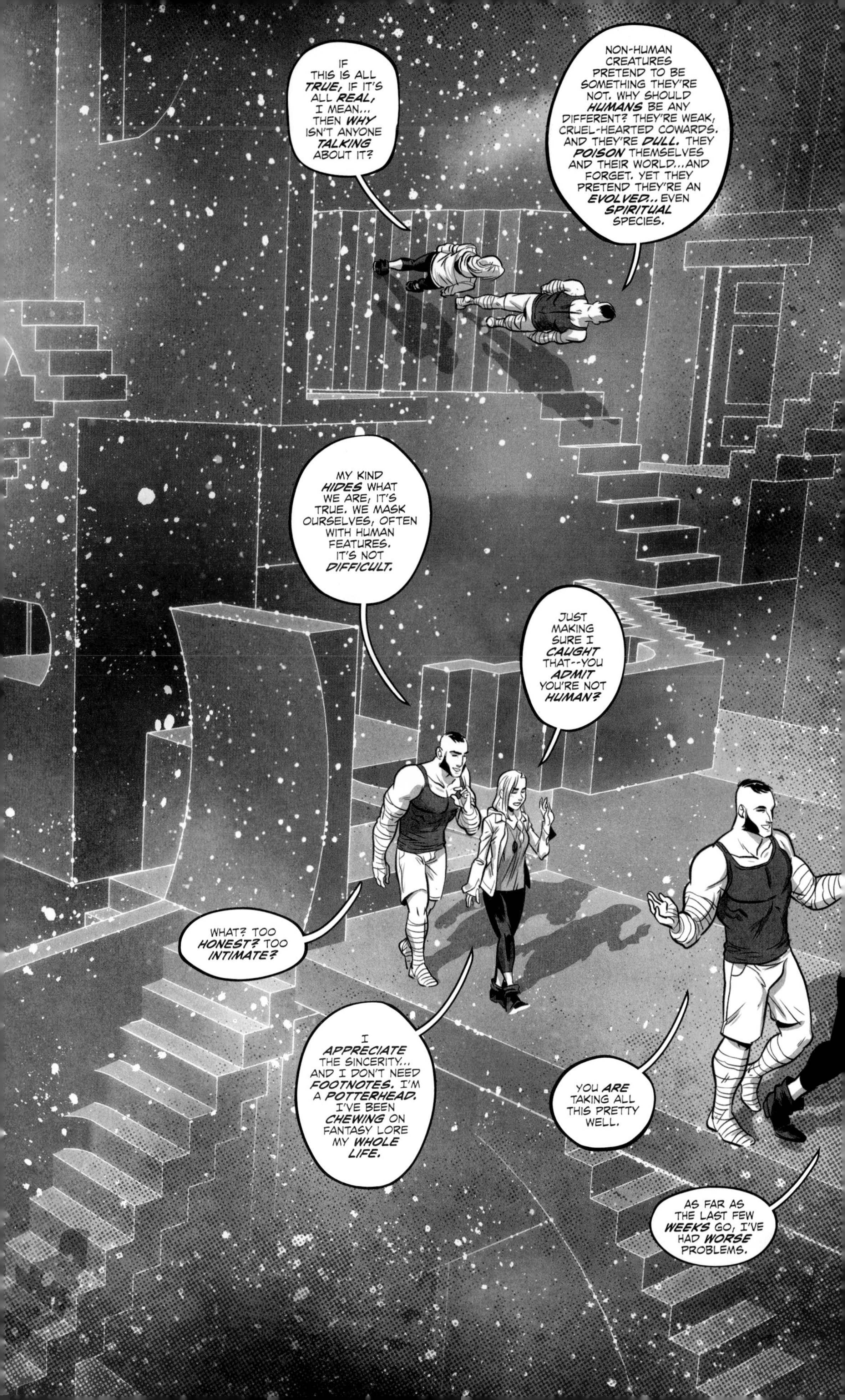
IF THIS IS ALL TRUE; IF IT'S ALL REAL, I MEAN... THEN WHY ISN'T ANYONE TALKING ABOUT IT?
NON-HUMAN CREATURES PRETEND TO BE SOMETHING THEY'RE NOT. WHY SHOULD HUMANS BE ANY DIFFERENT? THEY'RE WEAK, CRUEL-HEARTED COWARDS. AND THEY'RE DULL. THEY POISON THEMSELVES AND THEIR WORLD...AND FORGET. YET THEY PRETEND THEY'RE AN EVOLVED... EVEN SPIRITUAL SPECIES.
MY KIND HIDES WHAT WE ARE, IT'S TRUE. WE MASK OURSELVES, OFTEN WITH HUMAN FEATURES. IT'S NOT DIFFICULT.
JUST MAKING SURE I CAUGHT THAT--YOU ADMIT YOU'RE NOT HUMAN?
WHAT? TOO HONEST? TOO INTIMATE?
I APPRECIATE THE SINCERITY... AND I DON'T NEED FOOTNOTES. I'M A POTTERHEAD. I'VE BEEN CHEWING ON FANTASY LORE MY WHOLE LIFE.
YOU ARE TAKING ALL THIS PRETTY WELL.
AS FAR AS THE LAST FEW WEEKS GO, I'VE HAD WORSE PROBLEMS.

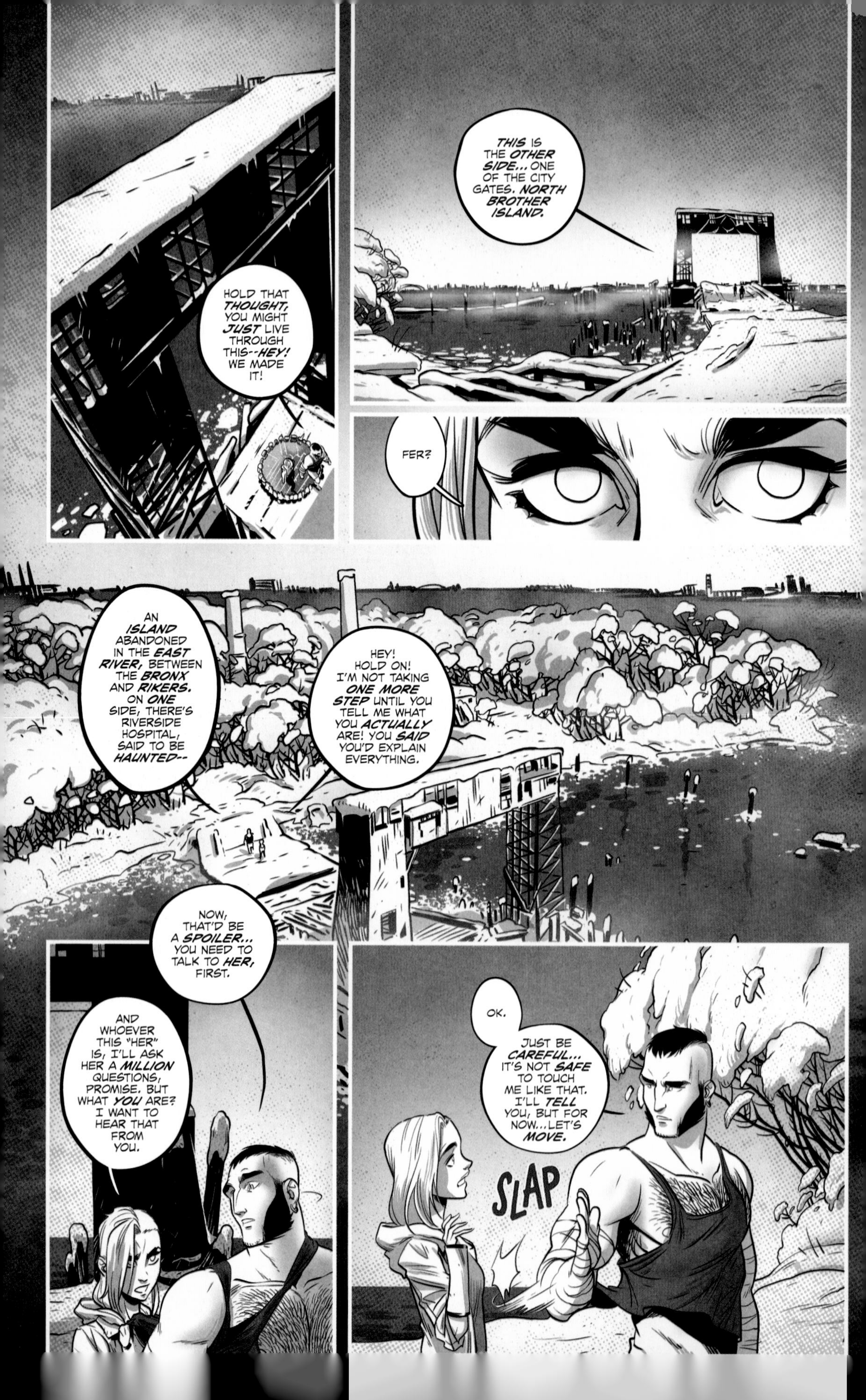
HOLD THAT THOUGHT, YOU MIGHT JUST LIVE THROUGH THIS--HEY! WE MADE IT!
THIS IS THE OTHER SIDE... ONE OF THE CITY GATES. NORTH BROTHER ISLAND.
FER?
AN ISLAND ABANDONED IN THE EAST RIVER, BETWEEN THE BRONX AND RIKERS. ON ONE SIDE, THERE'S RIVERSIDE HOSPITAL, SAID TO BE HAUNTED--
HEY! HOLD ON! I'M NOT TAKING ONE MORE STEP UNTIL YOU TELL ME WHAT YOU ACTUALLY ARE! YOU SAID YOU'D EXPLAIN EVERYTHING.
NOW, THAT'D BE A SPOILER... YOU NEED TO TALK TO HER, FIRST.
AND WHOEVER THIS "HER" IS, I'LL ASK HER A MILLION QUESTIONS, PROMISE. BUT WHAT YOU ARE? I WANT TO HEAR THAT FROM YOU.
OK.
JUST BE CAREFUL... IT'S NOT SAFE TO TOUCH ME LIKE THAT. I'LL TELL YOU, BUT FOR NOW...LET'S MOVE.
SLAP

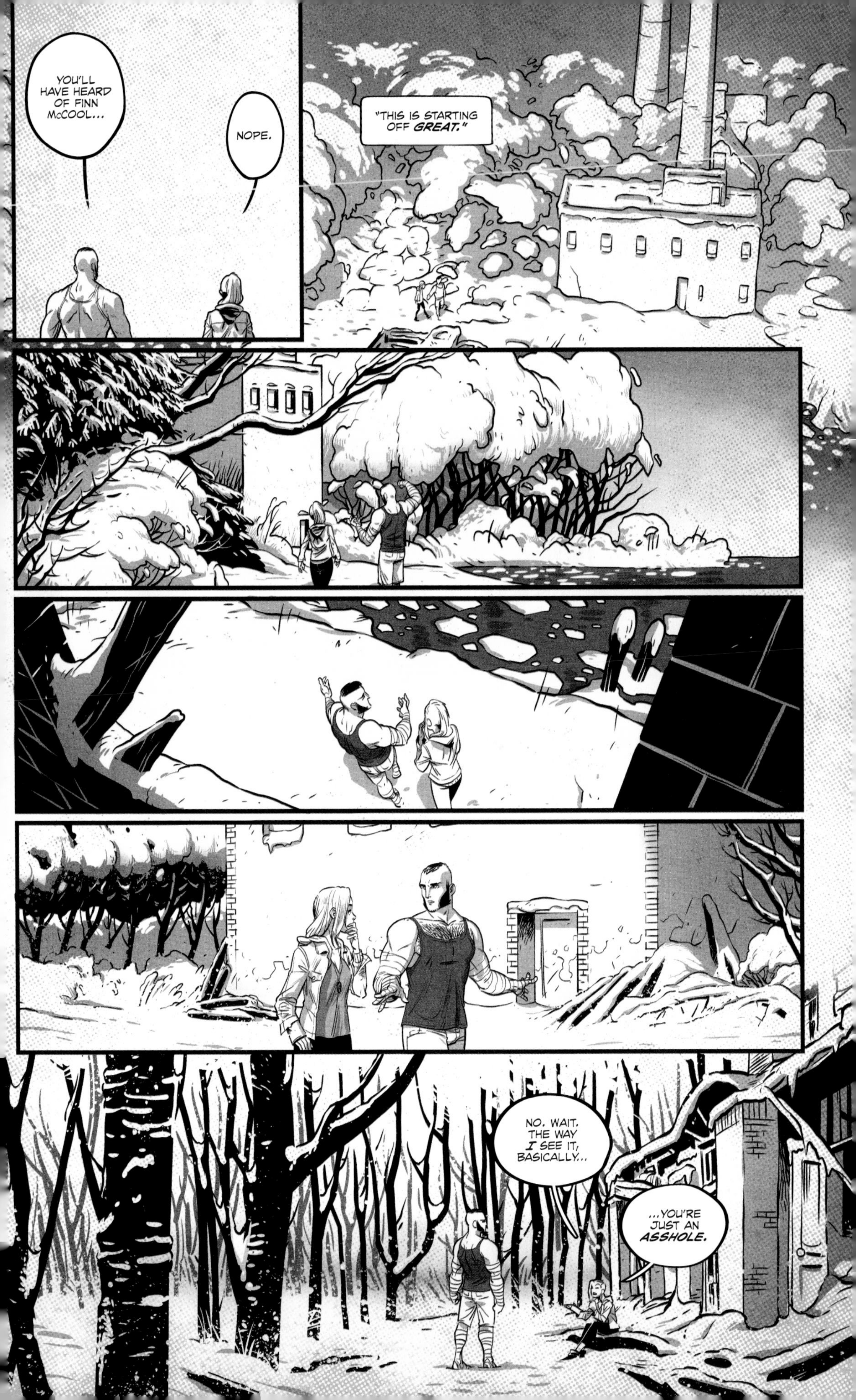
YOU'LL HAVE HEARD OF FINN McCOOL...
NOPE.
"THIS IS STARTING OFF GREAT."
NO. WAIT. THE WAY I SEE IT, BASICALLY...
...YOU'RE JUST AN ASSHOLE.

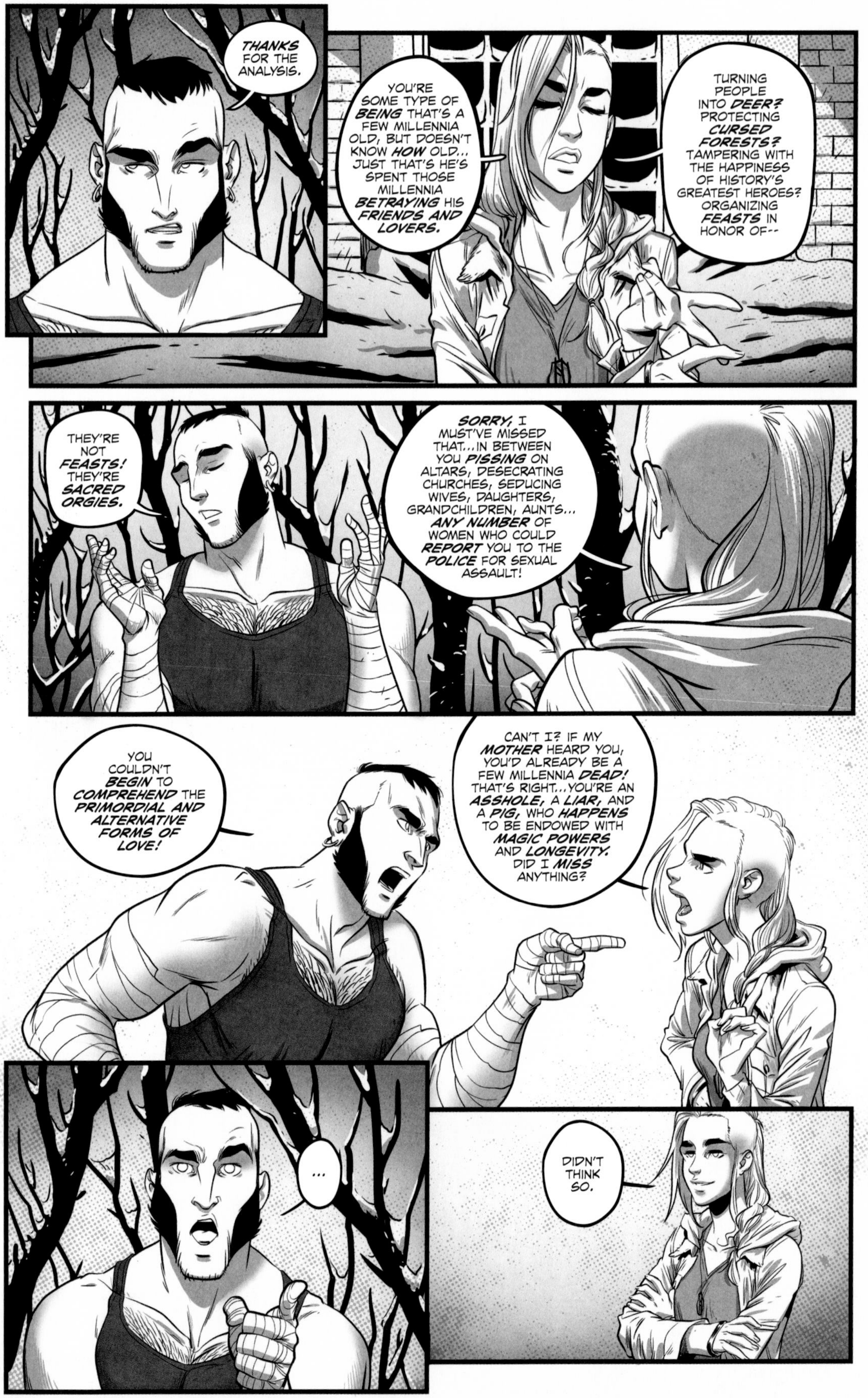
THANKS FOR THE ANALYSIS.
YOU'RE SOME TYPE OF BEING THAT'S A FEW MILLENNIA OLD, BUT DOESN'T KNOW HOW OLD... JUST THAT'S HE'S SPENT THOSE MILLENNIA BETRAYING HIS FRIENDS AND LOVERS.
TURNING PEOPLE INTO DEER? PROTECTING CURSED FORESTS? TAMPERING WITH THE HAPPINESS OF HISTORY'S GREATEST HEROES? ORGANIZING FEASTS IN HONOR OF--
THEY'RE NOT FEASTS! THEY'RE SACRED ORGIES.
SORRY, I MUST'VE MISSED THAT...IN BETWEEN YOU PISSING ON ALTARS, DESECRATING CHURCHES, SEDUCING WIVES, DAUGHTERS, GRANDCHILDREN, AUNTS... ANY NUMBER OF WOMEN WHO COULD REPORT YOU TO THE POLICE FOR SEXUAL ASSAULT!
YOU COULDN'T BEGIN TO COMPREHEND THE PRIMORDIAL AND ALTERNATIVE FORMS OF LOVE!
CAN'T I? IF MY MOTHER HEARD YOU, YOU'D ALREADY BE A FEW MILLENNIA DEAD! THAT'S RIGHT...YOU'RE AN ASSHOLE, A LIAR, AND A PIG, WHO HAPPENS TO BE ENDOWED WITH MAGIC POWERS AND LONGEVITY. DID I MISS ANYTHING?
...
DIDN'T THINK SO.

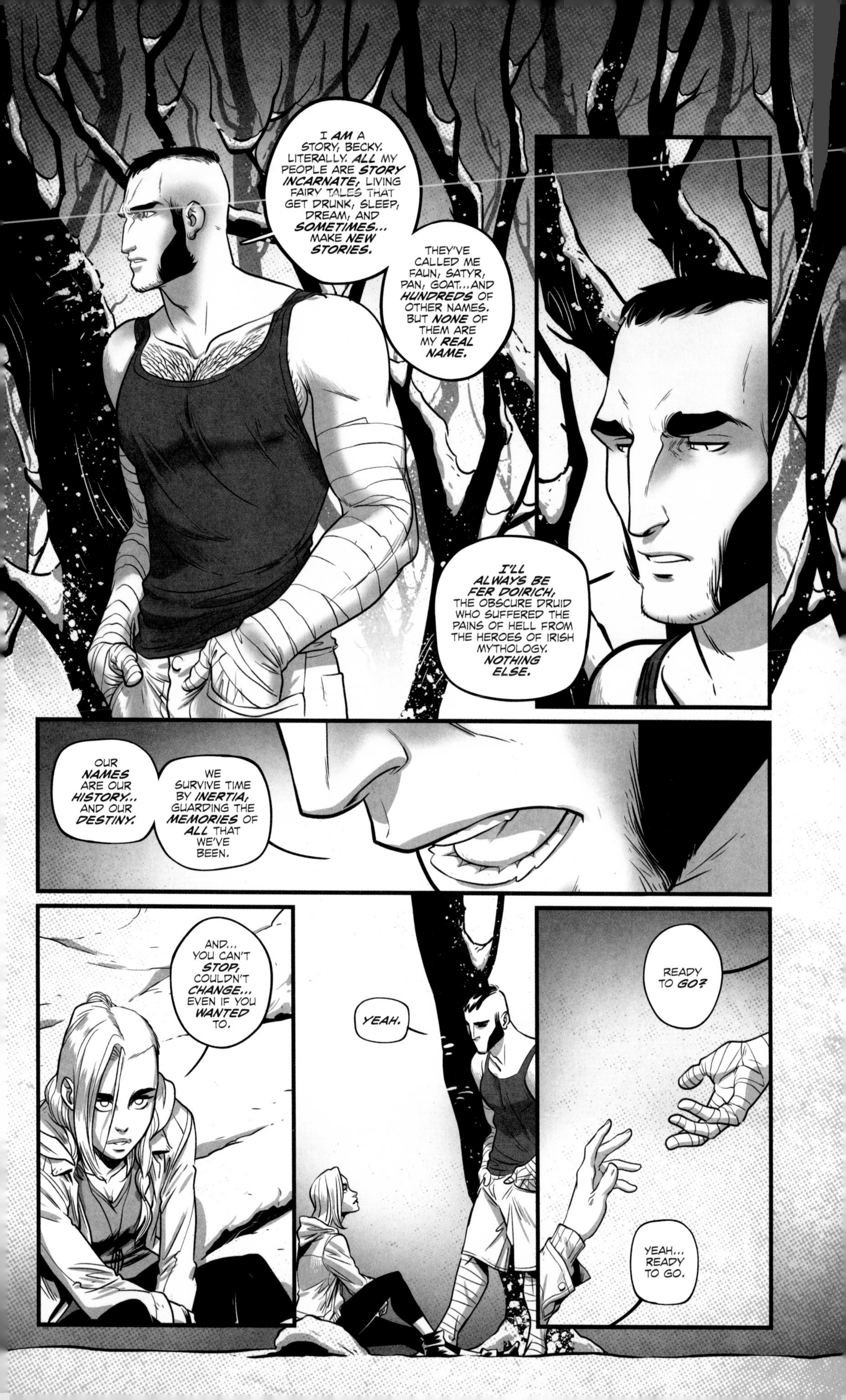
I AM A STORY, BECKY. LITERALLY. ALL MY PEOPLE ARE STORY INCARNATE, LIVING FAIRY TALES THAT GET DRUNK, SLEEP, DREAM, AND SOMETIMES... MAKE NEW STORIES.
THEY'VE CALLED ME FAUN, SATYR, PAN, GOAT...AND HUNDREDS OF OTHER NAMES. BUT NONE OF THEM ARE MY REAL NAME.
I'LL ALWAYS BE FER DOIRICH, THE OBSCURE DRUID WHO SUFFERED THE PAINS OF HELL FROM THE HEROES OF IRISH MYTHOLOGY. NOTHING ELSE.
OUR NAMES ARE OUR HISTORY... AND OUR DESTINY.
WE SURVIVE TIME BY INERTIA, GUARDING THE MEMORIES OF ALL THAT WE'VE BEEN.
AND... YOU CAN'T STOP, COULDN'T CHANGE... EVEN IF YOU WANTED TO.
YEAH.
READY TO GO?
YEAH... READY TO GO.

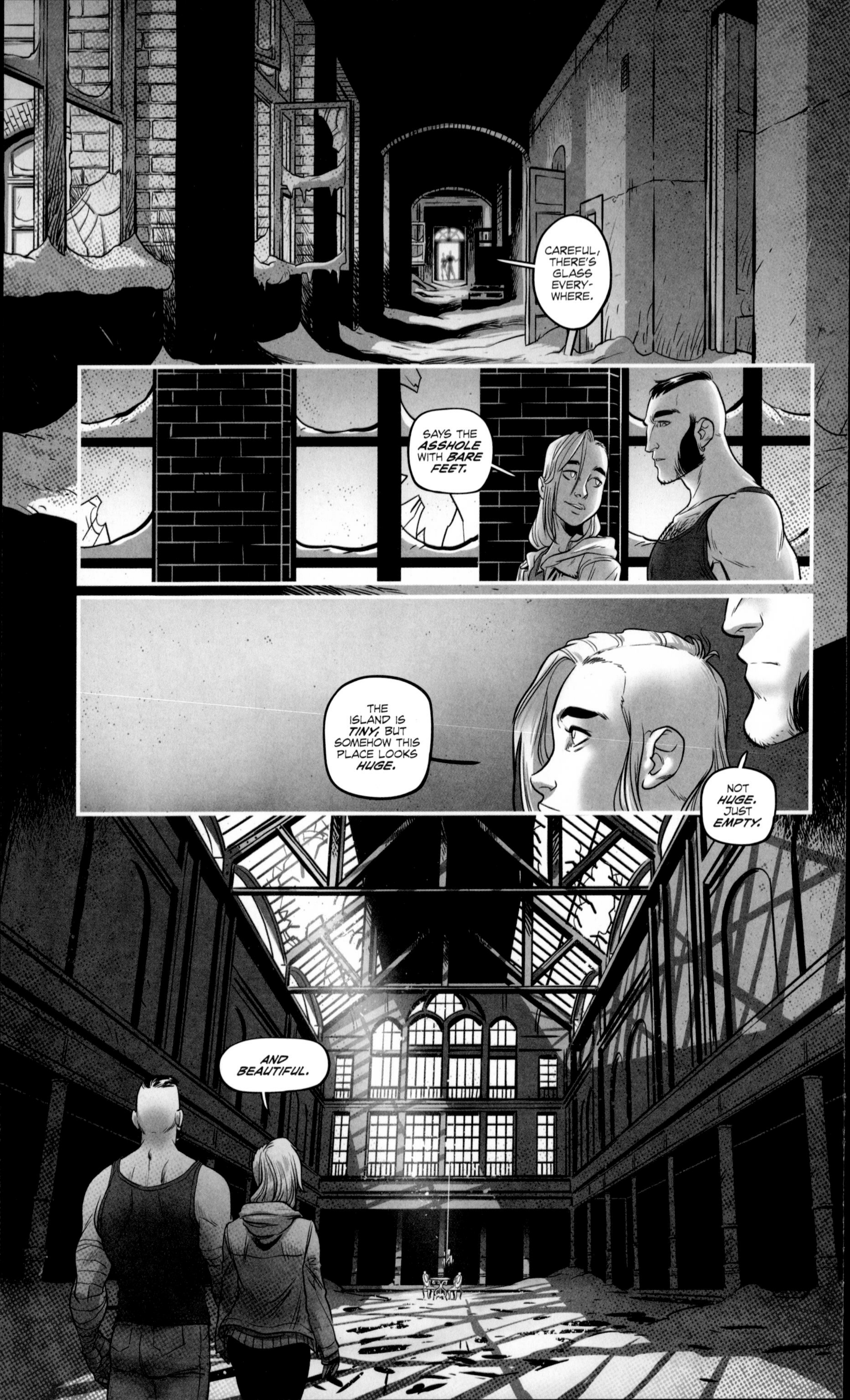
CAREFUL, THERE'S GLASS EVERY-WHERE.
SAYS THE *ASSHOLE* WITH *BARE FEET.*
THE ISLAND IS *TINY,* BUT SOMEHOW THIS PLACE LOOKS *HUGE.*
NOT *HUGE.* JUST *EMPTY.*
AND BEAUTIFUL.

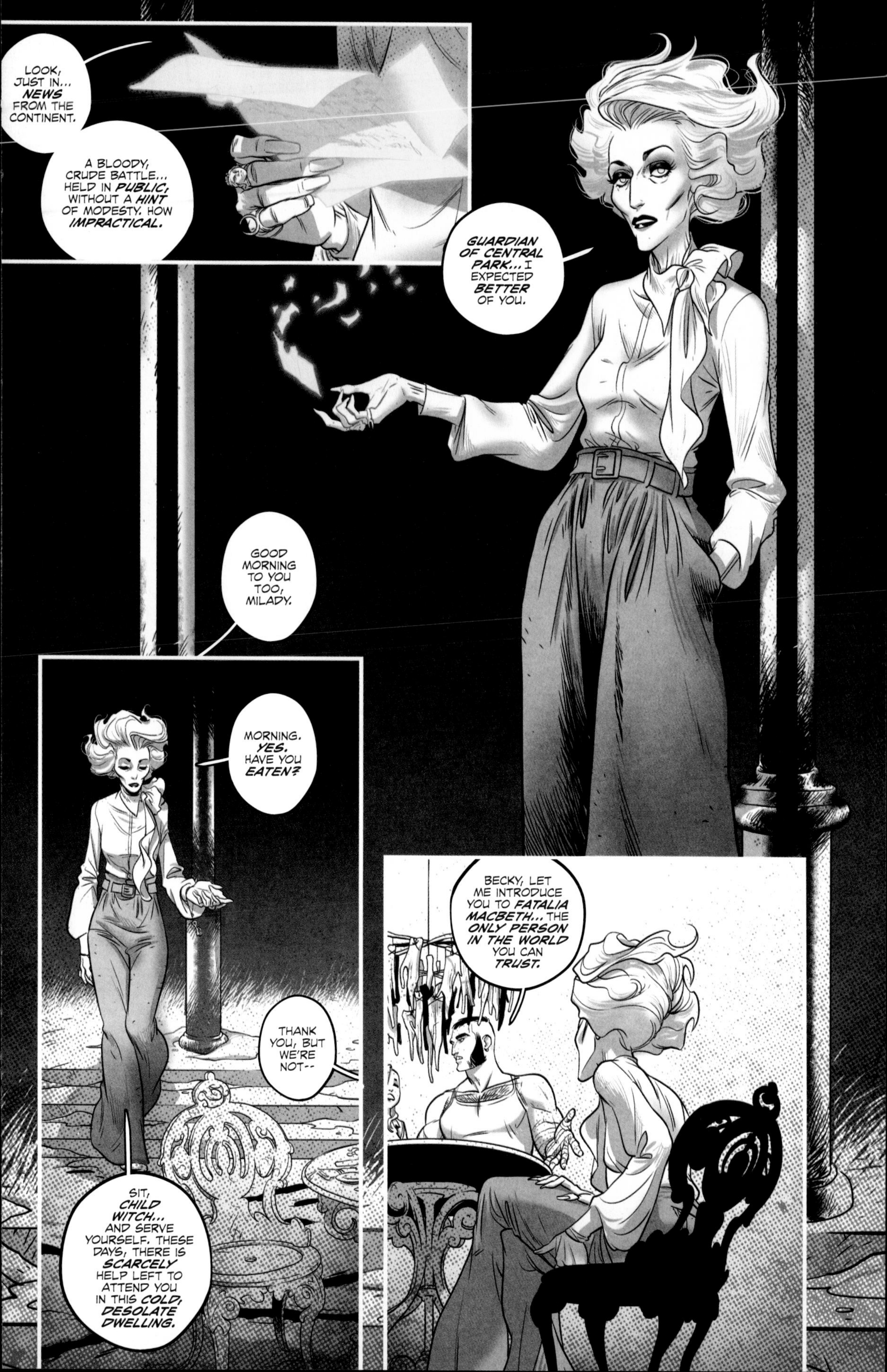
LOOK, JUST IN... NEWS FROM THE CONTINENT.
A BLOODY, CRUDE BATTLE... HELD IN PUBLIC, WITHOUT A HINT OF MODESTY. HOW IMPRACTICAL.
GUARDIAN OF CENTRAL PARK... I EXPECTED BETTER OF YOU.
GOOD MORNING TO YOU TOO, MILADY.
MORNING. YES. HAVE YOU EATEN?
THANK YOU, BUT WE'RE NOT--
SIT, CHILD WITCH... AND SERVE YOURSELF. THESE DAYS, THERE IS SCARCELY HELP LEFT TO ATTEND YOU IN THIS COLD, DESOLATE DWELLING.
BECKY, LET ME INTRODUCE YOU TO FATALIA MACBETH... THE ONLY PERSON IN THE WORLD YOU CAN TRUST.

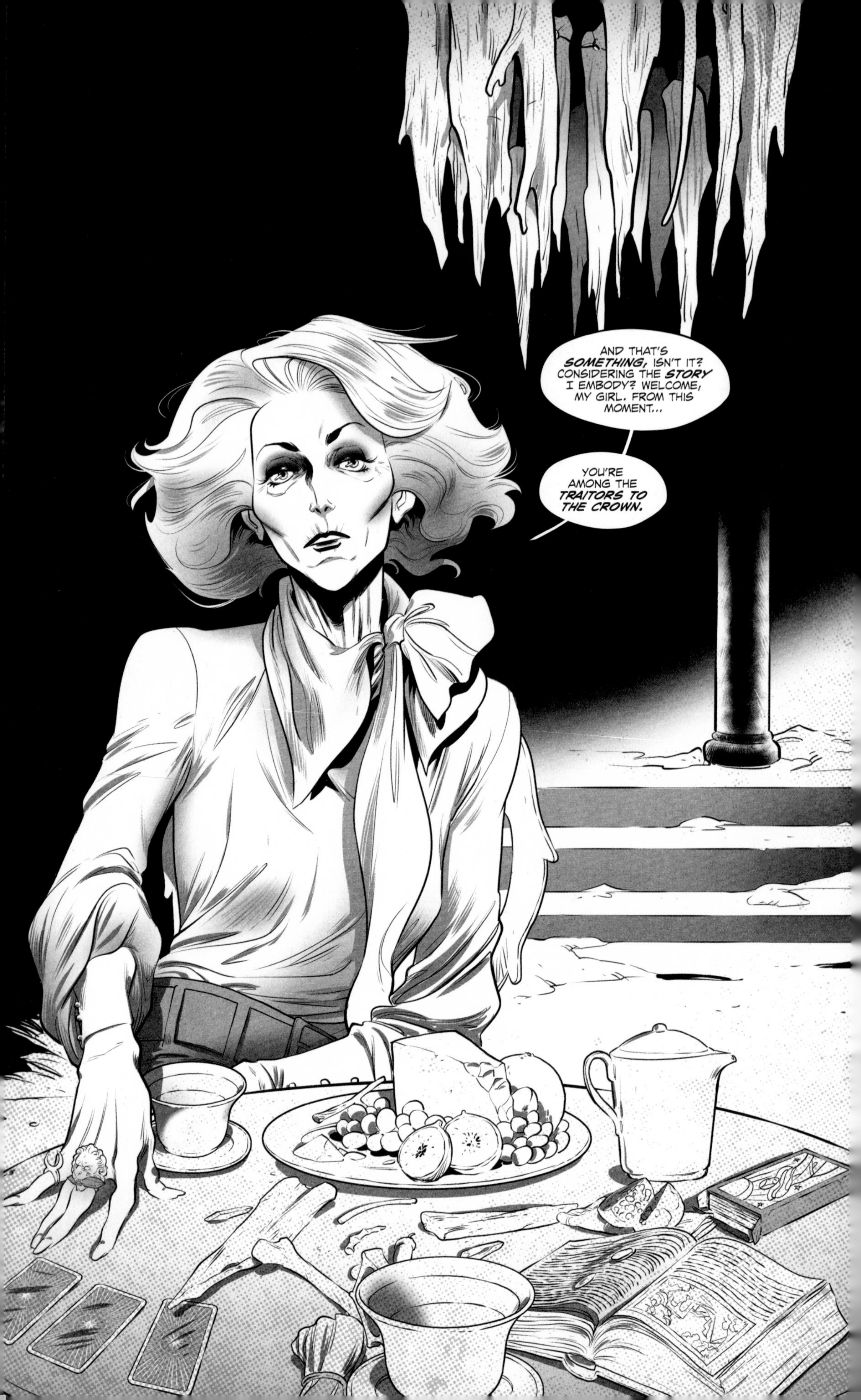
AND THAT'S SOMETHING, ISN'T IT? CONSIDERING THE STORY I EMBODY? WELCOME, MY GIRL. FROM THIS MOMENT...
YOU'RE AMONG THE TRAITORS TO THE CROWN.

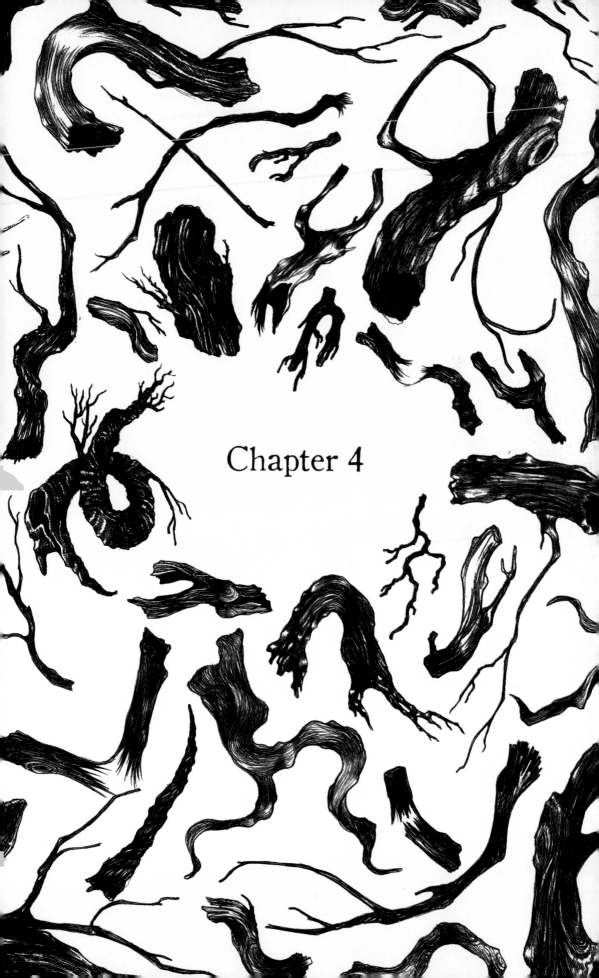

Chapter 4

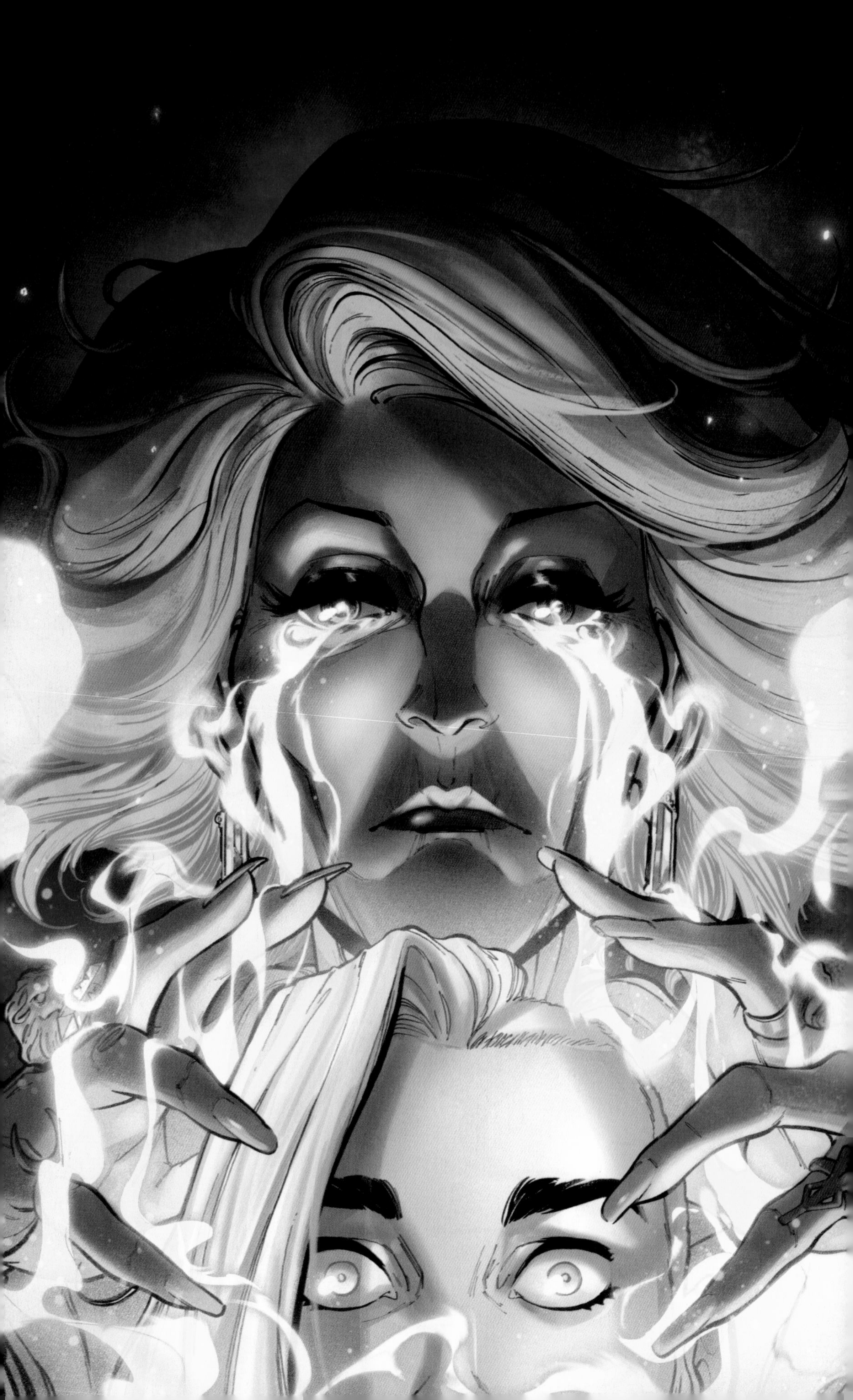

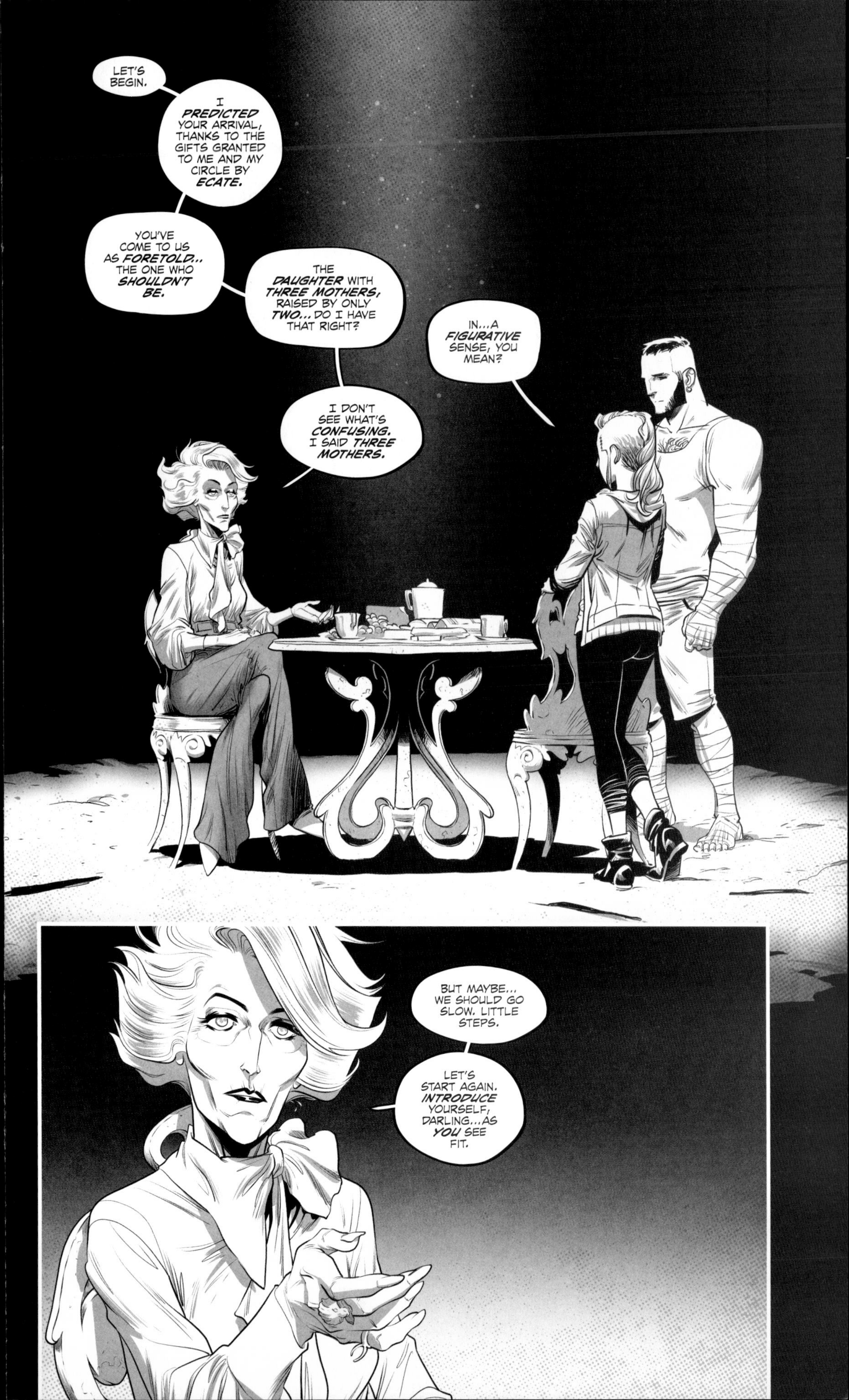
LET'S BEGIN.
I PREDICTED YOUR ARRIVAL, THANKS TO THE GIFTS GRANTED TO ME AND MY CIRCLE BY ECATE.
YOU'VE COME TO US AS FORETOLD... THE ONE WHO SHOULDN'T BE.
THE DAUGHTER WITH THREE MOTHERS, RAISED BY ONLY TWO... DO I HAVE THAT RIGHT?
IN...A FIGURATIVE SENSE, YOU MEAN?
I DON'T SEE WHAT'S CONFUSING. I SAID THREE MOTHERS.
BUT MAYBE... WE SHOULD GO SLOW. LITTLE STEPS.
LET'S START AGAIN. INTRODUCE YOURSELF, DARLING...AS YOU SEE FIT.

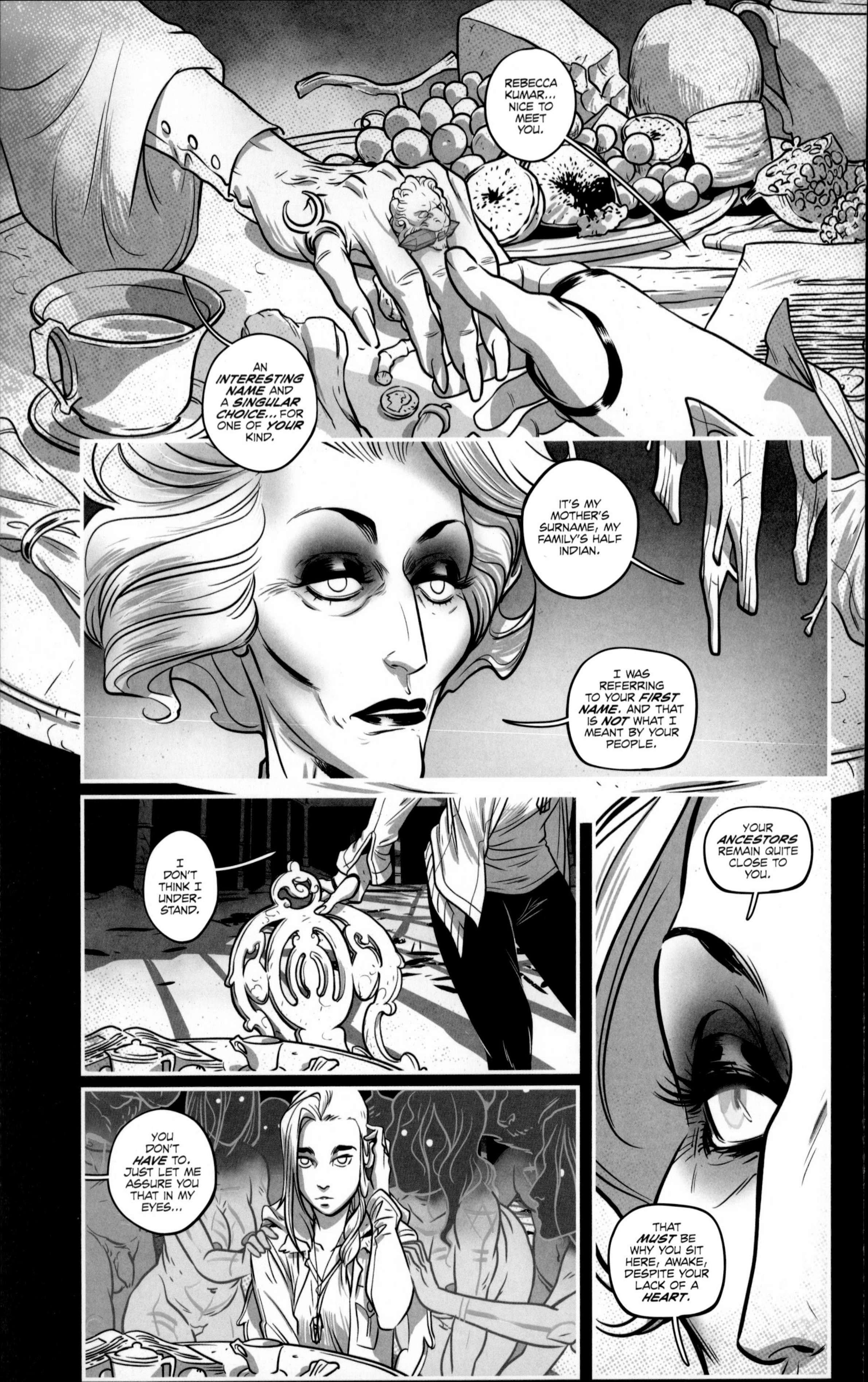
REBECCA KUMAR... NICE TO MEET YOU.
AN INTERESTING NAME AND A SINGULAR CHOICE... FOR ONE OF YOUR KIND.
IT'S MY MOTHER'S SURNAME, MY FAMILY'S HALF INDIAN.
I WAS REFERRING TO YOUR FIRST NAME. AND THAT IS NOT WHAT I MEANT BY YOUR PEOPLE.
I DON'T THINK I UNDER-STAND.
YOUR ANCESTORS REMAIN QUITE CLOSE TO YOU.
YOU DON'T HAVE TO. JUST LET ME ASSURE YOU THAT IN MY EYES...
THAT MUST BE WHY YOU SIT HERE, AWAKE, DESPITE YOUR LACK OF A HEART.

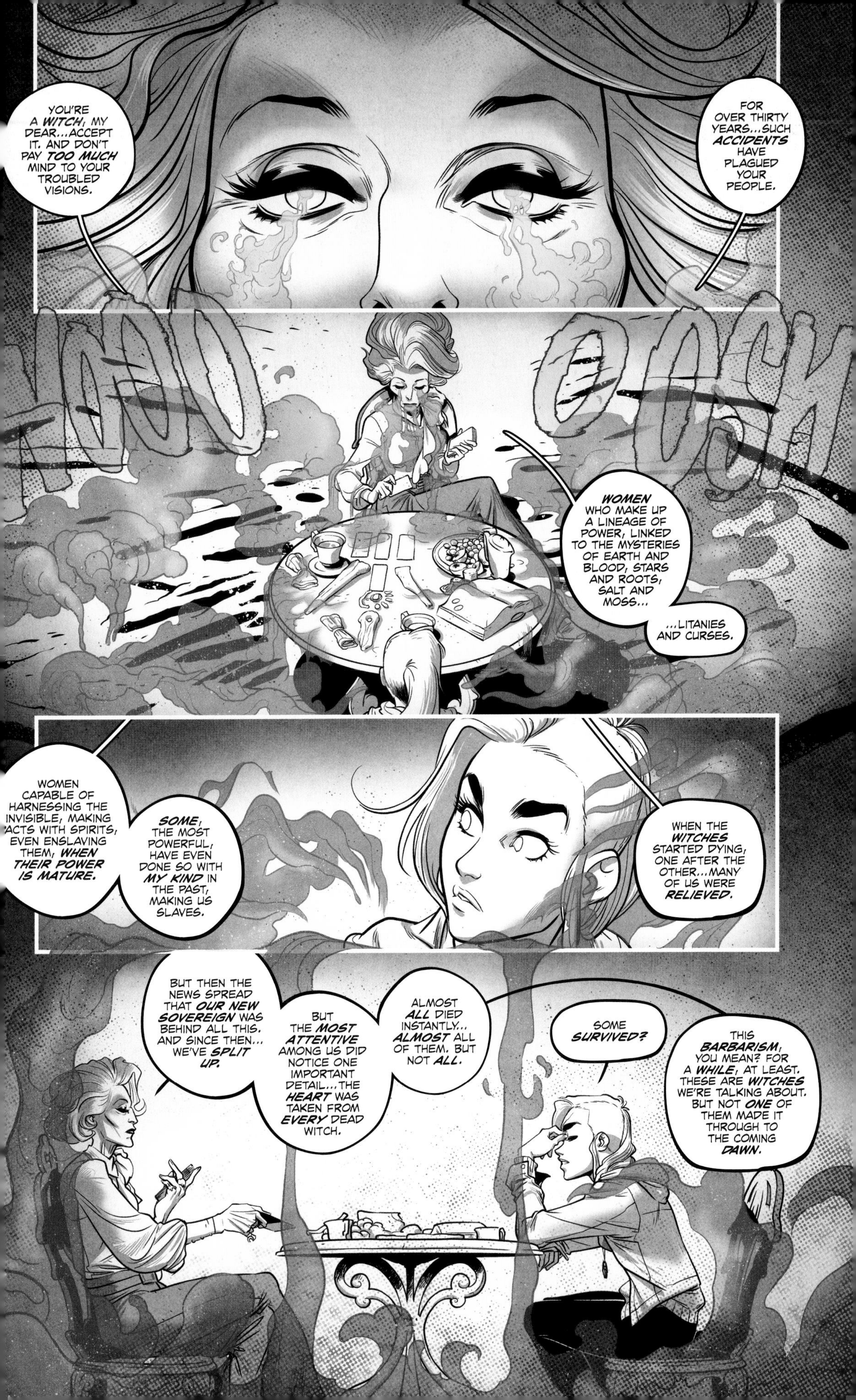
YOU'RE A WITCH, MY DEAR...ACCEPT IT. AND DON'T PAY TOO MUCH MIND TO YOUR TROUBLED VISIONS.
FOR OVER THIRTY YEARS...SUCH ACCIDENTS HAVE PLAGUED YOUR PEOPLE.
WOMEN WHO MAKE UP A LINEAGE OF POWER, LINKED TO THE MYSTERIES OF EARTH AND BLOOD, STARS AND ROOTS, SALT AND MOSS...
...LITANIES AND CURSES.
WOMEN CAPABLE OF HARNESSING THE INVISIBLE, MAKING ACTS WITH SPIRITS, EVEN ENSLAVING THEM, WHEN THEIR POWER IS MATURE.
SOME, THE MOST POWERFUL, HAVE EVEN DONE SO WITH MY KIND IN THE PAST, MAKING US SLAVES.
WHEN THE WITCHES STARTED DYING, ONE AFTER THE OTHER...MANY OF US WERE RELIEVED.
BUT THEN THE NEWS SPREAD THAT OUR NEW SOVEREIGN WAS BEHIND ALL THIS. AND SINCE THEN... WE'VE SPLIT UP.
BUT THE MOST ATTENTIVE AMONG US DID NOTICE ONE IMPORTANT DETAIL...THE HEART WAS TAKEN FROM EVERY DEAD WITCH.
ALMOST ALL DIED INSTANTLY... ALMOST ALL OF THEM. BUT NOT ALL.
SOME SURVIVED?
THIS BARBARISM, YOU MEAN? FOR A WHILE, AT LEAST. THESE ARE WITCHES WE'RE TALKING ABOUT. BUT NOT ONE OF THEM MADE IT THROUGH TO THE COMING DAWN.

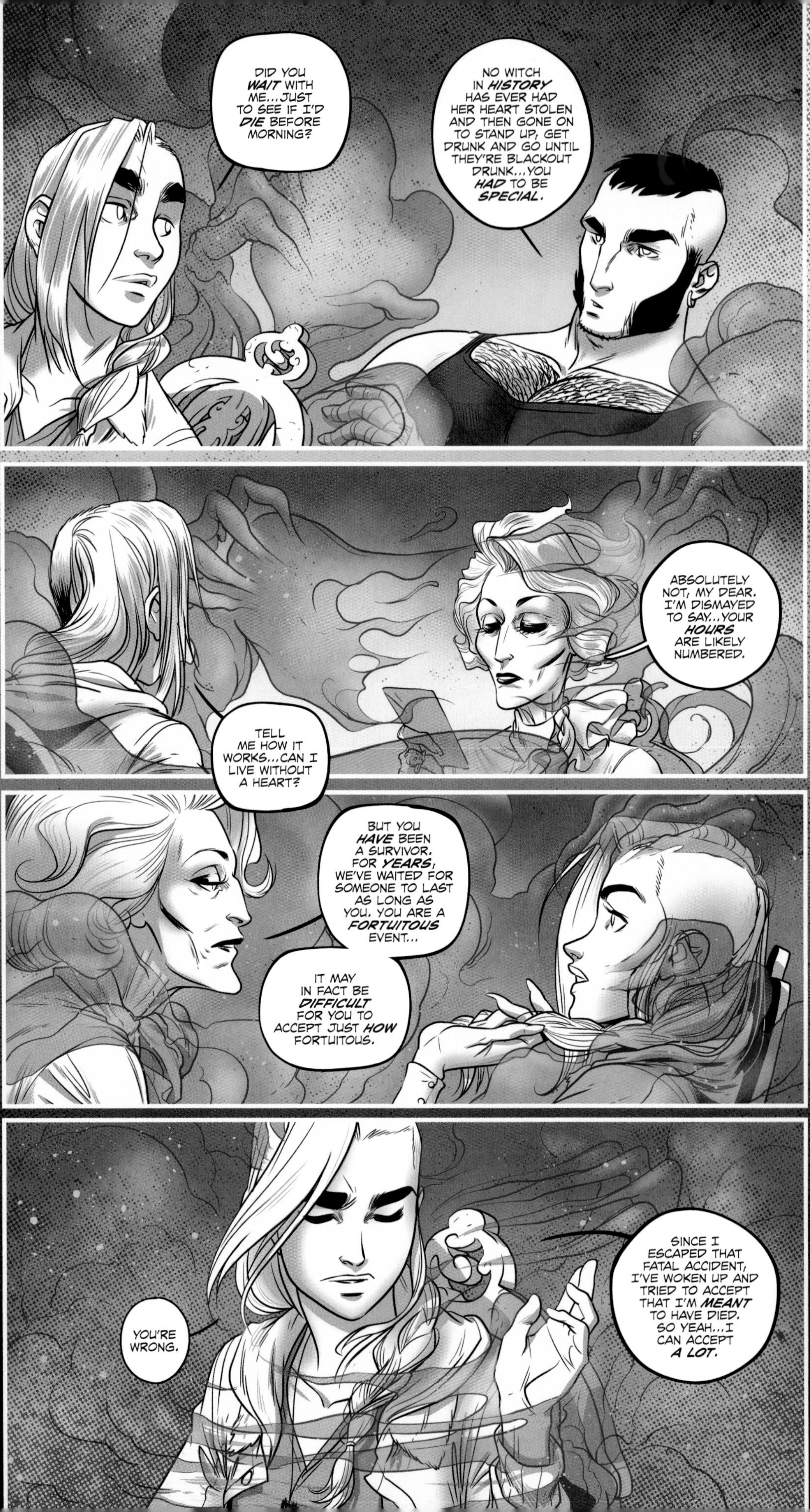
DID YOU WAIT WITH ME...JUST TO SEE IF I'D DIE BEFORE MORNING?
NO WITCH IN HISTORY HAS EVER HAD HER HEART STOLEN AND THEN GONE ON TO STAND UP, GET DRUNK AND GO UNTIL THEY'RE BLACKOUT DRUNK...YOU HAD TO BE SPECIAL.
ABSOLUTELY NOT, MY DEAR. I'M DISMAYED TO SAY...YOUR HOURS ARE LIKELY NUMBERED.
TELL ME HOW IT WORKS...CAN I LIVE WITHOUT A HEART?
BUT YOU HAVE BEEN A SURVIVOR. FOR YEARS, WE'VE WAITED FOR SOMEONE TO LAST AS LONG AS YOU. YOU ARE A FORTUITOUS EVENT...
IT MAY IN FACT BE DIFFICULT FOR YOU TO ACCEPT JUST HOW FORTUITOUS.
YOU'RE WRONG.
SINCE I ESCAPED THAT FATAL ACCIDENT, I'VE WOKEN UP AND TRIED TO ACCEPT THAT I'M MEANT TO HAVE DIED. SO YEAH...I CAN ACCEPT A LOT.

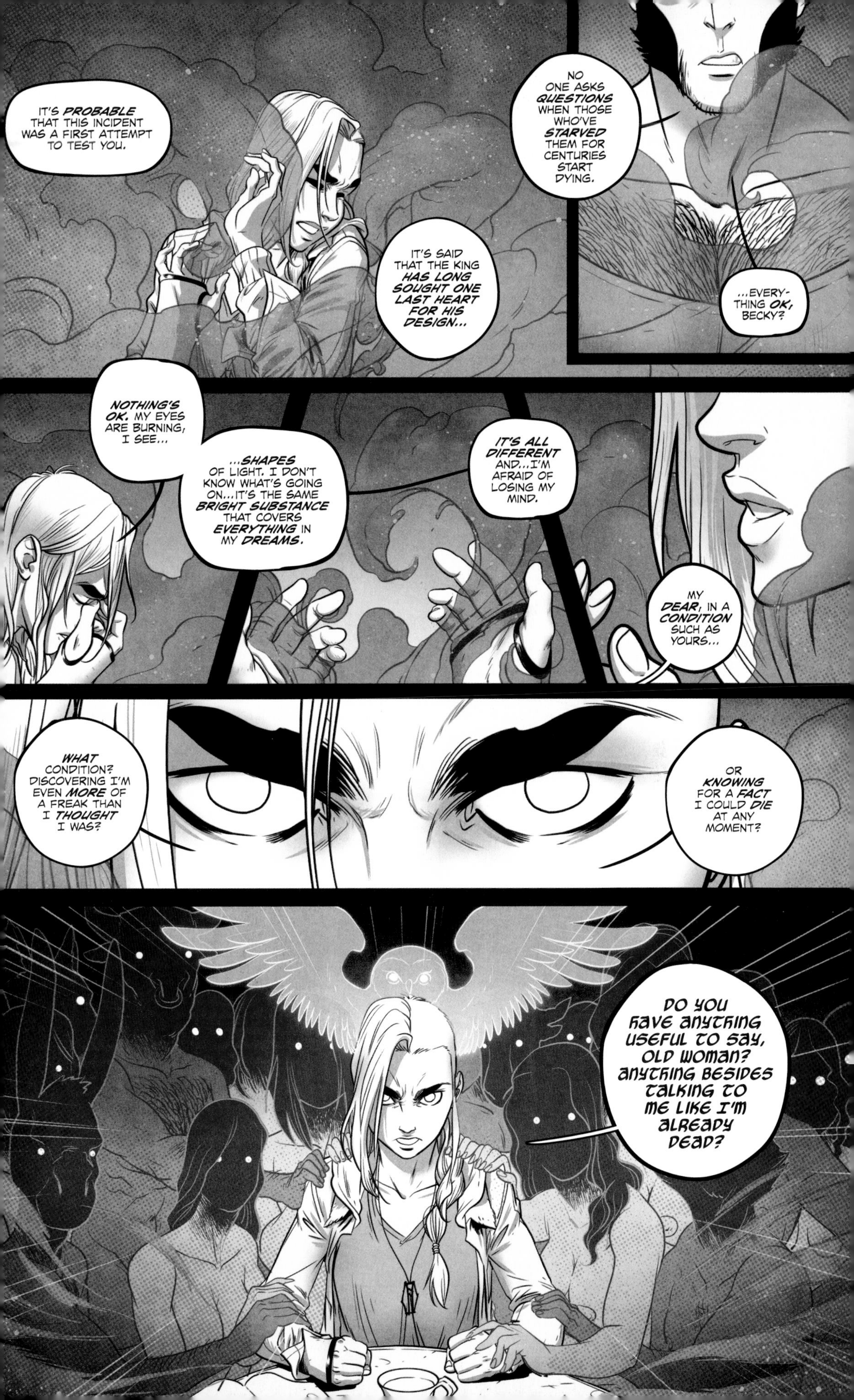

IT'S PROBABLE THAT THIS INCIDENT WAS A FIRST ATTEMPT TO TEST YOU.
IT'S SAID THAT THE KING HAS LONG SOUGHT ONE LAST HEART FOR HIS DESIGN...
NO ONE ASKS QUESTIONS WHEN THOSE WHO'VE STARVED THEM FOR CENTURIES START DYING.
...EVERY-THING OK, BECKY?
NOTHING'S OK. MY EYES ARE BURNING, I SEE...
...SHAPES OF LIGHT. I DON'T KNOW WHAT'S GOING ON...IT'S THE SAME BRIGHT SUBSTANCE THAT COVERS EVERYTHING IN MY DREAMS.
IT'S ALL DIFFERENT AND...I'M AFRAID OF LOSING MY MIND.
MY DEAR, IN A CONDITION SUCH AS YOURS...
WHAT CONDITION? DISCOVERING I'M EVEN MORE OF A FREAK THAN I THOUGHT I WAS?
OR KNOWING FOR A FACT I COULD DIE AT ANY MOMENT?
DO YOU HAVE ANYTHING USEFUL TO SAY, OLD WOMAN? ANYTHING BESIDES TALKING TO ME LIKE I'M ALREADY DEAD?

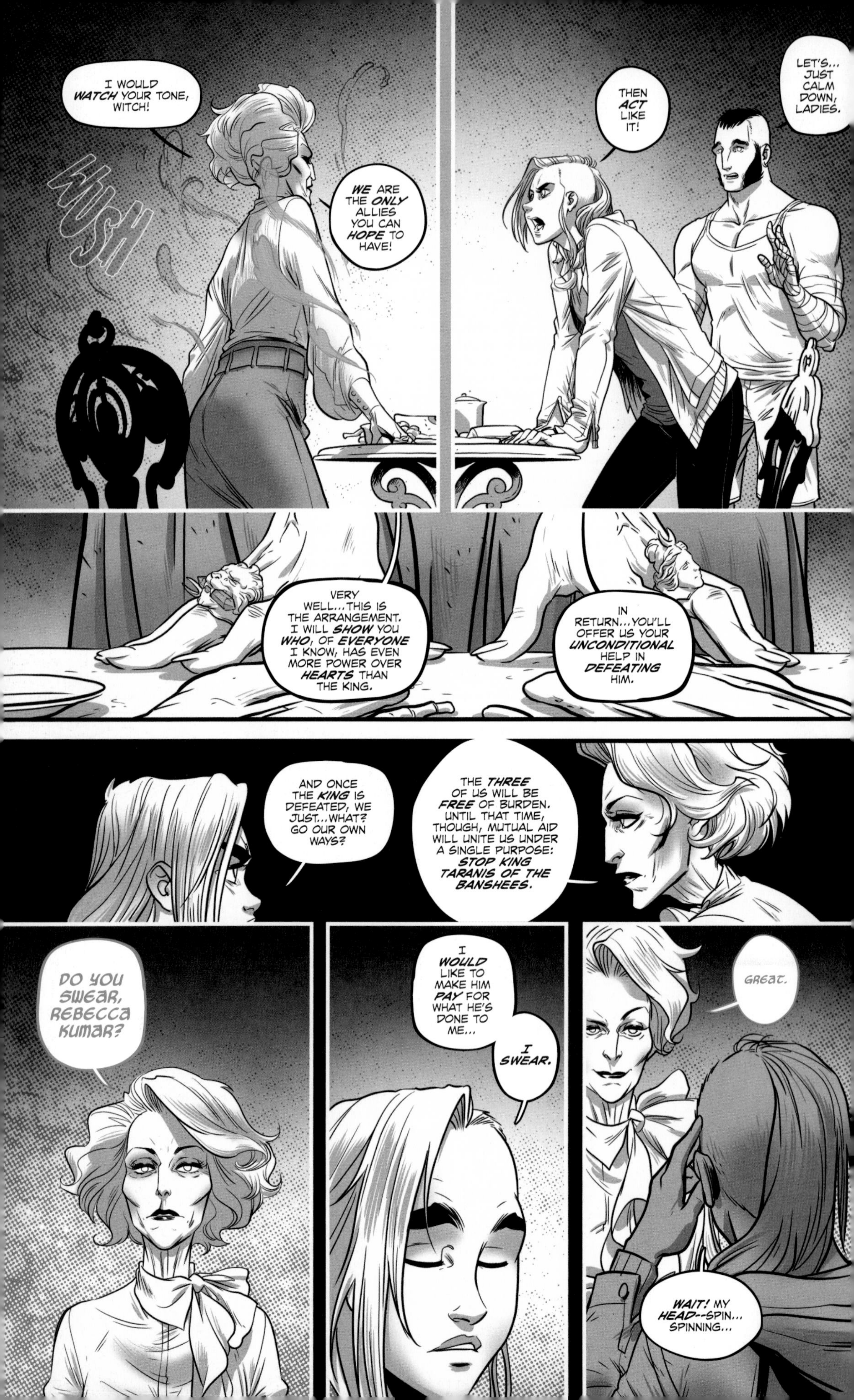
I WOULD WATCH YOUR TONE, WITCH!
WE ARE THE ONLY ALLIES YOU CAN HOPE TO HAVE!
WUSH
THEN ACT LIKE IT!
LET'S... JUST CALM DOWN, LADIES.
VERY WELL...THIS IS THE ARRANGEMENT. I WILL SHOW YOU WHO, OF EVERYONE I KNOW, HAS EVEN MORE POWER OVER HEARTS THAN THE KING.
IN RETURN...YOU'LL OFFER US YOUR UNCONDITIONAL HELP IN DEFEATING HIM.
AND ONCE THE KING IS DEFEATED, WE JUST...WHAT? GO OUR OWN WAYS?
THE THREE OF US WILL BE FREE OF BURDEN. UNTIL THAT TIME, THOUGH, MUTUAL AID WILL UNITE US UNDER A SINGLE PURPOSE: STOP KING TARANIS OF THE BANSHEES.
DO YOU SWEAR, REBECCA KUMAR?
I WOULD LIKE TO MAKE HIM PAY FOR WHAT HE'S DONE TO ME...
I SWEAR.
GREAT.
WAIT! MY HEAD--SPIN... SPINNING...

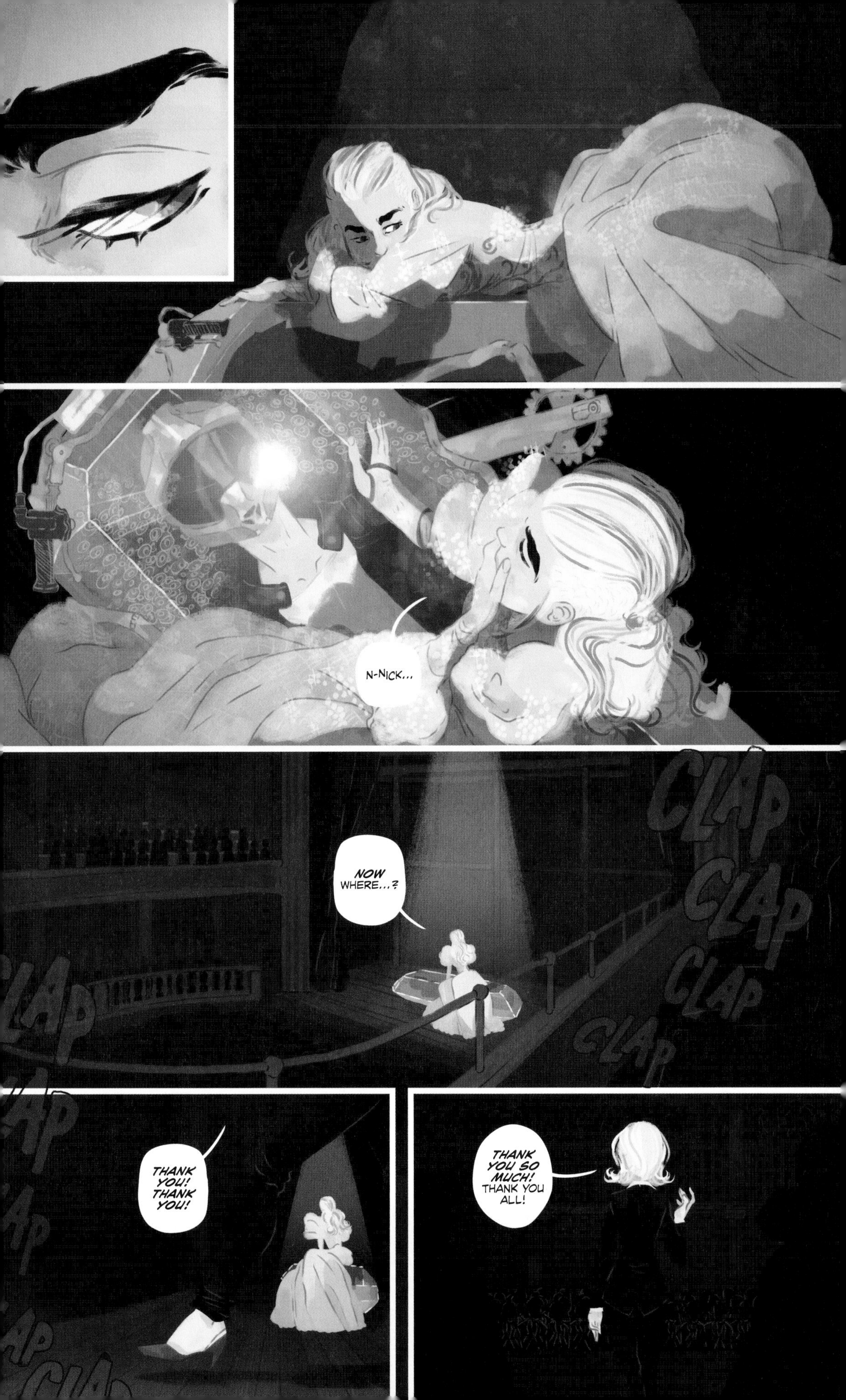
N-NICK...
NOW WHERE...?
CLAP
CLAP
CLAP
CLAP
CLAP
THANK YOU! THANK YOU!
THANK YOU SO MUCH! THANK YOU ALL!

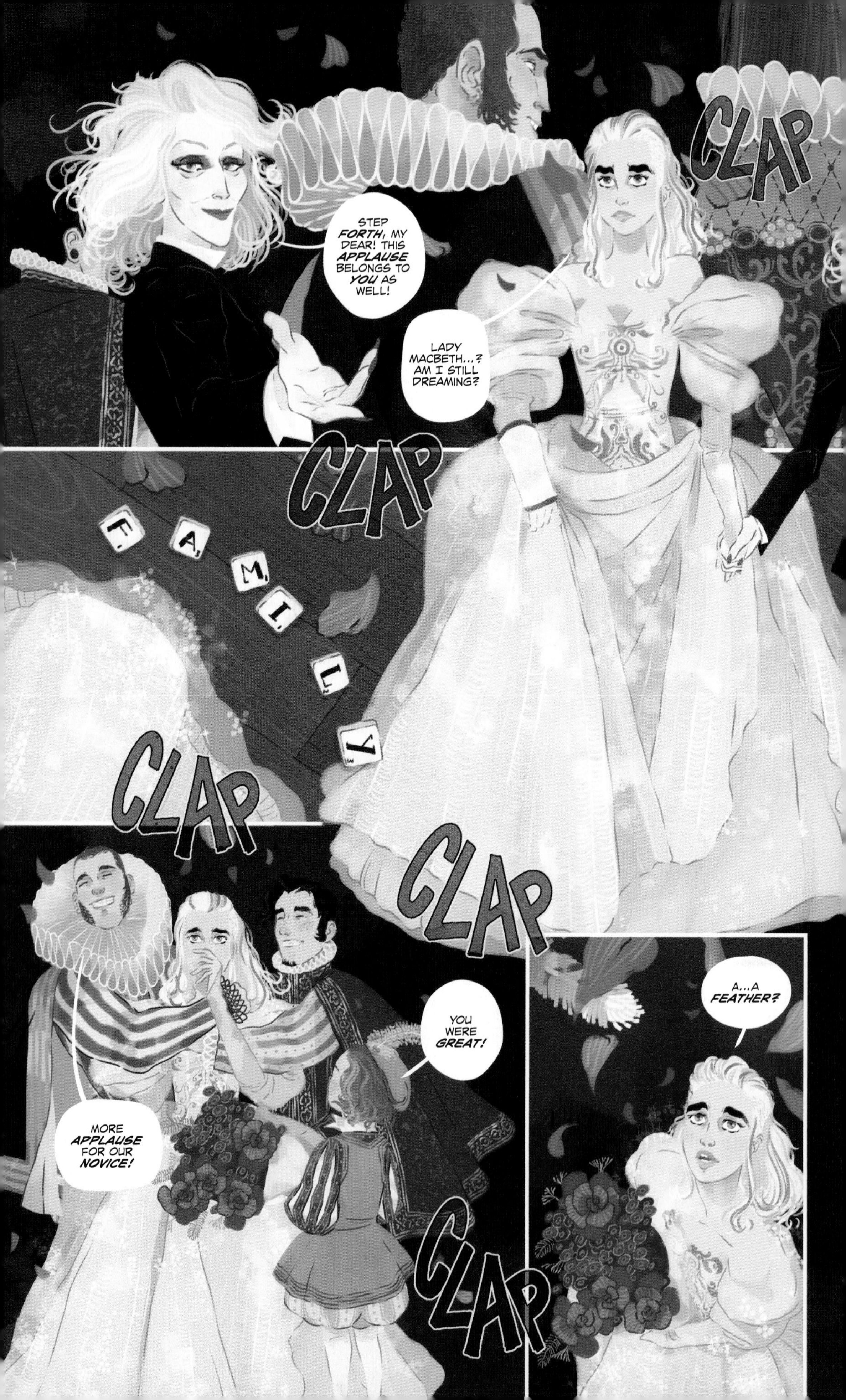
CLAP
STEP FORTH, MY DEAR! THIS APPLAUSE BELONGS TO YOU AS WELL!
LADY MACBETH...? AM I STILL DREAMING?
CLAP
FAMILY
CLAP
CLAP
MORE APPLAUSE FOR OUR NOVICE!
YOU WERE GREAT!
CLAP
A...A FEATHER?

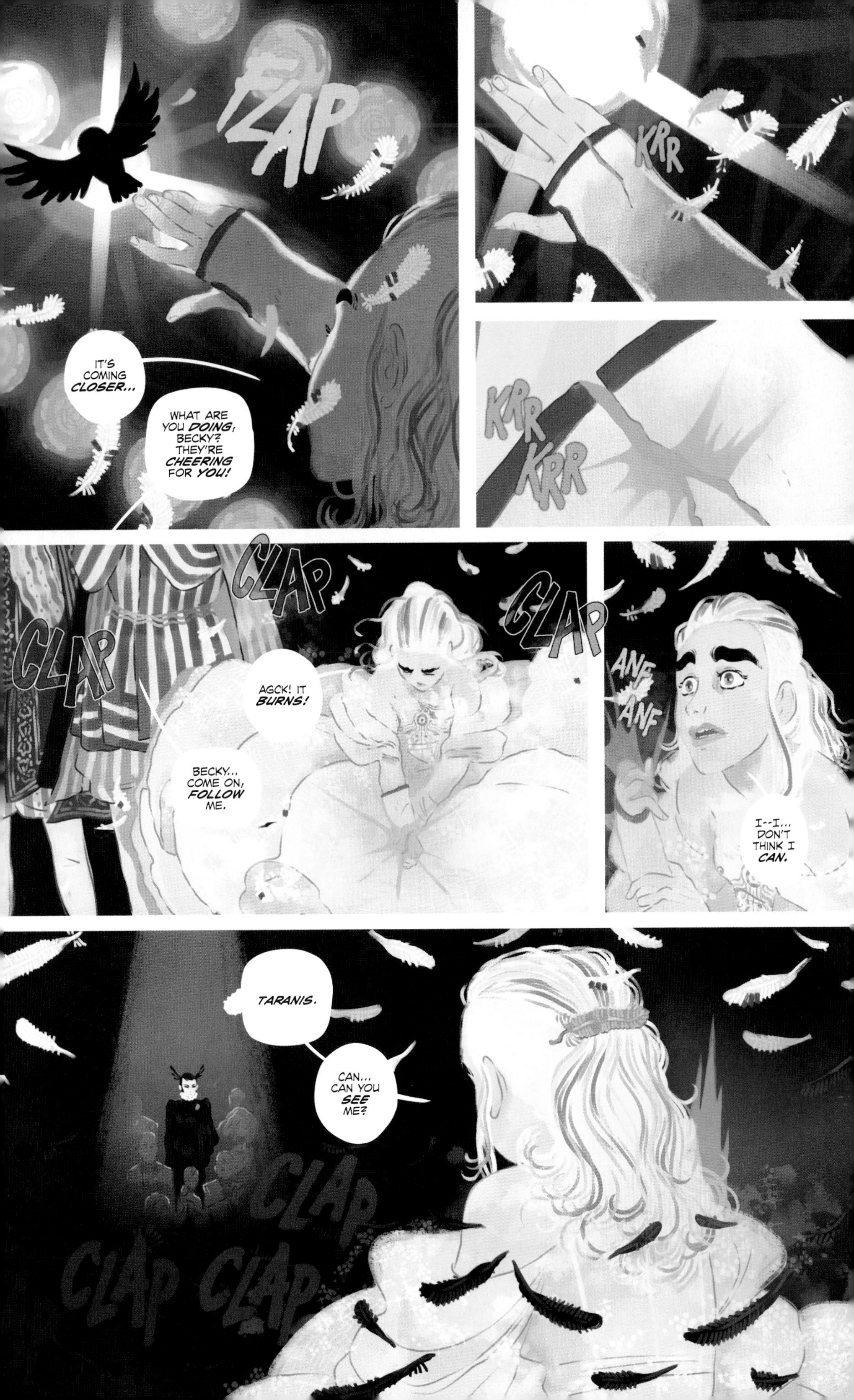
FLAP
IT'S COMING CLOSER...
WHAT ARE YOU DOING, BECKY? THEY'RE CHEERING FOR YOU!
KRR
KRR
KRR
CLAP
CLAP
CLAP
AGCK! IT BURNS!
BECKY... COME ON, FOLLOW ME.
ANF
ANF
I--I... DON'T THINK I CAN.
TARANIS.
CAN... CAN YOU SEE ME?
CLAP
CLAP
CLAP

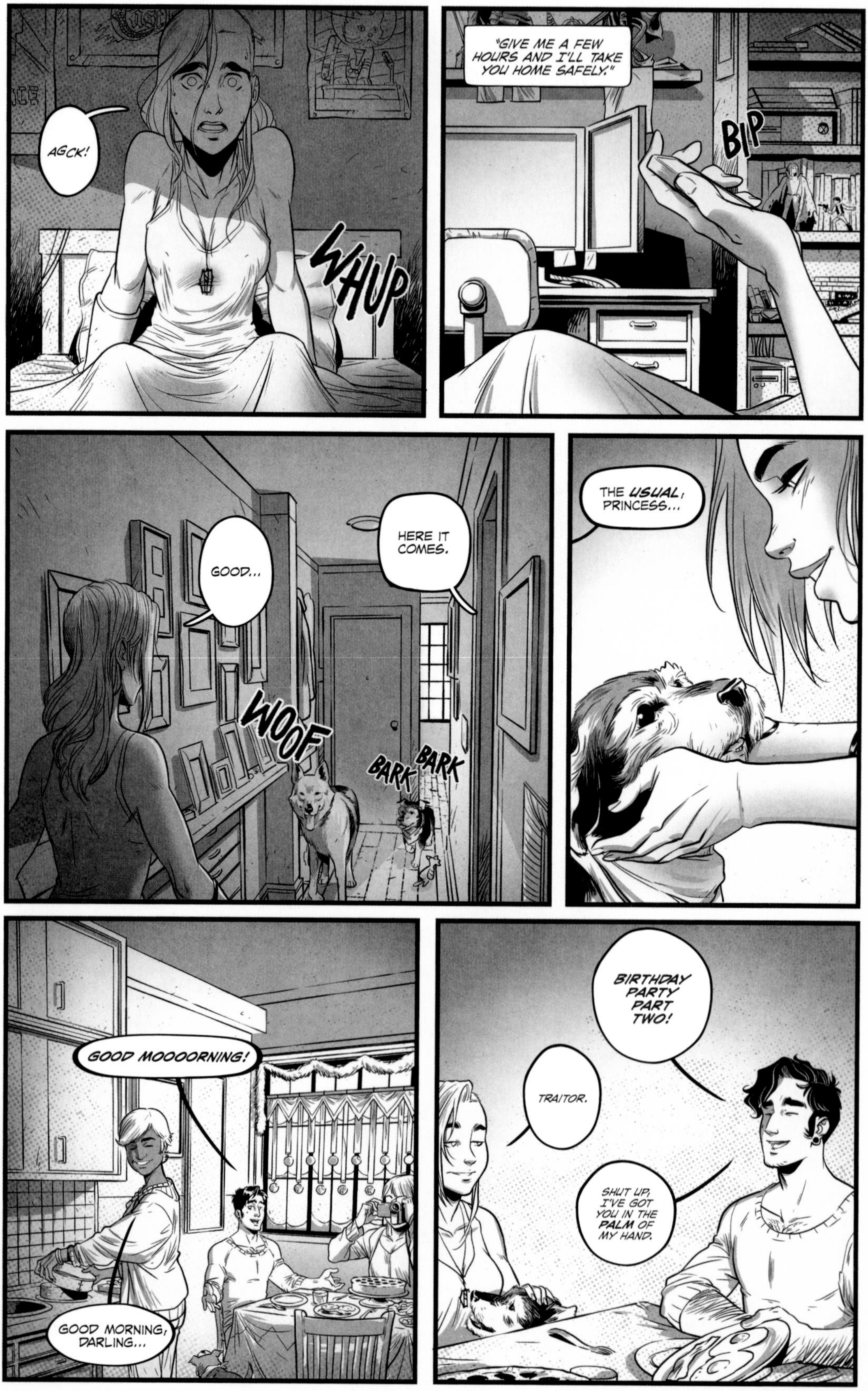
AGCK!
WHUP
"GIVE ME A FEW HOURS AND I'LL TAKE YOU HOME SAFELY."
BIP
GOOD...
HERE IT COMES.
WOOF
BARK
BARK
THE USUAL, PRINCESS...
GOOD MOOOORNING!
GOOD MORNING, DARLING...
BIRTHDAY PARTY PART TWO!
TRAITOR.
SHUT UP, I'VE GOT YOU IN THE PALM OF MY HAND.

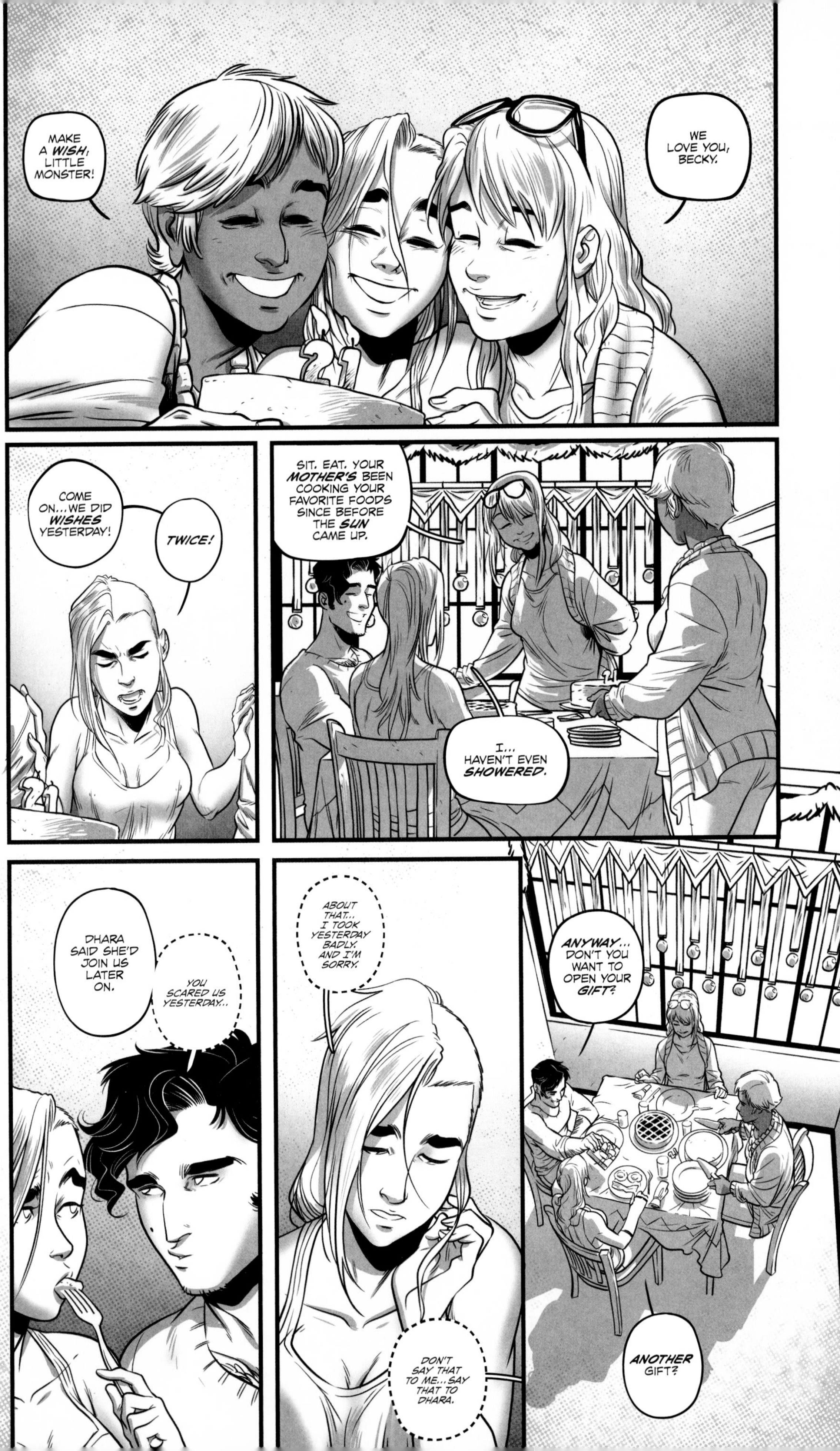
MAKE A WISH, LITTLE MONSTER!
WE LOVE YOU, BECKY.
COME ON... WE DID WISHES YESTERDAY!
TWICE!
SIT. EAT. YOUR MOTHER'S BEEN COOKING YOUR FAVORITE FOODS SINCE BEFORE THE SUN CAME UP.
I... HAVEN'T EVEN SHOWERED.
DHARA SAID SHE'D JOIN US LATER ON.
YOU SCARED US YESTERDAY...
ABOUT THAT... I TOOK YESTERDAY BADLY. AND I'M SORRY.
DON'T SAY THAT TO ME... SAY THAT TO DHARA.
ANYWAY... DON'T YOU WANT TO OPEN YOUR GIFT?
ANOTHER GIFT?

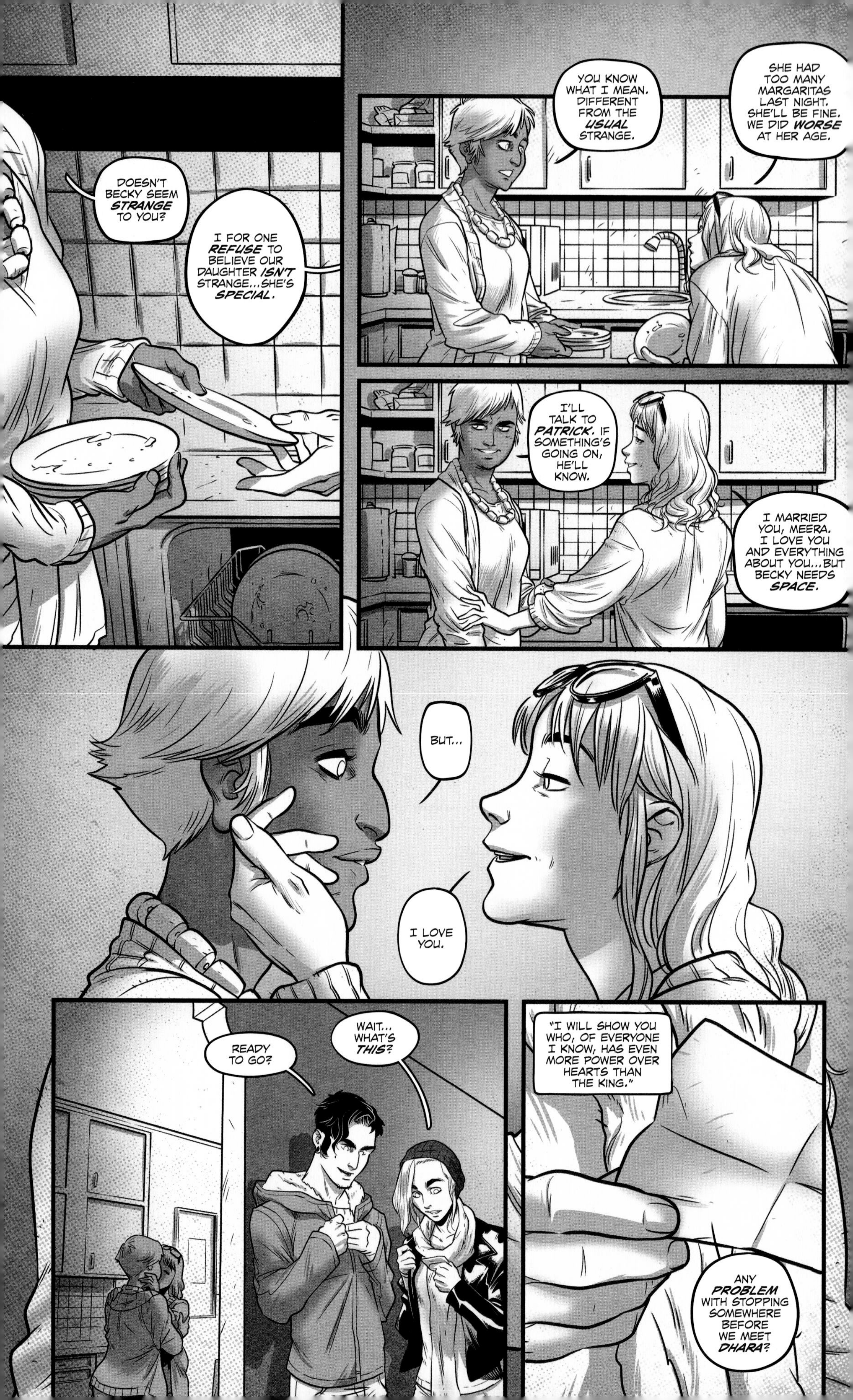
DOESN'T BECKY SEEM STRANGE TO YOU?
I FOR ONE REFUSE TO BELIEVE OUR DAUGHTER ISN'T STRANGE...SHE'S SPECIAL.
YOU KNOW WHAT I MEAN. DIFFERENT FROM THE USUAL STRANGE.
SHE HAD TOO MANY MARGARITAS LAST NIGHT. SHE'LL BE FINE. WE DID WORSE AT HER AGE.
I'LL TALK TO PATRICK. IF SOMETHING'S GOING ON, HE'LL KNOW.
I MARRIED YOU, MEERA. I LOVE YOU AND EVERYTHING ABOUT YOU...BUT BECKY NEEDS SPACE.
BUT...
I LOVE YOU.
READY TO GO?
WAIT... WHAT'S THIS?
"I WILL SHOW YOU WHO, OF EVERYONE I KNOW, HAS EVEN MORE POWER OVER HEARTS THAN THE KING."
ANY PROBLEM WITH STOPPING SOMEWHERE BEFORE WE MEET DHARA?

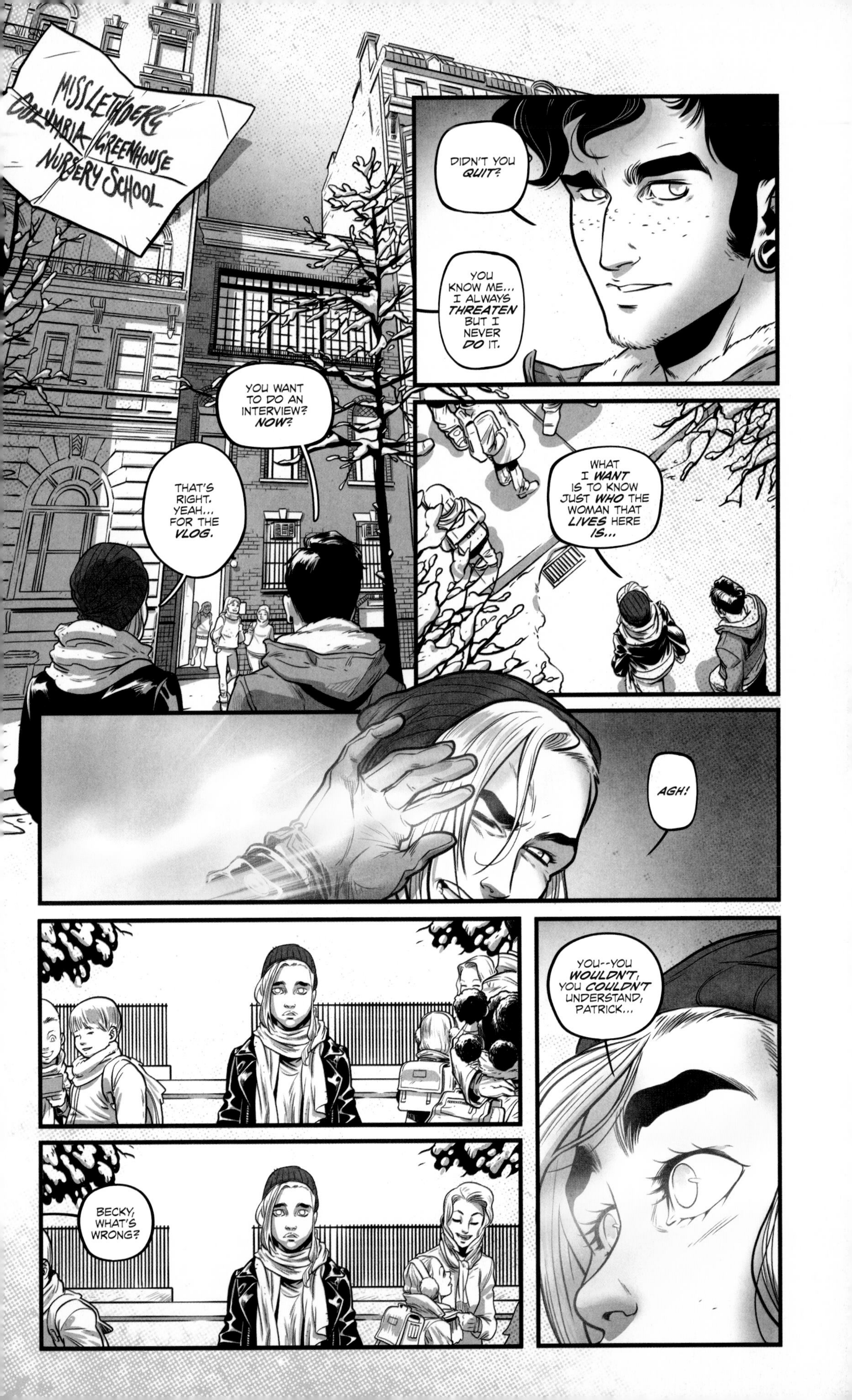
MISS LETHDERG
COLUMBIA GREENHOUSE
NURSERY SCHOOL
DIDN'T YOU QUIT?
YOU KNOW ME... I ALWAYS THREATEN BUT I NEVER DO IT.
YOU WANT TO DO AN INTERVIEW? NOW?
THAT'S RIGHT. YEAH... FOR THE VLOG.
WHAT I WANT IS TO KNOW JUST WHO THE WOMAN THAT LIVES HERE IS...
AGH!
BECKY, WHAT'S WRONG?
YOU--YOU WOULDN'T, YOU COULDN'T UNDERSTAND, PATRICK...

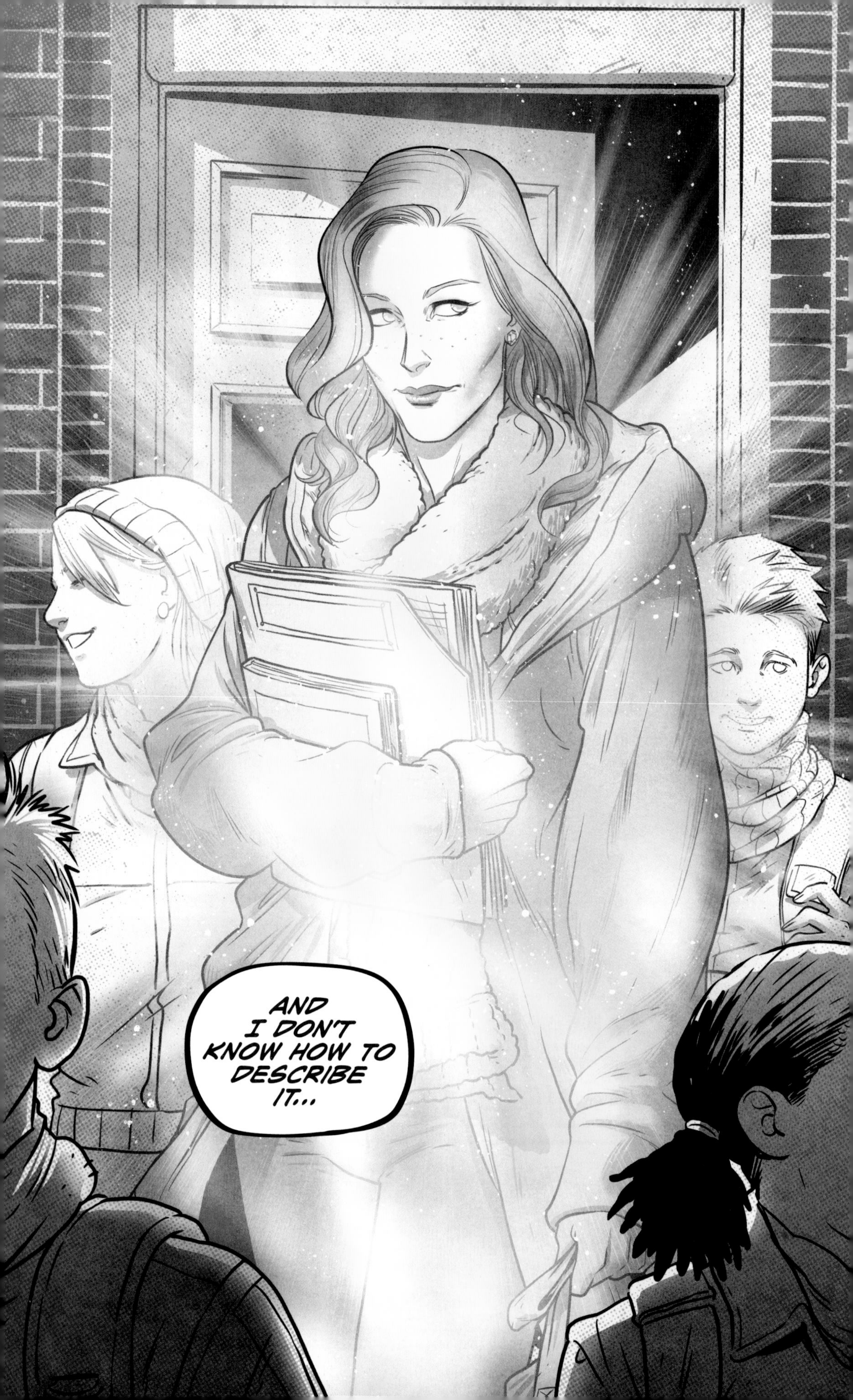
AND I DON'T KNOW HOW TO DESCRIBE IT...

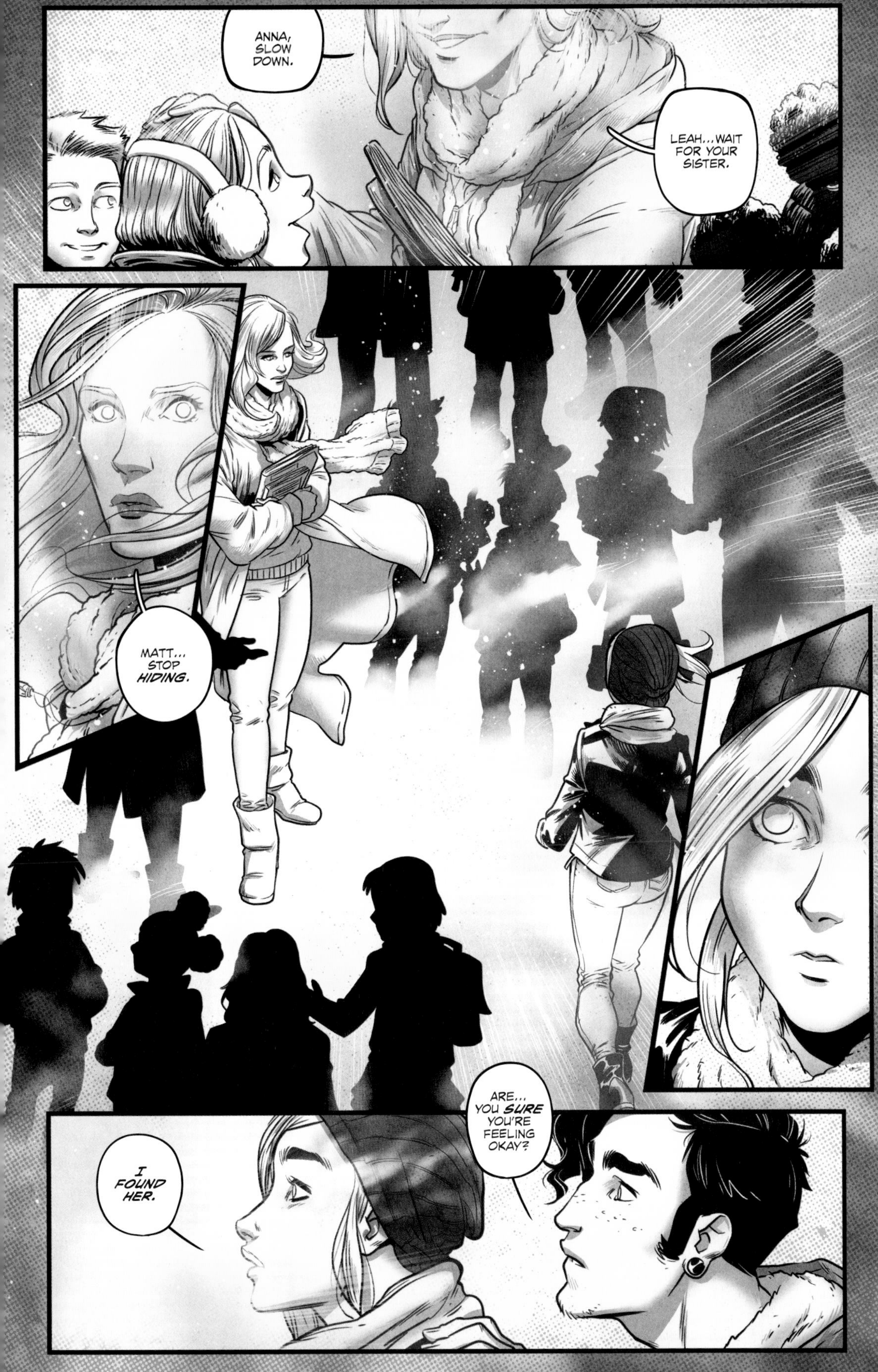
ANNA, SLOW DOWN.
LEAH... WAIT FOR YOUR SISTER.
MATT... STOP HIDING.
I FOUND HER.
ARE... YOU SURE YOU'RE FEELING OKAY?

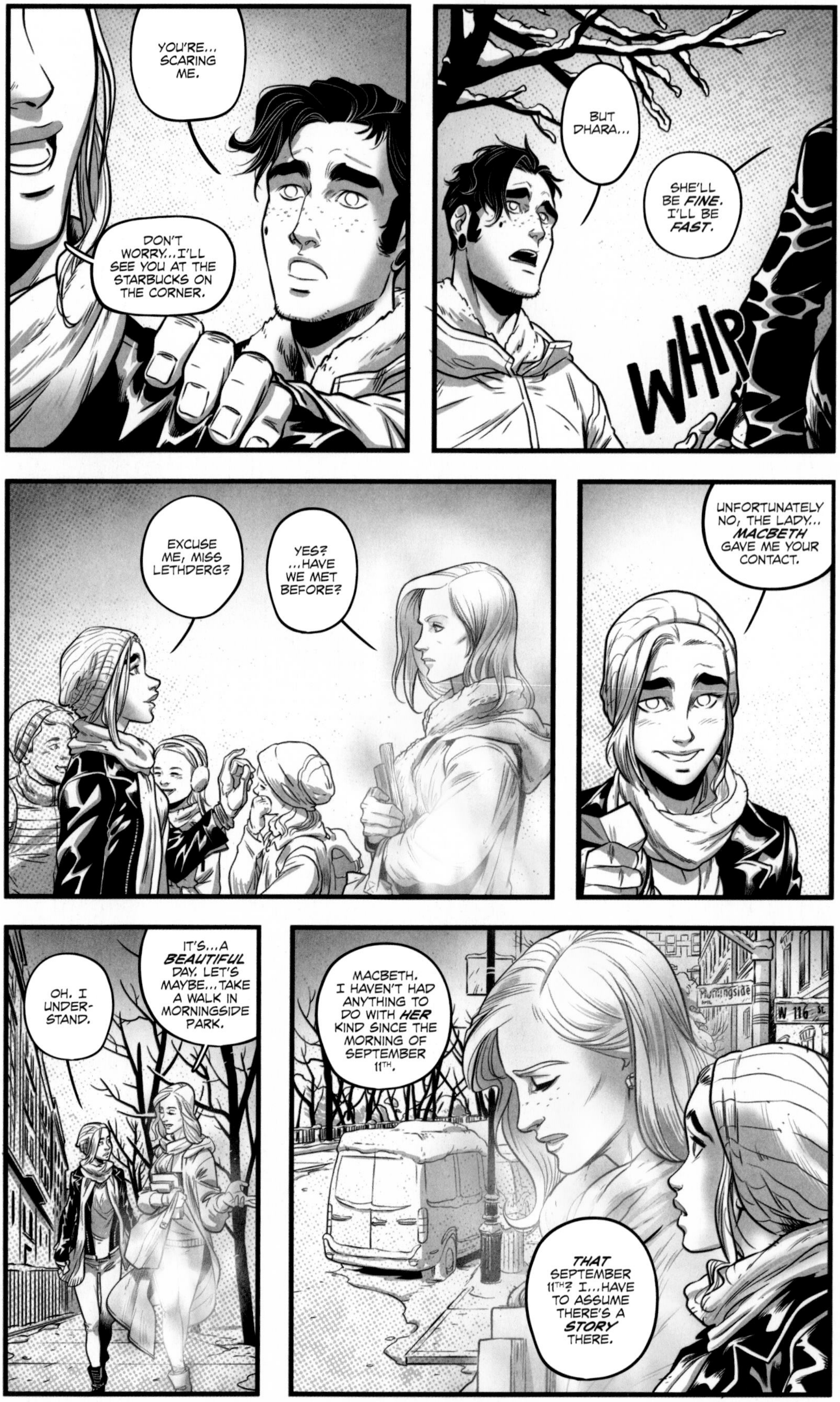
YOU'RE... SCARING ME.
DON'T WORRY...I'LL SEE YOU AT THE STARBUCKS ON THE CORNER.
BUT DHARA...
SHE'LL BE FINE. I'LL BE FAST.
WHIP
EXCUSE ME, MISS LETHDERG?
YES? ...HAVE WE MET BEFORE?
UNFORTUNATELY NO, THE LADY... MACBETH GAVE ME YOUR CONTACT.
OH. I UNDER-STAND.
IT'S...A BEAUTIFUL DAY. LET'S MAYBE...TAKE A WALK IN MORNINGSIDE PARK.
MACBETH. I HAVEN'T HAD ANYTHING TO DO WITH HER KIND SINCE THE MORNING OF SEPTEMBER 11TH.
Morningside
W 116 St
THAT SEPTEMBER 11TH? I...HAVE TO ASSUME THERE'S A STORY THERE.

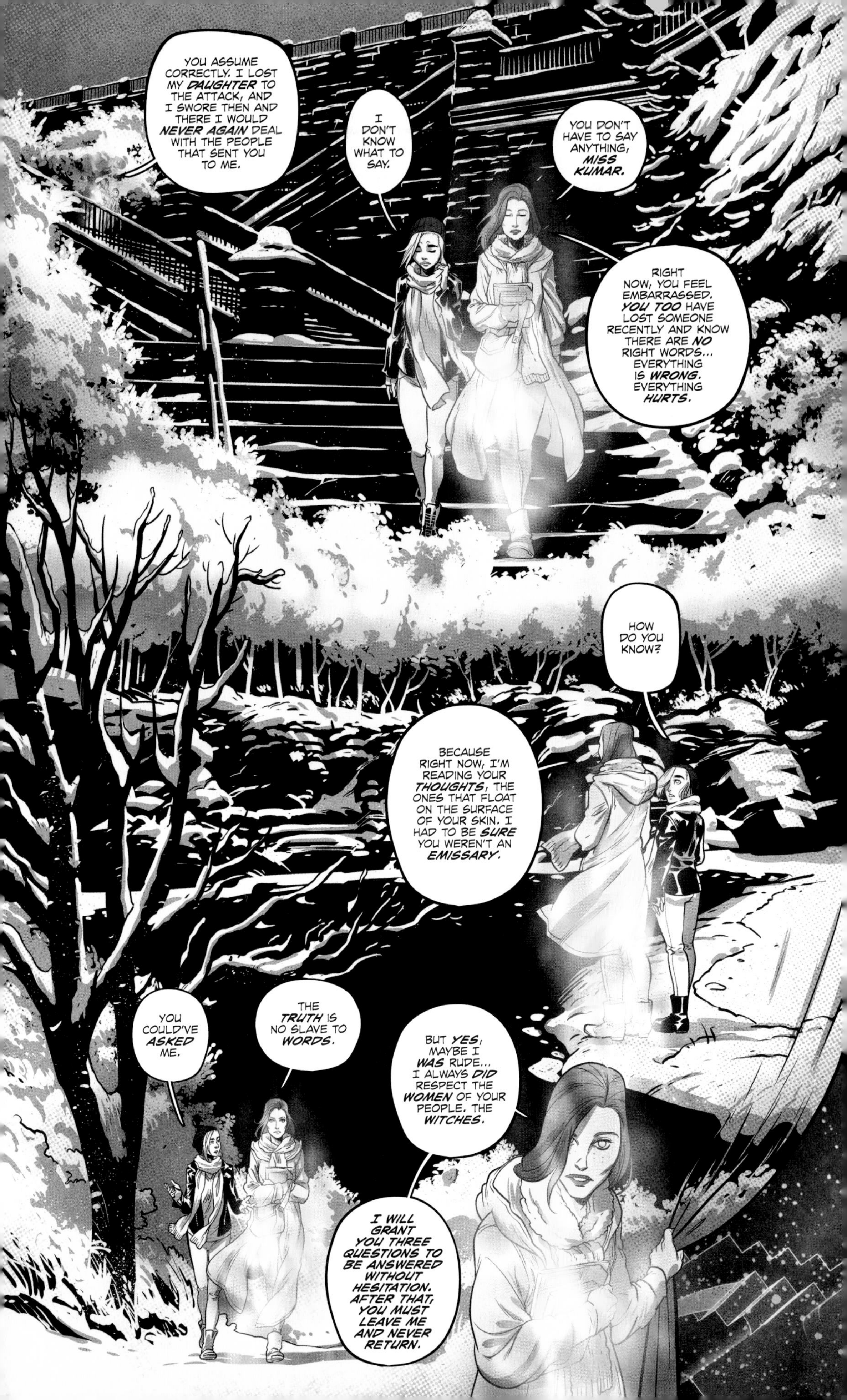
YOU ASSUME CORRECTLY. I LOST MY DAUGHTER TO THE ATTACK, AND I SWORE THEN AND THERE I WOULD NEVER AGAIN DEAL WITH THE PEOPLE THAT SENT YOU TO ME.
I DON'T KNOW WHAT TO SAY.
YOU DON'T HAVE TO SAY ANYTHING, MISS KUMAR.
RIGHT NOW, YOU FEEL EMBARRASSED. YOU TOO HAVE LOST SOMEONE RECENTLY AND KNOW THERE ARE NO RIGHT WORDS... EVERYTHING IS WRONG. EVERYTHING HURTS.
HOW DO YOU KNOW?
BECAUSE RIGHT NOW, I'M READING YOUR THOUGHTS, THE ONES THAT FLOAT ON THE SURFACE OF YOUR SKIN. I HAD TO BE SURE YOU WEREN'T AN EMISSARY.
YOU COULD'VE ASKED ME.
THE TRUTH IS NO SLAVE TO WORDS.
BUT YES, MAYBE I WAS RUDE... I ALWAYS DID RESPECT THE WOMEN OF YOUR PEOPLE. THE WITCHES.
I WILL GRANT YOU THREE QUESTIONS TO BE ANSWERED WITHOUT HESITATION. AFTER THAT, YOU MUST LEAVE ME AND NEVER RETURN.

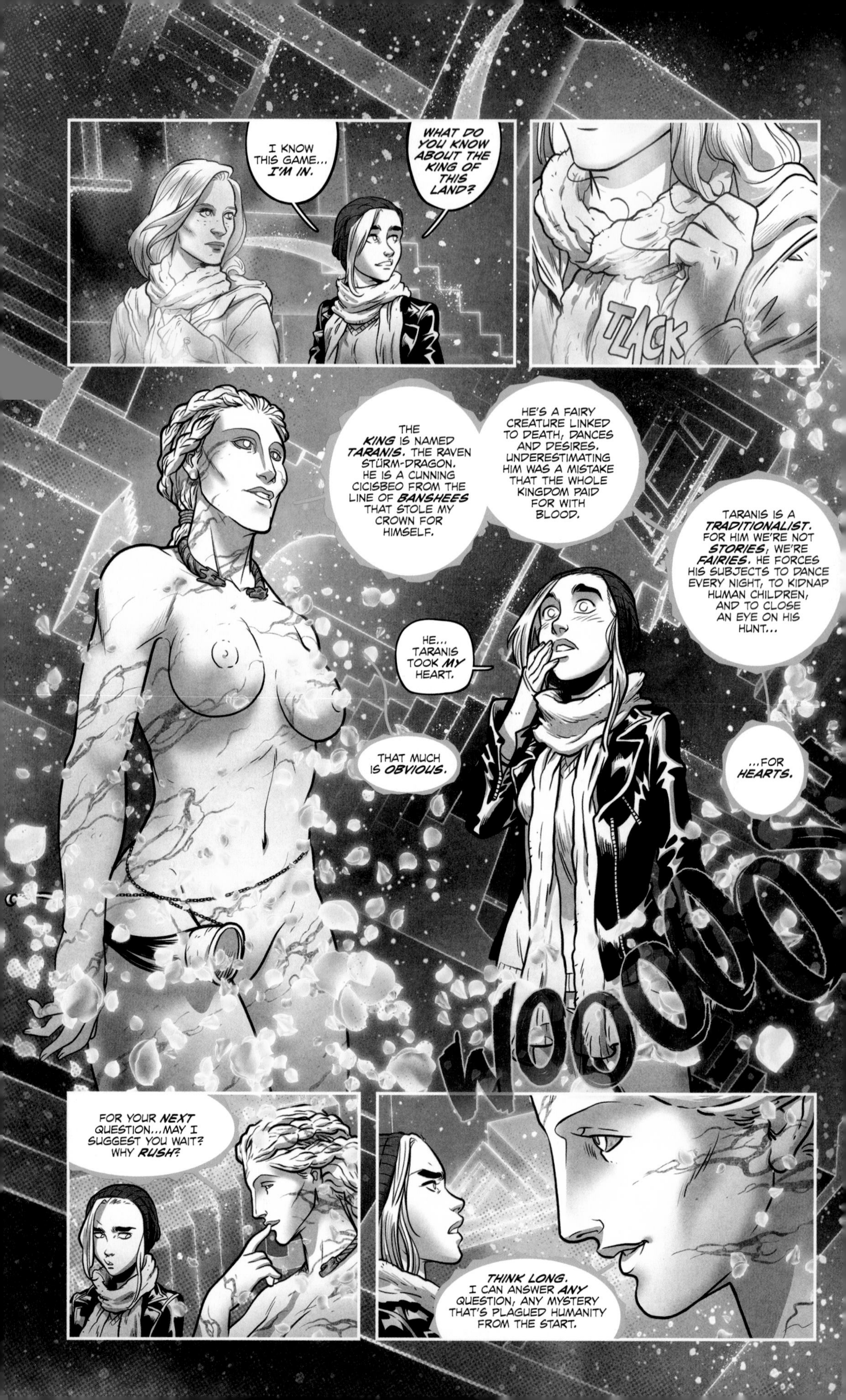
I KNOW THIS GAME... I'M IN.
WHAT DO YOU KNOW ABOUT THE KING OF THIS LAND?
TLACK
THE KING IS NAMED TARANIS. THE RAVEN STÜRM-DRAGON. HE IS A CUNNING CICISBEO FROM THE LINE OF BANSHEES THAT STOLE MY CROWN FOR HIMSELF.
HE'S A FAIRY CREATURE LINKED TO DEATH, DANCES AND DESIRES. UNDERESTIMATING HIM WAS A MISTAKE THAT THE WHOLE KINGDOM PAID FOR WITH BLOOD.
HE... TARANIS TOOK MY HEART.
THAT MUCH IS OBVIOUS.
TARANIS IS A TRADITIONALIST. FOR HIM WE'RE NOT STORIES, WE'RE FAIRIES. HE FORCES HIS SUBJECTS TO DANCE EVERY NIGHT, TO KIDNAP HUMAN CHILDREN, AND TO CLOSE AN EYE ON HIS HUNT...
...FOR HEARTS.
WOOOOOO
FOR YOUR NEXT QUESTION... MAY I SUGGEST YOU WAIT? WHY RUSH?
THINK LONG. I CAN ANSWER ANY QUESTION, ANY MYSTERY THAT'S PLAGUED HUMANITY FROM THE START.

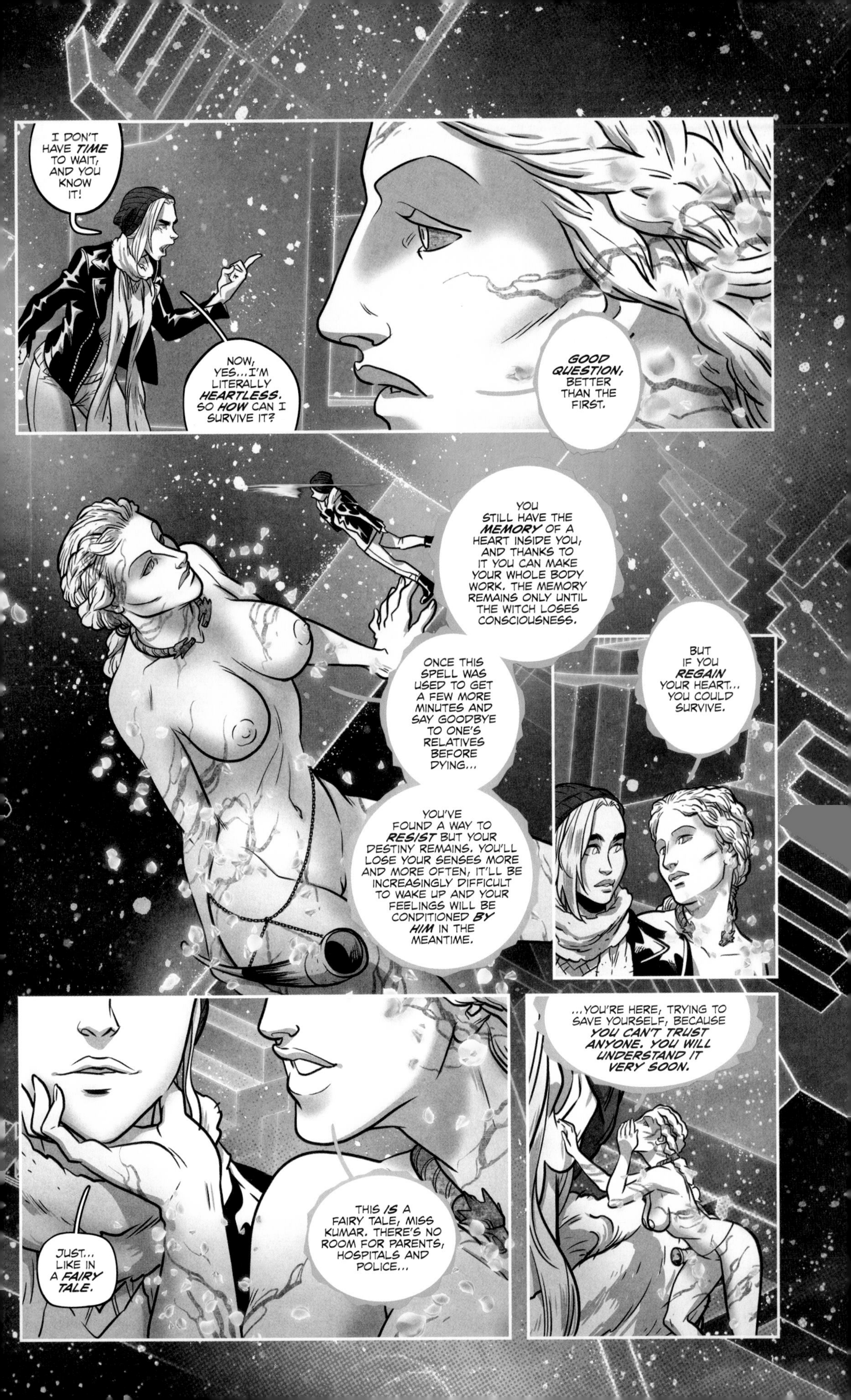
I DON'T HAVE TIME TO WAIT, AND YOU KNOW IT!
NOW, YES...I'M LITERALLY HEARTLESS. SO HOW CAN I SURVIVE IT?
GOOD QUESTION, BETTER THAN THE FIRST.
YOU STILL HAVE THE MEMORY OF A HEART INSIDE YOU, AND THANKS TO IT YOU CAN MAKE YOUR WHOLE BODY WORK. THE MEMORY REMAINS ONLY UNTIL THE WITCH LOSES CONSCIOUSNESS.
ONCE THIS SPELL WAS USED TO GET A FEW MORE MINUTES AND SAY GOODBYE TO ONE'S RELATIVES BEFORE DYING...
YOU'VE FOUND A WAY TO RESIST BUT YOUR DESTINY REMAINS. YOU'LL LOSE YOUR SENSES MORE AND MORE OFTEN, IT'LL BE INCREASINGLY DIFFICULT TO WAKE UP AND YOUR FEELINGS WILL BE CONDITIONED BY HIM IN THE MEANTIME.
BUT IF YOU REGAIN YOUR HEART... YOU COULD SURVIVE.
JUST... LIKE IN A FAIRY TALE.
THIS IS A FAIRY TALE, MISS KUMAR. THERE'S NO ROOM FOR PARENTS, HOSPITALS AND POLICE...
...YOU'RE HERE, TRYING TO SAVE YOURSELF, BECAUSE YOU CAN'T TRUST ANYONE. YOU WILL UNDERSTAND IT VERY SOON.

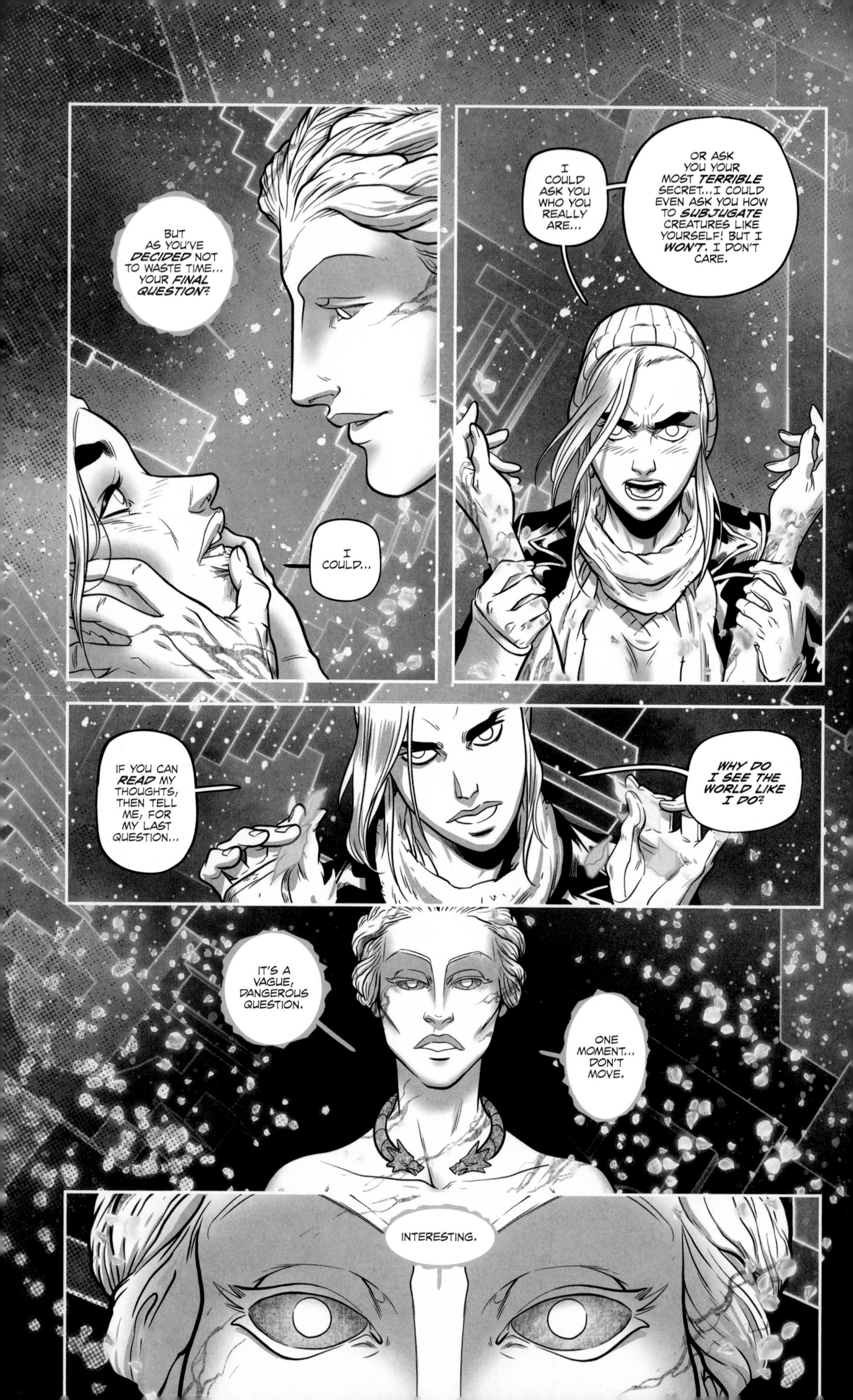
BUT AS YOU'VE *DECIDED* NOT TO WASTE TIME... YOUR *FINAL QUESTION*?
I COULD...
I COULD ASK YOU WHO YOU REALLY ARE...
OR ASK YOU YOUR MOST *TERRIBLE* SECRET...I COULD EVEN ASK YOU HOW TO *SUBJUGATE* CREATURES LIKE YOURSELF! BUT I *WON'T*. I DON'T CARE.
IF YOU CAN *READ* MY THOUGHTS, THEN TELL ME, FOR MY LAST QUESTION...
WHY DO I SEE THE WORLD LIKE I DO?
IT'S A VAGUE, DANGEROUS QUESTION.
ONE MOMENT... DON'T MOVE.
INTERESTING.

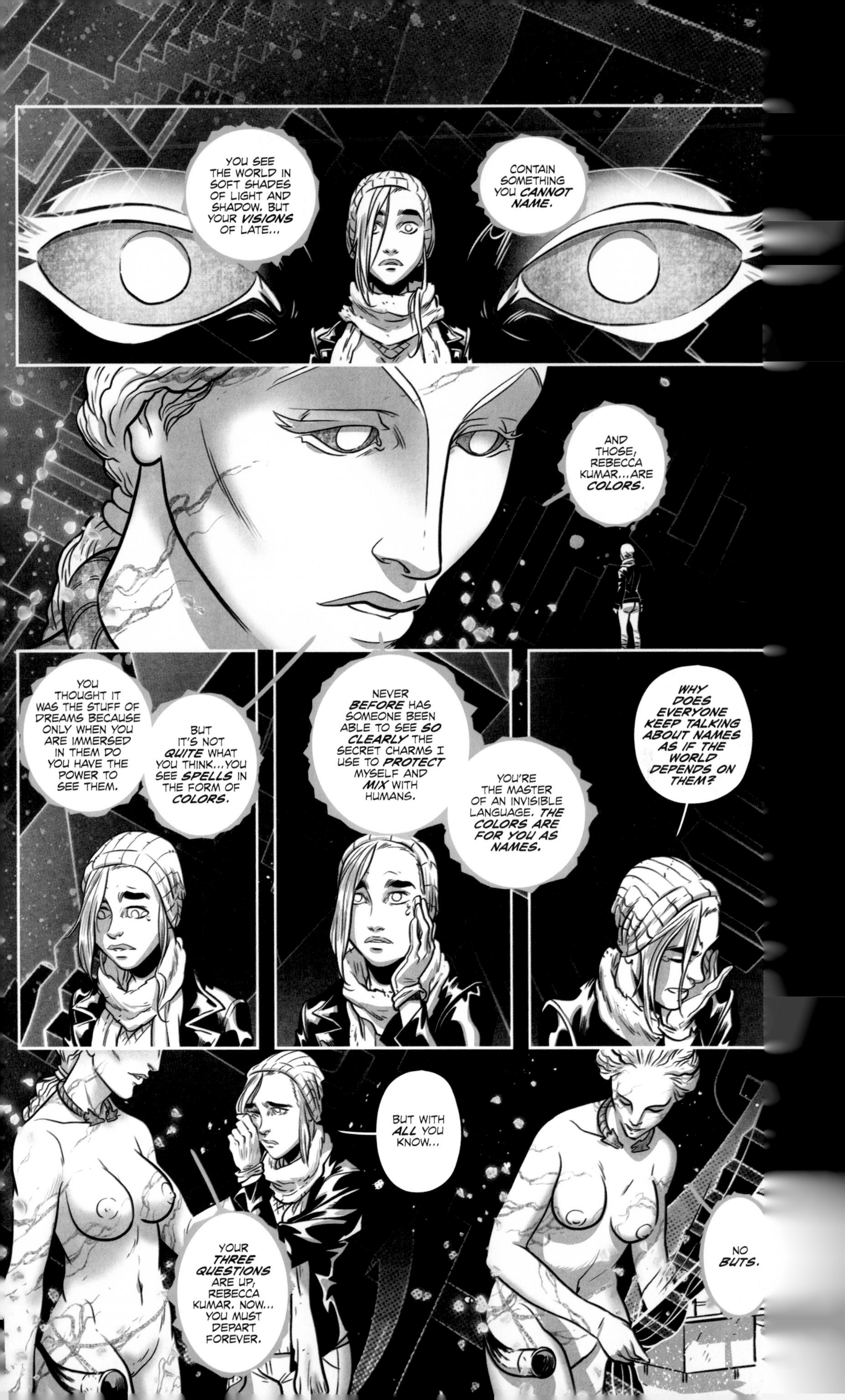
YOU SEE THE WORLD IN SOFT SHADES OF LIGHT AND SHADOW. BUT YOUR VISIONS OF LATE...
CONTAIN SOMETHING YOU CANNOT NAME.
AND THOSE, REBECCA KUMAR...ARE COLORS.
YOU THOUGHT IT WAS THE STUFF OF DREAMS BECAUSE ONLY WHEN YOU ARE IMMERSED IN THEM DO YOU HAVE THE POWER TO SEE THEM.
BUT IT'S NOT QUITE WHAT YOU THINK...YOU SEE SPELLS IN THE FORM OF COLORS.
NEVER BEFORE HAS SOMEONE BEEN ABLE TO SEE SO CLEARLY THE SECRET CHARMS I USE TO PROTECT MYSELF AND MIX WITH HUMANS.
YOU'RE THE MASTER OF AN INVISIBLE LANGUAGE. THE COLORS ARE FOR YOU AS NAMES.
WHY DOES EVERYONE KEEP TALKING ABOUT NAMES AS IF THE WORLD DEPENDS ON THEM?
BUT WITH ALL YOU KNOW...
YOUR THREE QUESTIONS ARE UP, REBECCA KUMAR. NOW... YOU MUST DEPART FOREVER.
NO BUTS.

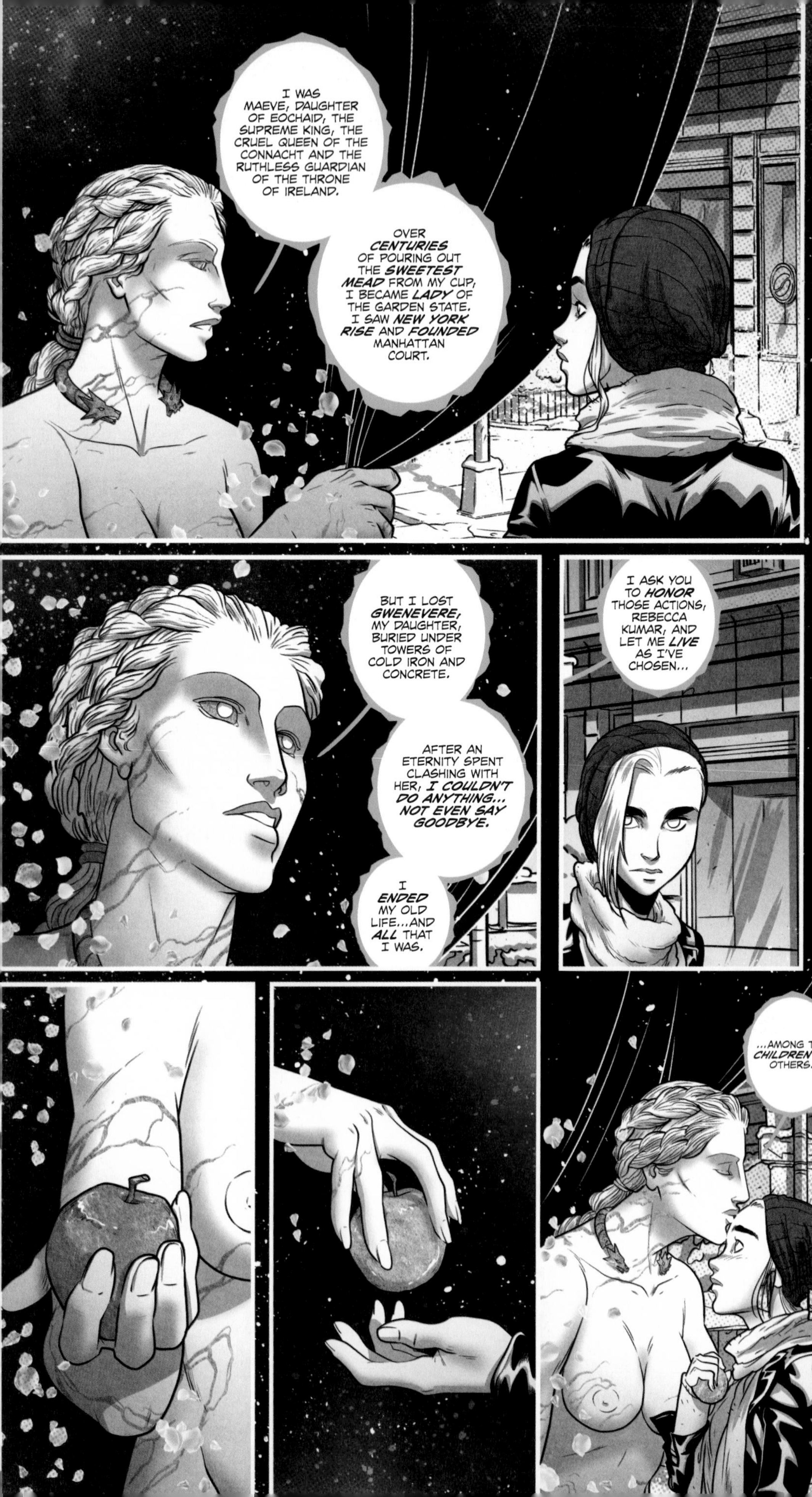

I WAS MAEVE, DAUGHTER OF EOCHAID, THE SUPREME KING, THE CRUEL QUEEN OF THE CONNACHT AND THE RUTHLESS GUARDIAN OF THE THRONE OF IRELAND.
OVER *CENTURIES* OF POURING OUT THE *SWEETEST MEAD* FROM MY CUP, I BECAME *LADY* OF THE GARDEN STATE. I SAW *NEW YORK RISE* AND *FOUNDED* MANHATTAN COURT.
BUT I LOST *GWENEVERE,* MY DAUGHTER, BURIED UNDER TOWERS OF COLD IRON AND CONCRETE.
AFTER AN ETERNITY SPENT CLASHING WITH HER, *I COULDN'T DO ANYTHING... NOT EVEN SAY GOODBYE.*
I *ENDED* MY OLD LIFE...AND *ALL* THAT I WAS.
I ASK YOU TO *HONOR* THOSE ACTIONS, REBECCA KUMAR, AND LET ME *LIVE* AS I'VE CHOSEN...
...AMONG T
CHILDREN
OTHERS.

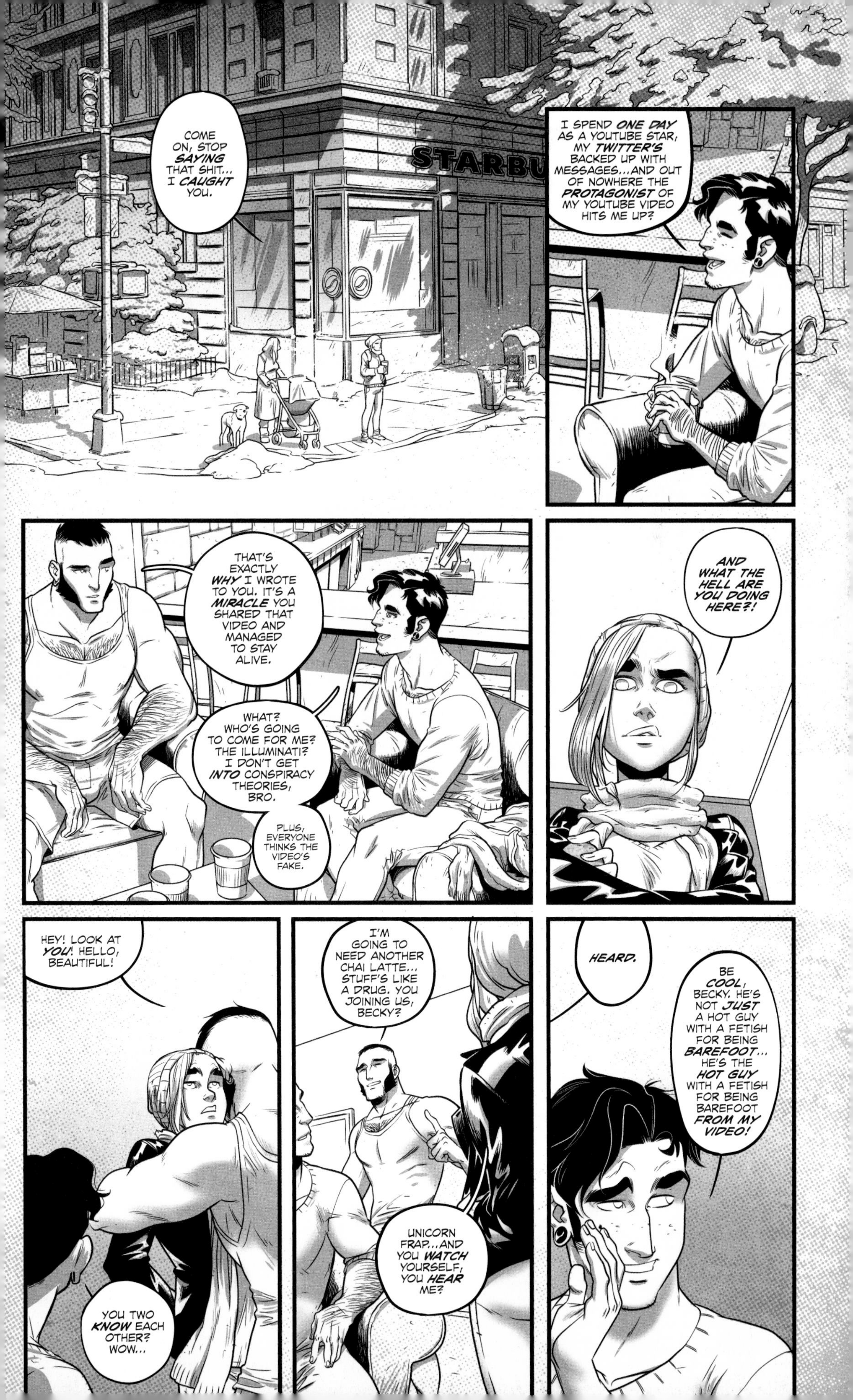

STARBU
COME ON, STOP SAYING THAT SHIT... I CAUGHT YOU.
I SPEND ONE DAY AS A YOUTUBE STAR, MY TWITTER'S BACKED UP WITH MESSAGES...AND OUT OF NOWHERE THE PROTAGONIST OF MY YOUTUBE VIDEO HITS ME UP?
THAT'S EXACTLY WHY I WROTE TO YOU. IT'S A MIRACLE YOU SHARED THAT VIDEO AND MANAGED TO STAY ALIVE.
WHAT? WHO'S GOING TO COME FOR ME? THE ILLUMINATI? I DON'T GET INTO CONSPIRACY THEORIES, BRO.
PLUS, EVERYONE THINKS THE VIDEO'S FAKE.
AND WHAT THE HELL ARE YOU DOING HERE?!
HEY! LOOK AT YOU! HELLO, BEAUTIFUL!
YOU TWO KNOW EACH OTHER? WOW...
I'M GOING TO NEED ANOTHER CHAI LATTE... STUFF'S LIKE A DRUG. YOU JOINING US, BECKY?
UNICORN FRAP...AND YOU WATCH YOURSELF, YOU HEAR ME?
HEARD.
BE COOL, BECKY. HE'S NOT JUST A HOT GUY WITH A FETISH FOR BEING BAREFOOT... HE'S THE HOT GUY WITH A FETISH FOR BEING BAREFOOT FROM MY VIDEO!

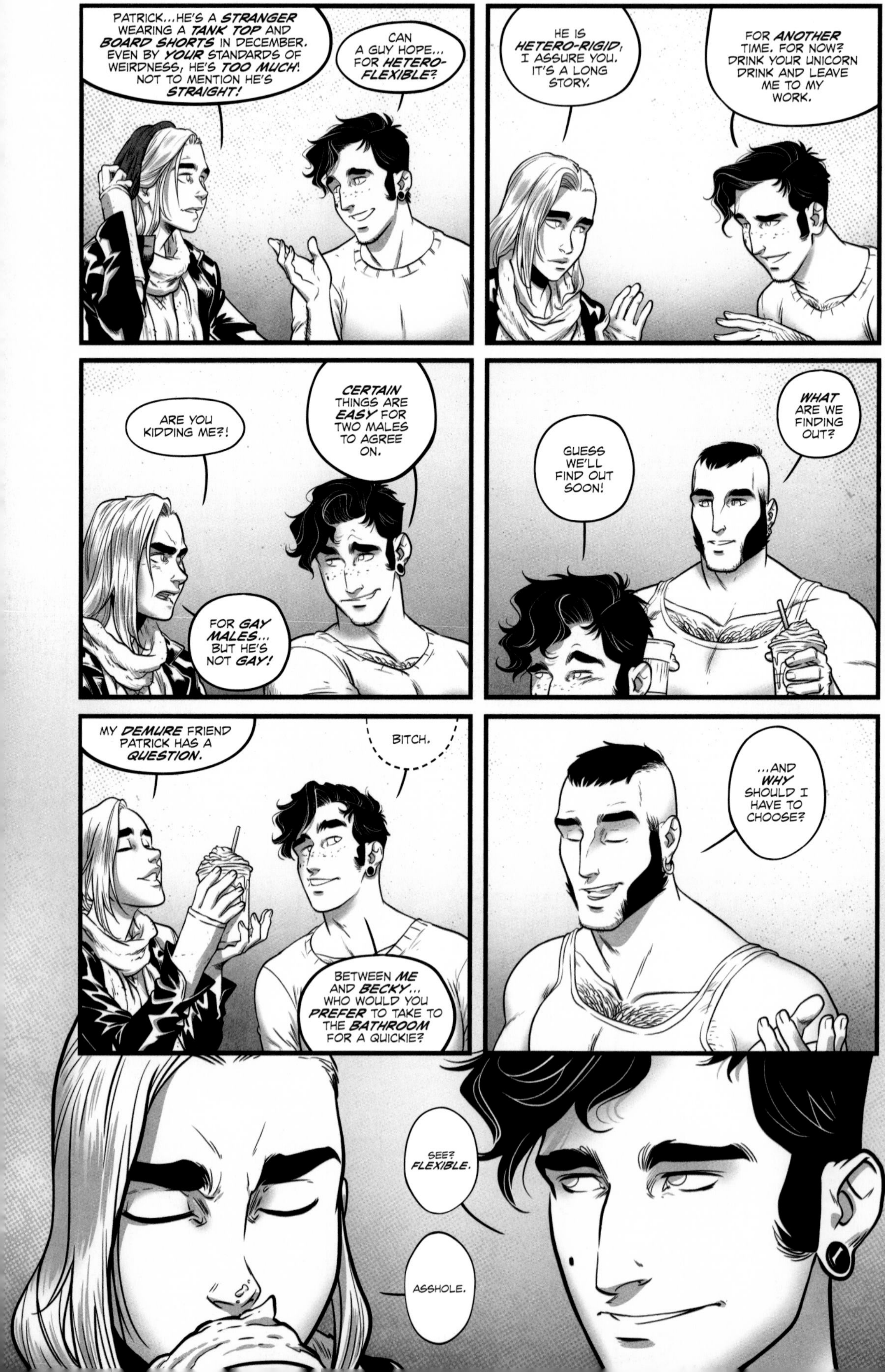
PATRICK...HE'S A STRANGER WEARING A TANK TOP AND BOARD SHORTS IN DECEMBER. EVEN BY YOUR STANDARDS OF WEIRDNESS, HE'S TOO MUCH! NOT TO MENTION HE'S STRAIGHT!
CAN A GUY HOPE... FOR HETERO-FLEXIBLE?
HE IS HETERO-RIGID, I ASSURE YOU. IT'S A LONG STORY.
FOR ANOTHER TIME. FOR NOW? DRINK YOUR UNICORN DRINK AND LEAVE ME TO MY WORK.
ARE YOU KIDDING ME?!
CERTAIN THINGS ARE EASY FOR TWO MALES TO AGREE ON.
FOR GAY MALES... BUT HE'S NOT GAY!
GUESS WE'LL FIND OUT SOON!
WHAT ARE WE FINDING OUT?
MY DEMURE FRIEND PATRICK HAS A QUESTION.
BITCH.
BETWEEN ME AND BECKY... WHO WOULD YOU PREFER TO TAKE TO THE BATHROOM FOR A QUICKIE?
...AND WHY SHOULD I HAVE TO CHOOSE?
SEE? FLEXIBLE.
ASSHOLE.

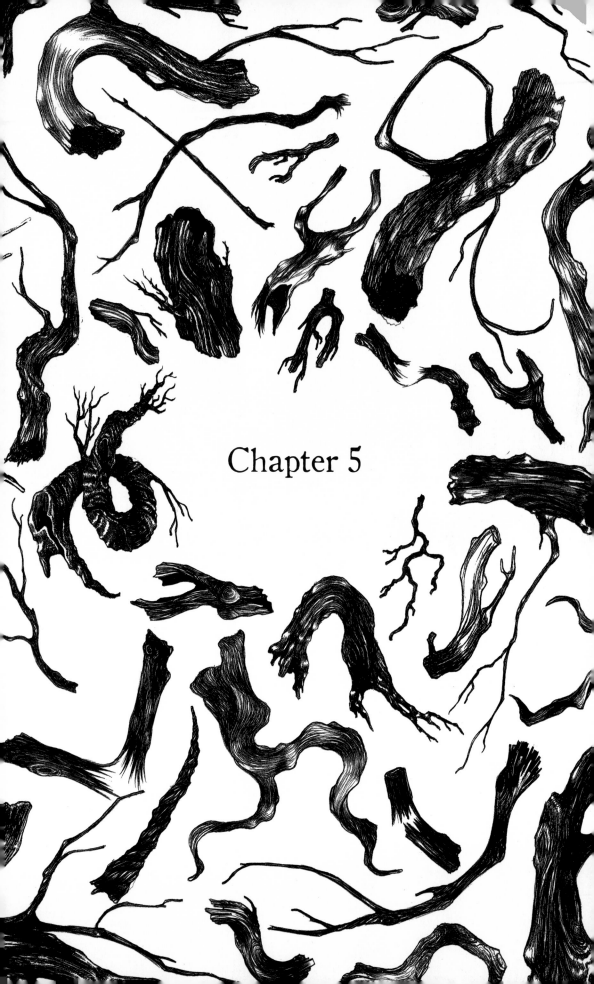

Chapter 5

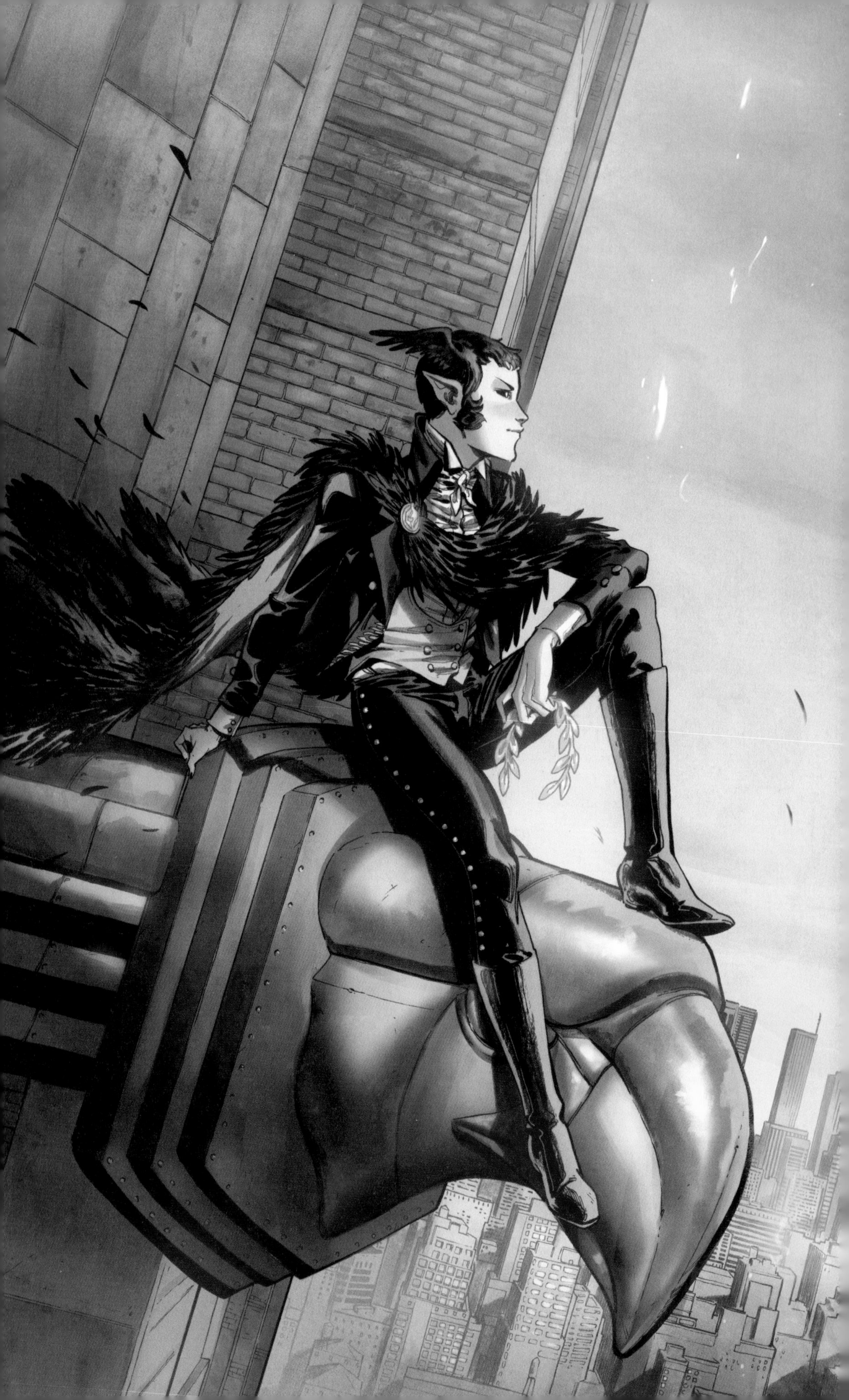

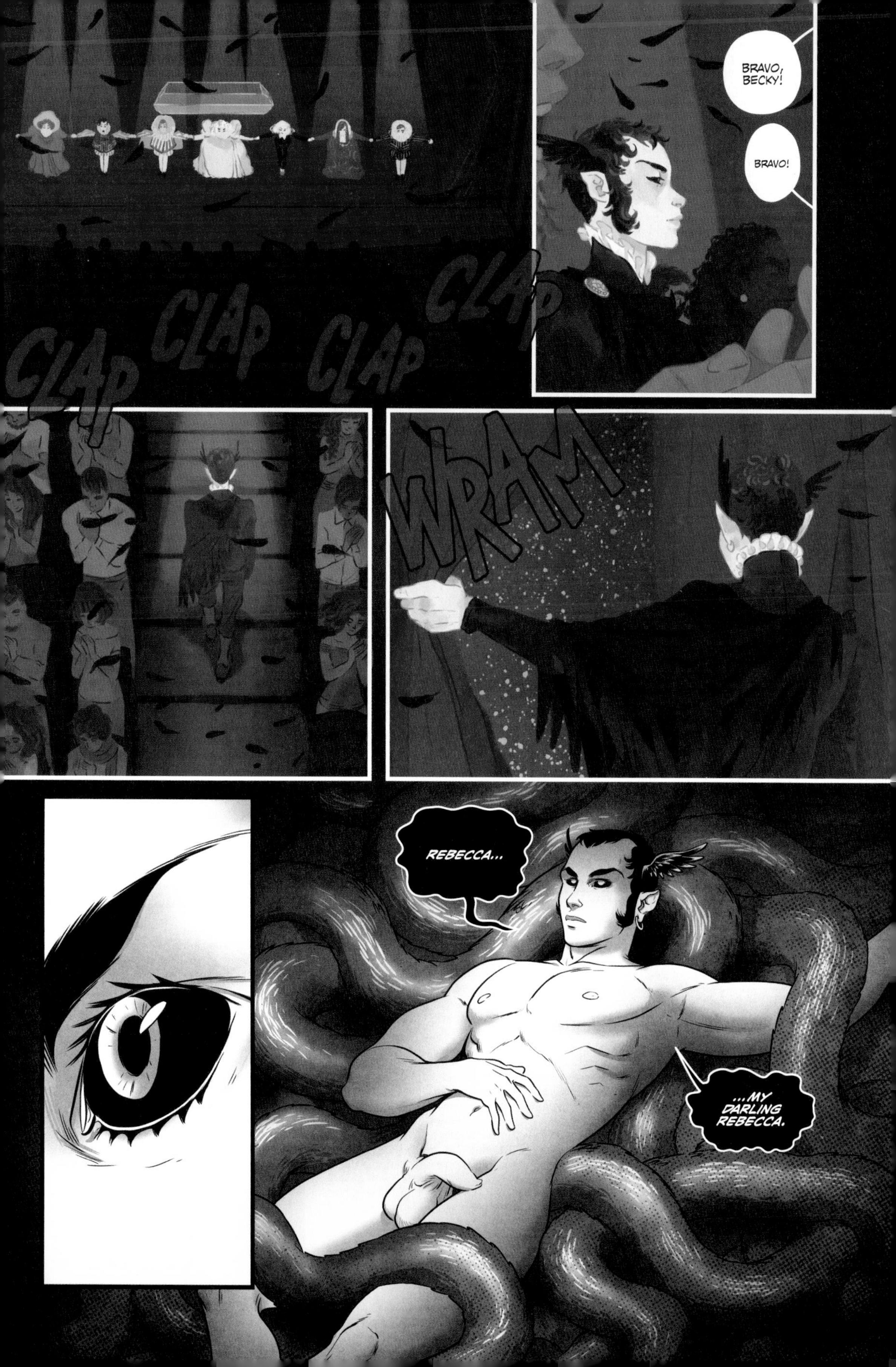
CLAP
CLAP
CLAP
CLAP
BRAVO, BECKY!
BRAVO!
WRAM
REBECCA...
...MY DARLING REBECCA.

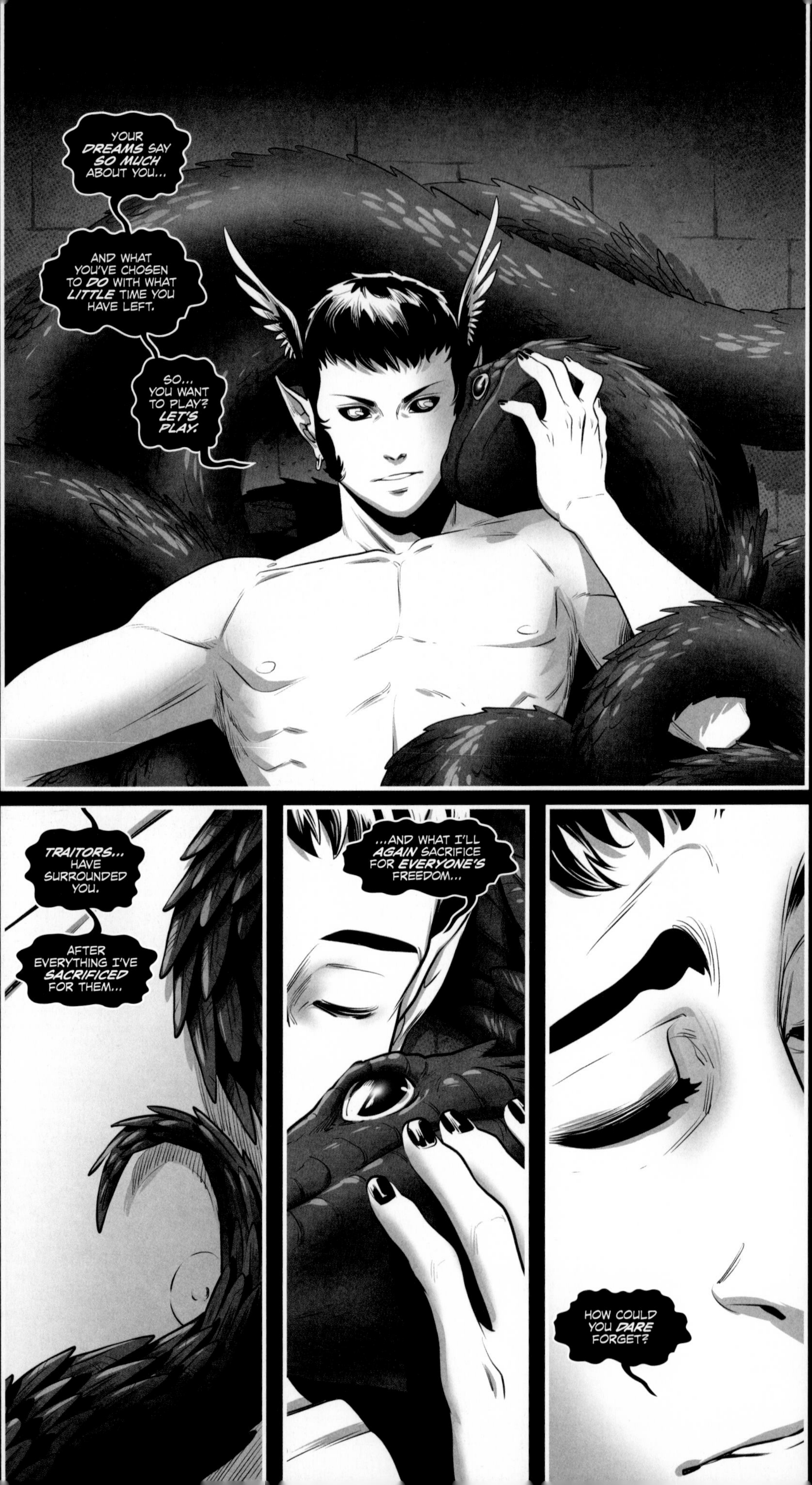
YOUR DREAMS SAY SO MUCH ABOUT YOU...
AND WHAT YOU'VE CHOSEN TO DO WITH WHAT LITTLE TIME YOU HAVE LEFT.
SO... YOU WANT TO PLAY? LET'S PLAY.
TRAITORS... HAVE SURROUNDED YOU.
AFTER EVERYTHING I'VE SACRIFICED FOR THEM...
...AND WHAT I'LL AGAIN SACRIFICE FOR EVERYONE'S FREEDOM...
HOW COULD YOU DARE FORGET?

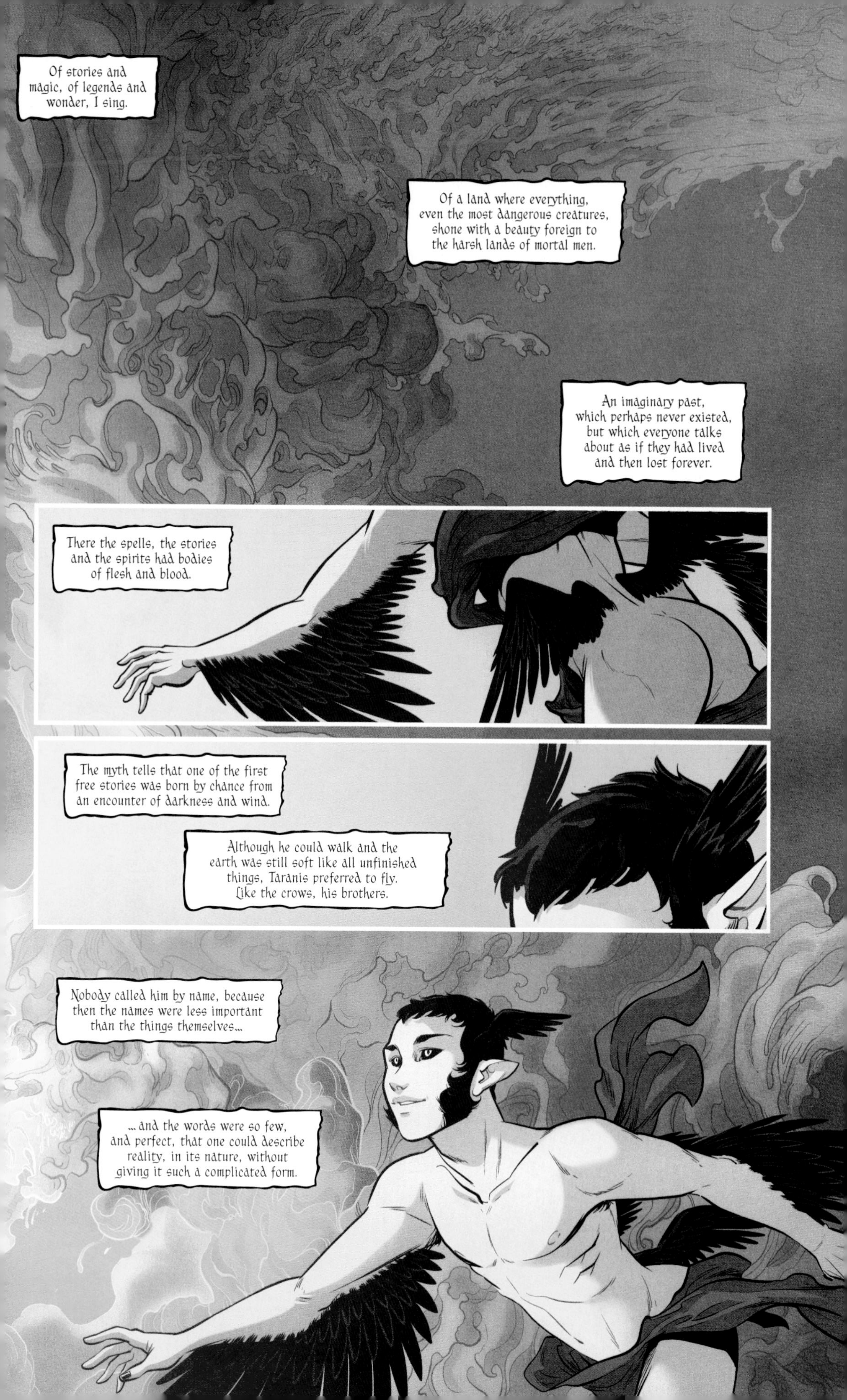
Of stories and magic, of legends and wonder, I sing.
Of a land where everything, even the most dangerous creatures, shone with a beauty foreign to the harsh lands of mortal men.
An imaginary past, which perhaps never existed, but which everyone talks about as if they had lived and then lost forever.
There the spells, the stories and the spirits had bodies of flesh and blood.
The myth tells that one of the first free stories was born by chance from an encounter of darkness and wind.
Although he could walk and the earth was still soft like all unfinished things, Taranis preferred to fly. Like the crows, his brothers.
Nobody called him by name, because then the names were less important than the things themselves...
...and the words were so few, and perfect, that one could describe reality, in its nature, without giving it such a complicated form.

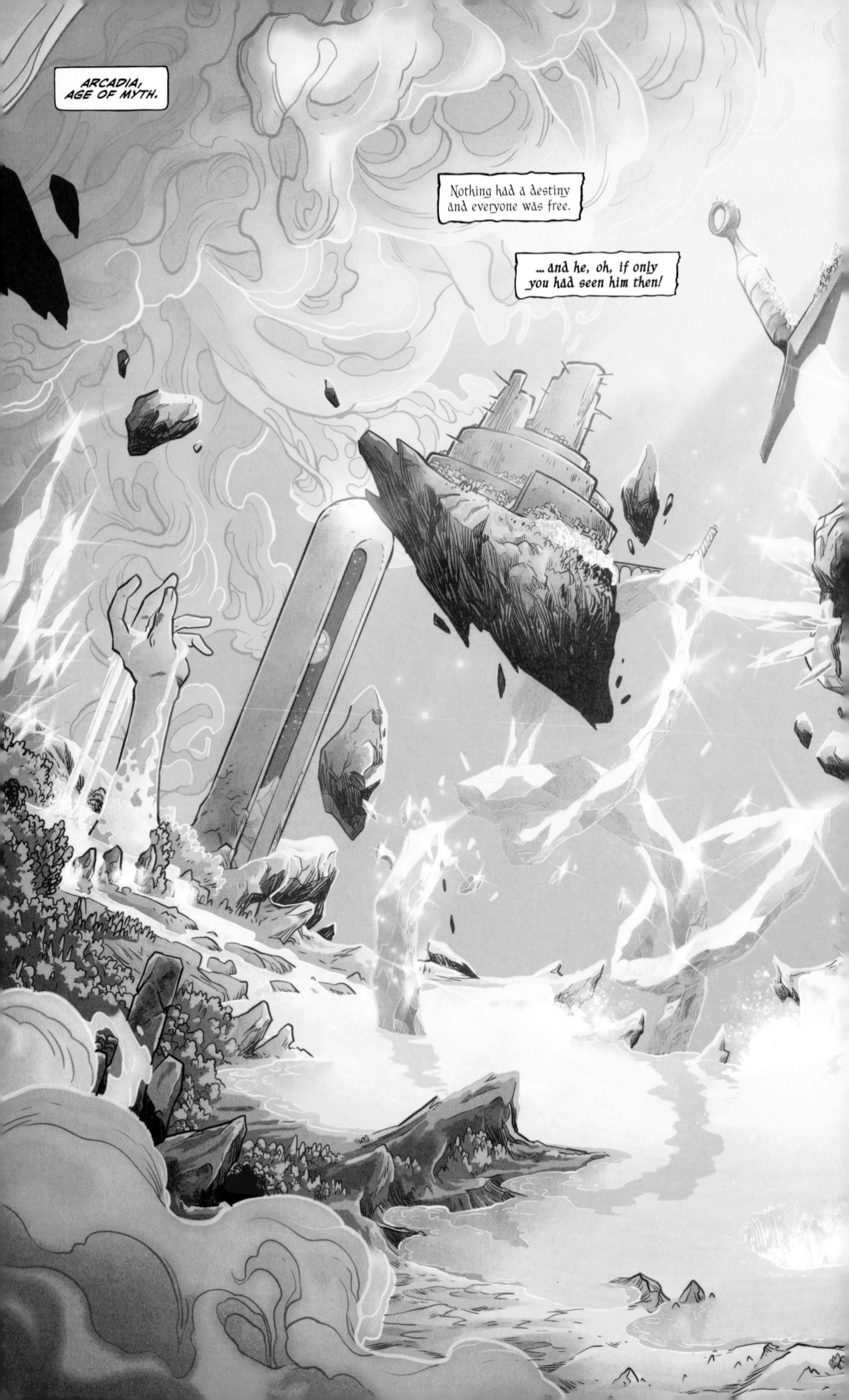
ARCADIA, AGE OF MYTH.
Nothing had a destiny and everyone was free.
...and he, oh, if only you had seen him then!

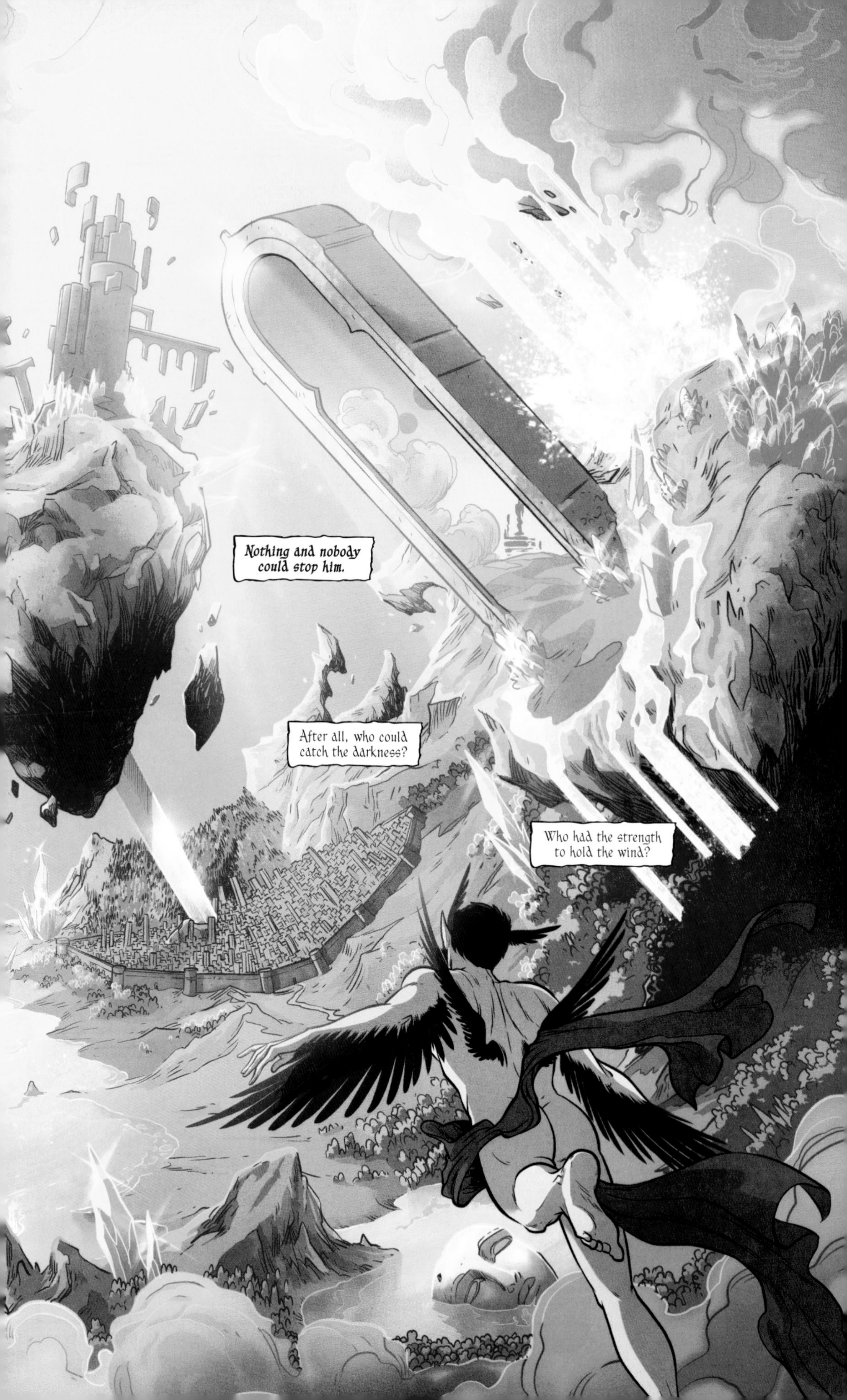
Nothing and nobody could stop him.
After all, who could catch the darkness?
Who had the strength to hold the wind?

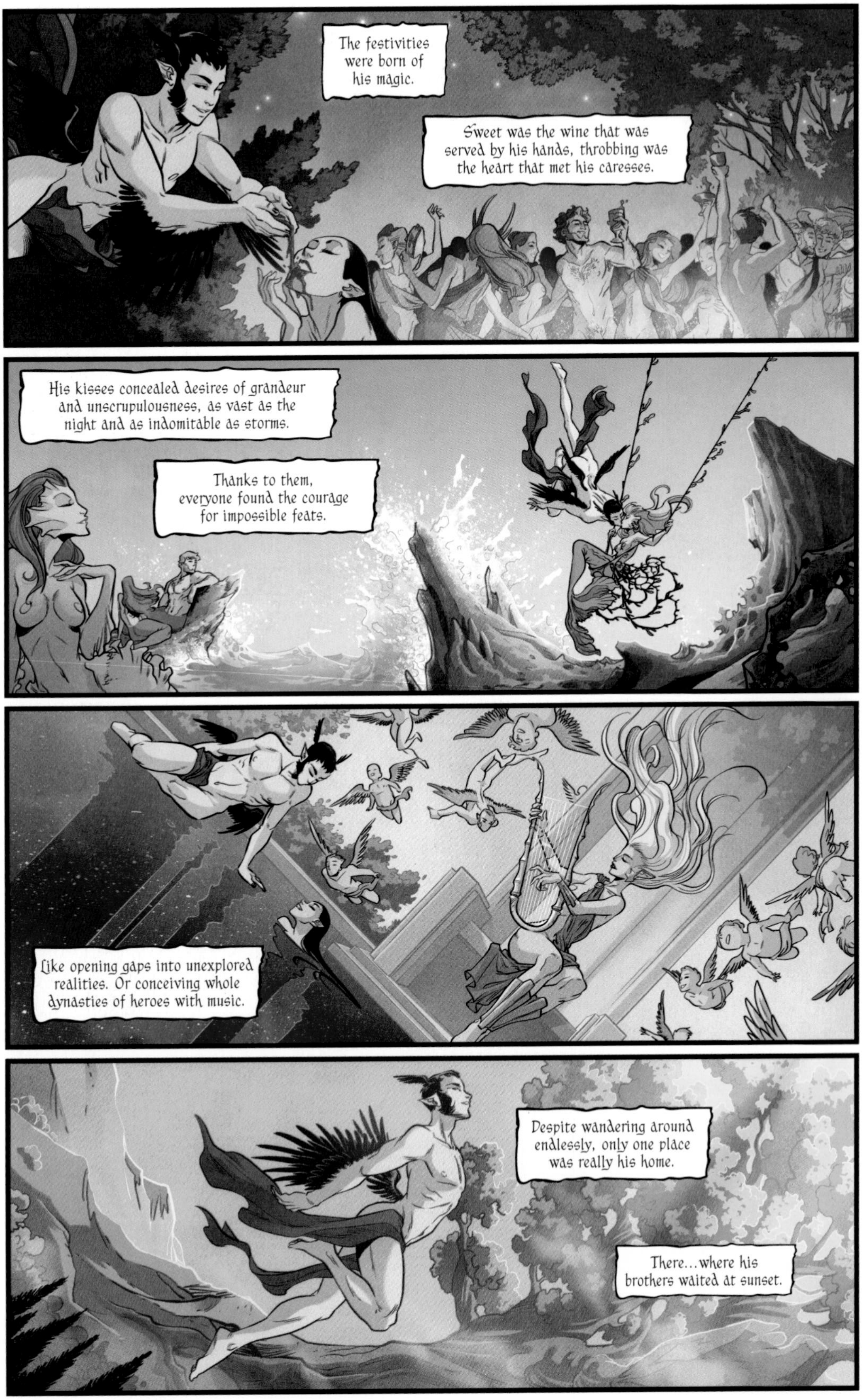
The festivities were born of his magic.
Sweet was the wine that was served by his hands, throbbing was the heart that met his caresses.
His kisses concealed desires of grandeur and unscrupulousness, as vast as the night and as indomitable as storms.
Thanks to them, everyone found the courage for impossible feats.
Like opening gaps into unexplored realities. Or conceiving whole dynasties of heroes with music.
Despite wandering around endlessly, only one place was really his home.
There...where his brothers waited at sunset.

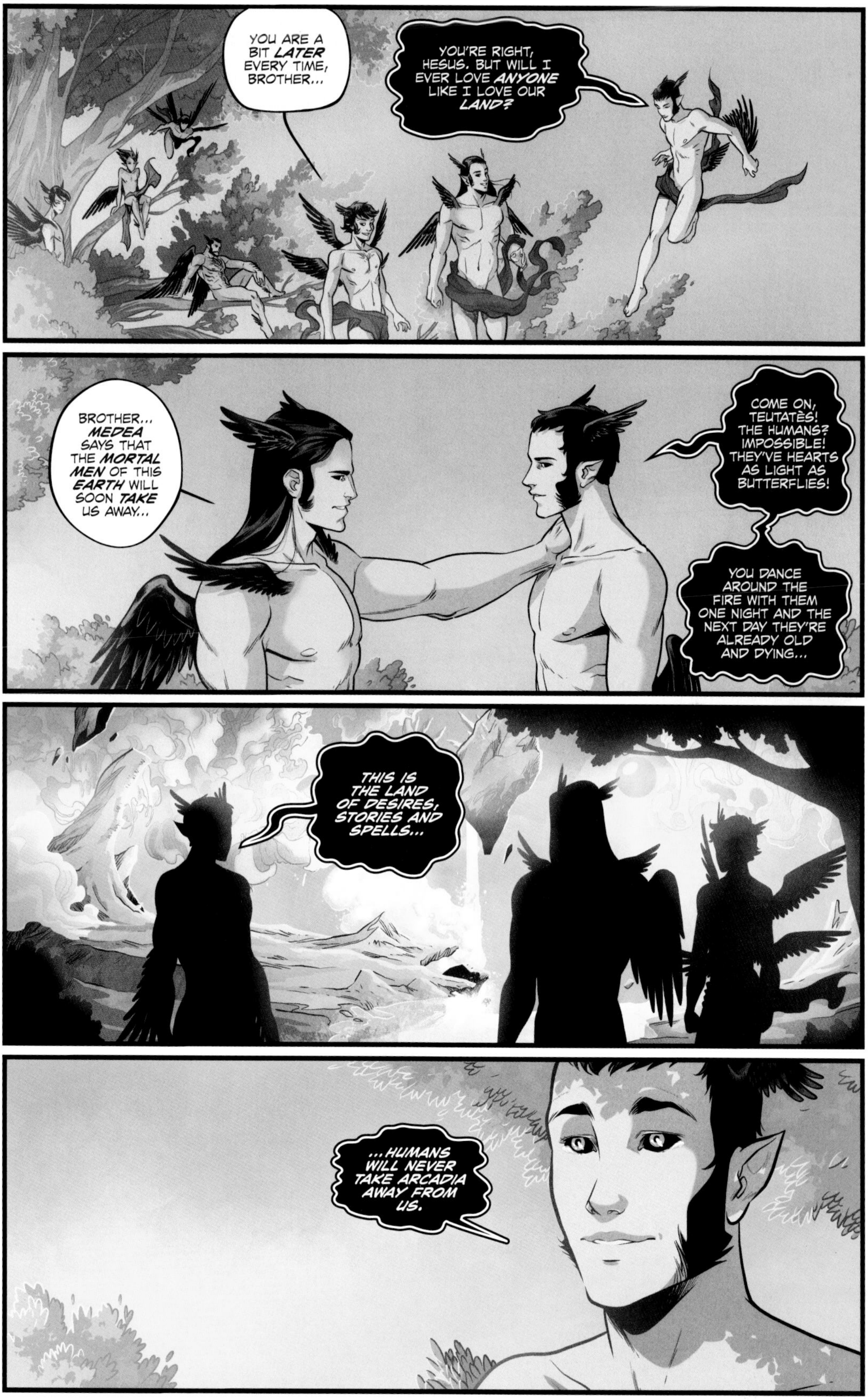
YOU ARE A BIT LATER EVERY TIME, BROTHER...
YOU'RE RIGHT, HESUS. BUT WILL I EVER LOVE ANYONE LIKE I LOVE OUR LAND?
BROTHER... MEDEA SAYS THAT THE MORTAL MEN OF THIS EARTH WILL SOON TAKE US AWAY...
COME ON, TEUTATÈS! THE HUMANS? IMPOSSIBLE! THEY'VE HEARTS AS LIGHT AS BUTTERFLIES!
YOU DANCE AROUND THE FIRE WITH THEM ONE NIGHT AND THE NEXT DAY THEY'RE ALREADY OLD AND DYING...
THIS IS THE LAND OF DESIRES, STORIES AND SPELLS...
...HUMANS WILL NEVER TAKE ARCADIA AWAY FROM US.

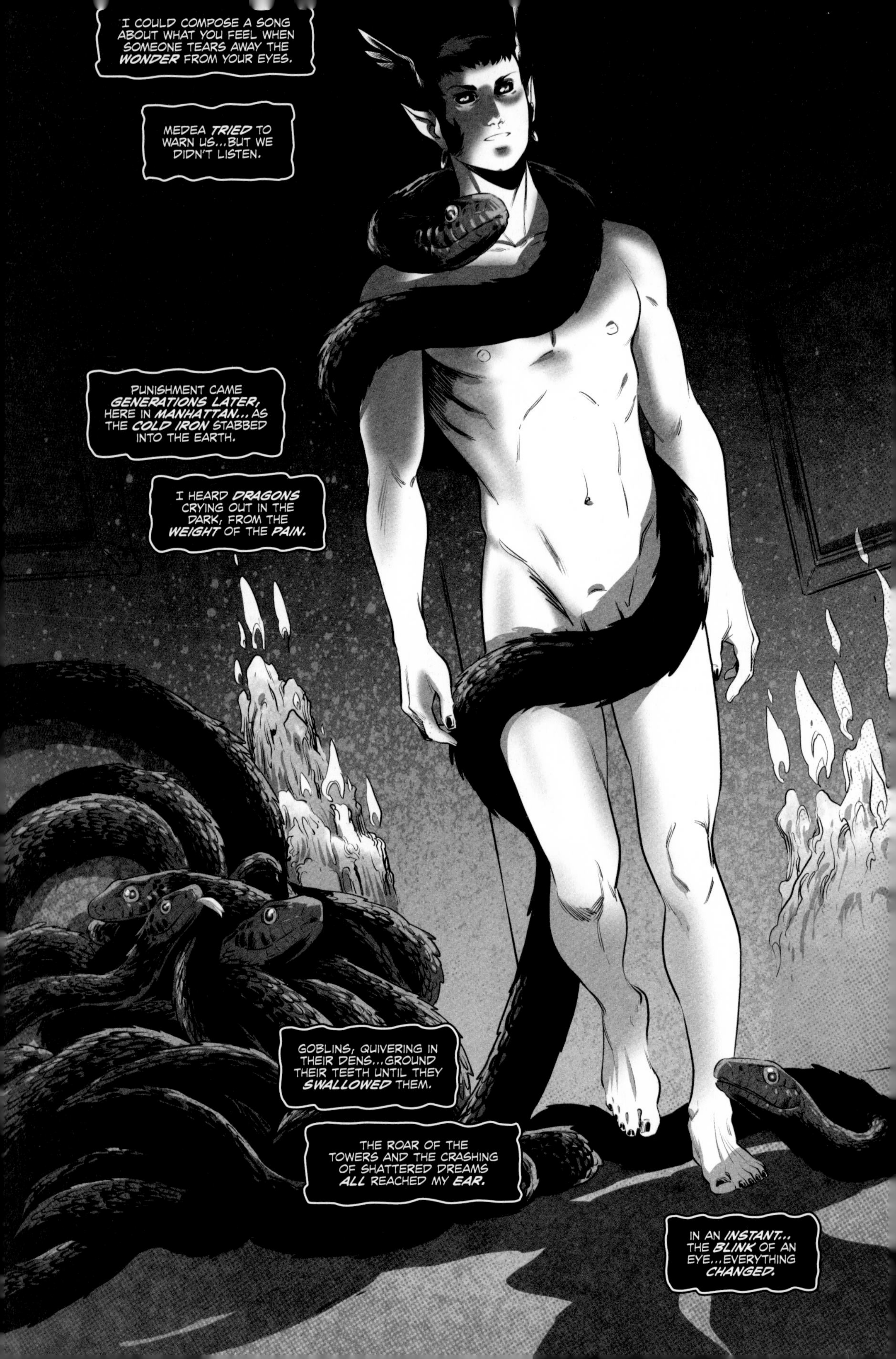

I COULD COMPOSE A SONG ABOUT WHAT YOU FEEL WHEN SOMEONE TEARS AWAY THE WONDER FROM YOUR EYES.
MEDEA TRIED TO WARN US...BUT WE DIDN'T LISTEN.
PUNISHMENT CAME GENERATIONS LATER, HERE IN MANHATTAN... AS THE COLD IRON STABBED INTO THE EARTH.
I HEARD DRAGONS CRYING OUT IN THE DARK, FROM THE WEIGHT OF THE PAIN.
GOBLINS, QUIVERING IN THEIR DENS...GROUND THEIR TEETH UNTIL THEY SWALLOWED THEM.
THE ROAR OF THE TOWERS AND THE CRASHING OF SHATTERED DREAMS ALL REACHED MY EAR.
IN AN INSTANT... THE BLINK OF AN EYE...EVERYTHING CHANGED.

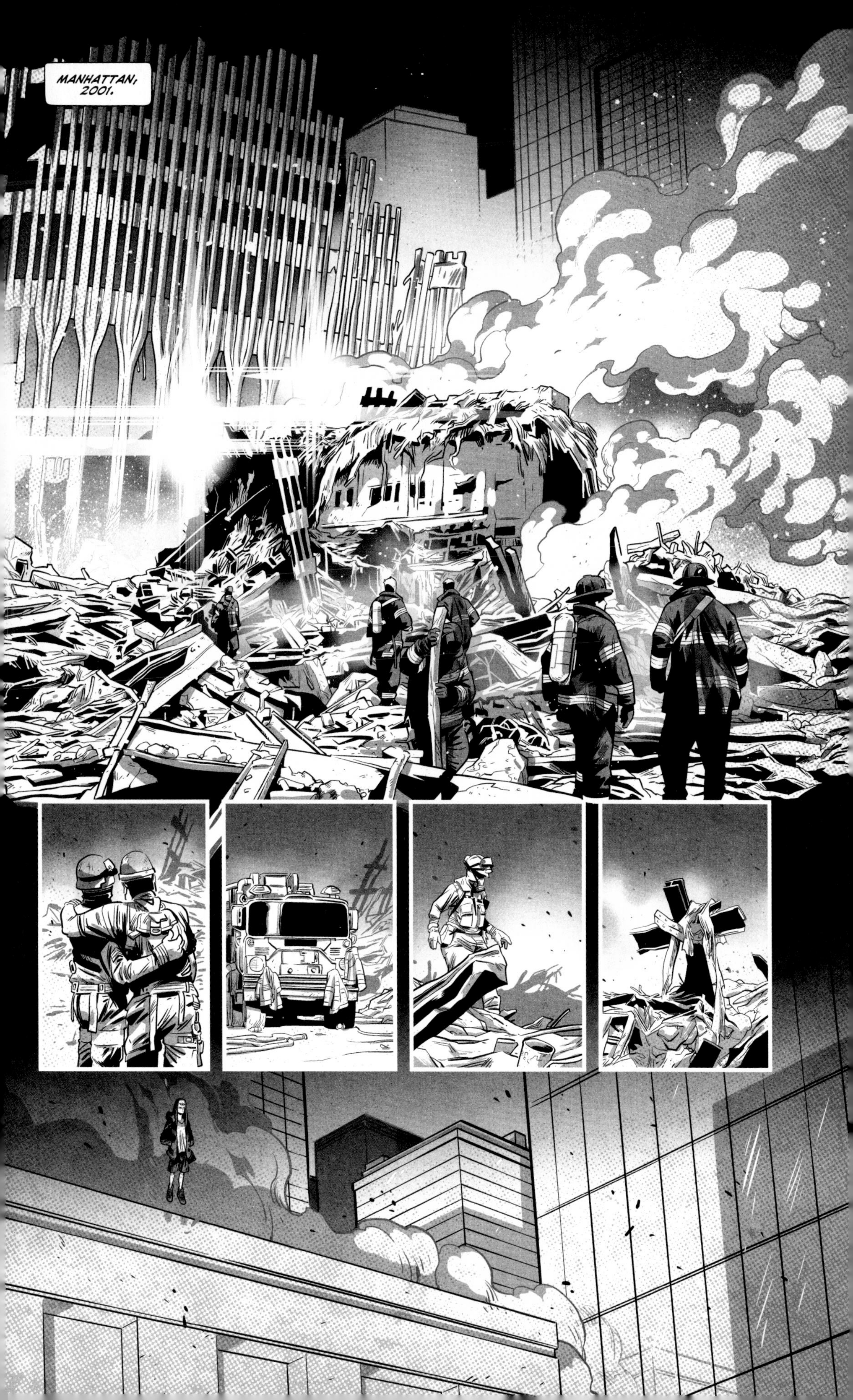
MANHATTAN, 2001.

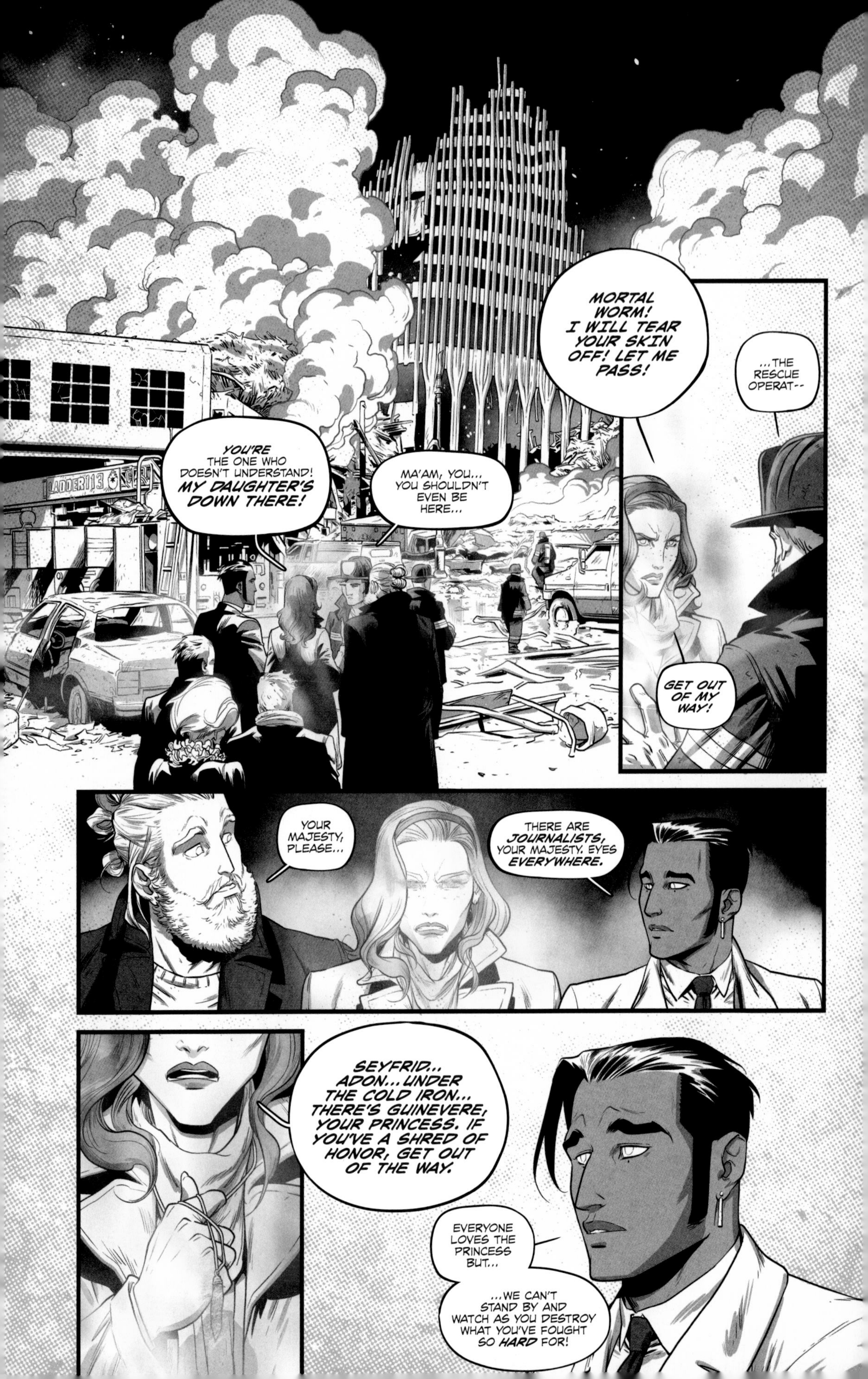
LADDER 113
YOU'RE THE ONE WHO DOESN'T UNDERSTAND! MY DAUGHTER'S DOWN THERE!
MA'AM, YOU... YOU SHOULDN'T EVEN BE HERE...
MORTAL WORM! I WILL TEAR YOUR SKIN OFF! LET ME PASS!
...THE RESCUE OPERAT--
GET OUT OF MY WAY!
YOUR MAJESTY, PLEASE...
THERE ARE JOURNALISTS, YOUR MAJESTY. EYES EVERYWHERE.
SEYFRID... ADON... UNDER THE COLD IRON... THERE'S GUINEVERE, YOUR PRINCESS. IF YOU'VE A SHRED OF HONOR, GET OUT OF THE WAY.
EVERYONE LOVES THE PRINCESS BUT...
...WE CAN'T STAND BY AND WATCH AS YOU DESTROY WHAT YOU'VE FOUGHT SO HARD FOR!

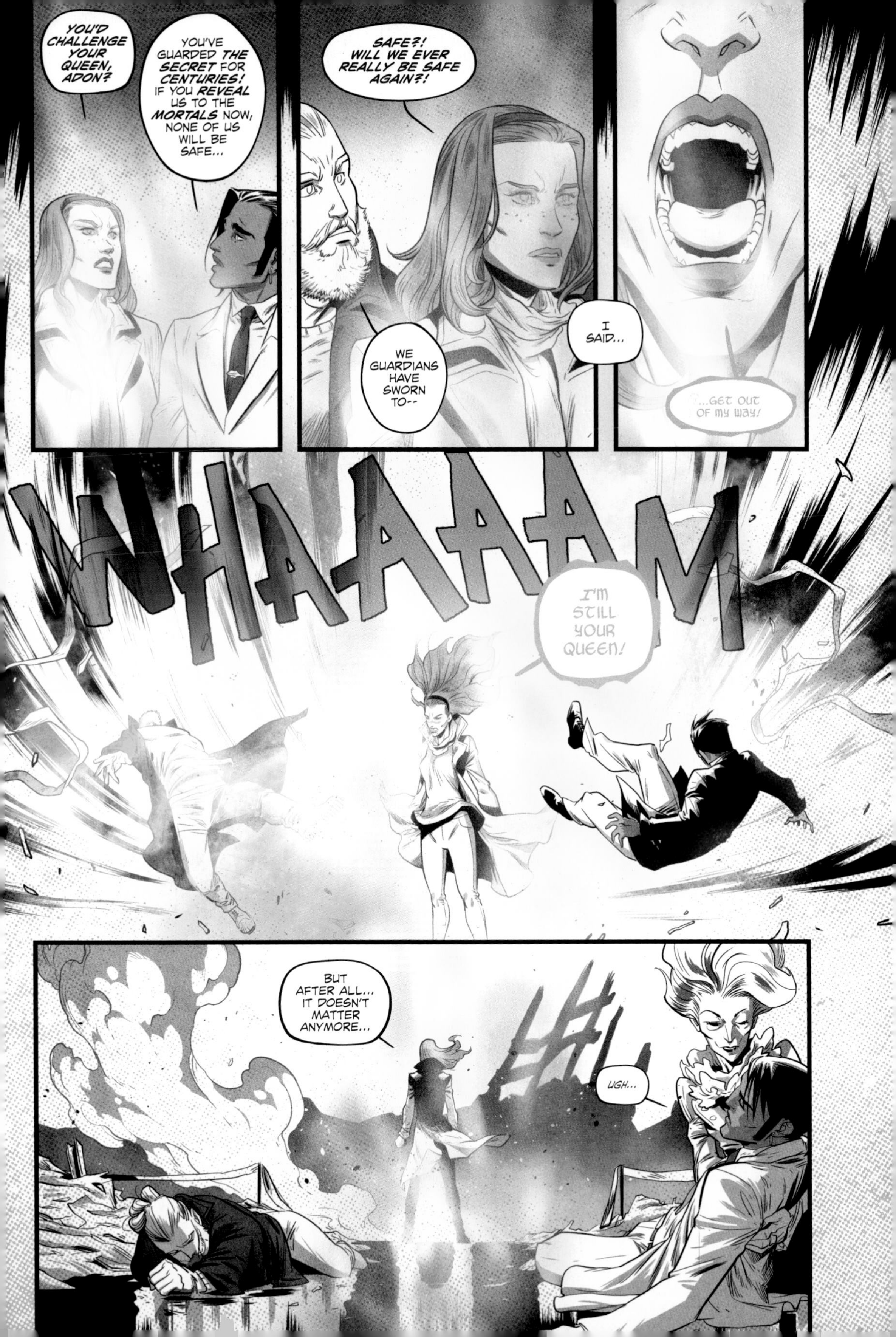
YOU'D CHALLENGE YOUR QUEEN, ADON?
YOU'VE GUARDED THE SECRET FOR CENTURIES! IF YOU REVEAL US TO THE MORTALS NOW, NONE OF US WILL BE SAFE...
SAFE?! WILL WE EVER REALLY BE SAFE AGAIN?!
WE GUARDIANS HAVE SWORN TO--
I SAID...
...GET OUT OF MY WAY!
WHAAAAM
I'M STILL YOUR QUEEN!
BUT AFTER ALL... IT DOESN'T MATTER ANYMORE...
UGH...

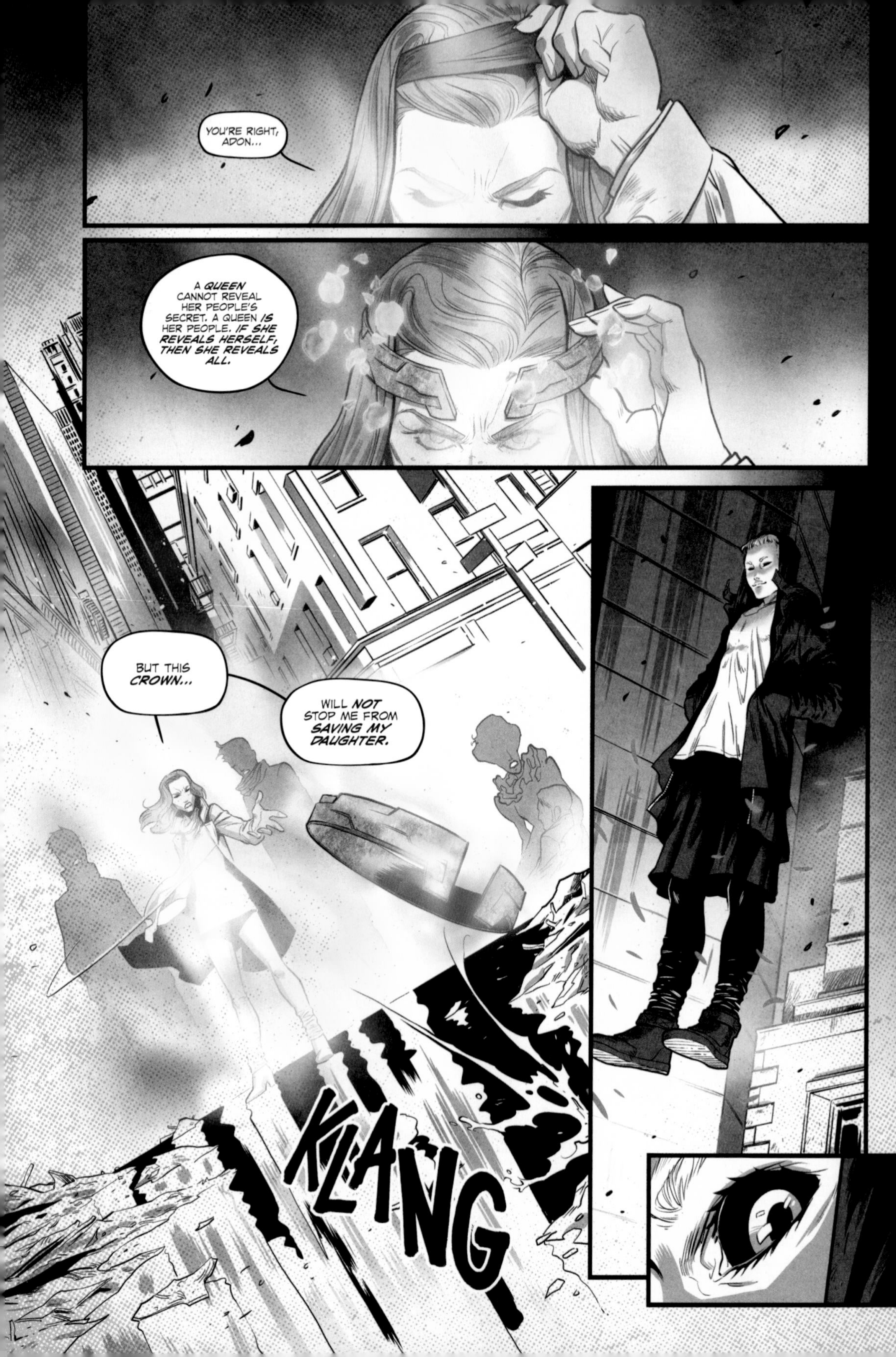

YOU'RE RIGHT, ADON...
A *QUEEN* CANNOT REVEAL HER PEOPLE'S SECRET. A QUEEN *IS* HER PEOPLE. *IF SHE REVEALS HERSELF, THEN SHE REVEALS ALL.*
BUT THIS *CROWN...*
WILL *NOT* STOP ME FROM *SAVING MY DAUGHTER.*
KLANG

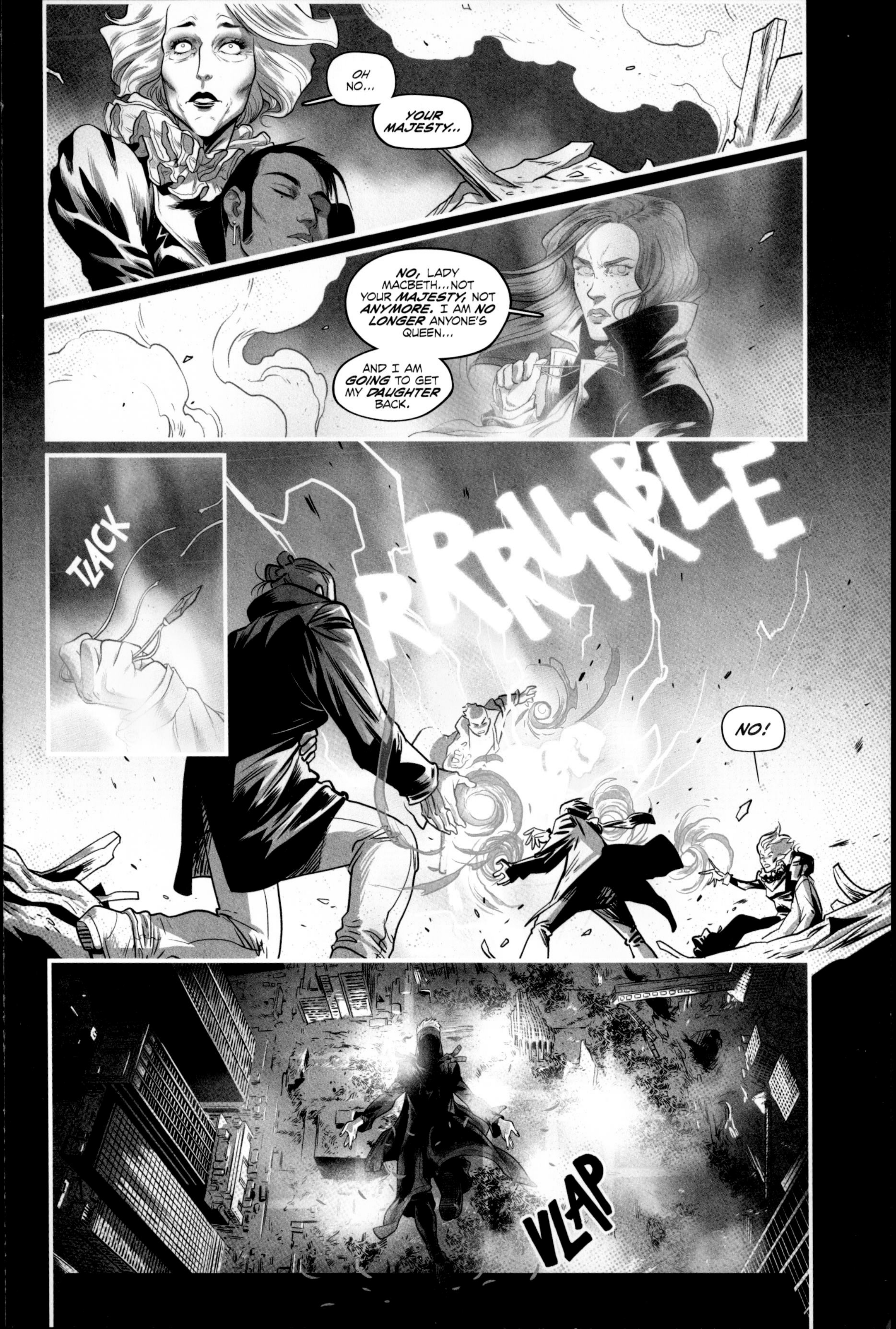
OH NO...
YOUR MAJESTY...
NO, LADY MACBETH...NOT YOUR MAJESTY, NOT ANYMORE. I AM NO LONGER ANYONE'S QUEEN...
AND I AM GOING TO GET MY DAUGHTER BACK.
TZACK
RRRUMBLE
NO!
VLAP

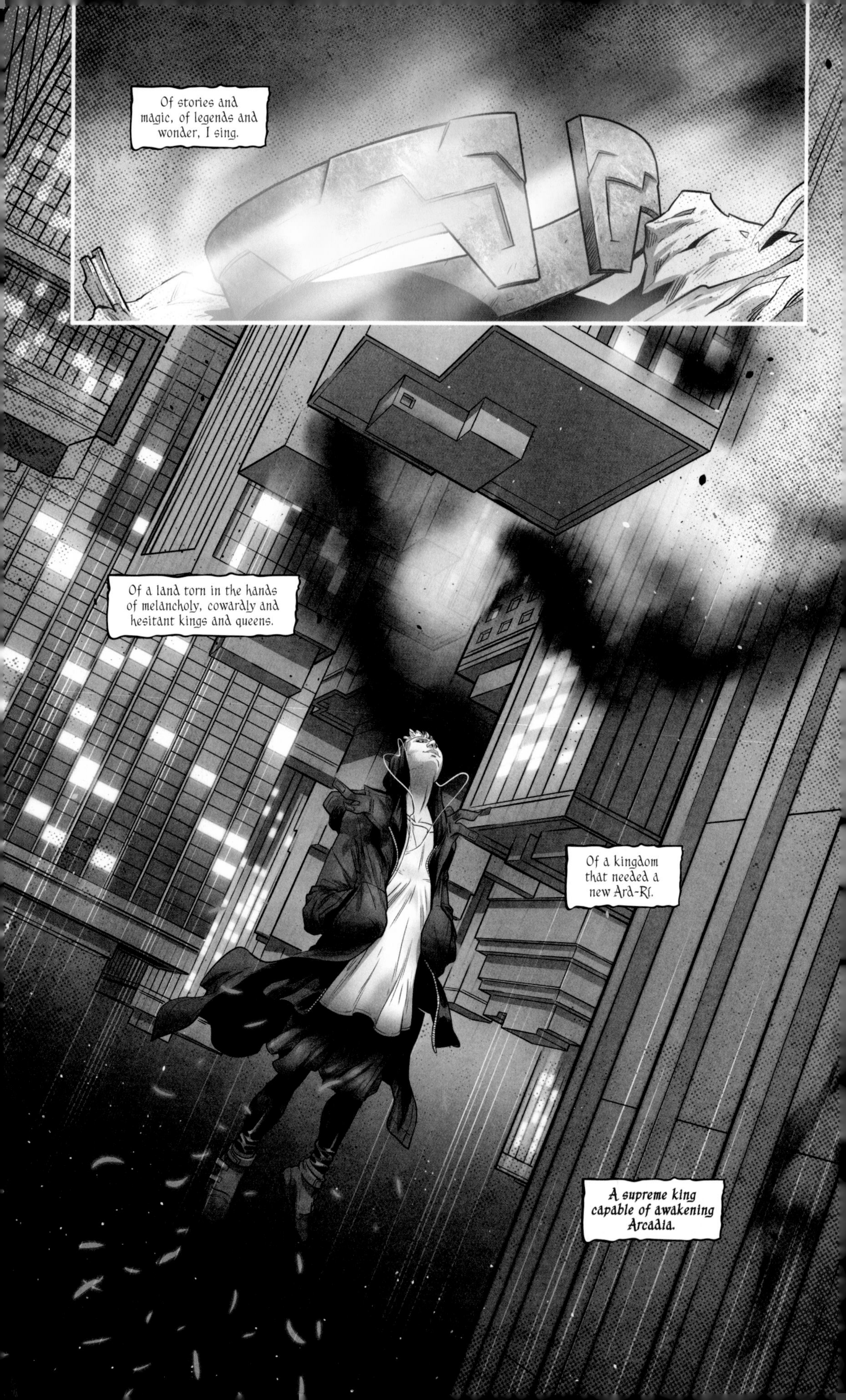
Of stories and magic, of legends and wonder, I sing.
Of a land torn in the hands of melancholy, cowardly and hesitant kings and queens.
Of a kingdom that needed a new Ard-Rí.
A supreme king capable of awakening Arcadia.

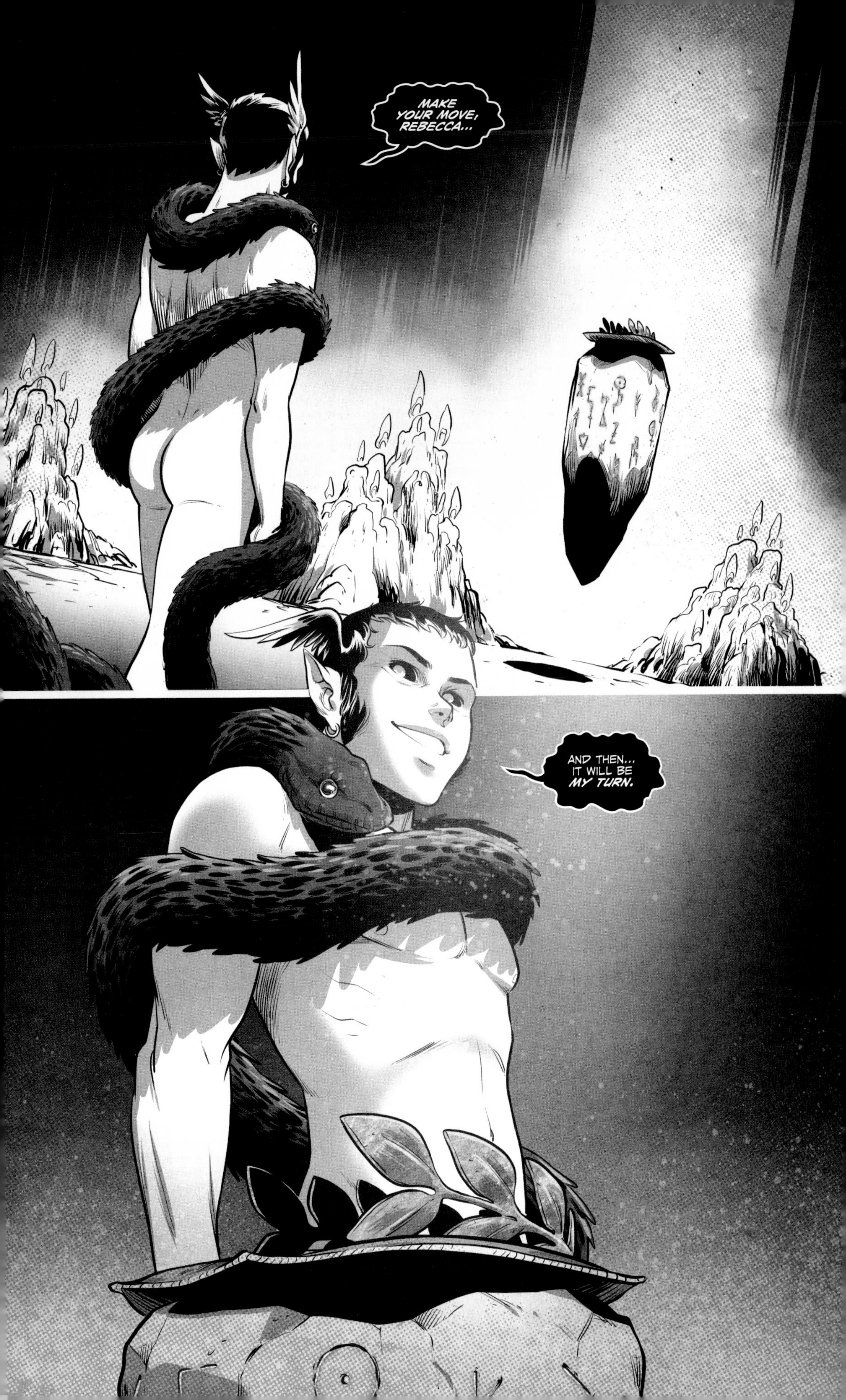
MAKE YOUR MOVE, REBECCA...
AND THEN... IT WILL BE MY TURN.

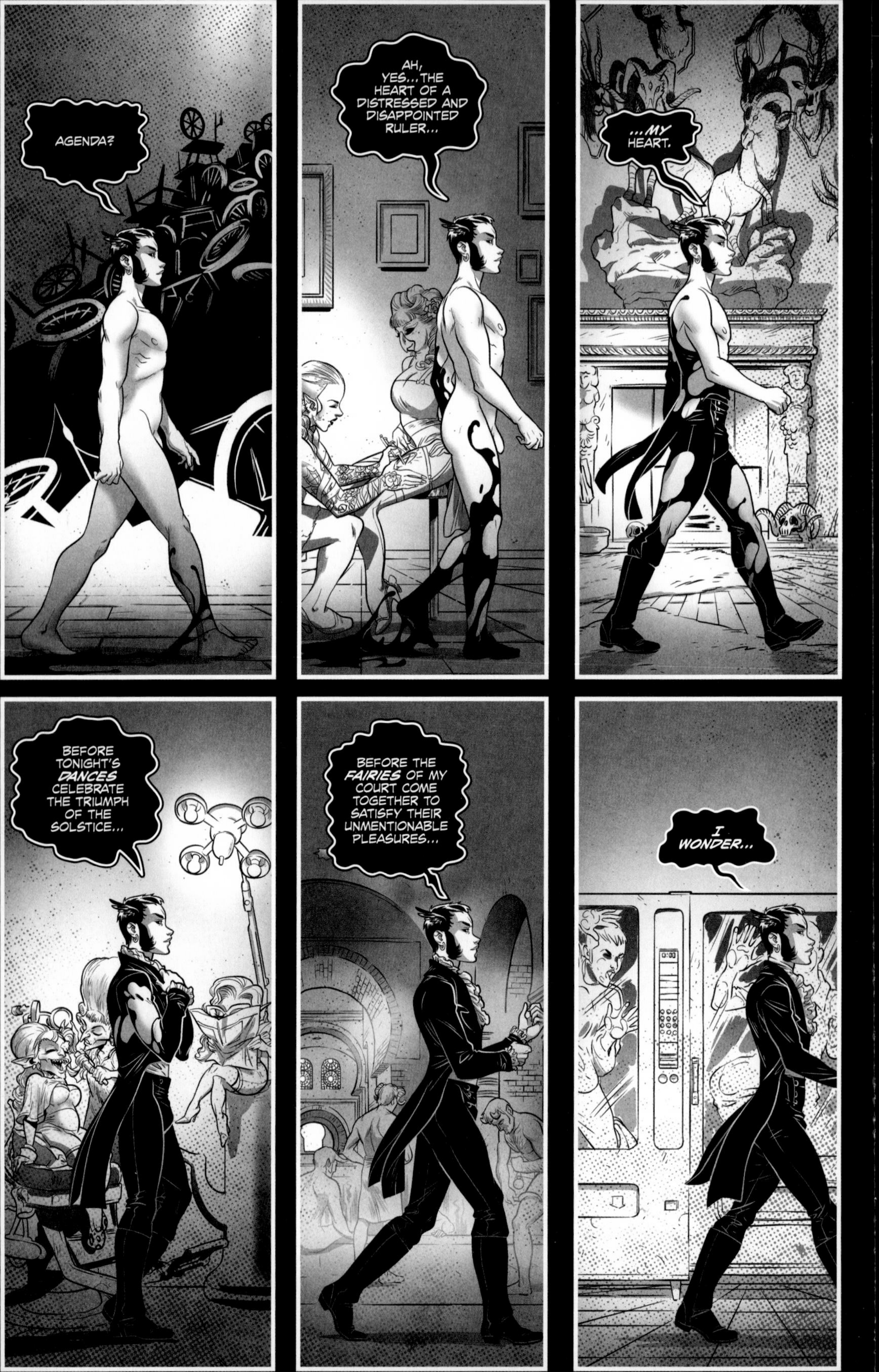
AGENDA?
AH, YES... THE HEART OF A DISTRESSED AND DISAPPOINTED RULER...
...MY HEART.
BEFORE TONIGHT'S DANCES CELEBRATE THE TRIUMPH OF THE SOLSTICE...
BEFORE THE FAIRIES OF MY COURT COME TOGETHER TO SATISFY THEIR UNMENTIONABLE PLEASURES...
I WONDER...

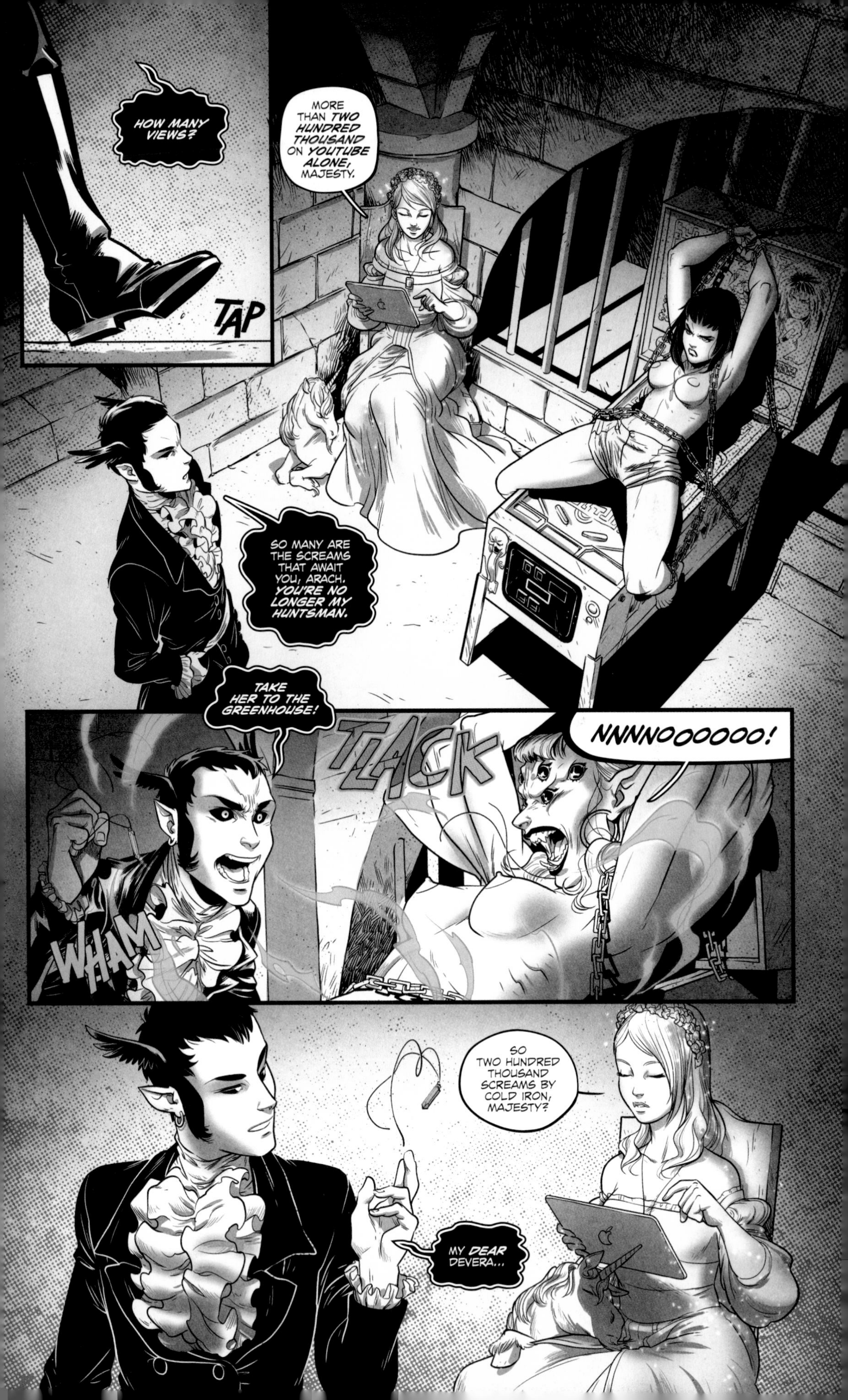

HOW MANY VIEWS?
TAP
MORE THAN TWO HUNDRED THOUSAND ON YOUTUBE ALONE, MAJESTY.
SO MANY ARE THE SCREAMS THAT AWAIT YOU, ARACH. YOU'RE NO LONGER MY HUNTSMAN.
TAKE HER TO THE GREENHOUSE!
TLACK
NNNNOOOOOO!
WHAM
SO TWO HUNDRED THOUSAND SCREAMS BY COLD IRON, MAJESTY?
MY DEAR DEVERA...

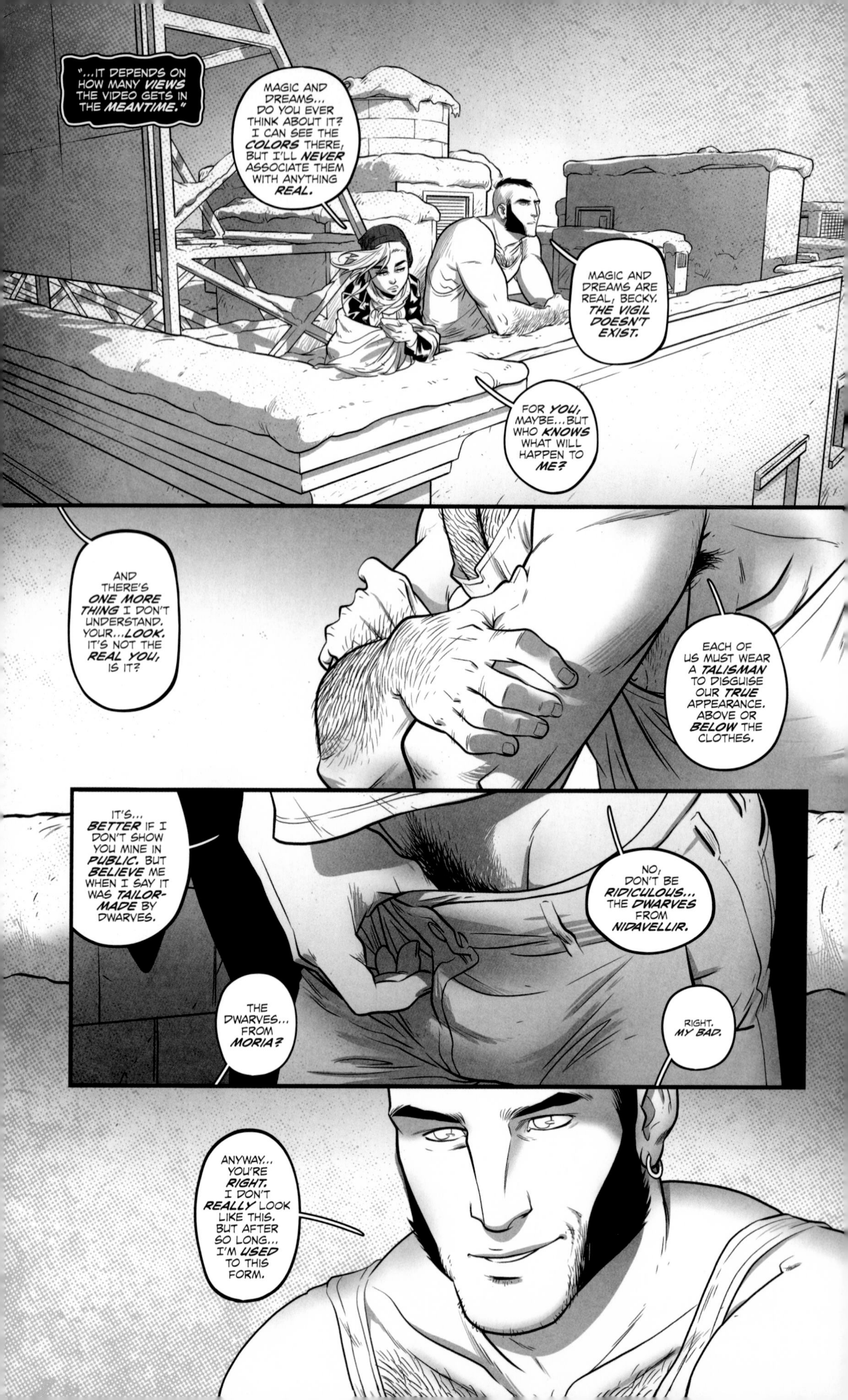
"...IT DEPENDS ON HOW MANY VIEWS THE VIDEO GETS IN THE MEANTIME."
MAGIC AND DREAMS... DO YOU EVER THINK ABOUT IT? I CAN SEE THE COLORS THERE, BUT I'LL NEVER ASSOCIATE THEM WITH ANYTHING REAL.
MAGIC AND DREAMS ARE REAL, BECKY. THE VIGIL DOESN'T EXIST.
FOR YOU, MAYBE...BUT WHO KNOWS WHAT WILL HAPPEN TO ME?
AND THERE'S ONE MORE THING I DON'T UNDERSTAND. YOUR...LOOK. IT'S NOT THE REAL YOU, IS IT?
EACH OF US MUST WEAR A TALISMAN TO DISGUISE OUR TRUE APPEARANCE. ABOVE OR BELOW THE CLOTHES.
IT'S... BETTER IF I DON'T SHOW YOU MINE IN PUBLIC. BUT BELIEVE ME WHEN I SAY IT WAS TAILOR-MADE BY DWARVES.
THE DWARVES... FROM MORIA?
NO, DON'T BE RIDICULOUS... THE DWARVES FROM NIDAVELLIR.
RIGHT. MY BAD.
ANYWAY... YOU'RE RIGHT. I DON'T REALLY LOOK LIKE THIS. BUT AFTER SO LONG... I'M USED TO THIS FORM.

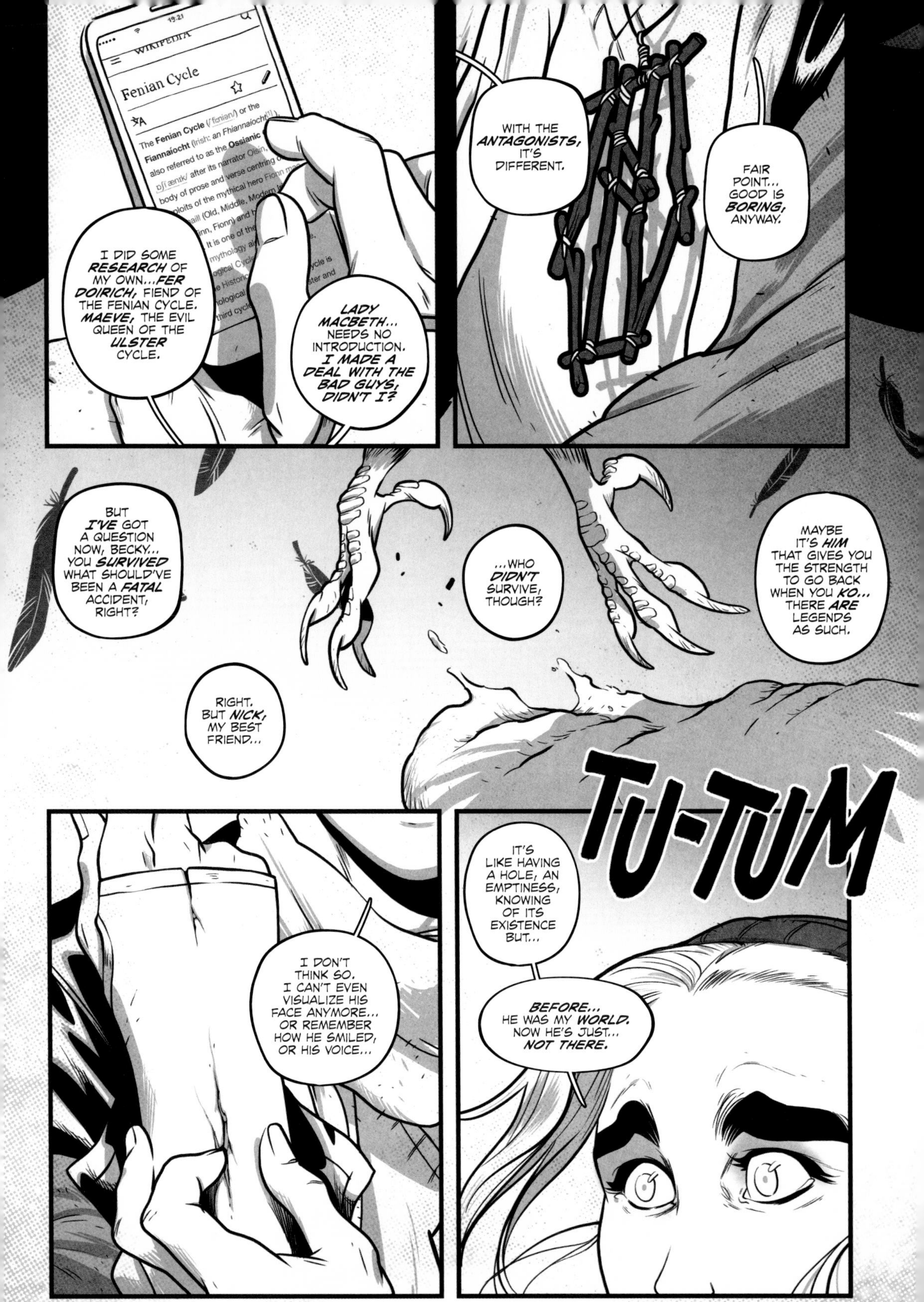
Fenian Cycle
I DID SOME RESEARCH OF MY OWN...FER DOIRICH, FIEND OF THE FENIAN CYCLE. MAEVE, THE EVIL QUEEN OF THE ULSTER CYCLE.
LADY MACBETH... NEEDS NO INTRODUCTION. I MADE A DEAL WITH THE BAD GUYS, DIDN'T I?
WITH THE ANTAGONISTS, IT'S DIFFERENT.
FAIR POINT... GOOD IS BORING, ANYWAY.
BUT I'VE GOT A QUESTION NOW, BECKY... YOU SURVIVED WHAT SHOULD'VE BEEN A FATAL ACCIDENT, RIGHT?
...WHO DIDN'T SURVIVE, THOUGH?
MAYBE IT'S HIM THAT GIVES YOU THE STRENGTH TO GO BACK WHEN YOU KO... THERE ARE LEGENDS AS SUCH.
RIGHT. BUT NICK, MY BEST FRIEND...
TU-TUM
I DON'T THINK SO. I CAN'T EVEN VISUALIZE HIS FACE ANYMORE... OR REMEMBER HOW HE SMILED, OR HIS VOICE...
IT'S LIKE HAVING A HOLE, AN EMPTINESS, KNOWING OF ITS EXISTENCE BUT...
BEFORE... HE WAS MY WORLD. NOW HE'S JUST... NOT THERE.

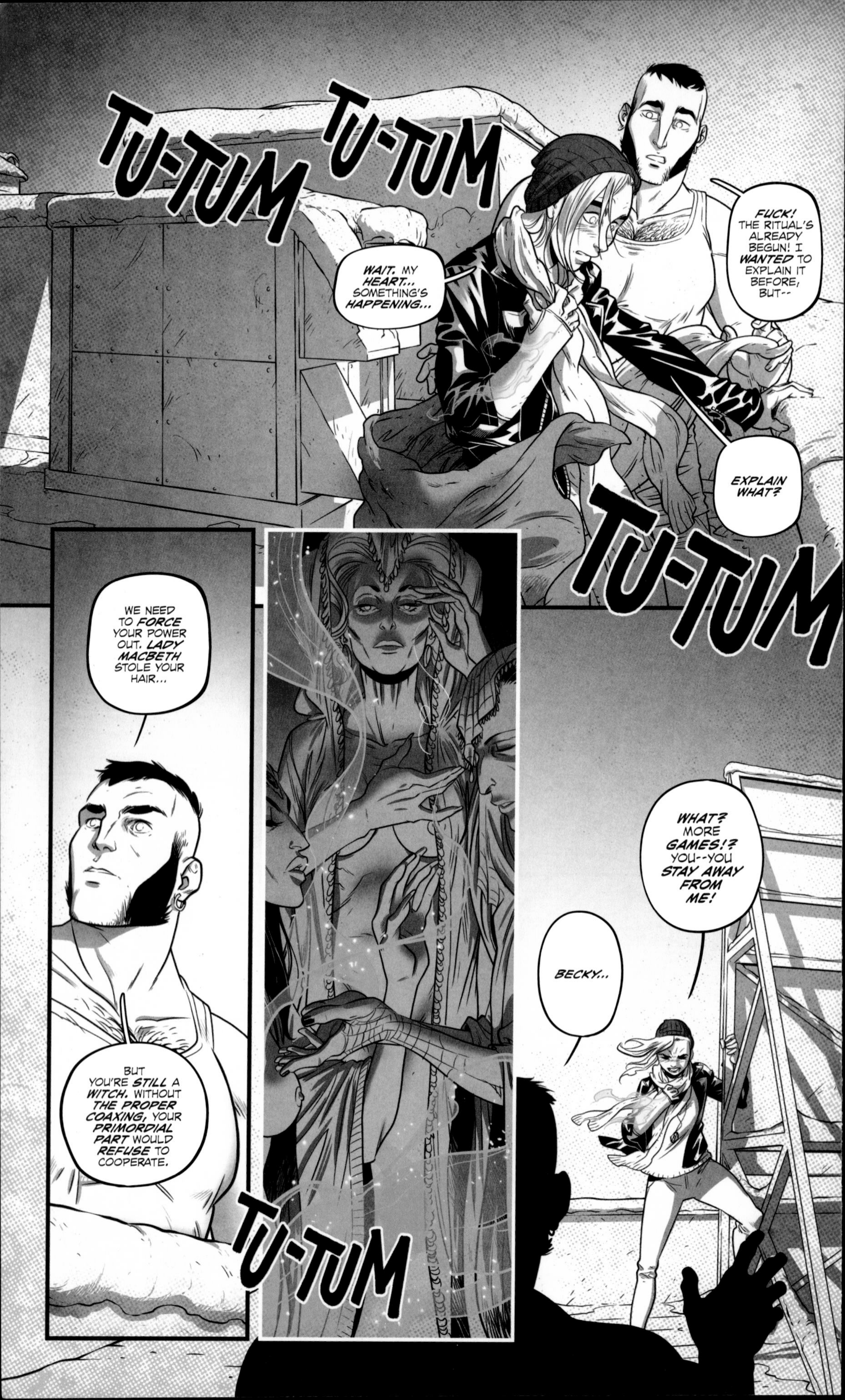
TU-TUM
TU-TUM
WAIT. MY HEART... SOMETHING'S HAPPENING...
FUCK! THE RITUAL'S ALREADY BEGUN! I WANTED TO EXPLAIN IT BEFORE, BUT--
EXPLAIN WHAT?
TU-TUM
WE NEED TO FORCE YOUR POWER OUT. LADY MACBETH STOLE YOUR HAIR...
BUT YOU'RE STILL A WITCH. WITHOUT THE PROPER COAXING, YOUR PRIMORDIAL PART WOULD REFUSE TO COOPERATE.
TU-TUM
WHAT? MORE GAMES!? YOU--YOU STAY AWAY FROM ME!
BECKY...

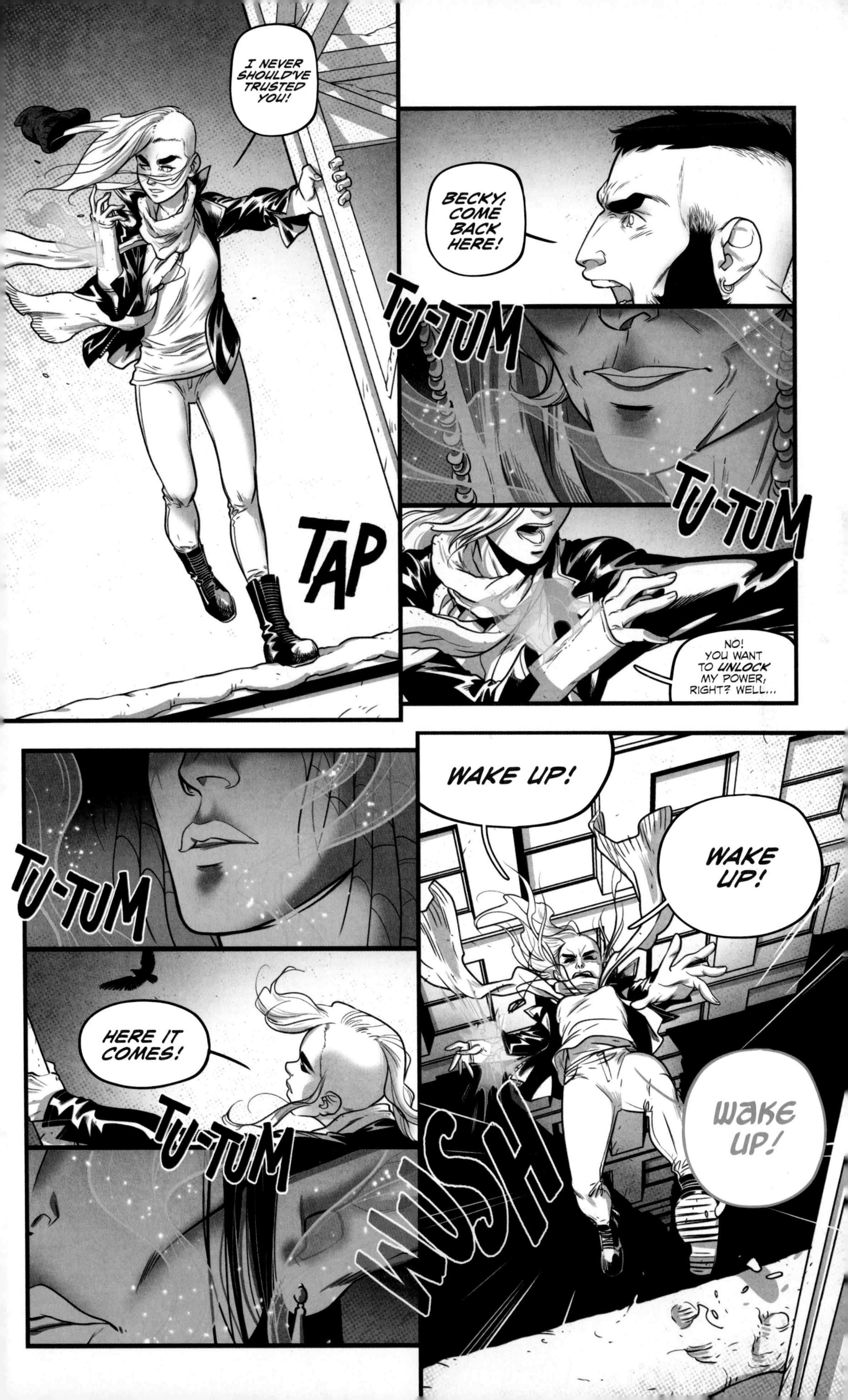
I NEVER SHOULD'VE TRUSTED YOU!
TAP
BECKY, COME BACK HERE!
TU-TUM
TU-TUM
NO! YOU WANT TO UNLOCK MY POWER, RIGHT? WELL...
TU-TUM
HERE IT COMES!
TU-TUM
WAKE UP!
WAKE UP!
WUSH
WAKE UP!

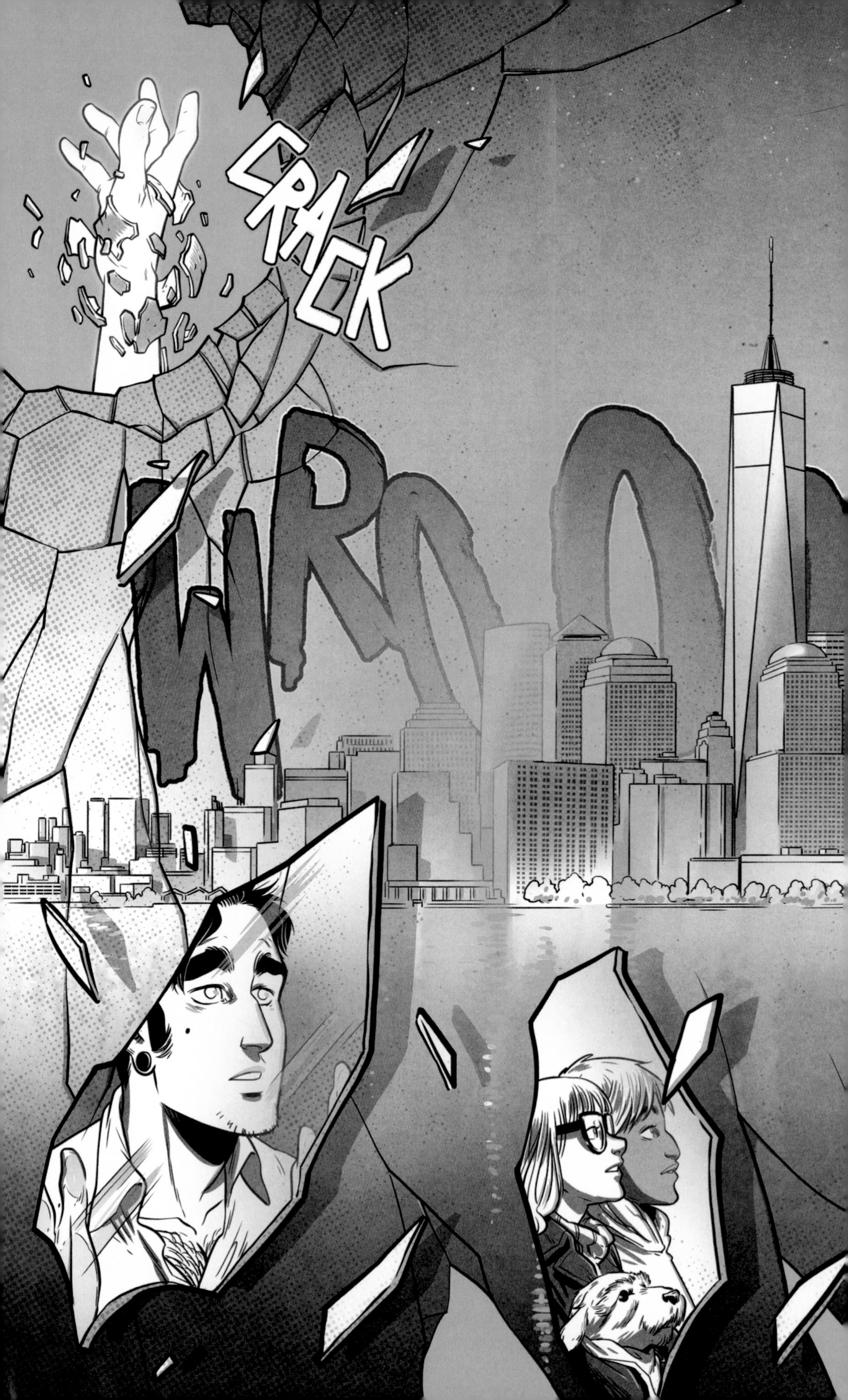
CRACK
WROO

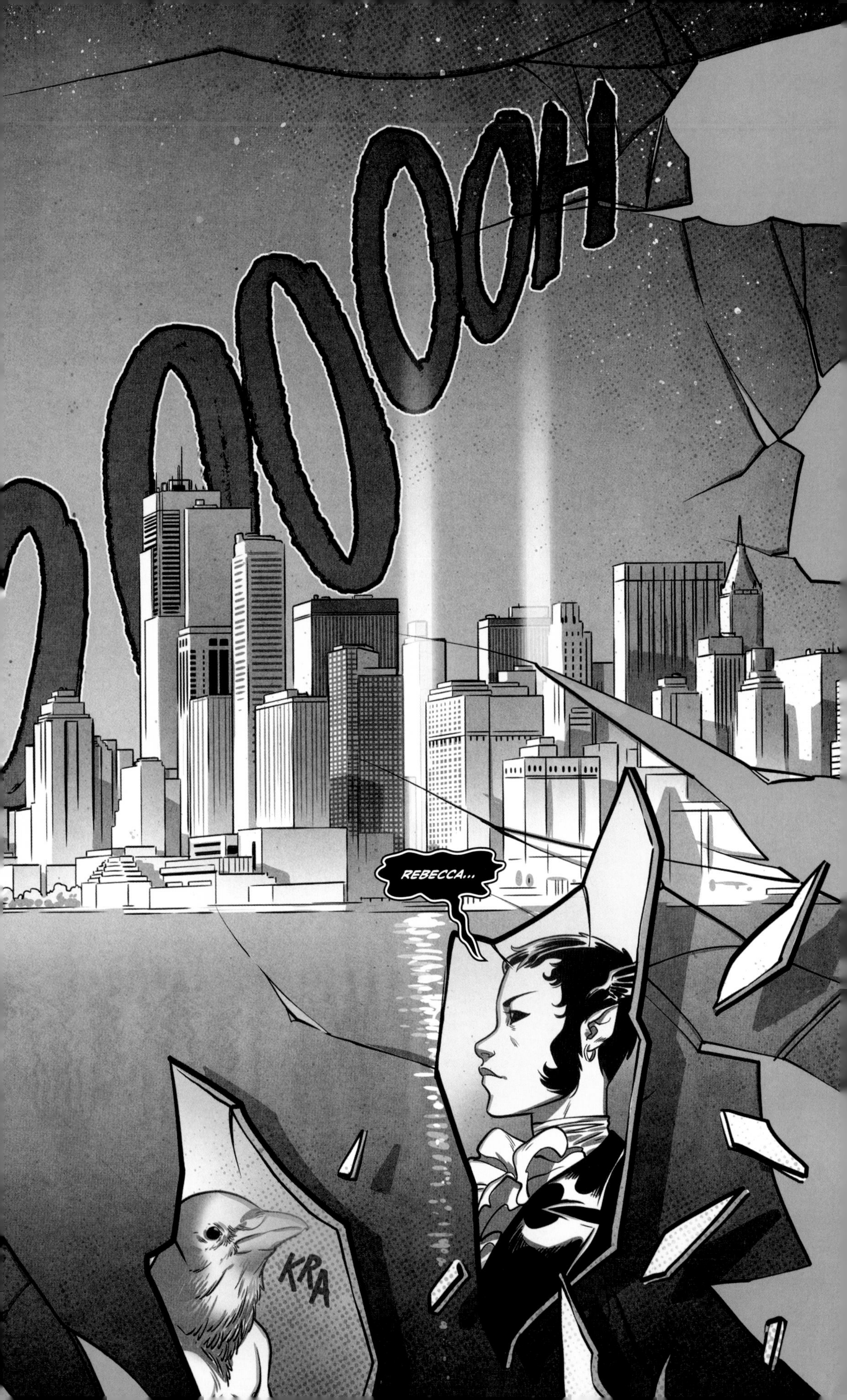
OOOOOOOH
REBECCA...
KRA

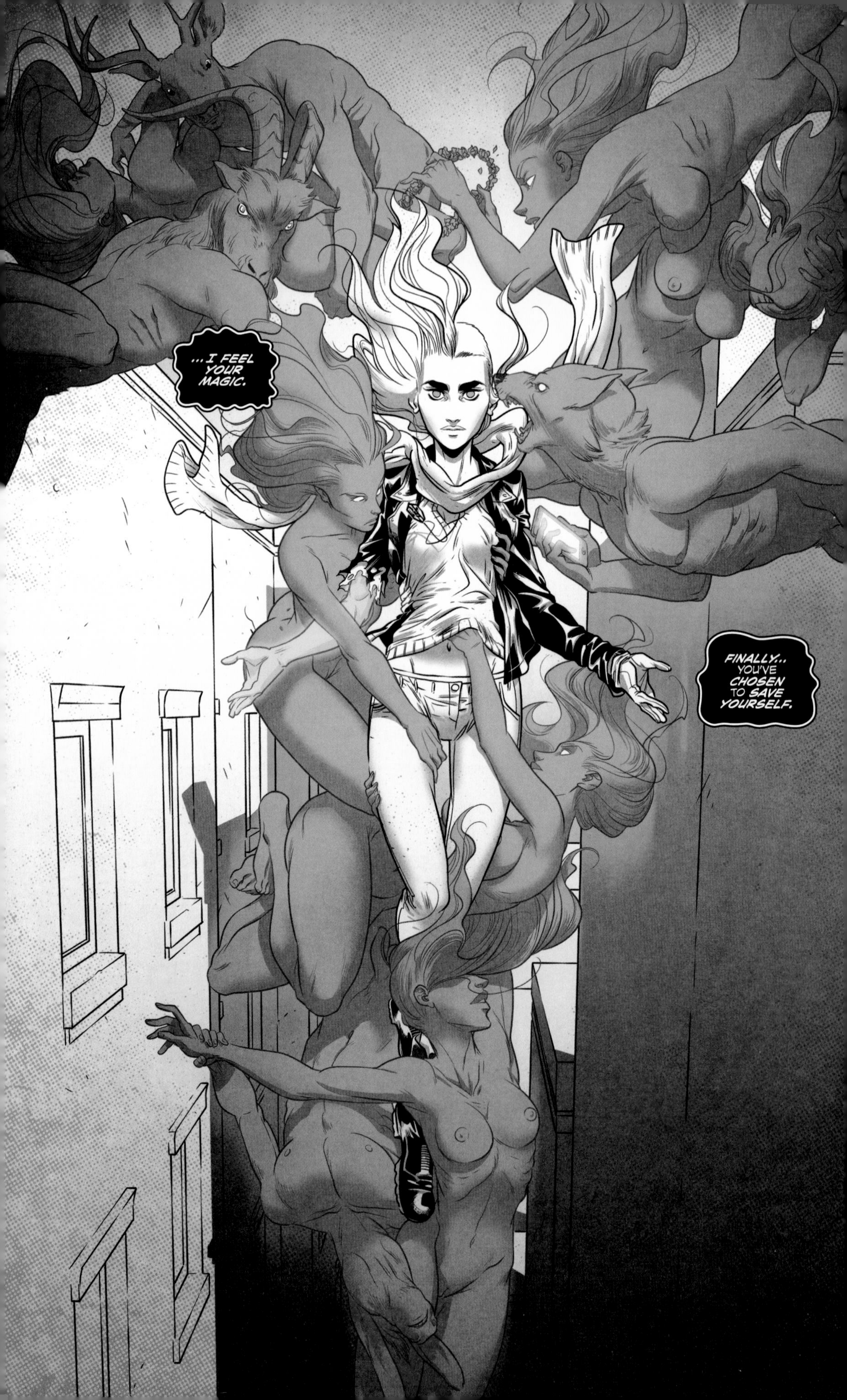
...I FEEL YOUR MAGIC.
FINALLY... YOU'VE CHOSEN TO SAVE YOURSELF.

WHAT IS THE SECRET?

or *How I learned to stop worrying by admitting that magic is real.*

An afterword by Marco B. Bucci

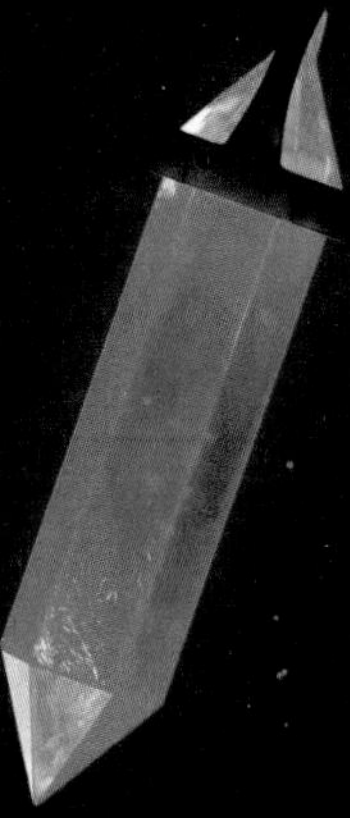

Magic is real. It's a phrase that I often repeat to myself, every day, in the most disparate moments. It helps me to overcome every obstacle, to turn around, to break it down into small parts. Magic is real, but it's also hidden and elusive, almost inaccessible. **Every gesture can become sacred, every word can invoke its strength, everything can become its symbol.** But to succeed we must overcome a veil of lies and mysteries, of illusions and ambiguity.

That's why I decided to write this story and that's why you've come to it. **Nomen Omen speaks of esoteric traditions, magical practices, supernatural creatures and how these affect the lives of those who practice Art.** And obviously it also speaks to the most devastating powers of Witches and Sorcerers, that of giving a name to something or someone to have power and control over its destiny. It's scary, isn't it? The power I mean. I've always been terrified by it. It was the part that frightened me the most in my journey. To have control over me and therefore also over the reality that surrounds me.

Becky is a bit like the daughter I wanted to protect from the truth. I wanted to tell a story of sentimental intrigues, of adventure, and perhaps also of love, why not? But reality is different from how it is represented. Becky is a special girl, it's true, but she will have to face trials much bigger than her. I wanted to keep the horror, loss and grief away from her. All the death that from the beginning fills the pages of *Nomen Omen*. But I can't. **Narrators are so unique in story, and wield such power. We are like mediums engaged in seances that never end.** Intermediaries between the world of the reader and the listener and the dreamy reality of all that has not yet been told.

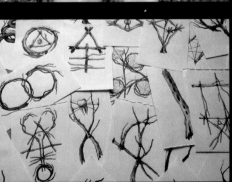

This will be a cruel story, as you might have noticed already. Everyone is in danger, even when it doesn't seem so, because all the magic has an unexpected price. That's how it works.

but we can't take a step backwards for that. **After all, Becky is the only girl I know to have three mothers.** One that carried her in her belly for a long time, one that gave her to the light and another that was always close to her. It's not surprising that this is the case. Myth is studded with peculiar births. Is it not true that Zeus carried out the gestation of Dionysus within his thigh? Not to mention that he had recently given birth to Athena from his head, thanks to a blow from Hephaestus' two-headed axe. **Special families have always existed and it's often from those that the greatest heroes come.**

Of course, it's strange to think that a nerdy girl who has an internship at Google and keeps a visual diary of her dreams on Instagram can become a real hero. This may not be her role. Certainly not the one she chose! But here it's no longer a question of what I want or what she wants.

This series is a group ritual. Every time you turn its pages, each chapter you patiently collect brings you closer to the very meaning of Magic. The real one that changed my life. That's why I welcome you here in this space beyond **The Secret.** Just a few warnings before moving on to other pressing matters. Never abandon the path, beware of what is too good to be true and never leave my hand after the sun has set.

But above all, please, pay attention to the Names. To give them, to accept them, to repeat them. Your life is at stake.

OTHER PRESSING MATTERS

If you've read the book already (and if you're reading this my best guess is you have) you understand, or you are beginning to understand, what the point of the situation is. **Supernatural creatures that instead of profile pictures on social networks wear a crystal that modifies their appearance in the human world.** It's not just illusions but a concrete presence. Their interaction with places, things or other living beings is conditioned by this avatar. The parallelism with the online world is obvious but in reality it has a much more rooted origin in my personal history.

Maybe one day I will tell you about the fact that as a child I could see things that should

not be seen. I didn't talk about it with my peers, on the contrary, I was ashamed of it. **It's in this separation between secrets and revelations, unmentionable truths and potential lies, that the supernatural world moves.** Masks, avatars, profiles, illusions, identity. Here's what the walls of the labyrinth are made of, a maze which keeps the presence of non-human creatures hidden within an apparently conquered, explained and solved world.

Those who are not human know that everything begins with names. **To define something means to know it. That's why legends exist. To pass on a truth that can only be told through a fantasy patina.** And that's why in *Nomen Omen* you'll find so many strange names. Some are just what remains of the original names, others are joined together, others are anagrams or simply crippled by magic. This is how you protect yourself from something, or how you control it. When I found myself describing the Wild Hunt of King Taranis I first found the supernatural creatures that hide behind illusions, then I had to change their names and finally imagine their avatars. It may seem strange but every part of *Nomen Omen* follows a specific ritual.

If you were a creature of thousands of years, who would you look like? What age would you be? Would you wear clothes that are fashionable or similar to those in the country where your legend has spread? Would you choose a face from a billboard or an old photo found in the attic of a stranger? Would you look like someone very famous or would you rather prefer completely anonymous features? **The answers to these questions are in my Hunters.** They are as dangerous as they are complex. Fruit of the game of names, of the great dance of identities. All liars in an urban and mortal reality that barely exists for them. Almost like a dream, or something abstract. Profiles that float on the net. **Just like us.**

THIS IS PERSONAL

I grew up in Italy in the 80s, being a few years younger than the kids on *Stranger Things*. A nerd without other nerds nearby. I was a strange child with red hair who didn't play football and rest assured not playing soccer in Italy in the 80s was definitely strange.

There was no Secret for me as I was born in the Vigil... **but I kept a very special one.** In fact, I never talked about the creatures that surrounded me when I was alone in the garden. I didn't pronounced their names, I didn't tell their stories and above all I didn't list the rules I had to follow to be able to see them. **I was strange, but not so strange as to reveal to everyone that I could see the fairies.** Indeed, I don't think I've ever done it publicly, not like I'm doing it now on these pages. I've seen them for years and I still can't explain those first questions related to mystery and magic. I still remember when I heard a classmate speak about ghosts. He had seen one inside an abandoned house and he told that to me. I didn't believe him, because *admitting* I believed him seemed too foolish at that time. I could not tell him that I too had seen things I could not explain. I left him alone, wearing a ring of doubt that I knew oh so well. That'd be the doubts that comes from the fear of being wrong, of having misinterpreted the world or of being a liar despite everything. It was terribly cruel, if not unjust. **I was afraid of being like him: one who is not believed.**

Fortunately, in my family we relied, more or less consciously, on witchcraft. This was decisive for the child who did not play soccer. At least I could try talking to someone about what I saw in the garden. Of course, confessing everything to an old aunt was not like talking about it with the best friend or the neighbor of my same age. Still it was very important. **Thanks to that little corner of "truth" I never felt really wrong, not entirely anyway.**

The oldest women in my family never used the word "magic". The word was considered an inconvenient bearer of bad luck. So we used to call it many different things in order to avoid of being heard by those "things" that carry small and big misfortunes or follow you in dreams. Grandmothers and Aunts did not use certain names especially in front of me, because I was a sleepwalker, and it was even more dangerous. **Knowing that anything could exist, even things generally considered impossible, helped me accept any kind of person.** Becky is an awful lot like me in this regard.

She read everything and played with everything and part of her firmly believes that there is something true in the stories created by imagination. She's passionate about fantasy novels, comics and video games. She plays role playing games, shares her passion for MMOs with her friends and has been a cosplayer at nerd events several times. For her, the revelation of a supernatural world is nothing but a confirmation. **An answer to a question that she never dared to ask.**

Her story could be mine or yours, it doesn't matter. We'll all need answers, sooner or later like the ones Fer, Lady Macbeth and Maeve gave to her. Little nuggets of truth that help us understand, and then tell to others, what magic really is.

nomen.omen

Becky's Auguries

Every time Becky dreams she finds a word waiting for her. She keeps a diary of her dreams on **Instagram** and she updates it as her life becomes more and more crazy and dangerous.

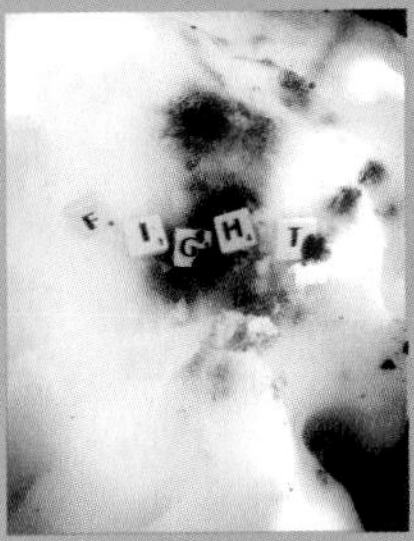
"Fight"

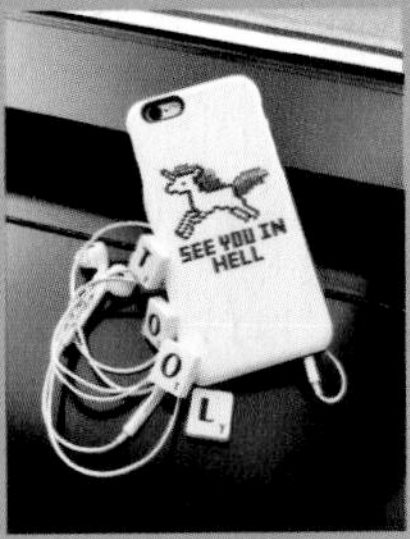
SEE YOU IN HELL
"Tool"

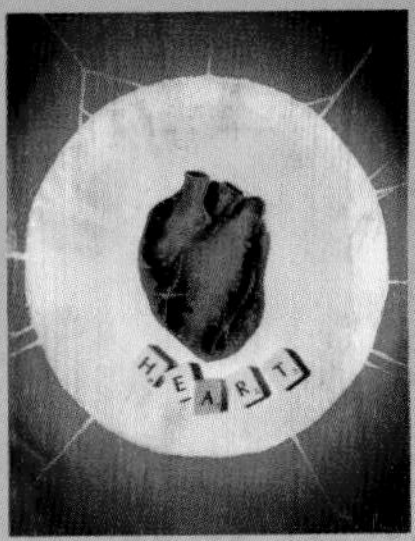
"Heart"

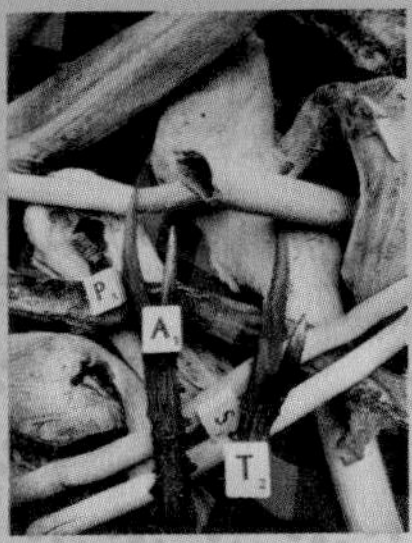
"Past"

Every dream could be a revelation about what the future holds for her!

COVER GALLERY

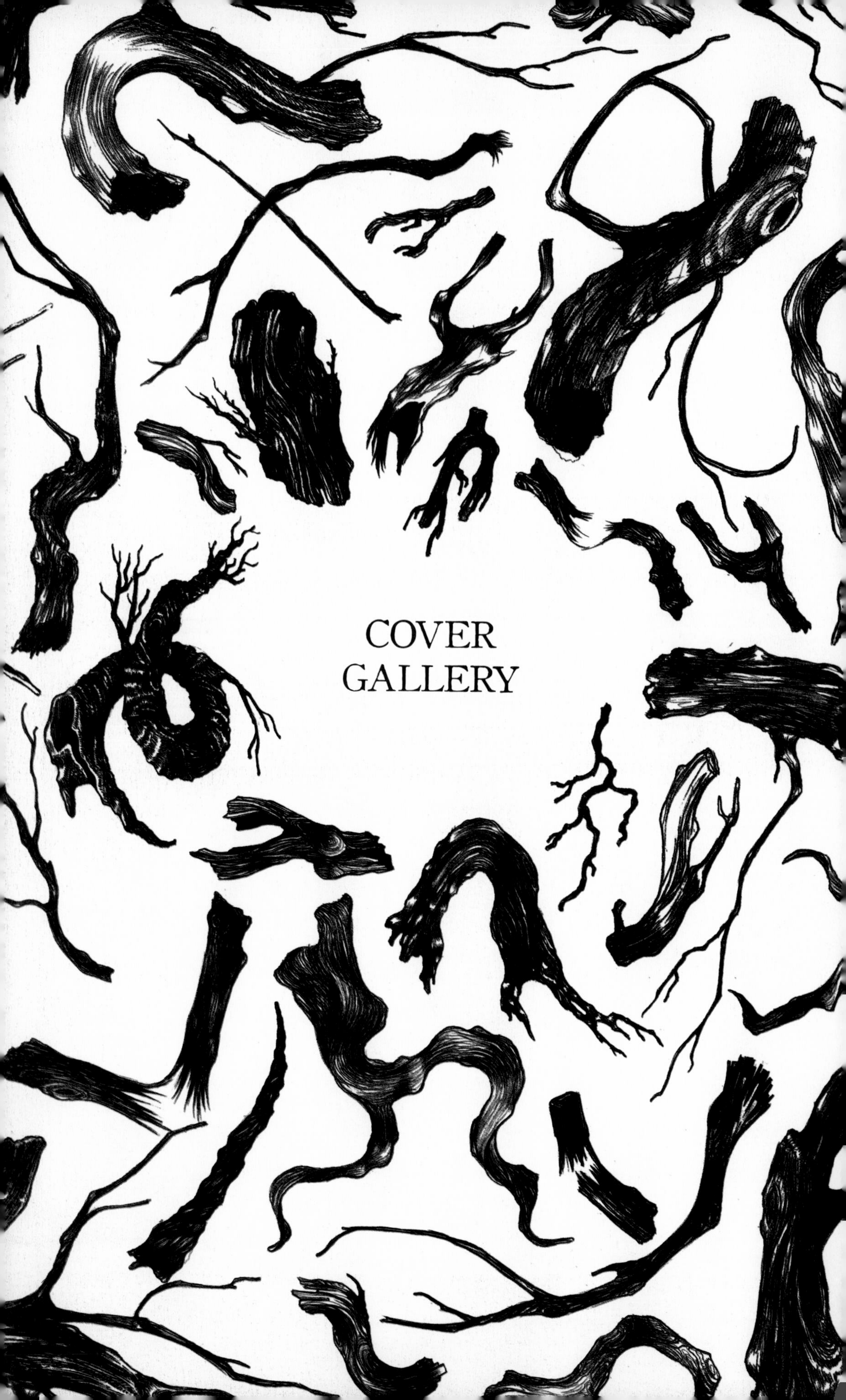

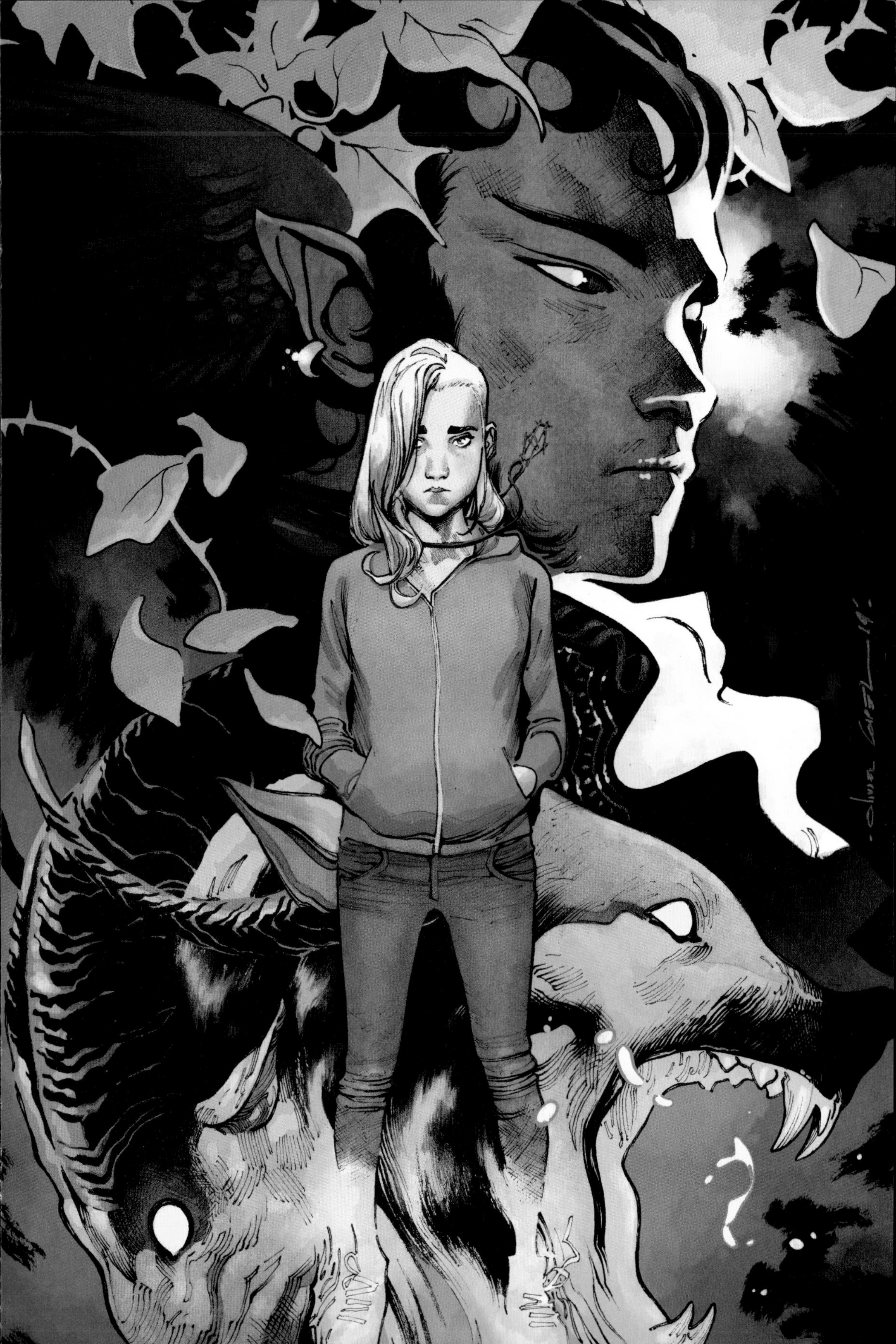

Issue 1 Variant by OLIVIER COIPEL
Colors by Dave Stewart

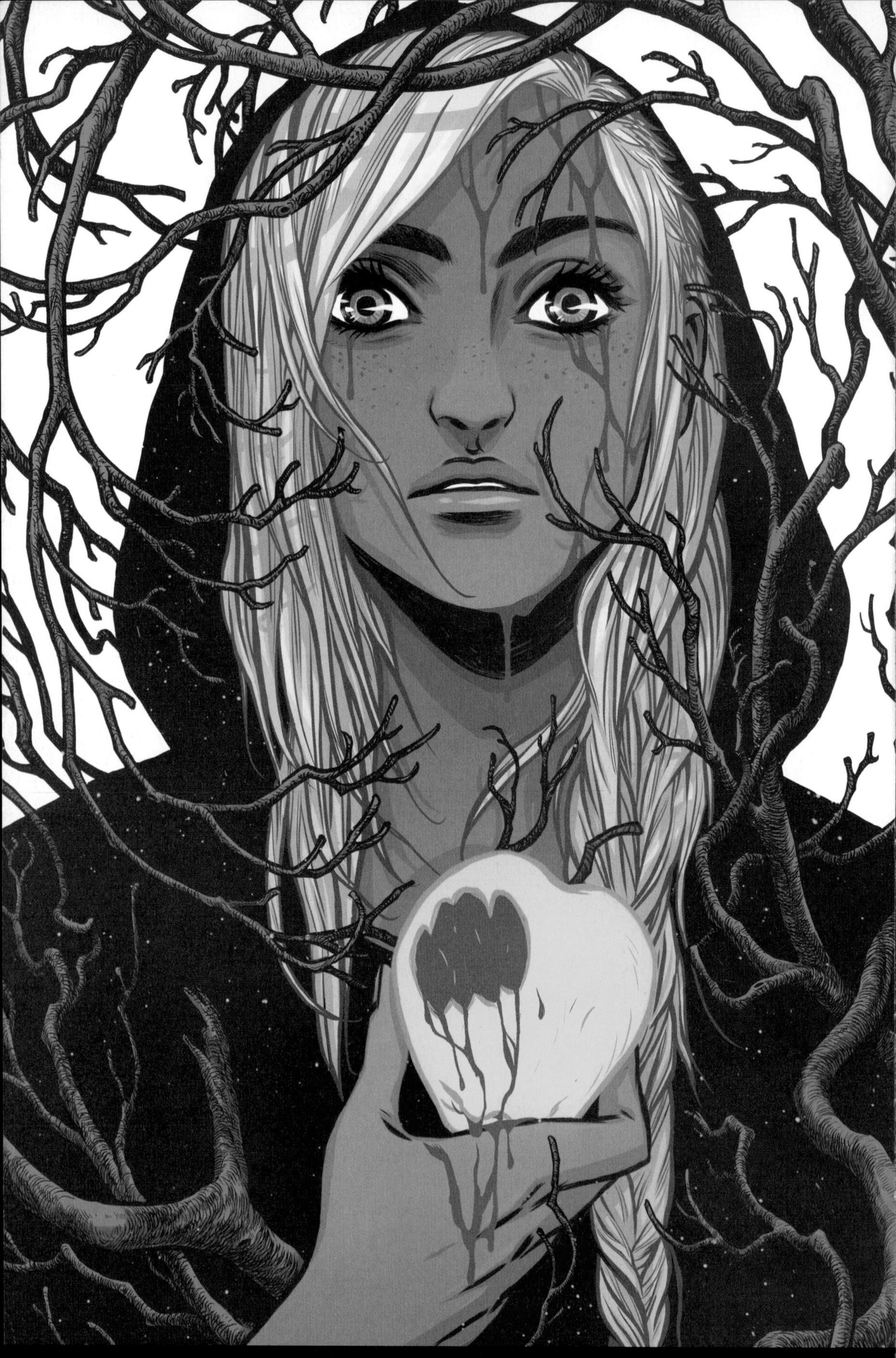

Issue 1 Variant by BECKY CLOONAN

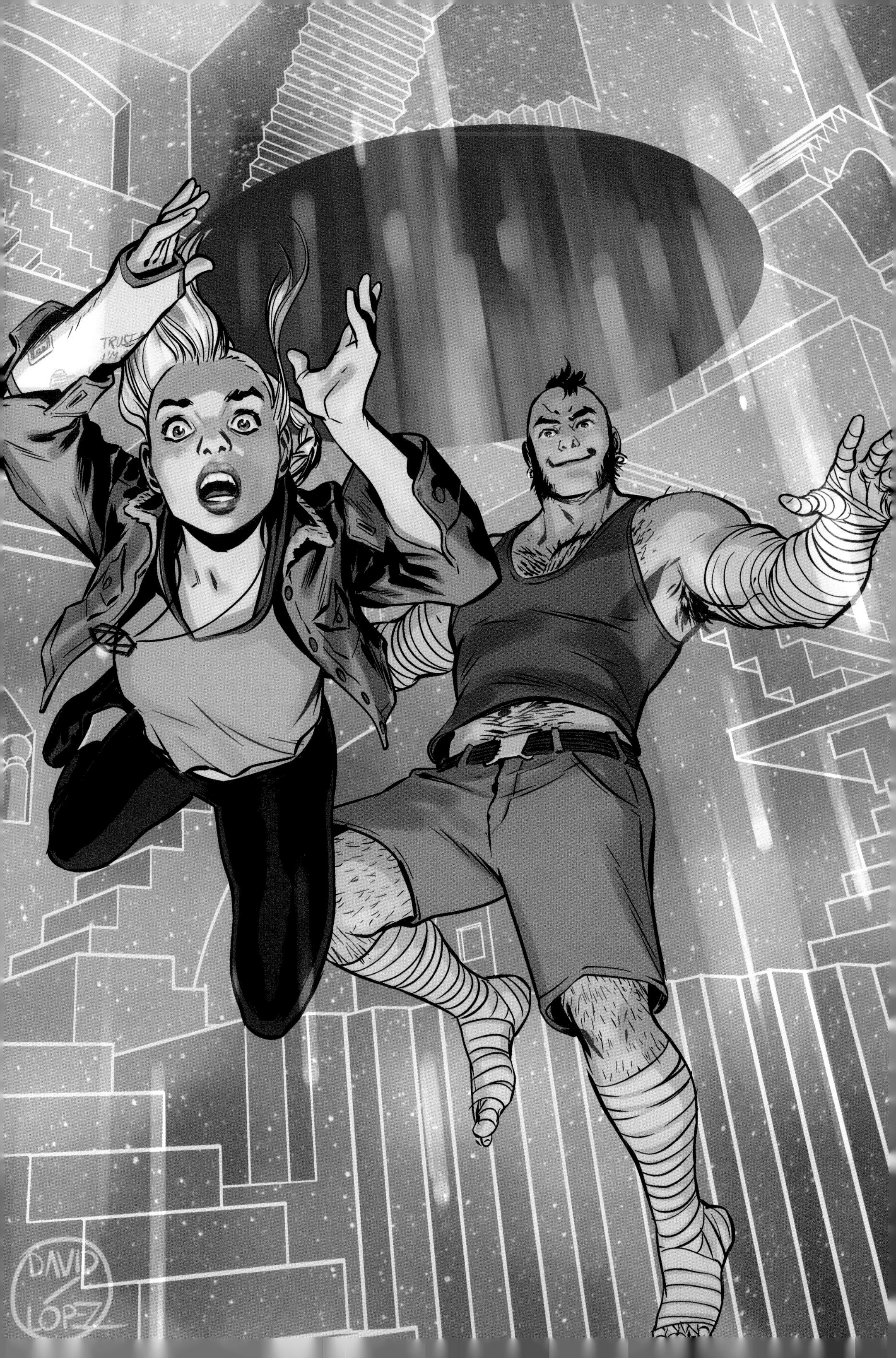
DAVID LOPEZ

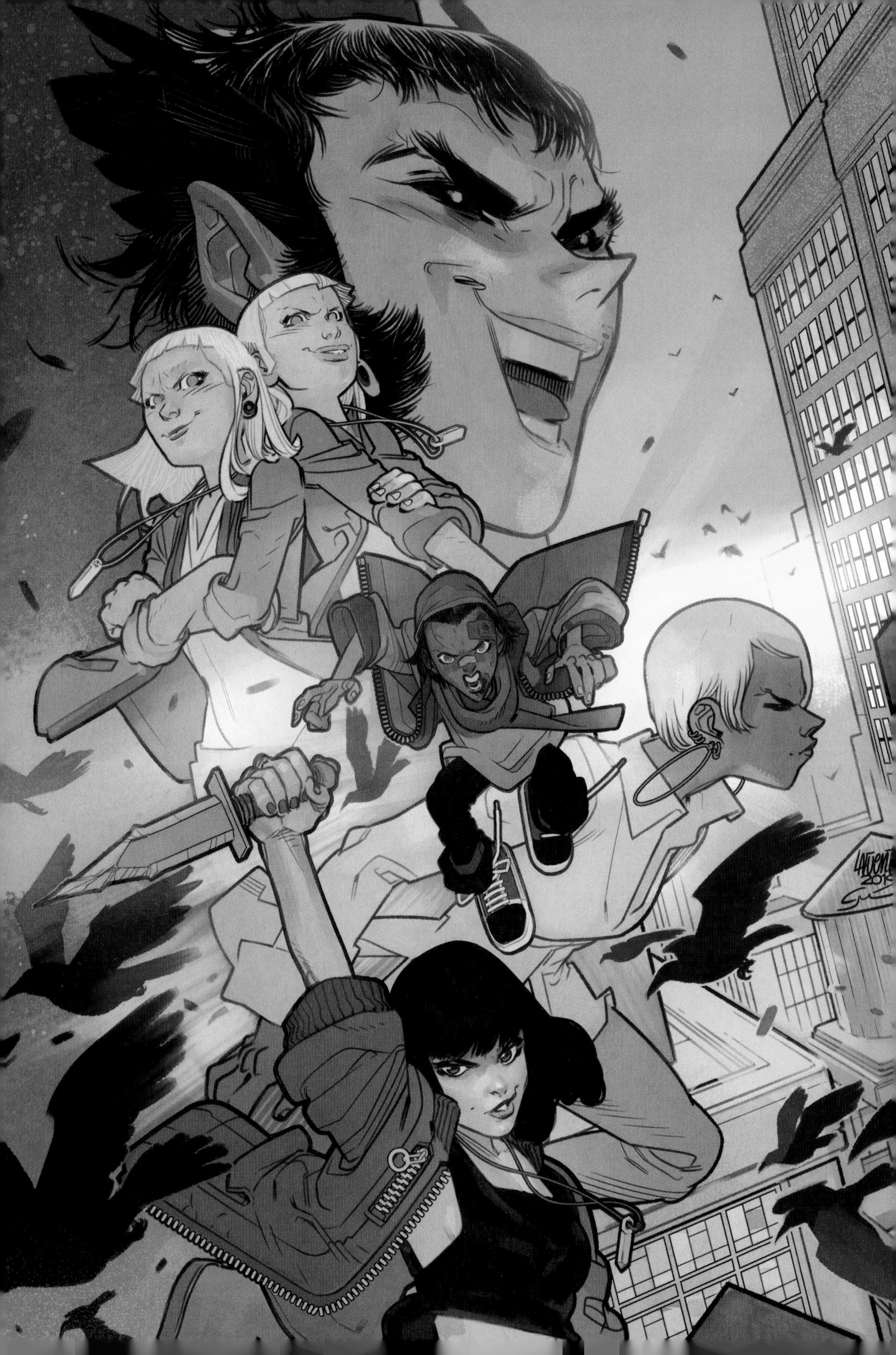

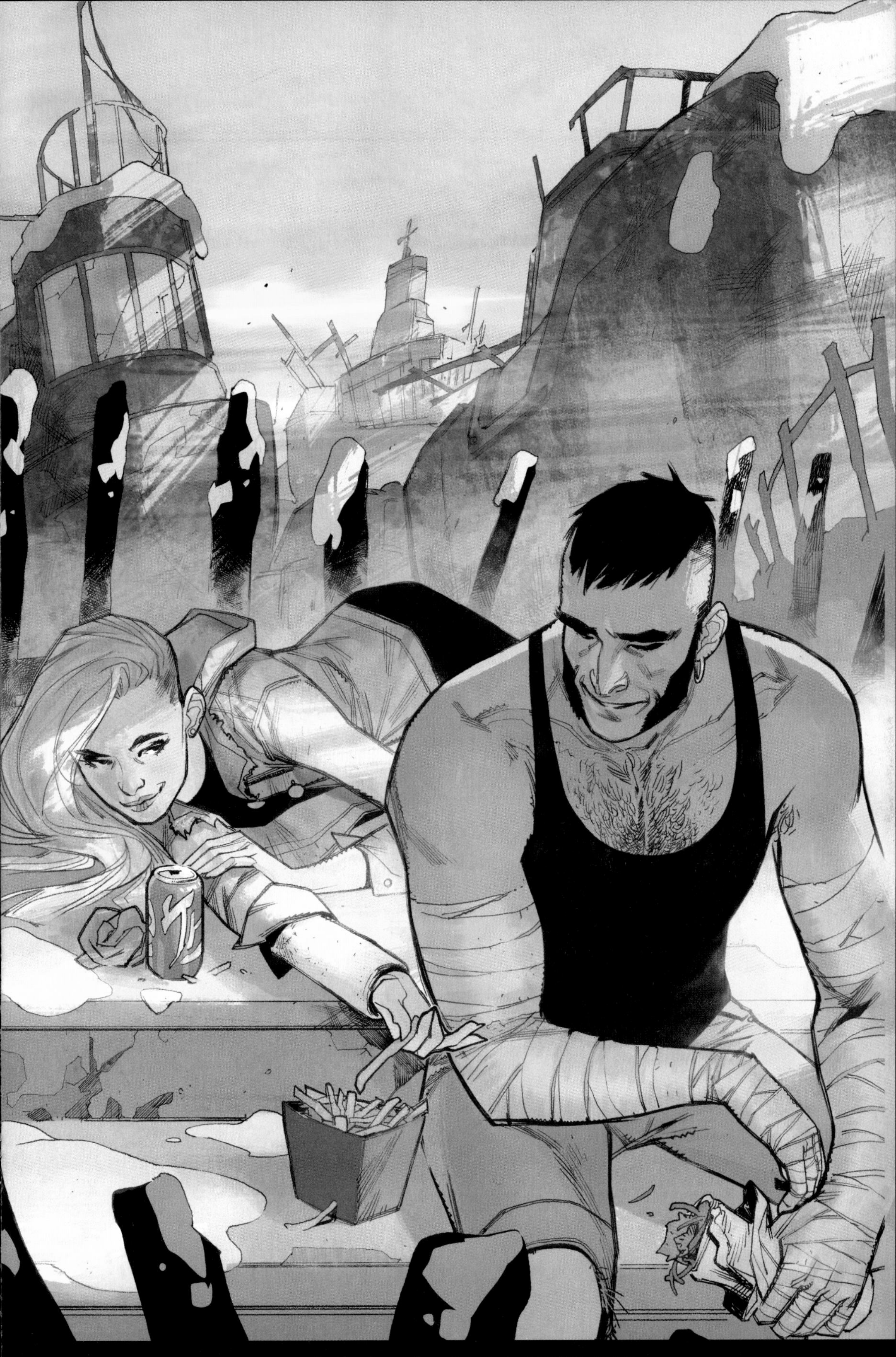

Issue 3 Variant by SARA PICHELLI
Colors by Giovanna Niro

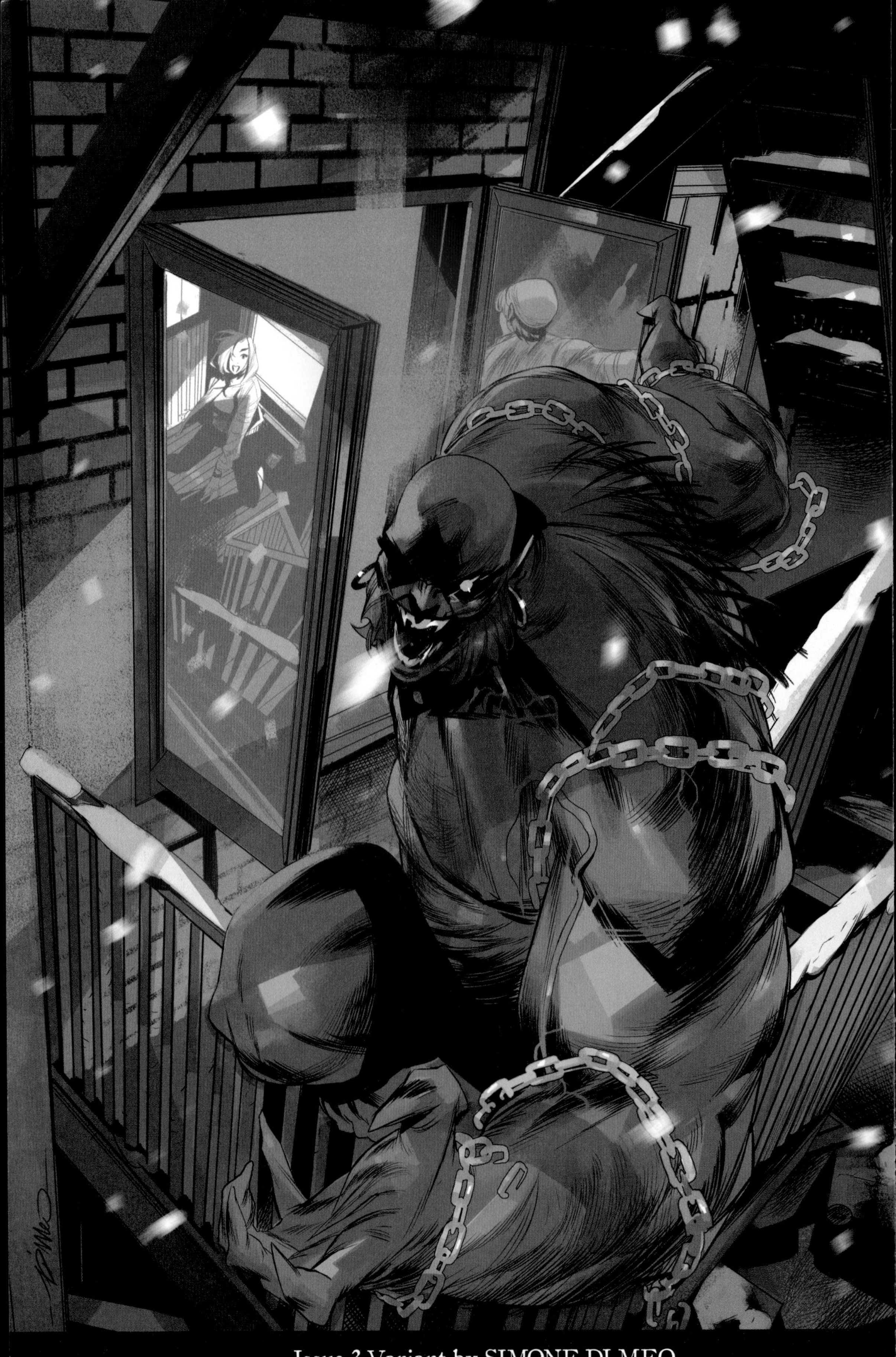

Issue 3 Variant by SIMONE DI MEO

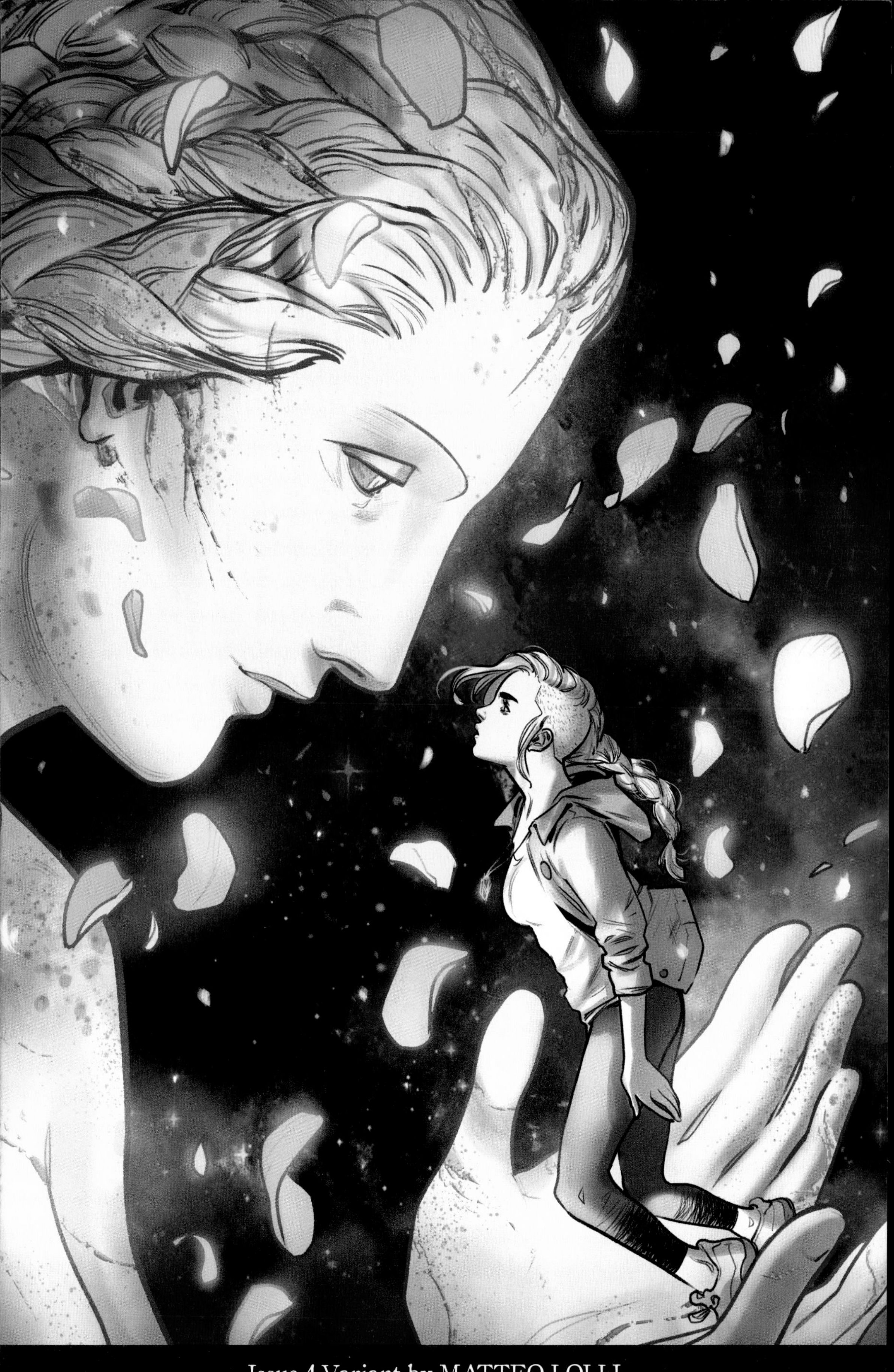

Issue 4 Variant by MATTEO LOLLI
Colors by Stefano Martinuz

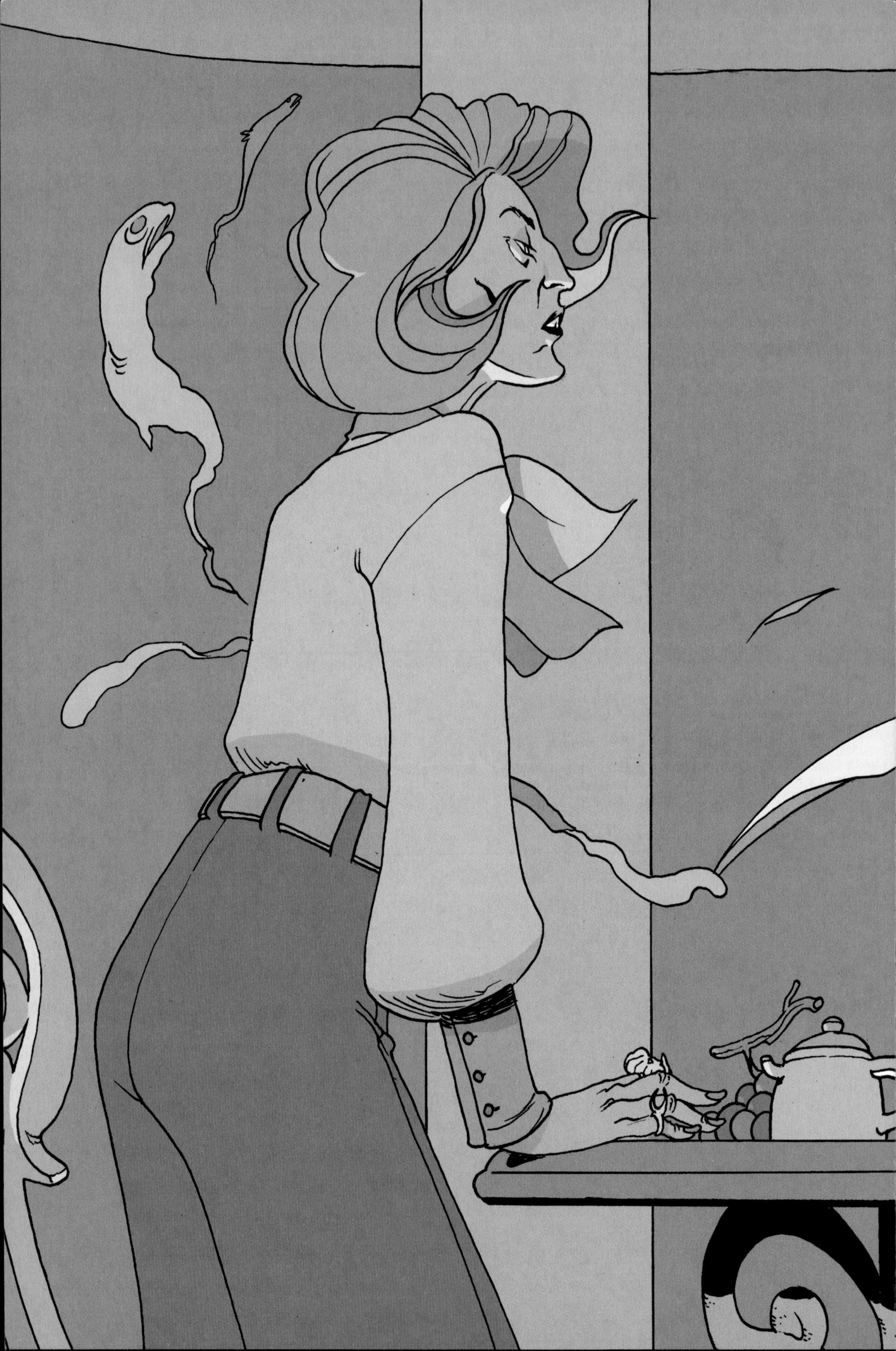

Issue 4 Variant by BRANDON GRAHAM

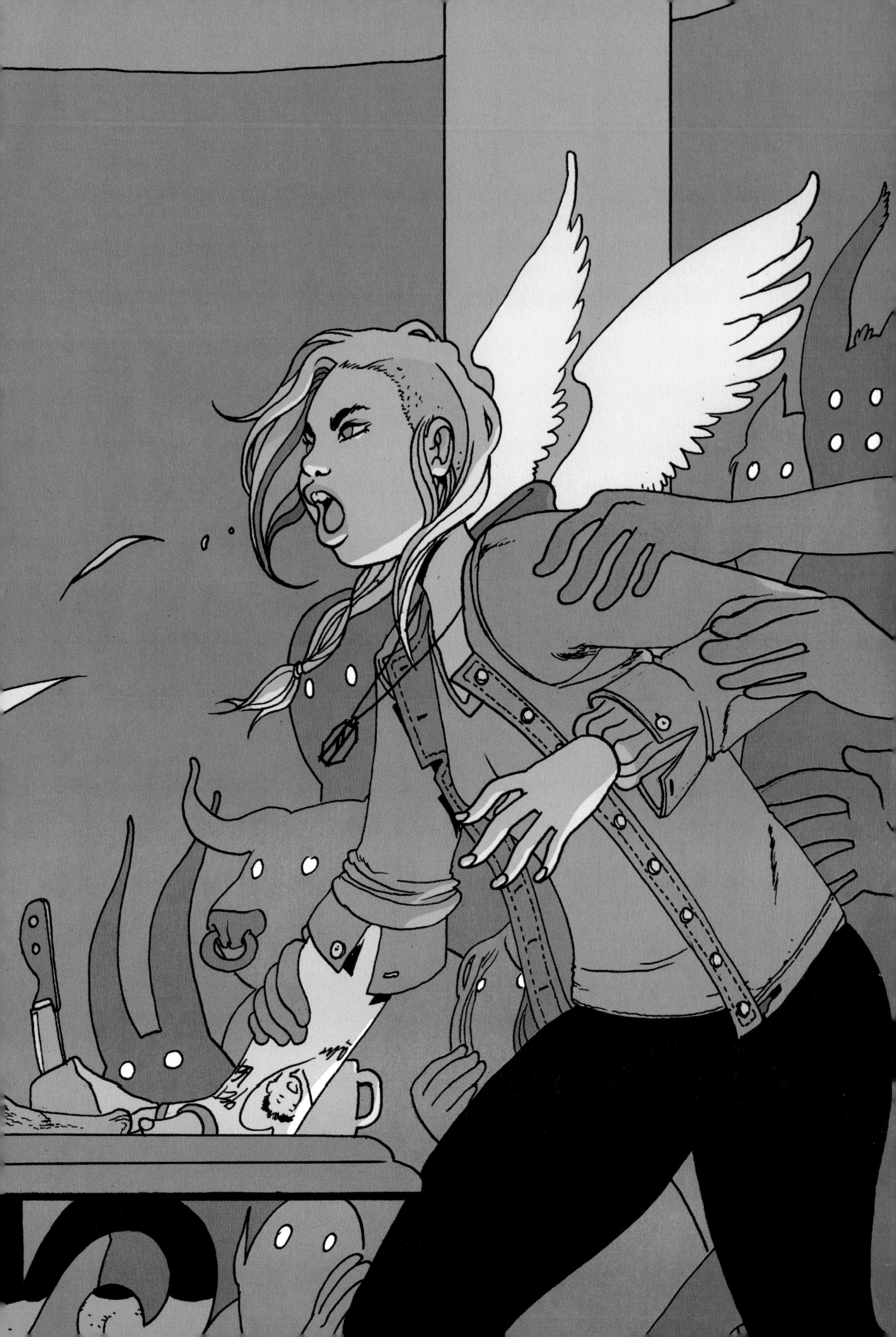

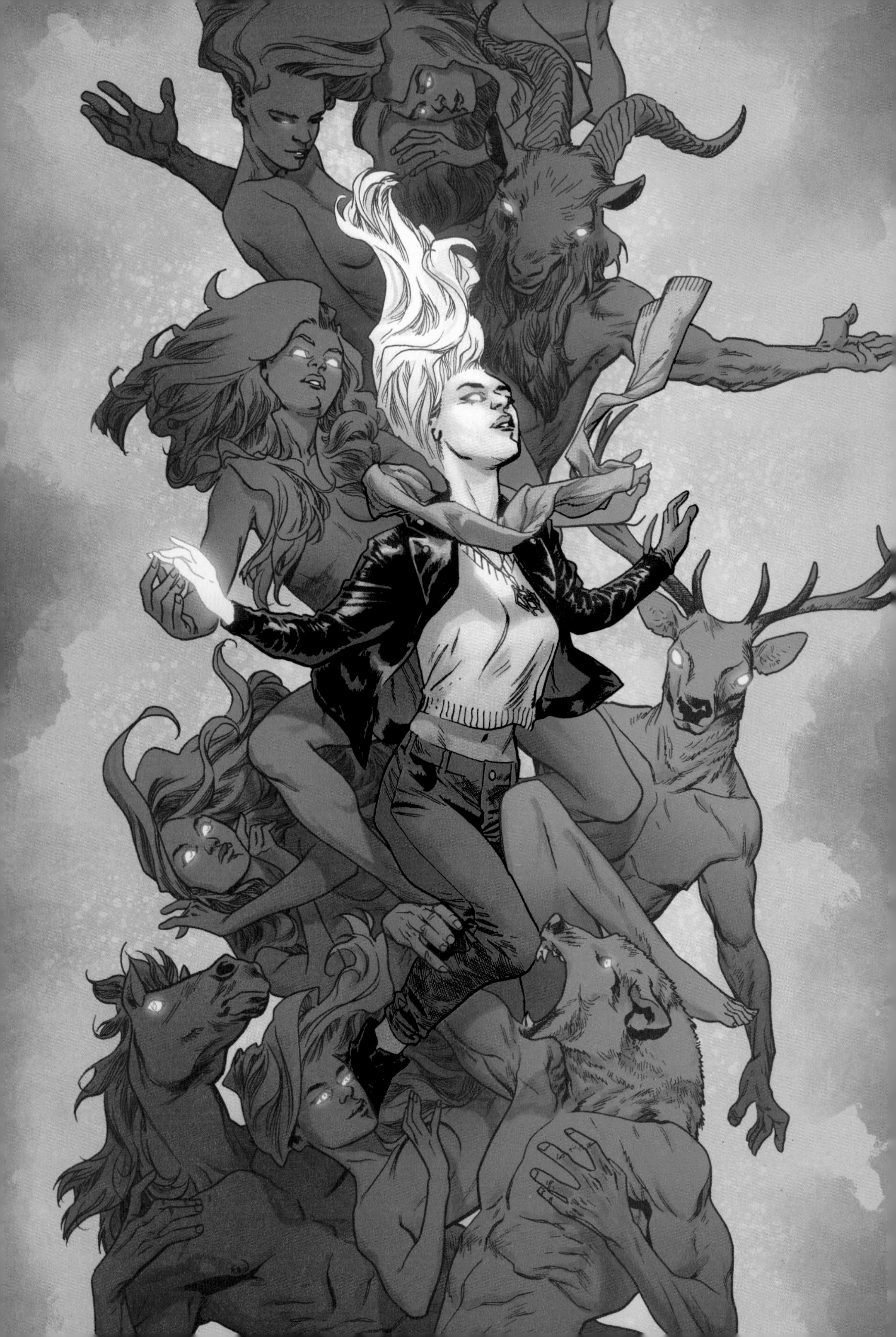

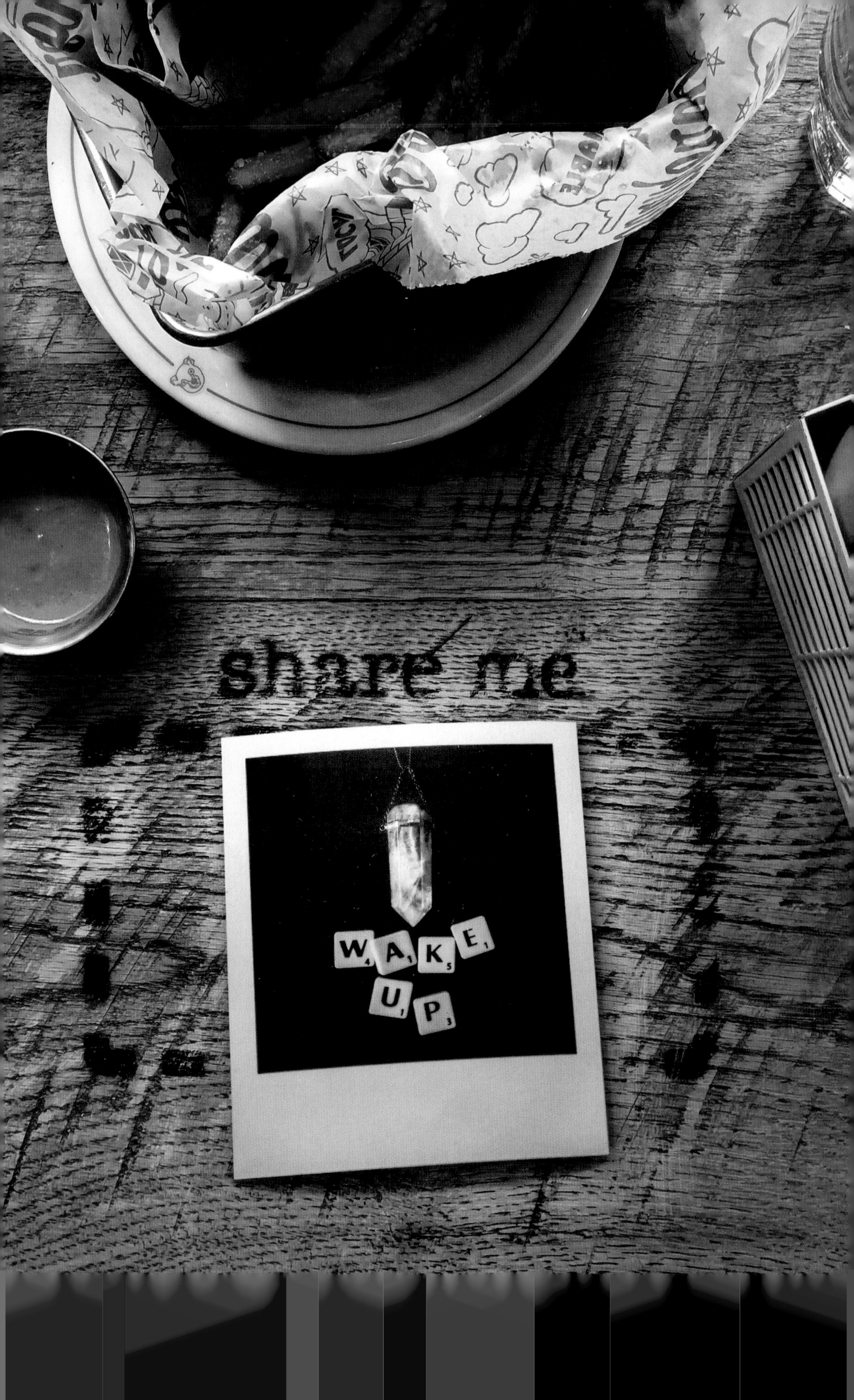
share me
WAKE
UP

BIOS

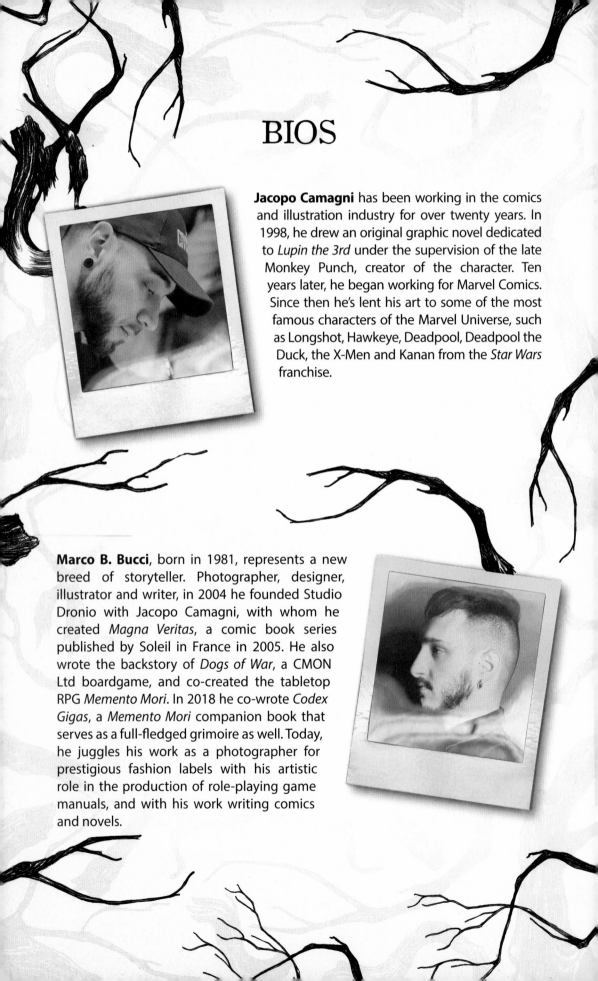

Jacopo Camagni has been working in the comics and illustration industry for over twenty years. In 1998, he drew an original graphic novel dedicated to *Lupin the 3rd* under the supervision of the late Monkey Punch, creator of the character. Ten years later, he began working for Marvel Comics. Since then he's lent his art to some of the most famous characters of the Marvel Universe, such as Longshot, Hawkeye, Deadpool, Deadpool the Duck, the X-Men and Kanan from the *Star Wars* franchise.

Marco B. Bucci, born in 1981, represents a new breed of storyteller. Photographer, designer, illustrator and writer, in 2004 he founded Studio Dronio with Jacopo Camagni, with whom he created *Magna Veritas*, a comic book series published by Soleil in France in 2005. He also wrote the backstory of *Dogs of War*, a CMON Ltd boardgame, and co-created the tabletop RPG *Memento Mori*. In 2018 he co-wrote *Codex Gigas*, a *Memento Mori* companion book that serves as a full-fledged grimoire as well. Today, he juggles his work as a photographer for prestigious fashion labels with his artistic role in the production of role-playing game manuals, and with his work writing comics and novels.